MERGERS AND ACQUISITIONS

THIRD EDITION

By

STEPHEN M. BAINBRIDGE

William D. Warren Distinguished Professor of Law
UCLA School of Law

CONCEPTS AND INSIGHTS SERIES®

FOUNDATION PRESS
2012

THOMSON REUTERS™

This publication was created to provide you with accurate and authoritative information concerning the subject matter covered; however, this publication was not necessarily prepared by persons licensed to practice law in a particular jurisdiction. The publisher is not engaged in rendering legal or other professional advice and this publication is not a substitute for the advice of an attorney. If you require legal or other expert advice, you should seek the services of a competent attorney or other professional.

Nothing contained herein is intended or written to be used for the purposes of 1) avoiding penalties imposed under the federal Internal Revenue Code, or 2) promoting, marketing or recommending to another party any transaction or matter addressed herein.

© 2003 FOUNDATION PRESS

© 2009 THOMSON REUTERS/FOUNDATION PRESS

© 2012 By THOMSON REUTERS/FOUNDATION PRESS
    1 New York Plaza, 34th Floor
    New York, NY 10004
    Phone Toll Free 1–877–888–1330
    Fax 646–424–5201
    foundation–press.com

Printed in the United States of America

ISBN 978–1–60930–132–3

Mat #41262336

For my Mother

PREFACE

Perhaps more than any other corporate transaction, mergers and acquisitions implicate a vast array of legal regimes. In any given transaction, issues may arise in such varied areas as corporate governance, securities regulation, tax and accounting, ERISA and other employment laws, successor liability and other tort doctrines, creditor rights, and, of course, antitrust. In deciding what subjects to cover in this text, I have kept in mind my primary target audience—namely, law students taking an advanced business law course such as Mergers & Acquisitions or Corporate Finance. (Of course, I hope the analysis will also prove useful to lawyers and judges seeking a fresh perspective on mergers and acquisitions.) Because most teachers of such courses focus on corporate and securities law issues, as do the several very fine casebooks in this area, I have focused on those subjects herein.

I have tried to produce a readable text, with a style that I hope is simple, direct, and reader-friendly. Even when dealing with complicated economic or financial issues, I tried to make them readily accessible to legal audiences. At the same time, however, I have not shied away from bringing theory to bear on doctrine. While the text has a strong emphasis on the doctrinal issues taught in today's M & A classes, it also places significant emphasis on providing an economic analysis of the major issues in that course. The text thus offers not only an overview of the black letter law, but also a unifying method of thinking about the subject.

I hasten to reassure the potentially worried reader that this text is designed for lawyers and law students—not graduate finance or economics students. Economic analysis is done solely qualitatively—no mathematical models or formal game theory—and kept as intuitive as possible. Even more important, economic analysis is never done for its own sake. In his well-known critique of modern legal scholarship, Judge Harry Edwards remarked: "Theory wholly divorced from cases has been of no use to me in practice."[1] My practice experience confirms that criticism, at least as long as we put strong emphasis on the phrase "wholly divorced." Theory brought to bear on specific legal issues often can be quite illuminat-

1. Harry T. Edwards, The Growing Disjunction Between Legal Education and the Legal Profession, 91 Mich. L. Rev. 34, 46 (1992) (quoting a former law clerk).

ing, as I hope to illustrate in this text. Economic analysis nevertheless is brought into play gradually and only in instances where it adds significant value.

In the interests of full disclosure, I should also note that this book is neither an encyclopedia nor a traditional hornbook. You will find no stultifying discussions of minutiae (I hope) or lengthy string citations of decades-old cases (or, at least, not very many).

A note on citation forms

In general, citations follow standard Blue Book form, but I have kept footnotes to the bare minimum. In particular, I refrained from using "id.," short form citations, and jump cites. Hence, unlike most modern law review articles, not every statement in the book is footnoted. Instead, I typically provide a source citation and allow interested readers to seek out pinpoint citations on their own. I strongly believe that this approach produced a more readable text. Finally, note that frequently referenced statutes and Restatements are cited in abbreviated form without dates, as follows:

ALI PRINCIPLES: American Law Institute, Principles of Corporate Governance: Analysis and Recommendations (1994).

CAL. CORP. CODE: California General Corporation Law, California Corporations Code § 100 et seq. (West 1998).

DGCL: Delaware General Corporation Law, Delaware Code Annotated tit. 8 (1999).

Exchange Act: Securities Exchange Act of 1934, as amended, 15 U.S.C. § 78a *et seq.* (1999).

MBCA: Model Business Corporation Act (1984 and supp.).

N.Y. Bus. Corp. L.: New York Business Corporation Law (McKinney 1999).

Rule: A rule adopted by the Securities and Exchange Commission under either the Securities Act or the Securities Exchange Act, 17 C.F.R. § 230.100 *et seq.* (1999) and 17 C.F.R. § 240.0–1 *et seq.* (1999), respectively.

Securities Act: Securities Act of 1933, as amended, 15 U.S.C. § 77a *et seq.* (1999).

TABLE OF CONTENTS

MERGERS AND ACQUISITIONS

Chapter 1

INTRODUCTION

It is difficult to imagine how a modern economy could function without something like our present corporate finance system. The numerous technological changes wrought by the Industrial Revolution, especially the development of modern mass production techniques in the nineteenth century, gave great advantages to firms large enough to achieve economies of scale. In turn, those advantages gave rise to giant industrial corporations. These firms required enormous amounts of capital, far exceeding the resources of any single individual or family. They could be financed only by aggregating many small investments, which was accomplished by selling stock or bonds to many investors— each of whom held only a tiny fraction of the firm's total capital.

Capital markets facilitated this process in at least two respects. First, the primary market gave issuers access to a large and ever growing pool of potential investors. Second, the secondary markets for corporate stocks and bonds gave investors essential liquidity and, accordingly, encouraged investment. In a liquid market, investors can freely sell their securities without involving the firm. Liquidity, in turn, makes it easier and cheaper for the company subsequently to raise capital in the primary market, because investors generally prefer (and will be willing to pay more) for liquid securities.

Few corporate finance transactions, in either the primary or secondary markets, rival corporate takeovers in size, media notoriety, public policy implications, or economic significance. Indeed, mergers and acquisitions are mega-business. Back in 1989, in a case involving the Time–Warner corporation, then-Delaware Chancellor William T. Allen opined that a transaction valued at $30 billion "would be rare" but was at least theoretically possible.[1] In 2000, Time–Warner was acquired by AOL in a transaction valued at over $100 billion. In the subsequent decade, transactions exceeding the $30 billion level became routine.

Merger and acquisition activity tends to be cyclical, usually coinciding with boom periods for the stock market. Economic historians have identified four major "merger waves" in U.S. history: 1897–1904, 1916–1929, 1965–1969, and 1984–1989.[2] Most also agree that a fifth wave

---

1. Paramount Communications Inc. v. Time Inc., 1989 WL 79880 at 22 (Del.Ch.), aff'd, 571 A.2d 1140 (Del.1989).

2. William J. Carney, Mergers and Acquisitions: Cases and Materials 2–13 (2000); Patrick A. Gaughan, Mergers, Acquisitions, and Corporate Restructurings 23–56 (3d ed.

1

began in the mid–1990s. That wave was characterized by the prevalence of negotiated over hostile acquisitions, the enormous dollar values involved, and a record-breaking pace both in terms of the number of deals and their aggregate dollar value.[3]

With the economic downturn in the opening years of the new century, and the concomitant stock market decline, the pace slackened somewhat but mergers and acquisitions nonetheless remained a very significant feature of the economic landscape. In 2001, for example, while the number of acquisitions dropped to the lowest level since 1998 and their aggregate dollar value dropped to the lowest level since 1997, there were still 8,265 deals worth an aggregate of more than $700 billion, including more than 100 transactions valued at $1 billion or more.[4]

The rate of M & A activity bottomed out in 2002 but then picked up significantly before peaking in 2007. The economic crisis and recession of 2008 again triggered a drop in the number of acquisition deals. By 2010, however, despite the slow pace of economic recovery, the volume of M & A activity had begun to recover. There were 9,116 acquisitions announced in 2010, a 34% increase over 2009. The total value of those deals was $690 billion, an increase of 24% over 2009. As a result, mergers and acquisitions remain a key part of the practice of corporate finance law.

§ 1.1 The Corporation

Because the asset traded in the market for corporate control is the corporation itself, a review of some basic concepts may be useful for some readers.

A leading legal dictionary defines the corporation as "an artificial person or legal entity created by or under the authority of the laws of a state or nation...."[5] Although technically correct, this definition is not especially enlightening. You may find it more helpful to think of the corporation as a legal fiction characterized by six attributes: formal creation as prescribed by state law;[6] legal personality; separation of

2002); Ronald J. Gilson and Bernard S. Black, The Law and Finance of Corporate Acquisitions 11–61 (2d ed. 1995).

3. William J. Carney, Mergers and Acquisitions: Cases and Materials 7–8 (2000).

4. M & A News and Trends, Mergerstat Rev., Jan. 2002.

5. Black's Law Dictionary 307 (5th ed. 1979).

6. Virtually all U.S. corporations are formed ("incorporated") under the laws of a single state by filing articles of incorporation with the appropriate state official. (A very few exceptions are formed under federal law.) The state in which the articles of incorporation are filed is known as the "state of incorporation." The founders of a company are free to select any state as the state of incorporation; they need not select the state in which the company is currently doing business. Selecting a state of incorporation has important consequences, because corporate law matters usually are governed by the law of the state of incorporation, irrespective of the jurisdiction in which suit is brought or the residence of the other parties to the dispute.

ownership and control; freely alienable ownership interests; indefinite duration; and limited liability.[7] Taken together, these six attributes give the corporate form considerable advantages for large businesses as compared to the other forms of business organizations available under U.S. law.

A. Some Fundamental Distinctions

Corporations come in a wide variety of flavors: business corporations, municipal corporations, and ecclesiastical corporations, to name a few. In this text, we are concerned solely with business corporations. Even with that limitation, however, here are a number of fundamental distinctions to bear in mind:

- *Not-for-profit versus for-profit corporations.* Many charitable organizations are organized as corporations, even though they do not carry on for-profit business activities. Special "non-profit" corporation statutes govern these organizations. Not-for-profit corporations can also qualify for special tax treatment under both state and federal law. As the name implies, the profit motive is what distinguishes business corporations from nonprofit corporations.

- *Public versus private corporations.* The term public corporation is sometimes used to refer to corporations created by the government (be it federal or state) to carry out some public function. In this terminology, private corporations are created by and owned by private individuals to carry out private functions. Almost all business corporations fall into the latter category. Because this text focuses solely on business corporations, we will exclusively use the term "public corporation" in the sense set forth in the next paragraph.

- *Close versus public corporations.* Business corporations generally are divided into two main categories: close corporations (a.k.a. closely held corporations) and public corporations (a.k.a. publicly held corporations). As a general rule of thumb, close corporations tend to be smaller than public corporations, but size is not what distinguishes the two categories. Instead, they are distinguished by the presence or absence of a secondary trading market for their shares of stock. Public corporations are those whose stock is listed for trading on a secondary market, such as the New York Stock Exchange or the NASDAQ system. Close corporations are those whose stock is not listed on such a market. In this text, the term public corporation will be used in this sense.

---

7. Note that the latter four of these attributes are default rules. Some corporations opt out of one or more of them. In particular, close corporations often unify ownership and control to one degree or another and/or restrict transfer of ownership interests.

Of these three distinguishing characteristics, the last is most salient for our purposes. Corporate securities, like all commodities, are traded in markets. Corporate lawyers distinguish between two basic types of markets in which a corporation's securities (such as stocks or bonds) are traded: the primary market and the secondary market. The primary market is the one in which the corporation sells its shares to investors. An initial public offering (IPO), for example, takes place on the primary market.

The secondary market is a trading market; the one in which investors trade stocks among themselves without any significant participation by the original corporate issuer of the shares. The New York Stock Exchange and the American Stock Exchange are well-known, highly organized, and thoroughly regulated examples of secondary markets. Market professionals working on these exchanges facilitate the trading process by matching buy and sell orders from investors.

Having a corporation's securities listed for trading on a secondary market is significant because it makes the securities liquid. In other words, investors can freely sell their securities without involving the firm. Liquidity, in turn, makes it easier and cheaper for the company subsequently to raise capital in the primary market, because investors generally prefer (and are willing to pay more) for liquid securities. The difference in liquidity of publicly held corporate stock and that of close corporation stock has important theoretical and doctrinal consequences.

B.   Sources of Corporation Law

Corporate law differs in two important respects from the common law courses taken by most law students during the first year of law school. First, statutes are far more important in corporate law than is the case in most of the so-called common law courses. When faced with a corporate law issue, the first place one always looks is the corporation statute of the state of incorporation.[8] Second, as far as public corporations are concerned, federal law is much more important in corporate law than is the case in common law subjects. Indeed, publicly held corporations can be said to function in a dual regulatory scheme: federal securities law and state corporate law. This is particularly the case with respect to mergers and other corporate acquisitions, where both state and federal law play very important regulatory roles.

---

8. Although one must pay careful attention to the applicable state corporation statute, judicial opinions remain quite important in corporate law. Corporation statutes almost never rise to the level of detail found in, say, the federal tax code. Many provisions of corporation statutes are quite vague. Worse yet, corporation statutes often fail to address important issues. Courts have filled the resulting gaps through a process far more closely resembling common law adjudication than statutory interpretation. The fiduciary duties of directors and officers are especially prominent examples of this process, but they are hardly the only ones.

1. State Corporate Law

Virtually all U.S. corporations are formed ("incorporated") under the laws of a single state by filing articles of incorporation with the appropriate state official. (A very few exceptions are formed under federal law.) The state in which the articles of incorporation are filed is known as the "state of incorporation." Selecting a state of incorporation has important consequences, because of the so-called "internal affairs doctrine"—a conflicts of law rule holding that corporate governance matters are controlled by the law of the state of incorporation. Virtually all U.S. jurisdictions follow the internal affairs doctrine, even if the corporation in question has virtually no ties to the state of incorporation other than the mere fact of incorporation.

Suppose, for example, that Acme, Inc., is incorporated in Delaware, but all of Acme's assets are located in Illinois. All of Acme's shareholders, directors, and employees reside in Illinois. Acme's sole place of business is located in Illinois. An Acme shareholder brings suit against the board of directors, alleging that its members violated their fiduciary duty of care. The lawsuit is filed in an Illinois court. Despite all these Illinois ties, the Illinois court nevertheless will apply Delaware law.[9]

The internal affairs doctrine takes on particular transactional significance when considered in conjunction with the constitutional restrictions on a state's ability to exclude foreign corporations.[10] With rare exceptions, states have always allowed foreign and pseudo-foreign corporations to do business within their borders. As early as 1839, for example, the U.S. Supreme Court held that federal courts should presume a state would recognize foreign corporations in the absence of an express statement to the contrary by the legislature.[11] A subsequent Supreme Court decision implied that states could not exclude foreign corporations from doing business within the state provided that the business constituted interstate commerce under the Commerce Clause of the U.S. Constitution.[12] These decisions effectively created a common market for corporate charters. If Illinois, for example, adopts a restrictive corporation law, its businesses are free to incorporate in a less

---

9. See, e.g., Paulman v. Kritzer, 219 N.E.2d 541, 543 (Ill.App.1966), aff'd, 230 N.E.2d 262 (Ill.1967) (applying Delaware fiduciary duties to the directors of a Delaware corporation).

10. A foreign corporation is one incorporated either by a state or nation other than the state in question. A pseudo-foreign corporation is one that has most of its ties to the state in question rather than to the state of incorporation. Many Delaware corporations are pseudo-foreign corporations. They are incorporated in Delaware, but most of their operations are located in one or more other states. In most states, there is no significant legal difference between a foreign and a pseudo-foreign corporation, and the internal affairs doctrine will be applied to invoke the law of the state of the incorporation. California and New York are the principal exceptions to this rule. Both states purport to apply parts of their corporate laws to pseudo-foreign corporations formed in other states but having substantial contacts with California or New York. See, e.g., Cal. Corp. Code § 2115; N.Y. Bus. Corp. L. §§ 1317–20.

11. Bank of Augusta v. Earle, 38 U.S. 519, 597 (1839).

12. Paul v. Virginia, 75 U.S. 168 (1868).

restrictive state, such as Delaware, while continuing to conduct business within Illinois.

Throughout the nineteenth century state corporation laws gradually moved in the direction of increased liberality, making the incorporation process simpler on the one hand, while at the same time abandoning any effort to regulate the substantive conduct of corporations through the chartering process. In later years, this process became known as the "race to the bottom."[13] Corporate and social reformers believed that the states competed in granting corporate charters. After all, the more charters (certificates of incorporation) the state grants, the more franchise and other taxes it collects. According to this view, because it is corporate managers who decide on the state of incorporation, states compete by adopting statutes allowing corporate managers to exploit shareholders.

Many legal scholars reject the race to the bottom hypothesis.[14] According to a standard account, investors will not purchase, or at least not pay as much for, securities of firms incorporated in states that cater too excessively to management. Lenders will not make loans to such firms without compensation for the risks posed by management's lack of accountability. As a result, those firms' cost of capital will rise, while their earnings will fall. Among other things, such firms thereby become more vulnerable to a hostile takeover and subsequent management purges. Corporate managers therefore have strong incentives to incorporate the business in a state offering rules preferred by investors. Competition for corporate charters thus should deter states from adopting excessively pro-management statutes. The empirical research appears to bear out this view of state competition, suggesting that efficient solutions to corporate law problems win out over time.[15]

---

13. See generally William L. Cary, Federalism and Corporate Law: Reflections Upon Delaware, 83 Yale L.J. 663 (1974) (classic statement of race to the bottom hypothesis); see also Lucian Ayre Bebchuk, Federalism and the Corporation: The Desirable Limits on State Competition in Corporate Law, 105 Harv. L. Rev. 1437 (1992).

14. See Ralph K. Winter, Jr., State Law, Shareholder Protection, and the Theory of the Corporation, 6 J. Legal Stud. 251 (1977) (the seminal response to Cary); see also William J. Carney, The Political Economy of Competition for Corporate Charters, 26 J. Legal Stud. 303 (1997); Frank H. Easterbrook, Managers' Discretion and Investors' Welfare: Theories and Evidence, 9 Del. J. Corp. L. 540, 654–71 (1984); Daniel R. Fischel, The "Race to the Bottom" Revisited: Reflections on Recent Developments in Delaware's Corporation Law, 76 Nw. U. L. Rev. 913 (1982); Roberta Romano, The

State Competition Debate in Corporate Law, 8 Cardozo L. Rev. 709 (1987); cf. Jonathan R. Macey and Geoffrey P. Miller, Toward an Interest Group Theory of Delaware Corporate Law, 65 Tex. L. Rev. 469 (1987) (public choice-based theory of state competition).

15. See Roberta Romano, The Genius of American Corporate Law (1993) (setting forth both an empirical analysis and theoretical arguments challenging race to the bottom hypothesis). As even many advocates of the race to the top hypothesis concede, however, state regulation of corporate takeovers appears to be an exception to the rule that efficient solutions tend to win out. See, e.g., Roberta Romano, Competition for Corporate Charters and the Lesson of Takeover Statutes, 61 Fordham L. Rev. 843 (1993); Ralph K. Winter, The "Race for the Top" Revisited: A Comment on Eisenberg, 89 Colum. L. Rev. 1526 (1989); see also

Whether state competition is a race to the bottom or the top, there is no question that Delaware is the runaway winner in this competition. More than half of the corporations listed for trading on the New York Stock Exchange and nearly 60% of the Fortune 500 corporations are incorporated in Delaware. Proponents of the race to the bottom hypothesis argue that Delaware is dominant because its corporate law is more pro-management than that of other states. Those who reject the race to the bottom theory ascribe Delaware's dominance to a number of other factors: There is a considerable body of case law interpreting the Delaware corporate statute (DGCL), which allows legal questions to be answered with confidence. Delaware has a separate court, the Court of Chancery, devoted largely to corporate law cases. The Chancellors have great expertise in corporate law matters, making their court a highly sophisticated forum for resolving disputes. They also tend to render decisions quite quickly, facilitating transactions that are often time sensitive.[16]

The most important alternative to Delaware law is the American Bar Association's Model Business Corporation Act (MBCA). The 1969 MBCA was adopted in whole or in large part by about 35 states. The 1984 MBCA is now in force in 24 states and has been adopted in part by many others. Delaware, California, and New York remain the commercially most important holdouts. Each has preserved a largely unique corporate statute, although each also has adopted some elements of the MBCA.

2. Federal Law

The issuance and trading of stocks and other corporate securities was largely unregulated until the passage of the first state "blue sky law" by Kansas in 1911. These laws were a response to widespread fraud in the sale of securities. Indeed, the name supposedly refers to unscrupulous promoters who would sell building lots in the clear blue sky. State regulation proved largely ineffective, however, because the statutes had a limited jurisdictional reach, many statutes contained numerous special interest exemptions, and states had limited enforcement resources.[17]

Lucian Ayre Bebchuk & Allen Ferrell, Federalism and Corporate Law: The Race to Protect Managers from Takeovers, 99 Colum. L. Rev. 1168 (1999) (contending that the race to the bottom in takeover regulation may be a general phenomenon).

16. See generally Jill E. Fisch, The Peculiar Role of the Delaware Courts in the Competition for Corporate Charters, 68 U. Cin. L. Rev. 1061 (2000).

17. In Securities Act § 18 and Securities Exchange Act § 28(a), Congress expressly protected state blue sky laws from being preempted by those Acts. Amend-

ments to those provisions in 1996 and 1998, however, created a complex preemption scheme that substantially limited the scope of the blue sky laws' potential application. Accordingly, while the blue sky laws remain on the books, the federal securities laws are now far more important in most situations. See generally David M. Levine & Adam C. Pritchard, The Securities Litigation Uniform Standards Act of 1998: The Sun Sets on California's Blue Sky Laws, 54 Bus. Law. 1 (1998); Richard W. Painter, Responding to a False Alarm: Federal Preemp-

In the aftermath of the Great Stock Market Crash of 1929 and the subsequent Great Depression, there was widespread agreement that the time had come for federal regulation of the securities markets. Between 1933 and 1940 Congress passed 7 statutes regulating various aspects of the industry, which have been amended on various subsequent occasions and joined by a few other highly specialized statutes.

The most important of these statutes for our purposes are the Securities Act of 1933 and the Securities Exchange Act of 1934. The Securities Act regulates primary market sales of securities by issuing corporations.[18] The Securities Exchange Act regulates a host of matters, but is generally concerned with trading of corporate securities on securities exchanges and other secondary markets.[19]

The New Deal Congress considered three models for regulating the securities markets: the fraud model, which would simply prohibit fraud in the sale of securities; the disclosure model, which would allow issuers to sell very risky or even unsound securities, provided they gave buyers enough information to make an informed investment decision; and the merit review model, which would require some government agency to review the merits of a security and to prohibit the sale of investments that were unsound or excessively risky. Although merit review was a common feature of state blue sky laws, Congress rejected that approach. Instead, it combined the fraud and disclosure models.

Accordingly, while the various federal statutes are concerned with different transactions, they have the same basic purposes. The first is requiring corporations and other issuers of securities to provide full disclosure to ensure that investors have all the information they need to make informed decisions about buying, selling, or voting securities. The second is to punish fraud committed in connection with securities transactions.[20]

The Securities Act follows a transactional disclosure model; i.e., it focuses attention on getting information concerning certain transactions from the issuer to investors. Accordingly, that act applies only when an issuer is actually selling securities. As long as a company can raise funds by other means, the Securities Act does not require it to provide any disclosures whatsoever. Obviously, this leaves a significant gap in the disclosure requirements.

tion of State Securities Fraud Causes of Action, 84 Cornell L. Rev. 1 (1998).

18. 15 U.S.C. §§ 77a–77z–3.

19. 15 U.S.C. §§ 78a–78mm. Subject to certain exemptions, all corporations that sell securities to the public are subject to the Securities Act. In contrast, the Securities Exchange Act applies to a narrower range of businesses. Although the Act has a

complex set of rules for deciding which provisions apply to which corporations, as a general rule of thumb it applies only to publicly held corporations.

20. See, e.g., Rubin v. United States, 449 U.S. 424, 431 (1981) ("these provisions were enacted to protect against fraud and promote the free flow of information in the public dissemination of securities").

The Securities Exchange Act addresses this problem by imposing a periodic disclosure system on certain issuers. It focuses attention on regularly and routinely getting information from the issuer to the market. In addition, the Securities Exchange Act includes a hodge-podge of other provisions, concerned with regulating secondary market trading and preventing fraud.

Our attention herein will be devoted almost exclusively to provisions of the Securities Exchange Act, especially those governing proxy solicitations and tender offers. Both of these provisions, like most of the Act, apply only to so-called "reporting companies." The name derives from the requirement noted above that certain firms comply with the periodic disclosure rules created by the Securities exchange Act.[21]

There are three basic categories of companies required to register under the Securities Exchange Act.[22] The first two are identified by §§ 12 and 13(a) of the Act. Section 13(a) requires periodic reports from any company registered with the SEC under Section 12 of the Act. In turn, § 12(a) requires that any class of securities listed and traded on a national securities exchange (such as the New York or American Stock Exchanges) must be registered under the Securities Exchange Act. In addition, § 12(g) and the rules there under require all other companies with assets exceeding $10 million and a class of equity securities held by 500 or more record shareholders to register that class of equity securities with the SEC. The third and final group of companies subject to the Securities Exchange Act is identified by § 15(d), which picks up any issuer that made a public offering of securities under the Securities Act. Issuers with less than 300 record shareholders, however, are not subject to this requirement except during the fiscal year in which they made the offering.

The Securities Exchange Act is also notable because it created the Securities and Exchange Commission (SEC), the primary federal agency charged with administering the various securities laws. The agency is headed by five Commissioners, who must be confirmed by the Senate. No

---

21. The periodic reports required by the Securities Exchange Act include: (1) Form 10, the initial Securities Exchange Act registration statement. It is only filed once with respect to a particular class of securities. It closely resembles a Securities Act registration statement. (2) Form 10–K, an annual report containing full audited financial statements and management's report of the previous year's activities. It usually incorporates the annual report sent to shareholders. (3) Form 10–Q, filed for each of first three quarters of the year. The issuer does not file a Form 10–Q for the last quarter of the year, which is covered by the Form 10–K. Form 10–Q contains unaudited financial statements and management's report of material recent developments. (4)

Form 8–K, which must be filed promptly within after certain important events affecting the corporation's operations or financial condition, such as bankruptcy, sales of significant assets, or a change in control of the company.

22. It is sometimes said that the Securities Exchange Act registers companies, while the Securities Act registers securities. In fact, the former registers classes of securities, but the point is otherwise well-taken. A corporation that has registered a class of securities under the Securities Exchange Act must nevertheless register a particular offering of securities of that class under the Securities Act.

more than three can belong to the same political party. Most of the agency's work, of course, is done not by the Commissioners but by the professional staff. The agency staff is organized into Divisions and Offices having various specialized responsibilities. The professional staff is comprised mainly of lawyers, although it also includes a number of accountants and economists. The staff has three primary functions: it provides interpretative guidance to private parties raising questions about the application of the securities laws to a particular transaction; it advises the Commission as to new rules or revisions of existing rules; and it investigates and prosecutes violations of the securities laws.

We will devote less attention to the Securities Act of 1933. The Securities Act does affect some M & A deals, however, because § 5(a) of the Act makes it unlawful to sell a security unless a registration statement is in effect with respect to the securities. In other words, unless an exemption is available, the prospective issuer must file a registration statement with the SEC and wait for the registration statement to become effective before selling securities.

Where some of all of the consideration paid target shareholders in an acquisition consist of securities issued by the acquirer (or any other company than the target, for that matter), the transaction constitutes a sale of those securities subject to the Securities Act registration requirements. As we'll see, this can affect both mergers and tender offers.

3.   *The Boundary Between State and Federal Law*

The U.S. Supreme Court has held repeatedly that the federal securities laws do not preempt state corporate law, but instead place only a limited gloss on the broader body of state law.[23] A fair rule of thumb is that state law is concerned with the substance of corporate governance, while federal law is concerned with disclosure and a limited number of procedural aspects of corporate governance (such as the solicitation of proxies and the conduct of a tender offer).[24] In certain areas, the dividing line between the federal and state role remains controversial. The two most important disputes concern shareholder voting rights and state regulation of takeovers.

C.   Separation of Ownership and Control

Above the corporate attributes noted above, the most important for our purposes is the fact that in corporations, unlike most other forms of

---

23. See, e.g., CTS Corp. v. Dynamics Corp. of Am., 481 U.S. 69 (1987); Burks v. Lasker, 441 U.S. 471 (1979); Santa Fe Indus. v. Green, 430 U.S. 462 (1977).

24. See, e.g., Business Roundtable v. SEC, 905 F.2d 406 (D.C.Cir.1990); see generally Robert B. Thompson, Preemption and Federalism in Corporate Governance: Protecting Shareholder Rights to Vote, Sell, and Sue, 62 Law & Contemp. Probs. 215 (1999); Stephen M. Bainbridge, The Short Life and Resurrection of SEC Rule 19c-4, 69 Wash. U. L.Q. 565 (1991).

business organizations, ownership of the firm is formally separated from its control. Although shareholders nominally own the corporation, they have virtually no decision-making powers—just the right to elect the firm's directors and to vote on an exceedingly limited—albeit not unimportant—number of corporate actions. Rather, management of the firm is vested by statute in the hands of the board of directors, who in turn delegate the day-to-day running of the firm to its officers, who in turn delegate some responsibilities to the company's employees.[25] The conflicts of interest created by this separation of ownership and control drive much of corporate law, especially the fiduciary obligations of officers and directors.

Although the separation of ownership and control is one of the corporation's essential attributes, it is also one of its most controversial ones. This controversy began taking its modern shape in what still may be the most influential book ever written about corporations, Berle and Means' *The Modern Corporation and Private Property*.[26] They identified three types of public corporations, classified according to the nature of share ownership within the firm:

- *Majority control*: A corporation having a dominant shareholder (or group of shareholders acting together) who owns more than 50% of the outstanding voting shares. Majority controlled corporations exhibit a partial separation of ownership and control: minority shareholders share in the corporation's ownership, but not in its control.

- *Minority control*: A corporation having a dominant shareholder (or group of shareholders acting together) who owns less than 50% of the outstanding voting shares, but is nevertheless able to exercise effective voting control. Minority controlled corporations also exhibit partial separation of ownership and control.

- *Managerial control*: A corporation in which no one shareholder (or group of shareholders acting together) owns sufficient stock to give him working control of the firm. Managerial controlled corporations exhibit complete separation of ownership and control.

The growth of managerial control occurred, according to Berle and Means, because stock ownership was dispersed amongst many shareholders, no one of whom owned enough shares to affect materially the corporation's management. In turn, Berle and Means believed that

---

25. Close corporations may differ. To be sure, the statutory separation of ownership and control applies to closely held corporations. Vesting formal decision-making power in the board of directors of a close corporation, however, is often unacceptable to the shareholders of such a firm. In this respect, a close corporation often closely resembles a partnership that for some business reason has been organized as a corporation. Under special statutory provisions, close corporations can be set up to give shareholders extensive management powers resembling those of partners.

26. Adolf A. Berle, Jr. and Gardiner C. Means, The Modern Corporation and Private Property (1932).

dispersed ownership was inherent in the corporate system. Important technological changes during the decades preceding publication of their work, especially the development of modern mass production techniques, gave great advantages to firms large enough to achieve economics of scale, which gave rise to giant industrial corporations. These firms required enormous amounts of capital, far exceeding the resources of most individuals or families. They were financed by aggregating many small investments, which was accomplished by selling shares to many investors, each of whom owned only a tiny fraction of the firm's stock.

Separation of ownership and control thus proved an essential prerequisite to corporate success. This conclusion is premised on two observations: (a) most investors in corporations prefer to be passive holders of stock; and (b) separating ownership and control results in various efficiencies in making decisions. Vesting decision-making power in the corporation's board of directors and managers allows shareholders to remain passive, while also preventing the chaos that would result from shareholder involvement in day-to-day decision making.

While separation of ownership and control facilitated the growth of large industrial corporations, Berle and Means recognized that that separation created the potential for shareholder and managerial interests to diverge. As the residual claimants on the corporation's assets and earnings, the shareholders are entitled to the corporation's profits. But it is the firm's management, not the shareholders, which decides how the firm's earnings are to be spent. Thus, there is a risk that management will expend firm earnings on projects that benefit management, rather than shareholders. Suppose the President of Acme, Inc., is musing over the following question: "I can either spend $100 million on a new corporate jet or I can distribute the $100 million to the shareholders by increasing the size of the dividend." Can you doubt that some (most?) managers will buy the jet? This is the so-called principal-agent problem, which we'll discuss in more detail in the next Chapter.

Corporate law has tried three policy responses to the potential divergence of shareholder and managerial interests created by the separation of ownership and control: (1) Some corporate laws try to reunite ownership and control, giving shareholders more control over the firm. The federal proxy rules are an example of such rules. Some legal scholars also believe that institutional investors will become more actively involved in corporate governance, at least partially reuniting ownership and control.[27] Whether this will prove true remains to be seen. (2) Some laws target the supposed lack of managerial accountability that purportedly is the basic problem caused by separating ownership and control. Because shareholders do not control the corporation, shareholders cannot discipline managers who put their self-interest ahead of the share-

---

27. For a critical analysis of this literature, see Stephen M. Bainbridge, The Poli-   tics of Corporate Governance, 18 Harv. J. L. & Pub. Pol'y 671 (1995).

holders' interests. Corporate governance therefore provides alternative mechanisms—some legal, but some market—for disciplining managers who abuse their positions. Examples of this approach include judicial review under the duties of care and loyalty and hostile corporate takeovers. (3) Some laws try to align management and shareholder interests. Examples of this approach include tax provisions encouraging management to own a larger percentage of the firm's shares.

D. Some Key Terminology

Bonds: Long-term debt securities.

Classes of shares: A class of shares is a type or category of stock. Thus, common stock is considered to be a class of stock. Preferred stock would be a second class of shares. Multiple classes must be authorized by the articles, which must set forth the number of shares of the class the corporation is authorized to issue and the class' basic rights.

Debentures: Unsecured long-term debt securities.

Directors: Although shareholders nominally own the corporation, they do not control it. Instead, control of the firm is vested in the board of directors, a body of individuals elected by the shareholders to manage the business.

Dividend: A pro rata distribution of the corporation's assets to shareholders. A liquidation dividend occurs when the firm dissolves and has assets remaining after all other claims have been satisfied. The residual assets are distributed pro rata to the corporation's shareholders as a final dividend.

Issuer: Used in connection with sales of securities to refer to the corporation that originally sold the securities.

Junk bonds: High yield, high-risk corporate bonds frequently used to finance takeovers.

Notes: Short-term debt securities, usually unsecured.

Series of shares: A series of shares is a subclass of stock. Thus, the corporation might have a class of preferred shares that is divided into series. All members of the class will have some preference over the common stock, but each series may have different rights and preferences from the others.

Shares: The units into which the ownership interest of a corporation is divided. Shares typically carry two basic rights: (1) voting rights, which allow their owners to elect the corporation's directors and to vote on certain other matters; and (2) economic rights, which entitle their owners to a pro rata share of dividends and, in the event of liquidation, any residual assets remaining after all other claims on the corporation have been paid.

Shareholder: Person or legal entity that owns shares.

Stock: Sometimes used interchangeably with the term "shares," but also used in a more technical sense to refer to the corporation's aggregate outstanding shares; hence the term, "a share of corporate stock."

§ 1.2 The Lawyer's Role

Corporate lawyers are one of three basic categories of advisors who play a critical role in virtually all corporate finance transactions (the others being accountants and investment bankers). Why? The reason people hire litigators is obvious—either they are being sued or they want to sue somebody else. Unauthorized practice of law statutes and bar admission rules give lawyers a near-total monopoly on litigation. The rationale for hiring transactional lawyers, by contrast, is less obvious. Much of the work of transactional lawyers entails giving advice that could be given by other professionals. Accordingly, it seems fair to ask: why does anybody hire transactional lawyers?

The question is neither an idle nor a rhetorical one. Business people often have a "quite uncharitable view of what business lawyers do. In an extreme version, business lawyers are perceived as evil sorcerers who use their special skills and professional magic to relieve clients of their possessions."[28] In his scathing attack on lawyers, *The Terrible Truth About Lawyers,* Mark H. McCormack, founder of the International Management Group, a major sports and entertainment agency, wrote that "it's the lawyers who: (1) gum up the works; (2) get people mad at each other; (3) make business procedures more expensive than they need to be; and now and then deep-six what had seemed like a perfectly workable arrangement. Accordingly, I would say that the best way to deal with lawyers is not to deal with them at all."[29] Pretty depressing stuff, especially if you hope to make a living as a transactional lawyer. Yet, even this cloud has a silver lining. Successful transactional lawyers build their practice by perceptibly adding value to their clients' transactions. From this perspective, the education of a transactional lawyer is a matter of learning where the value in a given transaction comes from and how the lawyer might add even more value to the deal.

Two competing hypotheses about how lawyers add value to a deal suggest themselves. The first might be termed the "Pie Division Role." In this version of the transactional lawyer story, lawyers strive to capture value—maximizing their client's gains from the deal. Although there are doubtless pie division situations in transactional practice, this explanation of the lawyer's role is flawed. Pie division assumes a zero

---

28. Ronald J. Gilson and Bernard S. Black, The Law and Finance of Corporate Acquisitions 5 (2d ed. 1995).

29. Mark H. McCormack, The Terrible Truth About Lawyers: How Lawyers Really Work and How to Deal With Them Success-

fully 15 (1987). Unfortunately, *The Terrible Truth* is now out of print. If you can find one in a used bookstore, however, it will prove a very educational read for a transactional lawyer of any age.

sum game in which any gains for one side come from the other side's share. Assume two sophisticated clients with multiple advisers, including competent counsel. Is there any reason to think that one side's lawyer will be able to extract significant gains from the other? No. A homely example may be helpful: You and a friend go out to eat. You decide to share a pizza, so you need to agree on its division. Would you hire somebody to negotiate a division of the pizza? Especially if they were going to take one of your slices as their fee?

The second hypothesis might be termed the "Pie Expansion Role." In this version of the story, people hire transactional lawyers because they add value to the deal. This conception of the lawyer's role rejects the zero sum game mentality. Instead, it claims that the lawyer makes everybody better off by increasing the size of the pie.

For the most part, lawyers increase the size of the pie by reducing transaction costs. One way of lowering transaction cost is through regulatory arbitrage. The law frequently provides multiple ways of effecting a given transaction, all of which will have various advantages and disadvantages. By selecting the most advantageous structure for a given transaction, and ensuring that courts and regulators will respect that choice, the transactional lawyer reduces the cost of complying with the law and allows the parties to keep more of their gains.

An example may be helpful. Acme Corporation wants to acquire Ajax, Inc., using stock as the form of consideration to be paid Ajax shareholders. Acme is concerned about the availability of appraisal rights to shareholders of the two corporations.[30] Presumably Acme doesn't care about the legal niceties of doing the deal—Acme just wants to buy Ajax at the lowest possible cost and, by hypothesis, with the minimal possible cash flow. In other words, the client cares about the economic substance of the deal, not the legal form it takes. As Acme's transactional lawyer, you know that corporate law often elevates form over substance—and that the law provides multiple ways of acquiring another company. A solution thus suggests itself: Delaware law only permits shareholders to exercise appraisal rights in connection with mergers. Appraisal rights are not allowed in connection with an acquisition structured as a sale of assets. Hence, while there is little substantive economic difference between an asset sale and a merger, there is a significant legal difference. By selecting one form over another, the transactional lawyer ensures that the deal is done at the lowest possible cost.

Parties would experience some transaction costs even in the absence of regulation, however. Reducing those nonregulatory costs is another function of the transactional lawyer. Information asymmetries are a good example. A corporation selling securities to an investor has considerably greater information about the firm than does the prospective

---

30. Appraisal rights permit shareholders to demand that their stock be bought for cash at a judicially-determined fair price.

buyer. The wise potential investor knows about this information asymmetry and, as a result, takes precautions. Worse yet, what if the seller lies? Or shades the truth? Or is itself uninformed? The wise investor also knows there is a risk of opportunistic withholding or manipulation of asymmetrically held information. Note that this is a species of what economists call the agency cost problem. One response to agency costs is monitoring, which in this context takes the form of investigation—due diligence—by the buyer. Another response to agency costs is bonding by seller, which in this context would take the form of disclosures including representations and warranties. In either case, by finding ways for the seller to credibly convey information to the investor, the transactional lawyer helps eliminate the information asymmetry between them. In turn, a variety of other transaction costs will fall. There is less uncertainty, less opportunity for strategic behavior, and less need to take costly precautions.

§ 1.3 A Preliminary Overview of Acquisition Mechanics

There are at least five major ways of acquiring control of a corporation: merger; purchase of all or substantially all of the target's assets; proxy contest; tender offer; negotiated or open market stock purchases. Subsequent chapters will describe their mechanics in more detail, but a quick overview may be helpful.

These five acquisition techniques can be classified in various ways. One might, for example, distinguish between negotiated and hostile acquisitions. Negotiated acquisitions are those in which the target is willing to be bought—indeed, the target may have initiated the transaction by searching out a buyer. Here the focus is on the mechanics by which the acquisition takes place, the duties of management in selecting and negotiating with a bidder, and the risk that competing bidders will try to buy the target out from under the initial bidder. Hostile acquisitions are those in which the target company's board of directors is unwilling to be acquired. Here the focus will be on how the target can defend itself against the bidder and what the bidder can do to defeat those defenses.

A more useful classification system, however, distinguishes between statutory and nonstatutory acquisition techniques.[31] The former category includes the merger, its variants, and the sale of all or substantially all corporate assets. The latter includes the proxy contest, the tender offer, and stock purchases. The role of the target board of directors is the chief distinction between the two categories. Statutory forms, such as a merger or asset sale, require approval by the target's board of directors. In contrast, the nonstatutory techniques do not. A proxy contest obviously does not require board approval, although a shareholder vote is still

---

31. The statute in question is the corporation code of the relevant state. Although the so-called nonstatutory techniques are largely unregulated by state corporation codes, they are governed by various other statutes, such as the federal securities laws.

required. A tender offer or stock purchase requires neither board approval nor a shareholder vote—if the buyer ends up with a majority of the shares, it will achieve control.

The need for board approval creates insurmountable barriers to use of a statutory form if the bidder is unable to secure board cooperation. The nonstatutory forms eliminate this difficulty by permitting the bidder to bypass the target's board and obtain control directly from the stockholders. But why would a board be unwilling to cooperate? Several reasons suggest themselves: (1) The board may refuse to sell at any price, perhaps out of concern for their positions and perquisites. (2) The board may hold out for a price higher than the bidder is willing to pay. (3) The board may hold out for side-payments.

A.   The Merger and its Variants

Although much planning and preparatory work must take place beforehand, a merger actually occurs when a document called the articles of merger is filed with the appropriate officials of the states of incorporation of the corporate parties to the transaction. Typically, articles of merger are filed with the same official with whom articles of incorporation are filed to create a corporation. In most states, this is the Secretary of State or some office subordinate thereto.

At the moment the articles are filed, two companies magically become one. This happens because a number of events take place by operation of law and without the need for further action after the merger becomes effective, including most notably: (1) the separate existence of all corporate parties comes to an end, with the exception of the surviving corporation; (2) title to all assets owned by each corporate party is automatically vested in the surviving corporation; (3) the surviving company succeeds to all liabilities of each corporate party; and (4) the consideration passes to non-dissenting shareholders.

Before it may take effect, a merger must be approved by the board of directors and shareholders of each of the constituent corporations (i.e., the corporations that are party to the transaction). In most states, the requisite vote is a majority of the outstanding shares. The requirement of shareholder approval can be a significant disadvantage to the merger in comparison to some other acquisition devices. Where public corporations are involved the process of obtaining shareholder approval is cumbersome and expensive. One must hire accountants to prepare the financial statements and to give an accounting opinion. Lawyers must be paid to prepare opinion letters on corporate, securities, and tax law questions. The lawyers will also draft, or at least review, the proxy statement that must be disseminated to shareholders in order to solicit their votes. A proxy solicitation firm usually will be retained to run the shareholder meeting and to solicit proxies. Finally, senior corporate officers must expend considerable time and effort. As a result, the cost of the shareholder approval process easily can run into seven figures.

In most mergers, the shareholders of the target corporation receive a premium for their shares over the market price that prevailed before the deal was announced. In the famous merger case of *Smith v. Van Gorkom*,[32] for example, the pre-announcement price was around $38 but the buyer paid $55 in the merger. Where two or more corporations combine in a so-called merger of equals, however, none of the constituent corporations' shareholders receive a premium for their shares. Instead, they all end up as shareholders of the combined entity.

1.   The Consolidation

A consolidation is a merger-like transaction that differs mainly in the identity of the surviving company. In a merger, two (or more) corporations combine with one of the constituent corporations surviving. In a consolidation, two (or more) corporations combine with none of the constituent corporations surviving. Instead, an entirely new corporation is created. The approval requirements and other procedural aspects are otherwise the same as for a merger.

2.   The Compulsory Share Exchange

Another transaction closely related to the merger is the so-called compulsory share exchange. In a share exchange, the acquiring corporation buys all of the outstanding shares of one or more classes of target corporation stock. Unlike a tender offer or other stock purchase transaction, in which each individual shareholder decides whether or not to sell, a share exchange is binding on all shareholders of the affected class of stock. See, e.g., MBCA § 11.03. As with a merger or consolidation, the share exchange must be approved by the board of directors and, subject to a limited but important exception, the shareholders of all constituent corporations. See, e.g., MBCA § 11.04. The exception just mentioned provides that shareholders of the acquiring corporation are not entitled to vote if the acquirer's articles of incorporation will not change, there is no change in the shareholders stock or rights, and the number of shares to be issued does not exceed 20% of the outstanding shares. See, e.g., MBCA § 11.04 (g). Although the Model Act provision for compulsory share exchanges has been adopted by over 40 states, Delaware has no comparable provision. Even in states where the procedure is available, moreover, it is rarely used.

3.   Short-form Mergers

In a short-form merger, a parent corporation merges with a majority-controlled subsidiary. Suppose Acme, Inc. owns 92% of the stock of Ajax Corporation, with the other 8% being owned by outside investors. If

---

32.   488 A.2d 858 (Del.1985).

Acme wishes to eliminate the outside investors so as to obtain 100% share ownership, a short-form merger is an attractive option. In particular, a short-form merger does not require a shareholder vote.

DGCL § 253 specifies the conditions that must be met in order for a short-form merger to be available. First, the acquiring parent must own at least 90% of each class of the subsidiary's stock that would be entitled to vote on the merger. (We examine shareholder voting rights in more detail in Chapter 5.) Second, the parent must file a statement of how much stock it owns and a certificate of merger with the state. The filing must include a resolution of the parent's board of directors authorizing the merger and setting forth "the terms and conditions of the merger, including the securities, cash, property, or rights to be issued, paid, delivered or granted by the surviving corporation upon surrender of each share of the subsidiary corporation or corporations not owned by the parent corporation, or the cancellation of some or all of such shares."

The ability to avoid a shareholder vote can make a short-form merger less expensive than a standard merger. One avoids the need to prepare and solicit proxies, as well as the necessity of a shareholder meeting and the other impedimenta of voting. With respect to the subsidiary's shareholders, this omission is not particularly controversial, because the result obviously is a foregone conclusion. The denial by the Delaware statute of voting rights for the parent corporation's shareholders, who are not allowed to vote on a short-form merger, is more controversial. Under MBCA §§ 8.04 and 8.05, by way of contrast, a vote by the parent's shareholders is required where the articles of merger would effect changes in the parent's articles of incorporation or where the parent—in order to use its own stock as consideration—issues shares collectively amounting to more than 20% of the parent's voting power.[33]

In both Delaware and Model Act states, the subsidiary's board of directors has no say in the transaction. Their approval is not required. The assumption underlying this omission is that the directors of a subsidiary with a parent that owns 90%-plus of its stock will not be independent. Accordingly, the power to effect such a merger is vested solely and exclusively in the parent's board of directors.

Minority subsidiary shareholders are not left solely to the tender mercies of the parent corporation. They will have appraisal rights, which give them the ability to go to court and have the judge determine the fair value of their shares (see Chapter 4). In many states, the parent corporation also owes fiduciary duties to the minority shareholders. In recent years, however, Delaware courts have exempted short-form mergers from the entire fairness standard typically applied to freeze-out mergers (See Chapter 4).

---

33. The text assumes the parent corporation is the surviving entity. Under both Delaware and the Model Act, parent corporation approval is required of so-called downstream mergers in which the subsidiary is the surviving entity.

Note: The short-form merger is but one of several techniques for effecting an important class of transactions variously known as freeze-outs, squeeze-outs, and take-outs. Regardless of which name is preferred, the gist of the transaction is the same. A controlling shareholder causes the corporation to effect a transaction pursuant to which the other shareholders are forced to swap their shares for cash or securities issued by the controlling shareholder. Such transactions are possible because merger statutes require the holders of all shares to participate in the transaction so long as the holders of at least 50% plus one of the shares votes in favor of it. We will examine freeze-out transactions in much more detail in Chapter 4.

B.   The Sale of All or Substantially All Assets

An acquisition by asset sale differs from a merger mainly in that the two companies do not combine. The target company remains in existence at least for a little while after the asset sale has been completed—and may remain in business indefinitely (with newly purchased assets, of course). Only title to the assets changes hands; both corporations remain alive. As a result, the mechanics of transferring control and consideration are more complex. Documents of transfer must be prepared with respect to every asset being sold and those documents must be filed with every applicable agency. For example, a deed of transfer will have to be properly filed with every county in which the target owns real estate. There must be a written assumption of liabilities. Finally, the process of distributing the consideration to the target's shareholders is more complicated. Since the target is still in existence one option is to distribute the consideration as a dividend. More often the target is formally dissolved and its remaining assets (including the consideration paid in the acquisition) are distributed to its shareholders in a final liquidating dividend.

C.   The Tender Offer

Although the tender offer has been around for a long time, it did not come into widespread use until the 1960s. Before then most takeovers were more or less friendly mergers. Granted, there was pressure and coercion in many transactions, but the necessity for target board of director approval meant the bidder ultimately had to negotiate with management. During the 1960s, however, the cash tender offer emerged as the most potent weapon in the hostile corporate acquirer's arsenal. One might almost say that it was the emergence of the cash tender offer that made the market for corporate control so economically important—it made hostile acquisitions possible.

The tender offer's growing popularity reflected the significant advantages it possessed over its principal alternative—a merger proposal.

As noted above, the requirement that the target's board approve a merger creates insurmountable barriers to the would-be hostile acquirer. The tender offer eliminated this difficulty by permitting the bidder to bypass the target's board and to buy a controlling share block directly from the stockholders. But while the tender offer is thus the key weapon in the hostile bidder's arsenal, most tender offers in fact are friendly transactions in which the target has agreed to be acquired. A tender offer is useful in negotiated acquisitions because it often can be effected much faster than can a merger transaction. The necessity of conducting a shareholder vote to approve a merger adds significant delay to the merger process.

Another important advantage the tender offer possessed during the 1960s was the almost total lack of legal rules applicable to cash tender offers. Mergers and proxy contests were subject to a complex web of federal and state laws. Among other things, the federal proxy rules and, where applicable, the federal Securities Act of 1933 and state blue sky statutes imposed substantial disclosure obligations on acquirers utilizing those techniques. The expensive process of preparing and vetting the requisite disclosure documents directly increased the transaction costs associated with such acquisitions. More subtly, the disclosures undoubtedly forced up the price the bidder needed to offer; presumably, the more the shareholders knew about why the proposal was being made (and, hence, the gains the bidder anticipated), the higher the price they would demand for their shares. In striking contrast, cash tender offers effectively fell through the cracks in the securities regulatory scheme—there simply were no important disclosure obligations attendant on such transactions. As a result, the transaction costs associated with the bid were lowered and, more important, bidders presumably were able to keep an greater percentage of the potential gains from the acquisition. This absence of disclosure formed the standard around which proponents of federal regulation rallied.

In 1965, decrying the "industrial sabotage" of raids on "proud old companies," Senator Harrison Williams introduced federal legislation that would have sharply restricted the viability of cash tender offers.[34] Among other things, the legislation would have required that bidders give target management 20 days notice of an impending tender offer. This provision alone would have substantially reduced the viability of the tender offer process, because a prenotification requirement gives target boards and managers a built-in delay period during which they can erect and pursue defensive strategies.[35] Indeed, Senator Williams acknowledged the bill's likely antitakeover effect, describing the legislation as being "designed to prevent, through appropriate disclosure, corporate takeovers by those interested merely in quick profits rather than legiti-

---

34. 111 Cong. Rec. S 28256–60 (Oct. 22, 1965).

35. Michael P. Dooley, Fundamentals of Corporation Law 492–93 (1995).

mate operation of businesses."[36] The 1965 bill was not adopted, but Senator Williams returned to the tender offer issue in 1967 and, in 1968, the Williams Act became law as a set of amendments to the Securities Exchange Act of 1934.[37] The final legislation, which was influenced by a growing perception that tender offers had both beneficial and detrimental economic effects, was considerably more balanced than the earlier proposal. In primarily focusing on disclosure and anti-fraud provisions, the Williams Act attempted to favor neither the target nor the offeror.[38] In any case, however, cash tender offers were now subject to the federal securities laws. As a result, each of the major takeover devices was now subject to relatively comprehensive regulation.

One of the curious things about the Williams Act is that it nowhere defines the term tender offer. Instead, developing a definition was left for the Securities and Exchange Commission (SEC) and the courts.[39] For present purposes, we can consider a tender offer to be a public offer, usually made to all shareholders of the target corporation, to purchase any and all target company shares tendered to the prospective acquirer. The bidder typically will offer to pay a price substantially greater than the market price prevailing before its intentions become public knowledge (the so-called "control premium").

On the day the offer commences, the bidder must file a disclosure document on Schedule 14D–1 with the SEC. Most of the information contained in the Schedule 14D–1 also must be disseminated to the target's shareholders, but the Williams Act gives the offeror two options as to how to effect that distribution. The first, and least used option, is so-called long-form publication of the offer in a newspaper. Alternatively, and more commonly, the offeror publishes a summary of the proposal in a newspaper advertisement and then mails a more detailed disclosure statement directly to the shareholders. Although this option is probably at least as expensive as the first, if not more so, there is a fair degree of certainty that all target shareholders will receive notice of the proposal by this means.

1. Partial Tender Offers

There are a number of important variations on basic tender offer theme. A partial tender offer is a tender offer for less than all of the target's outstanding shares (or for only one class of target shares).[40] One

---

36. 112 Cong. Rec. S 19003 (Aug. 11, 1966).

37. Pub. L. No. 90–439, 82 Stat. 454 (1968) (codified in scattered sections of 15 U.S.C.).

38. See generally Stephen M. Bainbridge, State Takeover and Tender Offer Regulations Post–MITE: The Maryland,

Ohio and Pennsylvania Attempts, 90 Dickinson L. Rev. 731, 735–36 (1986).

39. On the definition of a tender offer, see § 6.4.A; see also Ronald J. Gilson & Bernard S. Black, The Law and Finance of Corporate Acquisitions 959–84 (2d ed. 1995).

40. Typically, the bidder will seek tenders of at least enough shares to give it a

disadvantage of this type of offer is that it leaves minority shareholders in place. Failure to buy out all target shareholders may result in litigation over the fiduciary duties of controlling shareholders vis-à-vis the minority. Acquirers often solve this problem by a so-called freeze-out merger, in which the minority shareholders are squeezed out, although that transaction also raises fiduciary duty and disclosure problems. Another disadvantage of the partial offer is its vulnerability to competing bids; another would-be acquirer can often defeat a partial offer by making a cash any or all offer at a slightly higher price.

2.   Two–Tier Tender Offers

A closely related variant is the so-called two-tier offer. As the name implies, this offer is designed to proceed in two steps. First, the would-be acquirer makes a partial tender offer for a controlling block of target stock. At the same time the acquirer discloses its intention to effect a clean-up merger if the first step tender offer is successful. It is the fact that this intention exists and is disclosed from the outset that distinguishes this technique from the partial offer. This type of acquisition has the advantage of reducing, albeit not eliminating, the fiduciary duty and disclosure problems associated with partial offers. However, it can be vulnerable to competing any and all bids, because the acquirer often pays a lower price or uses non-cash consideration in the back end freeze-out merger.

3.   Three–Step Acquisitions

Whether a tender offer is friendly or hostile, it almost never results in acquisition of all the target's shares. Even in the case of a target board approved, cash offer for any and all of the outstanding shares at a very favorable price, it is almost unheard of for 100% of the target company's shares to be tendered. Accordingly, acquirers usually will need to plan on a freeze-out merger if the offer is successful.

In the 1970s, prominent takeover lawyer James Freund refined the process into a three-step technique. The acquirer opens with a large block purchase, then makes a friendly tender off for all remaining shares, followed by a freeze-out merger to clean up any untendered shares. Freund's approach differed from the two-tier offer in several important respects. First, it was intended for use in negotiated acquisitions, while the latter was almost always a tool for hostile acquirers. Second, the tender offer is for all shares rather than a partial offer. Third, the purpose was not to coerce shareholders into tendering, but to speed up the acquisition process so as to prevent competing bidders from entering the picture.[41]

controlling block of stock, although partial tender offers are occasionally used to effect a large investment in a firm over which the bidder does not seek control.

41.   James Freund & Richard Easton, The Three–Piece Suitor: An Alternative Ap-

4. Exchange Offers

An exchange offer is simply a tender offer in which all or part of the consideration is paid in the form of acquiring company stock or debt securities, rather than all in cash. As such, an exchange offer also can be structured as a partial or two-tier bid. Acquirers who are established public corporations most often use this option; target shareholders are unlikely to want stock or debt issued by some brand new company neither they nor their advisers have ever heard of. The other disadvantage associated with exchange offers is that the securities almost certainly will have to be registered with the SEC under the 1933 Act, adding to the delay period before the offer can be made. Delay is deadly to the hostile offer, because it allows time for management to erect takeover defenses and creates greater opportunities for competing bids.

5. Creeping Tender Offers

The so-called "creeping tender offer" does not involve an actual tender offer in the usual sense of the term. The acquirer simply keeps buying target shares on the open market or in privately negotiated block purchases until it has a controlling interest in the firm. It then wages a proxy contest to elect a board favorable to it. It may follow up with a freeze-out merger to eliminate remaining minority shareholders.

D. Negotiated or Open Market Stock Purchases

In his marvelous biography of the Krupp family, which for centuries owned a major German steel and munitions company, William Manchester described how one Krupp Magnate obtained control of a competitor by buying up its stock:

> In the spring of 1892 the shareholders of Gruson A.G. (*Aktiengesellschaft*—joint stock company) assembled and were astonished to find Friedrich Alfred Krupp among them. While Hermann [Gruson, the competitor's founder and an archrival of Krupp's father] stared across the table, his old foe's son counted out [stock certificates]. At the end he produced a pencil and did a simple sum. He owned 51 percent of the stock. Gruson now belonged to Krupp. Crushed, Hermann went home to die....[42]

Krupp's tactic would not work in the United States today. Securities Exchange Act § 13(d), adopted as part of the Williams Act, requires that any person who acquires more than 5% of a class of equity securities of a public corporation must file a disclosure statement on Schedule 13D disclosing his holdings and intentions. Once the Schedule 13D is filed, the market price of the target's stock tends to increase substantially as

proach to Negotiated Corporate Acquisitions, 34 Bus. Law. 1679 (1979).

42. William Manchester, The Arms of Krupp 199 (1964).

speculators anticipate a future merger or tender offer at a premium above the market price. For this reason, acquisition of control by open market purchases of stock is rare. The bidder will buy up as many shares as possible before being obliged to file its Schedule 13D and then shift gears to effect a merger, tender offer, or proxy contest. (Because the bidder is not obliged to file its Schedule 13D for 10 days after crossing the 5% threshold, bidders frequently acquire substantially more than 5% before disclosing their holdings.)

The short-swing profit provision of Securities Exchange Act § 16(b) provides another disincentive to acquiring control through stock purchases. Once the bidder crosses the 10% threshold, its profits on subsequent sales within the next six months may have to be disgorged to the target corporation. "Because a bidder typically realizes that it may be outbid if a bidding contest develops, it realizes that it may wish to sell out to the high bidder in the reasonably near future."[43] Consequently, most bidders are only willing to cross the 10% threshold in a transaction that will give it control of the target in a single step, such as a merger or tender offer.

Where a single shareholder (or, perhaps, a small and cohesive shareholder group) owns a controlling block of shares, however, a negotiated purchase of that block may be desirable. Acquisition of that block will give the purchaser immediate control of the corporation without the risks associated with a lengthy merger or tender offer process. As we shall see, however, such transactions entail significant fiduciary obligations on the part of both the selling and acquiring shareholders.

E. The Proxy Contest

In a proxy contest, the prospective acquirer nominates a slate of directors to be elected at the annual meeting of the shareholders. The contest arises because the insurgent slate is offered as an alternative to the incumbent members of the board. Alternatively, the insurgent shareholder may seek to hold a special shareholders meeting to remove the incumbent board and replace it with his nominees. Proxy contests, like tender offers, permit a bidder to end-run management. Proxy contests, however, suffer from a number of other drawbacks that render them the most expensive and the most uncertain, and therefore the least used, of the various techniques for acquiring corporate control. Among other things, the incumbent board's ability to use the corporate treasury to finance its reelection campaign gives the incumbents a significant advantage. In addition, the phenomenon of rational shareholder apathy, pursuant to which many shareholders pay little attention to the campaign, makes it difficult for the insurgent to make a persuasive case.

---

43. William J. Carney, Mergers and Acquisitions: Cases and Materials 15 (2000).

§ 1.4   Glossary of Takeover Terminology

Appraisal rights (a.k.a. dissenters' rights): A statutory right pursuant to which shareholders who oppose a merger (or, in some states, other extraordinary transactions) are entitled to be paid in cash the fair value of their shares as determined by a court.

Arbitrageur: An investment professional who profits from takeovers by buying the stock of a takeover target, or likely future takeover target, on the open market and then tendering the stock to the bidder.

Beachhead acquisitions: An initial block of target stock purchased on the open market or privately before the purchaser starts a tender offer, usually during the ten-day window before he must disclose his holdings.

Bidder: The individual or entity seeking to acquire shares by tender offer.

Bust-up takeover: Any acquisition in which the successful acquirer sells off target subsidiaries or other assets in order to repay debt incurred in the acquisition.

Conglomerate: A holding company that owns a diverse portfolio of subsidiaries in many different and unrelated industry sectors.

Consolidation: A combination of two or more corporations in which a new corporation is formed succeeding to the assets and liabilities of the constituent corporations and none of the constituent survives as a distinct entity.

Control share acquisition statutes: State laws that require a person seeking to purchase more than a certain percentage of target company stock to obtain prior shareholder approval, and which provide special provisions to ensure that such approval can be obtained without undue delay and in a manner which does not give an advantage either to the bidder or to the target company's management.

Corporate raider: Bidders, particularly those who do not actually acquire target companies but rather use the tender offer process to make quick profits through greenmail or by selling blocks of target stocks to other bidders.

Creeping tender offer: An acquisition technique that does not actually involve a tender offer at all. Rather, the bidder obtains control of the target company by purchasing blocks of its stock on the open market or through privately negotiated transactions.

De facto merger: Any acquisition that has the same substantive results as a merger but which is structured in some other form (such as an asset sale). The *de facto* merger doctrine is an equitable remedy pursuant to which courts may recharacterize such transactions, treating them as statutory mergers for such purposes as deciding whether shareholders are entitled to vote or to exercise appraisal rights.

Divestiture: The sale or other disposition of a substantial part of the selling corporation's business, such as the sale of an entire division. May be effected by a sale of assets, a merger of the subsidiary corporation to be sold with the buyer or a subsidiary thereof, or by a spin-off.

Fair price laws: State statutes that require that the shareholders who do not sell into a tender offer receive the same price paid in the offer in a subsequent merger, unless the shareholders approve the merger by a high percentage vote.

Fair price provision: An article of a corporation's charter or by-laws having the same effect as fair price statutes.

Forward triangular merger: A merger between the target corporation and a subsidiary of the acquiring corporation, in which the acquirer's subsidiary is the surviving entity.

Freeze-out merger: Where a subsidiary has minority shareholders, the controlling shareholder may wish to force those shareholders to sell their stock. A freeze-out is accomplished by merging the subsidiary with the parent or with a wholly-owned subsidiary of the parent pursuant to a merger agreement by which the minority shareholders receive cash or securities of the parent in exchange for their stock.

Golden parachutes: Employment contracts between a company and key employees which provide severance payments to the employee in the event he or she is fired after a change in control of company.

Going private transaction: An acquisition in which all of the public equity is acquired, after which the company's equity securities are delisted from the stock exchange and no longer traded.

Greenmail: The purchase by a target company of its own stock at a price above the prevailing market price from a corporate raider who has threatened to make or has made a hostile tender offer.

Horizontal merger: A combination of two corporations that previously competed in the same industry sectors.

Leveraged buyout (a.k.a. LBO): An acquisition in which the buyer uses debt, typically junk bonds, to finance the acquisition. Often followed by a bust-up transaction so as to pay down the resulting debt.

Lockup option: An agreement between a target company and a white knight giving the latter the right to buy a substantial block of target company shares or important target assets.

MBO: A management-sponsored buyout of the corporation, typically intended to take the company private and financed as a leveraged buyout.

Merger: The statutory combination of two or more corporations with one of the constituent entities surviving.

Merger of equals: A term of art used to describe mergers in which neither of the corporate parties is deemed to be the acquirer or the target. Instead, two putative equals combine. Typically, no premium is paid to the shareholders of either corporation; instead, the two companies swap stock. In most cases, the two corporations will have comparable market values, the shareholders of the constituent corporation will each end up owning 50% of the combined entity (plus or minus 5 percentage points), and the terms of the deal include some sharing of power among the boards and senior managers of the two companies.

Parking: Secret arrangements in which one person holds target company stock owned by another party so that the second party can avoid disclosing his holdings to the SEC and the issuer.

Partial tender offer: A tender offer in which the bidder only offers to buy part of the outstanding stock of the target company and makes no commitment to subsequently purchase the remaining shares held by other shareholders.

Poison pill: A takeover defense giving target company shareholders the right to purchase additional target or bidder stock, at a discount, if a change in control takes place. The deterrent effect of the poison pill comes from the resulting increase in the bidder's acquisition costs and/or dilution of the bidder's existing shareholders holdings. The target's board of directors typically can cancel its defensive effects by resolution to permit an acquisition to go forward. Also known as a "shareholder rights plan."

Reverse triangular merger: A merger between the target corporation and a subsidiary of the acquiring corporation, in which the target corporation is the surviving entity and thus becomes a subsidiary of the acquirer.

Shark repellents: Certain takeover defenses that are usually adopted as part of a corporation's charter or by-laws.

Short-form merger: A special statutory merger form typically limited to mergers between a parent and subsidiary corporation in which the minority shareholders of the subsidiary are denied voting rights.

Spin-off: The divestiture of a part of the selling corporation's business, effected by distributing stock of a subsidiary to the public shareholders of the parent (selling) corporation.

Sweeping the streets: An acquisition technique in which the bidder initially makes a tender offer, which has the effect of concentrating stock ownership in the hands of arbitragers, and then terminates the tender offer and purchases target company stock directly from the arbitragers.

Takeover defenses: Target company actions intended to defeat a takeover bid.

Target company: The company which is the subject of a tender offer or other takeover fight.

Ten-day window: Under § 13(d) of the Securities Exchange Act, a bidder need not report his holdings of target company stock until ten days after he acquires more than 5 percent of the company's shares.

Tender offer: An offer to purchase shares made by a bidder directly to the stockholders of a target company, sometimes subject to a minimum or a maximum number of shares that the bidder will accept, communicated to the shareholders by means of newspaper advertisements and (in most cases) by a general mailing to the entire list of shareholders, with a view to acquiring control of the target company. Termed a "hostile" offer when used in an effort to bypass a board of directors of the target company that is resisting acquisition.

Tin parachute: Employment contracts similar to golden parachutes, except that they typically are available to all, or almost all, corporate employees and provide smaller severance payments.

Two tier tender offers: An acquisition technique in which the bidder makes a partial tender offer and simultaneously announces an intention to subsequently acquire the remaining shares of the company in a subsequent merger. Often, the price paid in the second step merger is lower and not paid in cash.

Vertical merger: A combination of two corporations that operate in different sectors of a product stream, such as a merger between a manufacturer and a retailer.

White knight: A person or entity friendly to the target company that makes a tender offer in competition to that of the initial bidder.

Williams Act: The federal statute that regulates tender offers.

Chapter 2

THE BUSINESS CONTEXT OF
M & A TRANSACTIONS

§ 2.1 Introduction

Lawyer turned businessman Mark McCormack once observed that, "when lawyers try to horn in on the business aspects of a deal, the practical result is usually confusion and wasted time."[1] If lawyers are to successfully add value to a transaction, they must understand the business, financial, and economic aspects of the deal. In order to draft workable contracts and disclosure documents, conduct due diligence, or counsel clients, you need to have business savvy as well as a deep knowledge of the law.

§ 2.2 The Principal–Agent Problem

Organizing production within a firm creates certain costs. Among those costs, one of the most important classes for our purposes is that known as agency costs. Agency costs are defined as the sum of the monitoring and bonding costs, plus any residual loss, incurred to prevent shirking by agents.[2] In turn, shirking is defined to include any action by a member of a production team that diverges from the interests of the team as a whole. As such, shirking includes not only culpable cheating, but also negligence, oversight, incapacity, and even honest mistakes. In other words, shirking is simply the inevitable consequence of bounded rationality and opportunism within agency relationships.[3] It is worth

---

1. Mark H. McCormack, The Terrible Truth About Lawyers 87 (1987).

2. See Michael C. Jensen & William H. Meckling, Theory of the Firm: Managerial Behavior, Agency Costs and Ownership Structure, 3 J. Fin. Econ. 305 (1976) (seminal account of agency cost economics); see also Eric A. Posner, Agency Models in Law and Economics, in Chicago Lectures in Law and Economics 225 (2000) (good account of the current state of the art in agency cost economics).

3. A simple example of the agency cost problem is provided by the bail upon which alleged criminals are released from jail while they await trial. The defendant promises to appear for trial. But that promise is not very credible. The defendant will be tempted to flee the country. The court could keep track of the defendant—monitor him—by keeping him in jail or perhaps by means of some electronic device permanently attached to the defendant's person. Yet, such monitoring efforts are not free—indeed, keeping someone in jail is quite expensive (food, guards, building the jail, etc.). Alternatively, the defendant could give his promise credibility by bonding it, which is exactly what bail does. The defendant puts up a sum of money that he will forfeit if he fails to appear for trial. (Notice that the common use of bail bonds and the employment of bounty hunters to track fugitives further enhances the credibility of bail as a deterrent against flight.) Of course, despite these precautions, some defendants will escape jail and/or jump bail. Hence, there will always be some residual

spending some time exploring the implications of this concept, because much of transactional lawyering consists of dealing with the potential for shirking and opportunism.

A sole proprietorship with no agents will internalize all costs of shirking, because the proprietor's optimal trade-off between labor and leisure is, by definition, the same as the firm's optimal trade-off. Agents of a firm, however, will not internalize all of the costs of shirking: the principal reaps part of the value of hard work by the agent, but the agent receives all of the value of shirking. In a classic article, Professors Alchian and Demsetz offered the useful example of two workers who jointly lift heavy boxes into a truck.[4] The marginal productivity of each worker is difficult to measure and their joint output cannot be separated easily into individual components. In such situations, obtaining information about a team member's productivity and appropriately rewarding each team member are very difficult and costly. In the absence of such information, however, the disutility of labor gives each team member an incentive to shirk because the individual's reward is unlikely to be closely related to conscientiousness.

Although agents *ex post* have strong incentives to shirk, *ex ante* they have equally strong incentives to agree to a corporate contract containing terms designed to prevent shirking. Bounded rationality, however, precludes firms and agents from entering into the complete contract necessary to prevent shirking by the latter. Instead, there must be some system of *ex post* governance: some mechanism for detecting and punishing shirking. Accordingly, an essential economic function of management is monitoring the various inputs into the team effort: management meters the marginal productivity of each team member and then takes steps to reduce shirking. (No implication is intended that *ex post* governance structures are noncontractual.)

The process just described, of course, raises a new question: who will monitor the monitors? In any organization, one must have some ultimate monitor who has sufficient incentives to ensure firm productivity without himself having to be monitored. Otherwise, one ends up with a never-ending series of monitors monitoring lower level monitors. Alchian and Demsetz solved this dilemma by consolidating the roles of ultimate monitor and residual claimant. According to Alchian and Demsetz, if the constituent entitled to the firm's residual income is given final monitoring authority, he is encouraged to detect and punish shirking by the firm's other inputs because his reward will vary exactly with his success as a monitor.

loss in the form of defendants who escape punishment.

4. Armen A. Alchian & Harold Demsetz, Production, Information Costs, and Economic Organization, 62 Am. Econ. Rev. 777 (1972).

Unfortunately, this elegant theory breaks down precisely where it would be most useful. Because of the separation of ownership and control, it simply does not describe the modern publicly held corporation. As the corporation's residual claimants, the shareholders should act as the firm's ultimate monitors. But while the law provides shareholders with some enforcement and electoral rights, these are reserved for fairly extraordinary situations. In general, shareholders of public corporation have neither the legal right, the practical ability, nor the desire to exercise the kind of control necessary for meaningful monitoring of the corporation's agents.

The apparent lack of managerial accountability inherent in the modern corporate structure has troubled legal commentators since at least Adolf Berle's time.[5] To be sure, agency costs are an important component of any viable theory of the firm. A narrow focus on agency costs, however, easily can distort one's understanding of the firm. Corporate managers operate within a pervasive web of accountability mechanisms that substitute for monitoring by residual claimants. Important constraints are provided by a variety of market forces. The capital and product markets, the internal and external employment markets, and the market for corporate control all constrain shirking by firm agents. In addition, the legal system evolved various adaptive responses to the ineffectiveness of shareholder monitoring, establishing alternative accountability structures to punish and deter wrongdoing by firm agents, such as the board of directors.

An even more important consideration, however, is that agency costs are the inevitable consequence of vesting discretion in someone other than the residual claimant.[6] We could substantially reduce, if not eliminate, agency costs by eliminating discretion; that we do not do so suggests that discretion has substantial virtues. A complete theory of the firm thus requires one to balance the virtues of discretion against the need to require that discretion be used responsibly. Neither discretion nor accountability can be ignored, because both promote values essential to the survival of business organizations. Unfortunately, they are ultimately antithetical: one cannot have more of one without also having less of the other. Managers cannot be made more accountable without undermining their discretionary authority. Establishing the proper mix of discretion and accountability thus emerges as the central corporate governance question.

5. Adolf A. Berle, Jr. & Gardiner C. Means, The Modern Corporation and Private Property 6 (1932) ("The separation of ownership from control produces a condition where the interests of owner and of ultimate manager may, and often do, diverge, and where many of the checks which formerly operated to limit the use of power disappear.").

6. See generally Michael P. Dooley, Two Models of Corporate Governance, 47 Bus. Law. 461 (1992) (on which the following discussion draws).

§ 2.3   The Economics of Securities Markets

A.   Efficient Capital Markets

The efficient capital markets hypothesis (ECMH) is one of the most basic principles of modern corporate finance theory. Its influence on corporate law has been dramatic. ECMH, for example, has had an enormous impact on the SEC's disclosure rules and the elements of securities fraud. It also has been a crucial part of the debate over the desirability of insider trading prohibitions.

ECMH's fundamental thesis is that, in an efficient market, current prices always and fully reflect all relevant information about the commodities being traded.[7] In other words, in an efficient market, commodities are never over- or under-priced. The current price is an accurate reflection of the market's consensus as to the commodity's value. Of course, there is no real world condition like this, but the U.S. securities markets are widely believed to be close to this ideal.

Studies of the ECMH, as applied to the securities markets, have explored three forms of the theory.[8] Each tests a different level on which markets process information. The weak form posits that all information concerning historical prices is fully reflected in the current price. Put another way, the weak form predicts that price changes in securities are random.[9] Randomness does not mean that the stock market is like throwing darts at a dartboard. Stock prices go up on good news and down on bad news. If a company announces a major oil find, all other things being equal, the stock price will go up. Randomness simply means that stock price movements are serially independent: future changes in price are independent of past changes. In other words, investors cannot profit by using past price movements or trends to predict future prices.[10]

The ECMH's semi-strong form posits that current prices incorporate not only all historical information but also all current public information. This form predicts that investors cannot expect to profit from studying publicly available information about particular firms because the market almost instantaneously incorporates information into the

---

7. The classic (albeit somewhat dated) treatment of ECMH in the legal literature is Ronald J. Gilson and Reinier H. Kraakman, The Mechanisms of Market Efficiency, 70 Va. L. Rev. 549 (1984). For a highly accessible treatment of ECMH, see Burton G. Malkiel, A Random Walk Down Wall Street 137–221 (1996).

8. See Eugene F. Fama, Efficient Capital Markets: A Review of Theory and Empirical Work, 25 J. Fin. 383 (1970) (setting out the three forms).

9. Eugene F. Fama, The Behavior of Stock Market Prices, 38 J. Bus. 34 (1965); Paul Samuelson, Proof that Properly Antic- ipated Prices Fluctuate Randomly, 6 Indus. Mgmt. Rev. 41 (1965).

10. If the weak form of the hypothesis is true, charting—the attempt to predict future prices by looking at the past history of stock prices—cannot be a profitable trading strategy over time. And, indeed, empirical studies have demonstrated that securities prices do move randomly and, moreover, have shown that charting is not a long-term profitable trading strategy. See Burton G. Malkiel, A Random Walk Down Wall Street 196–204 (1996) (critiquing recent studies purporting to find violations of the weak form hypothesis).

price of the firm's stock. In other words, the semi-strong form predicts that prices will change only in response to new information. If information was previously leaked or anticipated, the price will not change when it is formally disclosed.

The ECMH's strong form predicts that prices incorporate all information, whether publicly available or not. As such, the strong form also predicts that no identifiable group can systematically earn positive abnormal returns from trading in securities. In other words, over time nobody outperforms the market. To some extent, this is true. The empirical evidence suggests that the vast majority of mutual funds that outperform the market in a given year falter in future years. Once adjustment is made for risks, it seems reasonably certain that most mutual funds do not systematically outperform the market over long periods.

In general, however, the ECMH's strongest form makes no intuitive sense. How can prices reflect information that only one person knows? In fact, empirical research suggests that strong form has only limited validity. There is good empirical evidence that corporate insiders, who have access to information not available to anyone else, consistently out perform the market.[11]

In an efficient stock market, the price of a share of corporate stock thus represents the consensus of all market participants as to the present discounted value of the future dividend stream in light of all currently available public information. In general, it is therefore meaningless to talk about the "intrinsic value" of corporate stock. As a marketable commodity, a share of stock has no value other than what someone else is willing to pay for it. In an efficient market, idiosyncratic valuations tend to wash out, and market price becomes the only meaningful value one can put on a share of stock.

The market thus builds consensus through trading. When new information is released, investors with high estimates of the firm's new net present value will buy, while those with lower estimates will sell. An equilibrium price quickly results.

This process necessarily assumes that investors are engaging in precisely the behavior the ECMH predicts they should eschew, namely searching out new information and seeking to capitalize on the information's value through stock trading. Accordingly, some suggest that there is a paradox behind the ECMH: markets may be efficient only if large numbers of investors do not believe in market efficiency. If everyone believed the ECMH, no one would engage in securities analysis to find "undervalued" or "overvalued" stocks. Only because a large number of investors engage in precisely this activity are the markets efficient.

---

11. See, e.g., Dan Givoly and Dan Palmon, Insider Trading and the Exploitation of Inside Information: Some Empirical Evidence, 58 J. Bus. 69 (1985).

More sophisticated analysis eliminates the apparent paradox behind the ECMH. The first analyst to correctly interpret new information can profit by being the first to buy or sell. Full-time professional investors capture enough of the value of new information to make the game one worth playing. It is trading by these investors that moves a stock's price to a new equilibrium in response to changed information. These investors thus set the price at which other investors trade.

The ECMH is widely regarded as one of the most well-established propositions in the social sciences.[12] Three important caveats to the ECMH are worth bearing in mind, however. First, most of the tests of the ECMH have been internal to the stock markets. In other words, researchers focused on whether the stock market is efficient in pricing stocks relative to one another. There is little good evidence with respect to whether the stock markets are efficient in an absolute sense. In other words, we do not know whether the stock market accurately measures the value of stocks relative to that of other commodities. The stock market could be efficient in this sense only if it were fundamentally efficient, which means that the market in fact accurately estimates the discounted present value of all future corporate dividends. There is some evidence that the market is not efficient in this sense.[13]

Noise theory purportedly offers additional evidence that the stock market is not fundamentally efficient.[14] Markets are made of human actors, who bring to bear their own individual foibles. Idiosyncratic valuations generate noise that may skew the market's valuation of stock prices. (Just as it is hard to carry on an accurate conversation in a noisy room, it is hard to accurately value stocks in a noisy market.) Research in cognitive psychology suggests that investor idiosyncrasies do not always cancel one another out.[15] Instead, investors sometimes act like a herd all running in the same direction, which can produce pricing errors.

12. As Michael Jensen famously claimed, "there is no other proposition in economics which has more solid empirical evidence supporting it than the Efficient Market Hypothesis." Michael C. Jensen, Some Anomalous Evidence Regarding Market Efficiency, 6 J. Fin. Econ. 95 (1978). During the 1990s there was something of a cottage industry of attacks on ECMH in the legal literature, the best examples of which include: Lawrence A. Cunningham, From Random Walks to Chaotic Crashes: The Linear Genealogy of the Efficient Capital Market Hypothesis, 62 Geo. Wash. L. Rev. 546 (1994); Donald C. Langevoort, Theories, Assumptions, and Securities Regulation: Market Efficiency Revisited, 140 U. Pa. L. Rev. 851 (1992); Lynn A. Stout, How Efficient Markets Undervalue Stocks: CAPM and ECMH Under Conditions of Uncertainty and Disagreement, 19 Cardozo L. Rev. 475 (1997); Lynn A. Stout, The Unim- portance of Being Efficient: An Economic Analysis of Stock Market Pricing and Securities Regulation, 87 Mich. L. Rev. 613 (1988).

13. Ronald J. Gilson and Bernard S. Black, The Law and Finance of Corporate Acquisitions 138–39 (2d ed. 1995).

14. See, e.g., Fischer Black, Noise, 41 J. Fin. 529 (1986); Andrei Shleifer & Lawrence H. Summers, The Noise Trader Approach to Finance, 4 J. Econ. Persp. 19 (1990). But see Eugene F. Fama, Efficient Capital Markets: II, 46 J. Fin. 1575 (1991) (criticizing early noise theory studies).

15. See generally Stephen M. Bainbridge, Mandatory Disclosure: A Behavioral Analysis, 68 U. Cin. L. Rev. 1023 (2000) (discussing cognitive psychology in capital markets).

Large speculative bubbles that appear out of nowhere and crash without apparent reason are the most visible form of this phenomenon.

Finally, U.S. stock markets exhibit some anomalous behaviors that are hard to explain in ECMH terms. Stocks tend to suffer abnormally large losses in December and on Mondays. Stocks with low price/earnings ratios tend to outperform the market, as do stocks of the smallest public corporations. Various explanations for these anomalies have been advanced, with varying degrees of persuasiveness.

The ECMH is often brought to bear on politically charged policy disputes, such as mandatory corporate disclosure and insider trading. Those who are troubled by the ECMH's implications in these areas find comfort in the foregoing caveats, asserting that these caveats argue against using the ECMH as a public policy tool. Many of those who support the ECMH's use in public policy admit the caveats, but deny their force. According to this view, it takes a theory to beat a theory, and no theory does a better job of explaining the vast bulk of stock market phenomena than the ECMH. At the moment, the fairest comment one can make probably is that the debate is likely to continue.

B. Portfolio Theory

Risk and return are positively correlated. A corporation seeking to sell risky securities therefore must pay a correspondingly high rate of return on that investment. The question addressed by portfolio theory is whether investors must be compensated for all risks that might effect a share of stock's value or only for certain risks. Modern portfolio theory claims that investors need to be compensated only for bearing certain risks.

In economic terms, risk is simply the probability that the actual outcome of an event will diverge from the expected outcome. As it becomes more likely that the actual and expected outcomes will differ, and as the spread of possible outcomes becomes wider, the riskiness of the event increases. Putting $1,000 in a federally-insured one-year bank certificate of deposit, for example, is not a very risky investment. The expected outcome of this investment is the return of your principal plus any accrued interest. It is highly unlikely that the actual outcome of this investment will differ from this expected outcome. If you had invested $1,000 in the stock market, however, that would be a very risky investment. Although you may expect to earn a certain return on your investment, there is a very high probability that the actual return will be different from what you expect. In addition, the breadth of possible outcomes is quite wide. At the end of one year, your investment might be worth much more than $1,000 or much less.

Attitudes towards risk vary considerably. Someone who is risk averse would rather have a sure thing than take a gamble, even if they have the same expected outcome. A risk preferrer would rather take the gamble than the sure thing, even if they have the same expected outcome. A risk neutral person would be indifferent between a sure thing and a gamble with the same expected outcome.[16]

Attitudes towards risk change over time as a person ages: When young, a person is less likely to be risk averse, but as they get older there comes a time when they become truly conscious of their own mortality and then their risk attitude begins to shift towards risk aversion. Attitudes towards risk also vary depending on the degree of risk present. Many people are risk preferrers with respect to small sums (witness state lotteries) but risk averse with respect to large sums (witness life insurance). Finally, risk aversion may also depend on whether you're gambling with your own money or somebody else's. As a general rule, however, most people are risk averse most of the time.

The proposition that most people are risk averse most of the time has very important implications for corporate finance, most notably in the relationship between risk and return. The idea that risk and return are positively correlated should not be controversial. We see examples all around us: Christmas club accounts at federally insured banks pay a lower interest rate than junk bonds issued by companies on the verge of insolvency.[17] This phenomenon is a direct consequence of risk aversion: because people prefer low risk to high risk, they must be compensated for bearing risk. The more risk you ask them to bear, the more compensation you must pay. Hence, risk and return are positively correlated. Issuers, however, only need compensate investors for certain types of risk—namely, systematic risks.

Unsystematic risk can be thought of as firm-specific risk. The risk that the CEO will have a heart attack, the firm's workers will go out on strike, or the plant will burn down are all firm-specific risks. In contrast, systematic risk might be regarded as market risk. Systematic risks affect all firms to one degree or another: changes in market interest rates; election results; recessions; and so forth. Portfolio theory acknowledges that risk and return are related: investors will demand a higher rate of return from riskier investments. In other words, a corporation issuing junk bonds must pay a higher rate of return than a company issuing investment grade bonds. Yet, portfolio theory claims that issuers of securities need not compensate investors for unsystematic risk. In other

---

16. Suppose, for example, that a gambler offers three people the following deal: "I'll give you a choice: you can have a dollar outright or we can flip a coin. Heads, you win $2; tails, you win nothing." Notice that the expected outcome of the sure thing and the gamble are the same, one dollar, because in the gamble there is a 50% probability of winning $2. The risk averse person will take the dollar outright, the risk preferrer will flip the coin, and the risk neutral person will be indifferent between the two.

17. On junk bonds, see generally William A. Klein, High–Yield ("Junk") Bonds as Investments and as Financial Tools, 19 Cardozo L. Rev. 505 (1997).

words, investors will not demand a risk premium to reflect firm-specific risks.

Investors can eliminate unsystematic risk by diversifying their portfolio. Diversification eliminates unsystematic risk, because things tend to come out in the wash. One firm's plant burns down, but another hits oil. A well-chosen portfolio of 20 stocks can virtually eliminate unsystematic risk.[18] Thus, even though the actual rate of return earned on a particular investment is likely to diverge from the expected return, the actual return on a well-diversified portfolio is less likely to diverge from the expected return. A well-diversified investor thus need not be concerned with unsystematic risk and therefore will not demand to be compensated for that risk. Systematic risk by definition cannot be eliminated by diversification, because it affects all stocks. Ergo investors will demand to be compensated for bearing systematic risk.

Although all stocks are affected by systematic risk, not all companies have the same exposure to systematic risk. A recession hurts almost all firms, for example, but it hurts cyclical manufacturing firms more than it hurts tobacco companies. If it were not so, of course, all stocks would pay identical rates of return. The capital asset pricing model (CAPM) was developed to quantify the relationship between systematic risk and return.[19]

CAPM was designed to answer a very specific question: what rate of return can we expect from an investment whose response to systematic risks differs from that of the market as a whole? In other words, suppose the market rate of return is 10%. Investment A is known to be more sensitive to systematic risk than the market as a whole: if the market goes up, Investment A goes up faster and higher; if the market goes down; Investment A goes down faster and lower. Because investors want to be compensated for systematic risk, they will want a higher rate of return for Investment A than the market rate. CAPM gives us a mathematical basis for figuring out how much higher Investment A's rate of return must be to compensate investors for bearing this additional risk.

The beta coefficient is the heart of the CAPM. Beta is simply a measurement of the investment's sensitivity to systematic risk. A beta of 1 shows that the firm tends to pay the same rate of return as the market as a whole. A beta greater than one suggests that the firm is more sensitive to systematic risk than is the market on average, so the firm will tend to pay higher rates of return. Beta thus gives us a way of comparing the riskiness of two securities by giving us a measure of each stock's sensitivity to systematic risk. Beta also gives us a way of

18. Burton G. Malkiel, A Random Walk Down Wall Street 245 (1996).

19. Franco Modigliani & Gerald A. Pogue, An Introduction to Risk and Return: Concepts and Evidence, Fin. Analysts J., May–June 1974, at 69.

measuring the impact of a proposed new investment on our portfolio. You can measure the beta of your portfolio by taking the weighted average of the betas of all the securities therein. By comparing that figure to the beta of the proposed investment, you know whether the investment would make your portfolio more or less risky.

Beta is calculated graphically by plotting market return on the X-axis and the firm's return on the Y-axis. After enough data points are assembled, you draw a regression line that fits the data best. The slope of that line is beta. Calculating beta thus involves lots of math, but we need not attempt it. Brokerage houses and investment advisors typically publish a stock's beta as part of their investor advising services.

Once beta is determined, one can use it to estimate the expected return on the asset in question using the following formula:

$$r = r_{rf} + [\beta \times (r_m - r_{rf})]$$

where r_{rf} is the risk free rate (usually measured by the current interest rate paid on short-term U.S. Treasury obligations), and r_m is the stock market's current rate of return (usually measured by reference to some market index, such as the S & P 500). As an example, assume the corporation's beta is 1.5, the market rate of return is 10%, and the risk-free rate of return is 5%. The company should pay a rate of return of 12.5%:

$$0.05 + 1.5(0.10 - 0.05) =$$

$$0.05 + 0.075 = 12.5\%$$

Beta and CAPM have been quite controversial in the financial economics literature. Critics contend that beta is not a complete measure of the risks that are priced by securities markets—in other words, that the market compensates investors for bearing some nonsystematic risks.[20] Various alternatives to CAPM have been proposed, most notably the Arbitrage Pricing Theory developed by Richard Roll and Stephen Ross.[21] As yet, however, CAPM remains state of the art in the legal literature. CAPM is still very widely used, for example, in valuing businesses for purposes of the statutory appraisal proceeding.[22]

20. See, e.g., Eugene F. Fama & Kenneth R. French, The Cross–Section of Expected Stock Returns, 47 J. Fin. 427 (1992).

21. See, e.g., Richard Roll & Stephen A. Ross, An Empirical Investigation of the Arbitrage Pricing Theory, 35 J. Fin. 1073 (1980).

22. See, e.g., Cede & Co. v. Technicolor, Inc., 1990 WL 161084 (Del.Ch.1990), rev'd on other grounds, 684 A.2d 289 (Del.1996); see also Hintmann v. Fred Weber, Inc., 1998 WL 83052 (Del.Ch.1998), modified, 1999 WL 182577 (Del.Ch.1999), modified, 2000 WL 376379 (Del.Ch.2000) (using CAPM to determine cost of equity); Le Beau v. M. G. Bancorporation, Inc., 1998 WL 44993 (Del.Ch.1998), aff'd, 737 A.2d 513 (Del.1999) (using CAPM to determine discount rate); Gilbert v. MPM Enters., Inc., 709 A.2d 663 (Del.Ch.1997), modified, 1998 WL 229439 (Del.Ch.1998), aff'd, 731 A.2d 790 (Del.1999) (using CAPM to determine cost of equity); Ryan v. Tad's Enters., Inc., 709 A.2d 682 (Del.Ch.1996), aff'd, 693 A.2d 1082 (Del.1997) (using CAPM to determine discount rate); TV58 Ltd. Partnership v. Weigel Broad. Co., 1993 WL 285850 (Del.Ch.1993) (using CAPM to determine dis-

§ 2.4 Putting the Tools to Work: Takeover Motives and Wealth Effects

Why would someone want to acquire a corporation? Obviously, there are many potential motivations. Yet, understanding the motivation driving a particular acquisition can help the transaction planner answer two critical questions: (1) What opportunities does the transaction offer by which one or both parties might behave opportunistically? In other words, how might one side try to get more than its "fair" share of the pie? Doing something about strategic behavior is a question as to which we as lawyers have a comparative advantage vis-à-vis other participants in mergers and acquisitions. Our expertise runs towards using laws and contracts to constrain behavior. (Alternatively, we may represent the party that wants to behave strategically, in which case our job is to figure out how to help them get more than their fair share.) (2) How does this transaction create value? This is a pie expansion rather than a pie division question. How can the lawyer expand the pie by adding additional value to the transaction?

A. The Urge to Merge: Various Motives for Takeovers

Takeovers sometimes create value by allowing the buyer to take advantage of specific legal rules. This is especially true with respect to tax and accounting rules. In the famous business judgment rule decision, *Smith v. Van Gorkom*, for example, the challenged acquisition was motivated by the desire to take advantage of investment tax credits that were about to expire unused.[23] These regulatory sources of value, however, lie outside the scope of this text. Instead, we will focus on two theories of more general application: displacement of inefficient management and strategic acquisitions.

1. Creating Value by Displacing Inefficient Managers

The agency cost literature describes two basic types of managerial inefficiency. The first is misfeasance: If managers worked harder, were smarter, or were more careful they would earn more money for shareholders. The second is malfeasance: Managers cheat the corporation or lavish perks on themselves. The annals of American business corporations are replete with examples of both forms of shirking, ranging from congenital unluckiness, to incompetence, to outright theft.

count rate); MacLane Gas Co. Ltd. Partnership v. Enserch Corp., 1992 WL 368614 (Del.Ch.1992), aff'd, 633 A.2d 369 (Del. 1993) (using CAPM to determine discount rate); Hodas v. Spectrum Tech., Inc., 1992 WL 364682 (Del.Ch.1992) (using CAPM to determine discount rate); In re Radiology Assocs., Inc. Litig., 611 A.2d 485 (Del.Ch.

1991) (using CAPM to determine discount rate); In re Appraisal of Shell Oil Co., 1990 WL 201390 (Del.Ch.1990), aff'd, 607 A.2d 1213 (Del.1992) (using CAPM to determine discount rate).

23. Smith v. Van Gorkom, 488 A.2d 858, 865 (Del.1985).

Experience teaches that most successful business people are smart, hard-working, and honest, however. Is it nevertheless possible that smart, hard-working, reasonably honest people might be "inefficient" and therefore in need of replacing? An affirmative answer is suggested by the so-called "free cash flow" theory: Successful managers end up with a lot of cash for which they have no good use. In technical terms, they end up with cash flows greater than the positive net present value investments available to the firm. Disbursing these free cash flows to shareholders in the form of dividends would (a) be costly because of the double taxation on dividends and (b) increase management risks because a smaller asset pool increases the risk of firm failure in the event of financial reverses. Accordingly, even well-meaning managers have an incentive to retain free cash flow by making negative net present value investments. A takeover releases most of those funds, while earning the acquirer a profit from the remainder.[24]

No matter the source or form of director or management shirking, it should be reflected in a declining market price for the stock of the company. Bad management is just another form of information that efficient markets are able to process. When a declining market price signals shirking by directors or management, among those who receive the signal are directors and managers of other firms, who possess the resources to investigate the reason for the potential target's deteriorating performance. Sometimes it will be something that is beyond anybody's ability to control, such as where highly specialized assets are languishing because of a permanent shift in consumer demand. Sometimes, however, it will be due to poor management, which presents real opportunities for gain if the personnel or policies causing the firm to languish can be corrected. A successful takeover gives the acquirer the ability to elect at least a majority of the board of directors and thereby control personnel and policy decisions. The resulting appreciation in value of the acquired shares provides the profit incentive to do so. It is partly for this reason that we refer to the takeover market as "the market for corporate control."[25]

---

24. See generally Michael C. Jensen, The Agency Costs of Free Cash Flow, Corporate Finance, and Takeovers, 76 Am. Econ. Rev. 323 (1986). The free cash flow story seems particularly useful as an explanation for leveraged acquisitions—i.e., those funded by borrowing. A leveraged acquisition results in a one-time disbursement of free cash to the shareholders and, moreover, forces the company to go forward with a highly leveraged capital structure. The additional debt forces the firm's board and management to continuing paying out free cash flows. Dividends are optional and flexible. Debt payments are mandatory and inflexible. You have to make them. Financial flexibility, in the form of free cash flow, large cash balances, and unused borrowing power provides managers with greater discretion over resources that is often not used in shareholders' interests. Debt limits management's discretion in useful ways. In effect, debt becomes a low cost mechanism by which management promises to refrain from spending free cash flows in ways detrimental to shareholder interests.

25. As is so often the case in the law and economics of corporations, the intellectual roots of this theory can be found in one of Henry Manne's articles. See Henry G. Manne, Mergers and the Market for Corporate Control, 73 J. Pol. Econ. 110 (1965).

The potential to create value through this market has important transactional and policy implications. The transactional implications should be obvious: nobody likes to be displaced, especially if the explanation for displacing them is their own incompetence or inefficiency. Hence, we can expect incumbent managers to resist takeovers motivated by a desire to displace them. Providing low-cost mechanisms for overcoming management resistance thus is one way in which transactional lawyers can add value to a prospective takeover.[26]

The market for corporate control argument also has important policy implications. Keeping the stock price up is one of the best defenses managers have against being displaced in a takeover. Accordingly, the market for corporate control is an important mechanism for preventing management shirking and thus for minimizing the agency costs associated with conducting business in the corporate form. Indeed, some scholars argue that the market for control is the ultimate monitor that makes the modern business corporation feasible.[27] If true, a variety of policy implications would follow. For example, one might well outlaw any target managerial resistance to takeovers. If there are alternative explanations of how takeovers create value, however, the market for corporate control loses some of its robustness as a policy engine. Put another way, awarding the lion's share of the gains to be had from a change of control to the bidder only makes sense if all gains from takeovers are created by bidders through the elimination of inept or corrupt target managers and none of the gains are attributable to the hard work of efficient target managers.

The empirical evidence suggests that takeovers produce gains for many reasons, of which the agency cost constraining function of the market for corporate control is but one. Studies of target corporation performance, for example, suggest that targets during the 1980s generally were decent economic performers.[28] Second, studies of post-takeover workforce changes find that managers are displaced in less than half of

---

See also Henry G. Manne, Cash Tender Offers for Shares—A Reply to Chairman Cohen, 1967 Duke L.J. 231. For appreciations of Manne's influence on the subsequent literature, see William J. Carney, The Legacy of "The Market for Corporate Control" and the Origins of the Theory of the Firm, 50 Case W. Res. L. Rev. 215 (1999); Fred S. McChesney, Manne, Mergers, and the Market for Corporate Control, 50 Case W. Res. L. Rev. 245 (1999).

26. Notice the relationship between this issue and the broader question of constraining strategic behavior. Management resistance to takeovers is a form of strategic behavior on their part.

27. See, e.g., Frank H. Easterbrook & Daniel R. Fischel, Auctions and Sunk Costs in Tender Offers, 35 Stan. L. Rev. 1 (1982); Frank H. Easterbrook & Daniel R. Fischel, The Proper Role of a Target's Management in Responding to a Tender Offer, 94 Harv. L. Rev. 1161 (1981); Ronald J. Gilson, The Case Against Shark Repellent Amendments: Structural Limitations on the Enabling Concept, 34 Stan. L. Rev. 775 (1982).

28. See, e.g., Edward S. Herman & Louis Lowenstein, The Efficiency Effects of Hostile Takeovers, in Knights, Raiders & Targets: The Impact of the Hostile Takeover 211 (John C. Coffee, Jr., et al. eds. 1988).

corporate takeovers.[29] Third, as already noted, acquiring company share-holders frequently lose money from takeovers. If displacing inefficient managers was the principal motivation for takeovers, acquiring company shareholders should make money from takeovers. Finally, there is little convincing evidence that acquired firms are better managed after the acquisition than they were beforehand. In sum, displacement of ineffi-cient managers is a plausible way in which takeovers create value, but it is hardly the only way—and it may not even be a particularly important way.

2. Strategic Acquisitions

A likely candidate as a motivation for many takeovers is the strate-gic acquisition. The bidder buys a well-managed company because it fits into the bidder's business plan. There are various ways this might happen:

Strategic acquisition for the sake of operating synergy: In a synergis-tic acquisition, the sum is greater than the whole of the parts. Synergy might be generated if two activities have greater value when conducted within an integrated firm than by separate firms. Suppose a movie studio merged with a magazine publisher, and the combined entity then merged with an Internet services provider. The magazines could cover a major movie release, while the ISP provided advertising, ticket sales, and the like. The combined efforts of the various divisions might significantly leverage the value of the movie in a way that a stand-alone studio could not.

Strategic acquisitions to redress potential hold up concerns: A com-mon efficiency-based justification for vertical integration is the elimina-tion of appropriate quasi-rents. Quasi-rents arise where investments in transaction specific assets create a surplus subject to expropriation by the contracting party with control over the assets.[30] A transaction specific asset is one whose value is appreciably lower in any other use than the transaction in question. Once a transaction specific investment has been made, it generates quasi-rents—i.e., returns in excess of that necessary to maintain the asset in its current use.[31] If such quasi-rents are appropriable by the party with control of the transaction specific asset, a hold up problem ensues. Vertical integration brings both parties within a single firm and, accordingly, is a common solution to the hold up problem.

---

29. See, e.g., David P. Baron, Tender Offers and Management Resistance, 38 J. Fin. 331 (1983); Ralph A. Walkling & Mi-chael S. Long, Agency Theory, Managerial Welfare, and Takeover Bid Resistance, 15 Rand J. Econ. 54 (1984).

30. See Benjamin R. Klein et al., Verti-cal Integration, Appropriable Rents, and the Competitive Contracting Process, 21 J. L. & Econ. 297, 298 (1978).

31. The asset may also generate true rents—i.e., returns exceeding that neces-sary to induce the investment in the first place—but the presence or absence of true rents is irrelevant to the opportunism prob-lem.

Strategic acquisition for the sake of market power: The bidder might buy one or more of its competitors so as to increase its market share and thus gain a competitive advantage. It is for this reason, of course, that the antitrust laws are concerned with takeovers. A related concept is the acquisition intended to allow entry into related markets with high entry barriers. An example may be the easiest way to explain this concept: ConAgra is a big agricultural and food products business. It wanted to enter the boxed beef business, which apparently is an industry with very high entry barriers. In other words, it is very difficult to get a new business going in the boxed beef area if one starts from scratch. So ConAgra simply bought an existing boxed beef company.[32]

Strategic acquisition for the sake of diversification: Around the middle of the 20th Century, the idea grew up that good managers could manage anything. This view was operationalized via conglomerate mergers, in which companies intentionally sought to diversify their product lines and business activities horizontally across a wide array of unrelated businesses. The theory was that a cyclical manufacturer could buy a noncyclical business, making the combined company stronger because some division would always be doing well. Diversification necessarily reduces the maximum gains a conglomerate can produce. When one segment is doing well, it is being pulled down by a segment that is doing less well. To be sure, diversification reduced the conglomerate's exposure to unsystematic risk. But so what? Investors can diversify their portfolios more cheaply than can a company, not least because the investor need not pay a control premium. Management of a conglomerate may be better off, because their employer is subject to less risk, but the empirical evidence is compelling that intra-firm diversification reduces shareholder wealth.[33] The self-correcting nature of free markets is demonstrated by what happened next: during the 1980s there was a wave of so-called "bust-up" takeovers in which conglomerates were acquired and broken up into their constituent pieces, which were then sold off. The process resulted in a sort of reverse synergy: the whole was worth less than the sum of its parts.[34]

Strategic acquisition for the sake of empire building: Bigger is typically better from management's perspective. Just like putting oriental rugs down on the floor, bigger organizational charts on the wall are a management perk. If size reduces the chances of firm failure, management even has a financial incentive to pursue such acquisitions. As with

32. ConAgra Inc. v. Cargill, Inc., 382 N.W.2d 576 (Neb.1986).

33. Yakov Amihud & Baruch Lev, Risk Reduction as a Managerial Motive for Conglomerate Mergers, 12 Bell J. Econ. 605 (1981); R. Hal Mason & Maurice Goudzwaard, Performance of Conglomerate Firms: A Portfolio Approach, 31 J. Fin. 39 (1976).

34. On the conglomerate merger phenomenon and bust-up mergers, see Gerald Davis et al., The Decline and Fall of the Conglomerate Firm in the 1980s: The Deinstitutionalization of an Organizational Form, 59 Am. Soc. Rev. 547 (1994); Andrei Shliefer & Robert W. Vishny, The Takeover Wave of the 1980s, 249 Sci. 745 (1990).

acquisitions motivated by a desire for intra-firm diversification, empire-building acquisitions doubtless reduce shareholder wealth. Free markets are self-correcting, however. Empirical studies confirm that bidders motivated by considerations other than shareholder wealth maximization themselves tend to become targets.[35]

B. Do Takeovers Create New Wealth?

In evaluating corporate takeovers, one needs to consider the wealth effects of such transactions on three sets of players: (1) target company shareholders; (2) acquiring company shareholders; and (3) society at large, which would include not only net gains to the shareholders of the constituent corporations, but also any externalities imposed on other creditors, employees, communities, and other constituencies. The question here is whether takeovers create new wealth or simply reshuffle existing wealth among the relevant players.

1. Target v. Acquirer Shareholders

Is it possible to have a takeover that increases the wealth of target shareholders, but decreases the wealth of acquiring company shareholders? In brief, sure. An auction of corporate control is the most likely situation in which such an outcome might result. Bidder One makes an offer for Target. Bidder Two then makes a competing, slightly higher bid. Several rounds of competitive bidding follow. In the end, the bidder with the highest reservation price should prevail. Yet, that bidder is the one most likely to overpay. In behavioral economics, this phenomenon is known as the "winner's curse." Suppose Target's stock was trading at $10 before the bidding began. Due to the familiar problems of uncertainty and complexity, nobody knows for sure what Target is really worth. Bidder One's reservation price is $20, Bidder Two's reservation price is $22. All else being equal, Bidder Two should win the auction. Suppose Bidder Two ends up paying its reservation price of $22, but later discovers that Target really was worth no more than $20. Bidder Two has experienced the winner's curse: it won the auction, but lost the war. It overpaid. Target shareholders are better off by $12, but Bidder Two's shareholders are worse off by $2. Net, investors as a class are better off, of course, but that fact may not assuage Bidder Two's shareholders.

The winner's curse does not always occur, even in a multi-bidder auction. The market for corporate control is thin, which reduces the probability that prices will be competed up to the reservation price of the highest-valuing user. Because better information means less risk of error on valuation, moreover, one can reduce the likelihood of bidder overpay-

35. Mark L. Mitchell & Kenneth Lehn,   J. Pol. Econ. 372 (1990).
Do Bad Bidders Become Good Targets?, 98

ment by reducing information asymmetries.[36] Nevertheless, there is evidence the winner's curse operates in the market for corporate control. The successful bidder typically pays a premium of 30–50%, sometimes even higher, over the pre-bid market price of the target's stock. Consequently, target shareholders demonstrably gain substantially—on the order of hundreds of billions of dollars—from takeovers.[37] In contrast, studies of acquiring company stock performance report results ranging from no statistically significant stock price effect to statistically significant losses.[38] By some estimates, bidders overpay in as many as half of all takeovers.

Even if it is quite common, of course, the winner's curse phenomenon does not preclude a conclusion that takeovers create new wealth. As long as target shareholders gain more than acquiring company shareholders lose, net new value is created. The evidence from the studies cited above suggests that takeovers produce net gains for shareholders.[39]

Should we worry about the distributional consequences of the difference between target and acquiring company shareholders? At first glance, well-diversified investors arguably should be indifferent as to how gains are divided between bidders and targets, because such investors are just as likely to be shareholders of one as the other. Hence, rational investors will prefer rules that maximize the net gain from changes of control. There are two difficulties with this line of reasoning, however. First, the analysis depends on both acquiring and target corporations being publicly held. If bidders are more likely to be privately held than are targets, or vice-versa, rational investors will be concerned with distributional effects. Second, and more important, the evidence recounted above suggests that target shareholders benefit from takeovers but that gains from takeovers are not passed on to acquiring company shareholders. Under such circumstances, rational investors would prefer that gains from takeovers be allocated to targets rather than acquirers. Accordingly, rational investors likely would prefer a rule maximizing the product of the number of takeovers and the average control premium to a rule simply maximizing the number of takeovers.

---

36. However, some behavioral economists contend that hubris on the part of acquiring company decision makers may cause them to persistently adhere to their chosen reservation price even in the face of objective evidence that they have overvalued the target. See, e.g., Richard Roll, The Hubris Hypothesis of Corporate Takeovers, 59 J. Bus. 197 (1986).

37. See, e.g., Bernard S. Black & Joseph A. Grundfest, Shareholder Gains from Takeovers and Restructurings Between 1981 and 1986, J. Applied Corp. Fin., Spring 1988, at 5; Gregg A. Jarrell et al., The Market for Corporate Control: The Empirical Evidence Since 1980, 2 J. Econ.

Persp. 49 (1988); Michael C. Jensen & Richard S. Ruback, The Market for Corporate Control: The Scientific Evidence, 11 J. Fin Econ. 5 (1983).

38. See, e.g., Julian Franks et al., The Postmerger Share–Price Performance of Acquiring Firms, 29 J. Fin. Econ. 81 (1991).

39. After reviewing numerous studies, Professors Gilson and Black conclude "that, on average, corporate acquisitions increase the combined shareholder market value of the acquiring and target companies." Ronald J. Gilson & Bernard S. Black, The Law and Finance of Corporate Acquisitions 309 (2d ed. 1995).

2. Investors v. Nonshareholder Constituencies

The question remains, whence comes the value created by takeovers? In particular, do takeovers transfer wealth from nonshareholder constituencies of the corporation to target shareholders? If so, takeovers generate negative externalities and the usual sorts of public policy implications follow.

There is a widely shared assumption that takeovers leave nonshareholder constituencies, especially employees, significantly worse off.[40] Admittedly, a fair bit of anecdotal evidence supports the claim. The AFL–CIO estimated, for example, that 500,000 jobs were lost as a direct result of takeover activity between 1983 and 1987 alone.[41] Acquiring companies also supposedly use funds taken out of the target company's pension plans to help finance the acquisition.[42] In light of such stories, prominent management author Peter Drucker spoke for many when he observed that "employees, from senior middle managers down to the rank and file in the office or factory floor, are increasingly being demoralized—a thoughtful union leader of my acquaintance calls it 'traumatized'—by the fear of a takeover raid."[43]

Corporate takeovers also affect the communities in which the corporation has plants and other facilities. In the wake of Boone Pickens' raid on Phillips Petroleum, for example, Phillips eliminated 2,700 jobs in its Bartlesville, Oklahoma headquarters. Because Bartlesville's population was only 36,000, this downsizing devastated the local community.[44] Similar tales of woe doubtless could be told of many communities affected by takeover-related corporate restructurings.

Highly-leveraged takeovers may adversely affect the interests of bondholders and other corporate creditors. As the theory goes, pre-takeover creditors assessed the corporation's creditworthiness and set their loan terms based on the corporation's existing assets and debt-equity ratios. In a highly-leveraged acquisition, the bidder finances the acquisition by borrowing against target corporation assets and/or selling target assets. This significantly lowers the corporation's creditworthiness, yet pre-takeover creditors are not compensated for this loss. Bondholders are particularly hard hit by this phenomenon. Bond rating agencies routinely downgrade a corporation's pre-takeover bonds to reflect the firm's increased riskiness post-takeover, which immediately

---

40. See Roberta Romano, The Future of Hostile Takeovers: Legislation and Public Opinion, 57 U. Cin. L. Rev. 457, 490–503 (1988).

41. S. Rep. No. 265, 100th Cong., 1st Sess. 14 (1987).

42. Leigh B. Trevor, Hostile Takeovers—The Killing Field of Corporate America, Address to the Financial Executives Institute, Mar. 11, 1986 at 15–16.

43. Peter F. Drucker, Taming the Corporate Takeover, Wall St. J., Oct. 30, 1984, at 30.

44. S. Rep. No. 265, 100th Cong., 1st Sess. 77 (1987) (separate views of Senators Sasser, Sanford, and Chaffee).

reduces those bonds' market value.[45]

A number of commentators have advanced theoretical bases for the claim that takeovers are detrimental to nonshareholder corporate constituents.[46] As the basic argument goes, many of the contracts making up the corporation are implicit and therefore judicially unenforceable.[47] Some of these implicit contracts are intended to encourage stakeholders to make firm-specific investments. Consider an employee who invests considerable time and effort in learning how to do his job more effectively. Much of this knowledge will be specific to the firm for which he works. In some cases, this will be because other firms do not do comparable work. In others, it will be because the firm has a unique corporate culture. In either case, the longer he works for the firm, the more difficult it becomes for him to obtain a comparable position with some other firm. An employee will invest in such firm-specific human capital only if rewarded for doing so. An implicit contract thus comes into existence between employees and shareholders. On the one hand, employees promise to become more productive by investing in firm-specific human capital. They bond the performance of that promise by accepting long promotion ladders and compensation schemes that defer much of the return on their investment until the final years of their career. In return, shareholders promise job security.[48] The implicit nature of these contracts, however, leaves stakeholders vulnerable to opportunistic corporate actions.

As the theory goes, this vulnerability comes home to roost in hostile takeovers. In all hostile acquisitions, the shareholders receive a premium for their shares. Where does that premium come from? Recall that the employees' implicit contract involved delaying part of their compensation until the end of their careers. If the bidder fires those workers before the

45. See Morey W. McDaniel, Bondholders and Stockholders, 13 J. Corp. L. 205 (1988).

46. See, e.g., John C. Coffee, Jr., Shareholders versus Managers: The Strain in the Corporate Web, 85 Mich. L. Rev. 1 (1986); Marleen A. O'Connor, The Human Capital Era: Reconceptualizing Corporate Law to Facilitate Labor–Management Cooperation, 78 Cornell L. Rev. 899 (1993); Marleen O'Connor, Restructuring the Corporation's Nexus of Contracts: Recognizing a Fiduciary Duty to Protect Displaced Workers, 69 N.C. L. Rev. 1189 (1991); Andrei Shleifer & Lawrence H. Summers, Breach of Trust in Hostile Takeovers, in Corporate Takeovers: Causes and Consequences 33 (Alan J. Auerbach ed. 1988). For critiques of such arguments, see William J. Carney, Does Defining Constituencies Matter?, 59 U. Cin. L. Rev. 385, 421–22 (1990); Jonathan R. Macey, Externalities, Firm–Specific Capital Investments, and the Legal Treatment of Fundamental Corporate Changes, 1989 Duke L.J. 173.

47. The long-term nature of the relationship between stakeholders and corporations forces the stakeholders to rely on implicit, rather than explicit, contracts. Bargaining is costly, especially where future contingencies are hard to predict. The longer the contractual term, the more costly bargaining becomes. Implicit contracts can be readjusted as needed and thus save all the parties bargaining costs.

48. While the employee-shareholder relationship is the paradigmatic implicit contract, other stakeholders supposedly make similar investments in firms. Communities, for example, often specialize around a given firm. The community receives a variety of services from the firm, but also provides the firm with a specialized infrastructure, tax breaks, and other benefits.

natural end of their careers, replacing them with younger and cheaper workers, or if the bidder obtains wage or other concessions from the existing workers by threatening to displace them or to close the plant, the employees will not receive the full value of the services they provided to the corporation. Accordingly, a substantial part of the takeover premium consists of a wealth transfer from stakeholders to shareholders. Or so the story goes.

There are any number of problems with this thesis, however. For one thing, there is no credible evidence that takeovers transfer wealth from nonshareholder constituencies to shareholders.[49] The theoretical justification for protecting nonshareholders is equally unpersuasive. Many corporate constituencies do not make firm specific investments in human capital (or otherwise). In contrast, the shareholders' investment in the firm always is a transaction specific asset, because the whole of the investment is both at risk and turned over to someone else's control. Consequently, shareholders are more vulnerable to director misconduct than are most nonshareholder constituencies. Relative to many non-shareholder constituencies, moreover, shareholders are poorly positioned to extract contractual protections. Unlike bondholders or unionized employees, for example, whose term-limited relationship to the firm is subject to extensive negotiations and detailed contracts, shareholders have an indefinite relationship that is rarely the product of detailed negotiations. In general, nonshareholder constituencies that enter voluntary relationships with the corporation thus can protect themselves by adjusting the contract price to account for negative externalities imposed upon them by the firm. Many nonshareholder constituencies have substantial power to protect themselves through the political process. Public choice theory teaches that well-defined interest groups are able to benefit themselves at the expense of larger, loosely defined groups by extracting legal rules from lawmakers that appear to be general welfare laws but in fact redound mainly to the interest group's advantage. Absent a few self-appointed spokesmen, most of whom are either gadflies or promoting some service they sell, shareholders—especially individuals—have no meaningful political voice. In contrast, cohesive, politically powerful interest groups represent many nonshareholder constituencies. As a result, the interests of nonshareholder constituencies increasingly are protected by general welfare legislation.

3. The Downward Sloping Demand Curve Hypothesis

In standard economic theory, a control premium is not inconsistent with the efficient capital markets hypothesis. The pre bid market price

---

49. See Ronald J. Gilson & Bernard S. Black, The Law and Finance of Corporate Acquisitions 623–27 (2d ed. 1995) (summarizing evidence); see also Amanda Acquisition Corp. v. Universal Foods Corp., 877 F.2d 496, 500 n. 5 (7th Cir.1989) ("no evidence of which we are aware suggests that bidders confiscate workers' and other participants' investments to any greater degree than do incumbents—who may (and frequently do) close or move plants to follow the prospect of profit").

represented the consensus of all market participants as to the present discounted value of the future dividend stream to be generated by the target—in light of all currently available public information. Put another way, the market price represents the market consensus as to the present value of the stream of future cash flows anticipated to be generated by present assets as used in the company's present business plans. A takeover bid represents new information. It may be information about the stream of future earnings due to changes in business plans or reallocation of assets. In any event, that pre bid market price will not have impounded the value of that information. To the extent the bidder has private information, moreover, the market will be unable to fully adjust the target's stock price.

Some commentators contend that the demand curves for stocks slope downwards and may even approximate unitary elasticity. If so, buying 50% of a company's stock would require a price increase of 50%.[50] If so, little or no new wealth is created by takeovers. Instead, takeover premia are largely an artifact of supply and demand.

Put another way, the downward sloping demand curve hypothesis takeover premium implies that many investors have a reservation price higher than the pre-bid market price of the target corporation's stock.[51] Indeed, because investors with a reservation price below the prevailing market price should already have sold, most investors' reservation price will be near or above the prevailing market price. Accordingly, a bidder must offer a control premium simply to induce those investors to sell. As to those investors, however, the portion of the control premium reflecting their reservation price really should not be considered new wealth.

---

50. See, e.g., Laurie Simon Bagwell, Dutch Auction Repurchases: An Analysis of Shareholder Heterogeneity, 47 J. Fin. 71 (1992); Andrei Shleifer, Do Demand Curves for Stocks Slope Down?, 41 J. Fin. 579 (1986); see generally Reinier Kraakman, Taking Discounts Seriously: The Implications of "Discounted" Share Prices as an Acquisition Motive, 88 Colum. L. Rev. 891 (1988); Lynn A. Stout, Are Takeover Premi- ums Really Premiums? Market Price, Fair Value, and Corporate Law, 99 Yale L.J. 1235 (1990).

51. The reservation price in this context refers to the minimum price investors would be willing to accept to sell their shares.

Chapter 3

MERGERS, ASSET SALES, AND OTHER STATUTORY ACQUISITIONS

§ 3.1 The Merger

In a merger, two corporations combine to form a single entity. Suppose, for example, Acme Company and Ajax Corporation are about to combine via merger. Filing the requisite documentation—typically so-called "articles of merger"—with the appropriate state official, not unlike the incorporation process by which the two companies were formed, effects their merger. After the merger, only one of the two companies will survive. But the survivor will have succeeded by operation of law to all of the assets, liabilities, rights, and obligations of the two constituent corporations.[1]

As MBCA § 11.07 more specifically explains, a merger has no fewer than 8 distinct effects on the merging corporations:

- The corporation designated in the merger agreement as the surviving entity continues its existence.

- The separate existence of the corporation or corporations that are merged into the survivor ceases.

- All property owned by, and every contract right possessed by, each constituent corporation is vested in the survivor.

- All liabilities of each constituent corporation are vested in the survivor.

- The surviving corporation's name may be substituted in any pending legal proceeding for the name of any constituent corporation that was a party to the proceeding.

- The articles of incorporation and bylaws of the survivor are amended to the extent provided in the merger agreement.

- The articles of incorporation or organizational documents of any entity that is created by the merger become effective.

- The shares of each constituent corporation are converted into whatever consideration was specified in the merger agreement

---

1. As a technical matter, a merger is defined as a combination of two or more corporations in which one of the constituent parties survives. In a consolidation, two or more corporations combine to form a new corporation. Because the articles of consolidation serve as the new entity's articles of incorporation, the distinction is mostly semantic from a corporate law perspective.

and the former shareholders of the constituent corporations are entitled only to the rights provided them in the merger agreement or by statute.

Under the Model Act, effecting a merger requires four basic steps. First, a plan of merger must be drafted, specifying the deal's terms and conditions.[2] The board of directors must approve the plan of merger.[3] The shareholders then must approve the plan.[4] Finally, articles of merger must be filed with the requisite state agency—usually the Secretary of State. The process is essentially the same in non-Model Act states, except we'll see in Chapter 5 that the vote required for the merger to receive shareholder approval varies from state to state.

§ 3.2   The Sale of All or Substantially All Corporate Assets

The board of directors has essentially unconstrained authority to sell, lease, mortgage, or otherwise dispose of corporate assets except where the board attempts to dispose of all or substantially all corporate assets. In the latter case, shareholder approval is required.[5]

"All or substantially all" is not exactly a bright-line standard. Given the expense and other burdens associated with shareholder approval, and the potentially severe consequences of guessing wrong, determining whether the sale qualifies as "all or substantially all" becomes a critical issue for transaction planners. Two classic Delaware opinions usefully illustrate the problem.

In *Gimbel v. Signal Companies*, the defendant conglomerate had multiple lines of business, including aircraft and aerospace technology, truck manufacturing, and oil.[6] The latter once was Signal's core business, but over time had become something of a sideline. The board of directors decided to sell the oil division at a price exceeding $480 million. The plaintiff shareholder challenged the sale on various grounds, including a claim that the transaction constituted a sale of substantially all Signal's assets. The Chancellor used a number of metrics to determine the percentage of assets being sold: revenues, earnings, assets, net worth, return on assets, and return on net worth. In each case, the contribution of the oil business was compared to the other lines of business. The precise percentage attributable to the oil business varied substantially depending on which metric was chosen. For example, the oil business represented 41% of Signal's total net worth, but represented

---

2. MBCA § 11.02(c).

3. MBCA § 11.04(a).

4. MBCA § 11.04(b)–(e). The voting requirements become more complex, of course, if group voting is required or if the terms of the deal trigger voting rights for classes of stock that otherwise lack such rights.

5. DGCL § 271. In 1999, the Model Act adopted amendments incorporating a new terminology. Under revised MBCA § 12.02(a), shareholder approval is required if the transaction "would leave the corporation without a significant continuing business activity."

6. Gimbel v. Signal Companies, Inc., 316 A.2d 599 (Del.Ch.1974).

only 26% of total assets, and generated only 15% of revenues and earnings. As a purely quantitative matter, the court therefore held, the sale did not entail a disposition of all or substantially all of Signal's assets. In dicta, however, the court went on to apply a second standard based on qualitative considerations. Signal had become a conglomerate whose main occupation was buying, operating, and selling businesses of various types. Oil may have been where the company started, but it was now just one line of business among many. Selling off the oil subsidiary did not mean that the company was going out of business or even changing the nature of its business. Consequently, the court indicated, the sale did not rise to the level of a sale of all or substantially all Signal's assets.

In *Katz v. Bregman*, the corporation sold off a series of unprofitable divisions.[7] When it proposed to sell one of its principal remaining subsidiaries, however, a shareholder sued claiming the transaction would entail a sale of all or substantially all the remaining assets. Through its various subsidiaries, the company had been in the business of manufacturing steel storage and shipping drums. Using the proceeds of its various sales, the company planned to go into the business of manufacturing plastic shipping and storage drums. In assessing whether shareholder approval was required, the Chancellor began with quantitative metrics. The subsidiary to be sold represented 51% of the firm's remaining assets, which generated 44.9% of total revenues and 52.4% of pre-tax earnings. Turning to qualitative measures, the court opined that the planned switch from steel to plastic drums would be "a radical departure," by which the corporation would sell off the core part of the business in order to go into an entirely new line of business. Taken together, the nature of the transaction, plus the fairly high percentage of assets being sold, satisfied the "all or substantially all" standard and shareholder approval therefore was required.

The *Katz* opinion seems problematic from a number of perspectives. On the one hand, switching from steel to plastic drums hardly seems like a "radical departure." Imagine a company that for many years profitably manufactured wooden baseball bats. Because almost nobody except professional players uses wooden bats anymore, the business has suffered. The company therefore decides to sell its wood lathes and other manufacturing equipment and to invest the proceeds in equipment for manufacturing aluminum baseball bats. Making this sort of product line decision is a quintessential business judgment for the board of directors. In relying on qualitative considerations, the *Katz* opinion thus improperly inserted shareholders into a decision reserved by statute for the board.[8]

---

7. Katz v. Bregman, 431 A.2d 1274 (Del. Ch.1981).

8. See DGCL § 141(a) ("The business and affairs of every corporation organized under this chapter shall be managed by or

As a transactional planning matter, the absence of a bright-line rule creates unfortunate complications. Consider the plight of a transactional lawyer asked by the seller's board of directors to opine as to the necessity of a shareholder vote. A well-known rule of thumb suggests assuming that a sale of more than 75% of balance sheet assets by market value[9] is a sale of substantially all corporate assets and that a sale of less than 25% is not.[10] Between those yard lines, one must make an educated guess based on qualitative considerations of the sort identified by *Gimbel* and *Katz*. In practice, one throws a few junior associates into the library with instructions to scour the reported decisions looking for cases from the jurisdiction in question—plus all the Delaware cases—that might match up to the facts of the deal at hand. One then writes as narrowly tailored an opinion letter as possible.

§ 3.3   Choosing Between a Merger and an Asset Sale

A given transaction often can be accomplished in more than one way. For example, suppose Ajax, Inc., is a unitary corporation with 5 unincorporated divisions: Defense; Consumer Electronics; Computers; Automotive; Trucking. Ajax proposes to sell the Defense division to the Acme Company. Because the divisions are part of a single corporation, it may seem that a sale of assets is the only choice. But the transaction readily could be structured as a merger. The transaction planner will cause Ajax to set up a shell corporation called NewCo. Ajax will then transfer the assets of the Defense division to NewCo in return for NewCo's stock. NewCo and Acme will then merge. Having said that, however, mergers and asset sales do differ in some rather fundamental ways, of which the following seem most significant:

Ease of transferring control: When a merger becomes effective, the separate existence of constituent corporations, except the surviving corporation, comes to an end. As we have seen, a number of key events

under the direction of a board of directors").

9. In general, corporate assets are carried on the books at their historical cost, but current market value obviously is more important and, usually, more accurate. The sale price offers a good proxy for the market value of the assets being sold, of course. As for the value of the assets being retained, one typically obtains an appraisal by an investment banking firm. If litigation results, of course, a battle of expert witnesses as to proper valuation follows. If the assets being sold constitute an identifiable line of business, such as a specific subsidiary or division, some other metrics become available. In these cases, you can often figure out what percentage of your earnings, revenues or sales the assets produce. For example, in *Gimbel*, the firm was selling off its oil subsidiary. So it was fairly easy to compute the percentage of revenues and earnings the subsidiary produced.

10. Leo Herzel et al., Sales and Acquisitions of Divisions, 5 Corp. L. Rev. 3, 25 (1982). The 1999 amendments to the Model Act create a formal safe harbor for transactions below the 25% threshold: "If a corporation retains a business activity that represented at least 25% of total assets at the end of the most recently completed fiscal year, and 25% of either income from continuing operations before taxes or revenues from continuing operations for that fiscal year, in each case of the corporation and its subsidiaries on a consolidated basis, the corporation will conclusively be deemed to have retained a significant continuing business activity." MBCA § 12.02(a).

thereupon take place by operation of law and without the need for further action. In an asset sale, the target company remains in existence with its incumbent directors and shareholders. Virtually nothing happens by operation of law, which significantly raises transaction costs.

Ease of transferring assets: In a merger, title to all assets owned by each constituent corporation is automatically vested in the surviving corporation. In an asset sale, documents of transfer must be prepared with respect to each and every asset being sold and those documents must be filed with every applicable agency. For example, a deed of transfer will have to be properly filed with every county in which the target owns real estate.

Ease of passing consideration: In a merger, the consideration passes directly to non-dissenting shareholders. In an asset sale, the process of distributing the consideration to the target's shareholders is more complicated. (Assuming this is desired. In some cases, the proceeds will be invested in a new line of business.) Because the selling corporation still exists, one option is to distribute the consideration as a dividend. More often, the target is formally dissolved and liquidated. After creditors have been paid off, any remaining assets (including the consideration paid in the acquisition) are distributed to its shareholders in a final liquidating dividend.

Tax treatment: If the buying corporation pays cash in an asset acquisition, the proceeds of that sale typically will be taxed twice. The selling corporation will pay corporate tax on the proceeds. Assuming the seller is then liquidated, its shareholders will pay personal income tax on the liquidation dividend. In contrast, if the buyer uses its own common stock as consideration in the asset acquisition, the transaction can qualify as a tax-free C reorganization. Although dividends have been taxed at the same rate as capital gains since the 2001 Bush tax cuts, the double taxation remains a significant disadvantage for cash for asset transactions. As a result, such transactions are rare.

Mergers are taxed at most only once, with the shareholders of the target paying capital gains tax on any gains realized on their shares in the transaction. In many instance, moreover, it is possible to structure the merger as a tax-free reorganization. The merger thus possesses significant tax advantages.

Successor liability: In a merger, the surviving company succeeds to all liabilities of each constituent corporation. In an asset sale, subject to some emerging exceptions in tort law, the purchaser does not take the liabilities of the selling company unless there has been a written assumption of liabilities.

Shareholder voting: Avoiding shareholder voting is the goal of most transaction planners most of the time. In the case of public corporations, the process of obtaining shareholder approval is cumbersome and expensive. Proxies must be solicited, which requires preparation of a proxy statement. Accountants must prepare financial statements and give an accounting opinion. Lawyers must prepare opinion letters on corporate, securities and tax law questions. The lawyers will also draft, or at least review, the proxy statement. The firm typically will hire a proxy solicitation firm to run the shareholder meeting and to solicit proxies. Senior corporate officers must expend time going over documents and gathering materials. And so on. As a result, the cost of the shareholder approval process easily can run well into seven figures. In a straight two-party merger, approval by both company's boards and by both company's shareholders is required. In an asset sale, by contrast, the purchasing corporation's shareholders generally are not entitled to vote on the transaction.

Appraisal rights: Appraisal rights give dissenting shareholders the right to demand that the corporation buy their shares at a judicially determined fair market value. The prospect that a significant number of shareholders might force the firm to buy them out for cash can threaten the acquisition, especially if the buyer is strapped for cash. So the transaction planner tries to minimize the availability of appraisal rights. In a straight two-party merger, shareholders of both corporations are eligible for appraisal rights. In most states, shareholders of the selling company are entitled to appraisal rights in a sale of all or substantially all corporate assets, but not the purchasing corporation's shareholders. In Delaware, appraisal is limited solely to mergers. In an asset sale, neither corporation's shareholders are entitled to appraisal.

Summary: On the last three criteria, a sale of all or substantially all corporate assets seems preferable to a merger. An asset sale minimizes successor liability problems and restricts both shareholder voting and appraisal rights relative to a straight two-party merger. Is there a way to get these transaction cost-minimizing advantages of an asset sale, while also getting the advantages of a merger? Indeed, there is a simple solution: the triangular merger.[11]

§ 3.4 Triangular Transactions

In a triangular merger, the acquiring corporation sets up a shell subsidiary. The shell is capitalized with the consideration to be paid to target shareholders in the acquisition—such as cash or securities of the acquiring corporation.[12] The shell is then merged with the target corporation. In a forward triangular merger, the shell is the surviving entity. In a reverse triangular merger, the target survives. The point is the same in either case. The target company ends up as a wholly owned

---

11. Note that an asset sale also can be structured as a triangular transaction.

12. Formally, the acquiring corporation transfers the consideration to the shell, which in turn issues all of its shares to the parent acquiring company.

subsidiary of the acquirer. The former target shareholders either become shareholders of the acquirer or are bought out for cash.[13]

In a triangular merger, nothing changes from the target's perspective. Exactly the same approval process must be followed. From the acquiring corporation's perspective, however, much has changed. Only shareholders of a constituent corporation are entitled to vote or to exercise appraisal rights. In a triangular transaction, the constituent parties are the target and the shell. As a result, the parent acquiring corporation is not a formal party to the transaction, and its shareholders are entitled neither to voting nor appraisal rights.

A triangular merger also addresses the problem of successor liability. After a triangular merger, the target remains in existence as a wholly owned subsidiary of the true acquirer. As such, the target remains solely responsible for its obligations. Unless a plaintiff is able to pierce the corporate veil, and thus reach the parent, the parent acquiring corporation's exposure to successor liability is limited to its investment in the acquired subsidiary.[14]

Again, the take home lesson is that there are many forms a given deal can take. To the extent the law elevates form over substance, as it generally does in this area, the transaction planner has substantial opportunity to engage in regulatory arbitrage. This potentially permits the planner to add substantial value to a transaction. Contrary to conventional wisdom, good lawyering actually can create wealth.

§ 3.5   Deciding to Merge

A.   The Role of the Board of Directors

Modern corporation statutes give primary responsibility for negotiating a merger agreement to the target's board of directors. The target's board possesses broad authority to determine whether to merge the firm and to select a merger partner. The initial decision to enter into a negotiated merger transaction is thus reserved to the board's collective business judgment, shareholders having no statutory power to initiate merger negotiations.[15] The board also has sole power to negotiate the terms on which the merger will take place and to arrive at a definitive merger agreement embodying its decisions as to these matters.[16]

To be sure, most mergers require shareholder approval. If the target's board rejects the initial bidder, however, the merger process

---

13. One important technical difference is that a reverse triangular merger typically will not trigger either group voting or voting rights for non-voting stock, as discussed in Chapter 5.

14. In addition, leaving the target in place as a separate entity may have other advantages in terms of employee and customer relations.

15. Smith v. Van Gorkom, 488 A.2d 858, 873 (Del.1985).

16. DGCL § 251(b).

comes to a halt without shareholder involvement. If the board approves a merger agreement, the shareholders become somewhat more involved, but only slightly. Shareholders have no statutory right to amend or veto specific provisions, their role being limited to approving or disapproving the merger agreement as a whole, with the statute requiring only approval by a majority of the outstanding shares.[17]

Allocating the principal decision-making role to the board of directors reflects the general deference corporation law gives board decisions. It also makes good sense from a governance perspective. The board knows much more than its shareholders about the company's business goals and opportunities. The board also knows more about the extent to which a proposed merger would promote accomplishment of those goals. The board is also a more manageable body. The familiar array of collective action problems that plague shareholder participation in corporate decision making obviously preclude any meaningful role for shareholders in negotiating a merger agreement. Rational shareholders will expend the effort to make an informed decision only if the expected benefits of doing so outweigh its costs. Because merger proxy statements are especially long and complicated, there are unusually high opportunity costs entailed in attempting to make an informed decision. In contrast, shareholders probably do not expect to discover grounds for opposing the proposed transaction in the proxy statement. Frequently there are none, and even where grounds exist they will often be very difficult to discern from the proxy statement. Accordingly, shareholders can be expected to assign a relatively low value to the expected benefits of careful consideration. As a result, negotiated acquisitions are likely to be approved even where approval is not the decision an informed shareholder would reach. This is why corporate law gives the board sole power to negotiate mergers. It is also why corporate law requires shareholders to vote on the merger agreement as a whole, rather than allowing them to approve or disapprove specific provisions.

As with any conferral of plenary authority, the board's power to make decisions about negotiated acquisitions gives rise to the potential for abuse. Inherent in all corporate takeovers is a well-documented conflict between the interests of target managers and target shareholders. Although the tension between shareholders and managers is perhaps most obvious in hostile takeovers, where there is a substantial risk incumbent directors and managers will be fired if the acquisition is successful, similar conflicts of interest arise in negotiated acquisitions. Because approval by the target's board of directors is a necessary prerequisite to most acquisition methods, the modern corporate statutory scheme gives management considerable power in negotiated acquisitions. To purchase the board's cooperation the bidder may offer side payments to management, such as an equity stake in the surviving

---

17. DGCL § 251(c).

entity, employment or non-competition contracts, substantial severance payments, continuation of existing fringe benefits or other compensation arrangements.[18] Although it is undoubtedly rare for side payments to be so large as to materially affect the price the bidder would otherwise be able to pay target shareholders, side payments may affect management's decision making by causing them to agree to an acquisition price lower than that which could be obtained from hard bargaining or open bidding.[19]

Even where management is not consciously seeking side-payments from the bidder, a conflict of interest can still arise:

> There may be at work [in negotiated acquisitions] a force more subtle than a desire to maintain a title or office in order to assure continued salary or perquisites. Many people commit a huge portion of their lives to a single large-scale business organization. They derive their identity in part from that organization and feel that they contribute to the identity of the firm. The mission of the firm is not seen by those involved with it as wholly economic, nor the continued existence of its distinctive identity as a matter of indifference.[20]

Although such motivations are understandable, they conflict with the shareholders' economic interests.

Corporate acquisitions thus are a classic example of what game theorists refer to as "final period problems." In repeat transactions, the risk of self-dealing by one party is constrained by the threat that other party will punish the cheating party in future transactions. In a final period transaction, this constraint disappears. Because the final period transaction is the last in the series, the threat of future punishment disappears.

Just so, the various extrajudicial constraints imposed on management in the operational context break down in corporate acquisitions. Target management is no longer subject to shareholder discipline because the acquirer will buy out the target's shareholders. Target management is no longer subject to market discipline because the target by definition will no longer operate in the market as an independent agency. As a result, management is no longer subject to either sharehold-

---

18. E.g., Samjens Partners I v. Burlington Industries, Inc., 663 F.Supp. 614 (S.D.N.Y.1987) (white knight offered target management equity stake); Singer v. Magnavox Co., 380 A.2d 969 (Del.1977) (target directors offered employment contracts); Gilbert v. El Paso Co., 490 A.2d 1050 (Del. Ch.1984) (plaintiff alleged tender offeror modified bid to benefit target managers).

19. E.g., Pupecki v. James Madison Corp., 382 N.E.2d 1030 (Mass.1978) (plaintiff claimed that consideration for sale of assets was reduced due to side-payments to controlling shareholder); Barr v. Wackman, 368 N.Y.S.2d 497, 329 N.E.2d 180 (1975) (plaintiff claimed target directors agreed to low acquisition price in exchange for employment contracts).

20. Paramount Communications Inc. v. Time Inc., [1989] Fed.Sec.L.Rep. (CCH) ¶ 94,514 at 93,268–69 (Del.Ch.1989), aff'd, 571 A.2d 1140 (Del.1989).

er or market penalties for self-dealing. Accordingly, there is good reason to be skeptical of management claims to be acting in the shareholders' best interests.

Despite these significant accountability concerns, the Delaware cases consistently apply the business judgment rule to board decisions to approve a merger. Courts often refer to the business judgment rule as "a presumption" that the directors or officers of a corporation acted on an informed basis, in good faith, and in the honest belief that the action taken was in the best interests of the company.[21] This phraseology is unfortunate, at best. The business judgment rule is not a presumption "in the strict evidentiary sense of the term."[22] Instead, it is more in the nature of an assumption; namely, courts assume they should not review director decisions absent fraud, illegality, or self-dealing. In any event, the bottom line is that even clear mistakes of judgment rarely result in personal liability on the part of corporate directors.

Put another way, the business judgment rule reflects a balance pursuant to which directors are given substantial discretion, but are not allowed to put their own interests ahead of those of the shareholders. In other words, we give them carte blanche to make decisions that might turn out badly, but no discretion to make selfish decisions. This balance is reflected in the various preconditions courts have identified that must be satisfied before directors may avail themselves of the rule's protection.

An exercise of judgment. The business judgment rule is relevant only where directors have actually exercised business judgment. A decision to refrain from action is protected just as much as a decision to act, but there is no protection where directors have made no decision at all.[23] Instead, the consequences of inaction are subject to review under the duty of care.[24]

Disinterested and independent decision makers. The business judgment rule "presupposes that the directors have no conflict of interest."[25] Hence, self-dealing is one of the classic triad of ways in which the business judgment rule's presumptions are rebutted. "A director is interested if he will be materially affected, either to his benefit or detriment, by a decision of the board, in a manner not shared by the corporation and the shareholders."[26] Consequently, for example, a di-

---

21. See, e.g., Panter v. Marshall Field & Co., 646 F.2d 271, 293 (7th Cir.), cert. denied, 454 U.S. 1092 (1981); Aronson v. Lewis, 473 A.2d 805, 812 (Del.1984).

22. R. Franklin Balotti & James J. Hanks, Jr., Rejudging the Business Judgment Rule, 48 Bus. Law. 1337, 1345 (1993).

23. See, e.g., Rosenblatt v. Getty Oil Co., 493 A.2d 929, 943 (Del.1985) (holding that "an informed decision to delegate a

task is as much an exercise of business judgment as any other").

24. See, e.g., In re Caremark Int'l Inc. Deriv. Litig., 698 A.2d 959 (Del.Ch.1996).

25. Lewis v. S. L. & E., Inc., 629 F.2d 764, 769 (2d Cir.1980).

26. Seminaris v. Landa, 662 A.2d 1350, 1354 (Del.Ch.1995).

rector who sells or leases property to or from the corporation is interested in that transaction. Similarly, a director who contracts to provide services to the corporation is interested in that transaction.

Directors also can be interested in a transaction by virtue of indirect connections. In *Bayer v. Beran*,[27] for example, the corporation hired the wife of its president. Their spousal relationship gave the president an indirect interest in the transaction. Similarly, in *Globe Woolen Co. v. Utica Gas & Electric Co.*,[28] a director of the defendant was also the president and chief stockholder of the plaintiff. By virtue of those business relationships, he was deemed interested in the transaction even though he was not a party to the contract.

In addition to lacking a personal interest in the transaction in question, a director must be independent. "A director is independent if he can base his decision 'on the corporate merits of the subject before the board rather than extraneous considerations or influences.' "[29] In order to prove that the directors were not independent, plaintiff therefore must establish personal or business relationships by which the directors are either beholden to or controlled by the interested party.[30]

Where the board has acted collectively, it is not enough to show that a single director was interested or lacked independence. The business judgment rule will still insulate the board's decision from judicial review unless plaintiff can show that a majority of the board was interested and/or lacked independence.[31]

Absence of fraud or illegality. The business judgment rule will not insulate from judicial review decisions tainted by fraud or illegality.[32]

Rationality. In *Sinclair Oil Corp. v. Levien*, the Delaware supreme court held that so long as the board's decision could be attributed to any rational business purpose the business judgment rule precluded the court from substituting its judgment as to the merits of the decision for those of the board.[33] Similarly, in *Brehm v. Eisner*, the court held that

---

27. 49 N.Y.S.2d 2 (Sup.Ct.1944).

28. 121 N.E. 378 (N.Y.1918). Consequently, directors are deemed to be interested when they "stand in a dual relation which prevents an unprejudiced exercise of judgment." Stoner v. Walsh, 772 F.Supp. 790, 802 (S.D.N.Y.1991) (quoting United Copper Sec. Co. v. Amalgamated Copper Co., 244 U.S. 261, 264 (1917)).

29. Seminaris v. Landa, 662 A.2d 1350, 1354 (Del.Ch.1995) (quoting Aronson v. Lewis, 473 A.2d 805, 816 (Del.1984)).

30. See Aronson v. Lewis, 473 A.2d 805, 815 (Del.1984); see also Odyssey Partners, L.P. v. Fleming Cos., Inc., 735 A.2d 386, 407 (Del.Ch.1999). In Kahn v. Tremont

Corp., 694 A.2d 422 (Del.1997), a committee of nominally independent directors approved a corporate acquisition. Two of the three directors were wholly passive, acquiescing in the decisions of the committee chairman, who had a significant financial relationship with a controlling shareholder. The directors' decision was not protected by the business judgment rule.

31. See Odyssey Partners, L.P. v. Fleming Cos., Inc., 735 A.2d 386, 407 (Del.Ch.1999).

32. See, e.g., Shlensky v. Wrigley, 237 N.E.2d 776, 778 (Ill.App.1968).

33. Sinclair Oil Corp. v. Levien, 280 A.2d 717, 720 (Del.1971).

the business judgment rule does not apply when the board has "act[ed] in a manner that cannot be attributed to a rational business purpose."[34]

The reference to a "rational business purpose," properly understood, does not contemplate substantive review of the decision's merits. "*Sinclair*'s use of [the word] rational is to be equated with conceivable or imaginable and means only that the court will not even look at the board's judgment if there is any possibility that it was actuated by a legitimate business reason. It clearly does not mean, and cannot legitimately be cited for the proposition, that individual directors must have, and be prepared to put forth, proof of rational reasons for their decisions."[35] Consequently, as Chancellor Allen has stated:

> [W]hether a judge or jury considering the matter after the fact, believes a decision substantively wrong, or degrees of wrong extending through "stupid" to "egregious" or "irrational", provides no ground for director liability, so long as the court determines that the process employed was either rational or employed in a *good faith* effort to advance corporate interests. To employ a different rule— one that permitted an "objective" evaluation of the decision—would expose directors to substantive second guessing by ill-equipped judges or juries, which would, in the long-run, be injurious to investor interests.[36]

Instead, as Chancellor Allen observed elsewhere, "such limited substantive review as the rule contemplates (i.e., is the judgment under review 'egregious' or 'irrational' or 'so beyond reason,' etc.) really is a way of inferring bad faith."[37] Put another way, inquiry into the rationality of a decision is a proxy for an inquiry into whether the decision was tainted by self-interest.

An informed decision (a.k.a. process due care). It is frequently said that the exercise of "reasonable diligence and care" is a precondition for the business judgment rule's application.[38] This phraseology is most unfortunate. It implies the necessity to inquire into the care exercised by the board, which in turn easily slides into the error of treating compliance with the duty of care as an essential prerequisite for invoking the rule. The problem reduces to one of mere semantics, however, if we understand the requirement of "reasonable diligence and care" as being limited to the process by which the decision was made. Numerous Delaware decisions confirm that judicial references to a requirement of due care really go to the adequacy of the decision-making process—what

---

34. Brehm v. Eisner, 746 A.2d 244, 264 n. 66 (Del.2000).

35. Michael P. Dooley, Two Models of Corporate Governance, 47 Bus. Law. 461, 478–79 n.58 (1992).

36. In re Caremark International Inc. Derivative Litig., 698 A.2d 959, 967 (Del. Ch.1996) (emphasis in original).

37. In re RJR Nabisco, Inc. Shareholders Litig., 1989 WL 7036 at *13 n. 13 (Del. Ch.1989).

38. See, e.g., S. Samuel Arsht, The Business Judgment Rule Revisited, 8 Hofstra L. Rev. 93, 100 (1979).

the court has begun calling "process due care."[39] It would be better to follow the lead of those decisions and simply stop talking about whether the board exercised "reasonable diligence and care." Instead, the requisite precondition would be better stated as a rational and good faith decision-making process.

Assuming the foregoing preconditions are satisfied, courts asked to review a board decision to approve a merger—standing alone—will invoke the business judgment rule as the standard of review. By doing so, they ensure that the considerable latitude conferred upon the board by statute may exercised without significant risk of judicial intervention.

Why aren't courts more worried about the conflict of interest identified above? In a plain vanilla arms-length merger, the board's potential conflict of interest is policed by a variety of non-legal constraints. Independent directors and shareholders must be persuaded to approve the transaction. The reputational consequences of self-dealing may cause bother the directors and managers problems in the internal and external job markets. Ill-advised acquisitions are likely to cause the acquiring firm problems in the capital markets, which may constrain its willingness to divert gains from target shareholders to the target's board and managers.

In addition to those monitoring mechanisms, negotiated acquisitions are subject to the constraining influences of the market for corporate control. Where side payments persuade management to accept a low initial offer, a second bidder may—and often does—succeed by offering shareholders a higher-priced alternative. Indeed, to the extent side payments affect the initial bidder's ability to raise its offer in response to a competing bid, the threat of competing bids becomes particularly important. In such cases, the second bidder is almost certain to prevail. True, the competing bidder's transaction cannot be structured as a merger or asset sale if it is unable to persuade target management to change sides. But the intervener has a formidable alternative: the tender offer, which eliminates the need for target management's cooperation by permitting the bidder to bypass the target's board and to buy a controlling share block directly from the stockholders.

B.　The Necessity of Process Due Care when Deciding to Merge

Although courts routinely apply the business judgment rule to a

---

39. Brehm v. Eisner, 746 A.2d 244, 264 (Del.2000) ("Due care in the decisionmaking context is *process* due care only."; emphasis in original); Citron v. Fairchild Camera & Instrument Corp., 569 A.2d 53, 66 (Del.1989) ("our due care examination has focused on a board's decision-making process"); In re Caremark Int'l Inc. Deriv. Litig., 698 A.2d 959, 967 (Del.Ch.1996) ("compliance with a director's duty of care can never appropriately be judicially determined by reference to *the content of the board decision* that leads to a corporate loss, apart from consideration of the good faith *or* rationality of the process employed"; emphasis in original).

board's decision to merge, this does not mean that there is no judicial review of that decision. As we saw above, the exercise of process due care by the board of directors is an essential precondition for application of the business judgment rule. *Smith v. Van Gorkom*,[40] the seminal process case, illustrates the special import of this requirement in judicial review of a board's decision to merge. In 1980, Trans Union's CEO and chairman, Van Gorkom, negotiated a merger between Trans Union and an entity controlled by financier Pritzker. Trans Union's board and shareholders approved the deal. Plaintiff-shareholder Smith sued, alleging that the board's approval of the deal merger violated the Trans Union directors' duty of care. The defendant directors contended that their decision to sell the company should be protected by the business judgment rule.

The court began its analysis by noting that the business judgment rule provides a presumption that in making a decision the directors acted on an informed basis, in good faith and in the honest belief that the decision was in the firm's best interests. None of the usual triad of exceptions to the rule—i.e., fraud, illegality, or self-dealing—was present in this case, as the court acknowledged.[41] The protection provided by the business judgment rule is unavailable, however, if the directors failed to inform themselves of all material information reasonably available to them. In the course of its opinion, the court focused closely on issues of board process. Indeed, one can plausibly read *Van Gorkom* as providing a procedural roadmap by which corporate decisions, at least of this magnitude, ought to be made. Accordingly, it seems appropriate to identify those aspects of the Trans Union board's conduct by which the court was troubled.

Consultations. During his negotiations with Pritzker, Van Gorkom consulted only with Trans Union's controller (Peterson). Worse yet, once he told other senior managers about the impending deal, their initial reaction was strongly negative. In particular, Romans (Trans Union's CFO) objected that the price was too low, the transaction would have adverse tax consequences for some shareholders, and an option given Pritzker to buy Trans Union shares amounted to a "lock-up" that would inhibit competing offers. Such evidence likely proved quite damning in the court's own decision-making process. Having evidence in the record

---

40.   488 A.2d 858 (Del.1985).

41.   One could perhaps construct a self-dealing argument by focusing on the fact that Van Gorkom was very close to the mandatory retirement age and owned 75,-000 shares of Trans Union stock. At $55 per share, those shares would be worth over $4 million; on the stock market, the shares had recently traded in a range of $30 to $39 per share. Even at the high end of that range, those shares were worth less than $3 million. One thus could argue that Van Gorkom's large stockholdings and his imminent mandatory retirement meant that he had an incentive to sell the company. If so, however, his incentive clearly is to get the best possible price. The more money for which Trans Union was sold, the more money Van Gorkom would have in retirement. Consequently, his self-interest was directly in-line with the interests of the shareholders, who presumably also would want the best possible price.

of these types of internal disagreements obviously raised questions about the fairness of the transaction. The take-away lesson is that deal-makers should, early in the process, consult with senior management and get them "on board." In addition, Van Gorkom would have been well-advised to consult in advance with the board of directors and kept them informed as to the progress of the negotiations.

Setting the price. When selling an entire business, whether the sale is nominally structured as a merger or not, the board of directors "must focus on one primary objective—to secure the transaction offering the best value reasonably available for all stockholders."[42] In his negotiations with Pritzker, it was Van Gorkom who proposed the price of $55. In evaluating the potential for a management-sponsored leveraged buyout, Romans had earlier determined that such a buyout would be easy at a price of $50 but very difficult at a price of $60. Van Gorkom then seemingly split the difference, picking $55 out of the air as a price he would accept for his shares.

The court emphasized that the price thus was based on an evaluation of the feasibility with which a leveraged deal could be financed, rather than the Trans Union's value.[43] To the extent the court's analysis rests on the idea that a company has some intrinsic value, the decision is seriously flawed. As with any other asset, a company is worth only what somebody is willing to pay for it. Although the company's only value thus is its market value, an asset can have different values in different markets. (Otherwise, arbitrage would never be profitable.) Two distinct markets are implicated in this setting. On the one hand, there is the ordinary stock market in which Trans Union's shares trade. On the other, however, there is the market for corporate control. Prices in the latter market typically exceed those in the former. Hence, we speak of a "control premium" that is paid when someone buys all of the shares of a company's stock.

Trans Union's board made no effort to determine what control was worth to Pritzker, such as by ordering a valuation study, and in the absence of such a determination had no basis for deciding whether the price was a fair one. Put another way, the real issue, which is not well-framed in the majority opinion, is what the firm was worth to Pritzker and, accordingly, whether the board of directors did a good job in capturing that value on behalf of their shareholders. Trans Union's own estimate suggested that a price of up to $60 per share feasibly could be financed, albeit with some difficulty.[44] The feasibility study, moreover,

---

42. McMullin v. Beran, 765 A.2d 910, 918 (Del.2000).

43. See, e.g., Smith v. Van Gorkom, 488 A.2d 858, 874 (Del.1985) (noting that the directors "were uninformed as to the intrinsic value of the Company").

44. The difference between $60 and the $55 Pritzker agreed to pay is only $5 per share, but $5 per share times roughly 12.5 million outstanding shares works out to about $63 million, which is not chump change.

was prepared internally by an officer who presumably did not do such studies for a living. Although the court explicitly stated that boards are not obliged to hire outside financial experts, investment bankers in fact do valuation and feasibility studies for a living. The well-advised board thus obtains a fairness opinion that, at least in theory, gives them some basis for evaluating what the prospective buyer could afford, and would be willing, to pay. Not surprisingly, *Van Gorkom* is sometimes referred to as the "Investment Bankers' Full Employment Act."[45]

Negotiations. Van Gorkom's negotiations with Pritzker appear to have been less than demanding. Van Gorkom asked for a meeting, at which he basically said "if you'll pay $55, here's how you can finance the deal." Pritzker counter-offered with $50 per share, which Van Gorkom rejected. Pritzker then agreed to $55. Pritzker's quick acceptance of the price suggests that he thought he was getting a bargain, which enhances our questions about the adequacy of the price.

Time pressures. Pritzker imposed a tight time deadline in order to prevent leaks and the increased stock price that usually follows such leaks. As a result, the process went quite quickly and many decisions were made under significant time constraints. All of which evidently troubled the court, as it several times noted that there was no crisis or emergency justifying such speed. Does *Van Gorkom* thus imply that the board can never make quick decisions? Probably not. The speed with which the decision was made likely would have been unobjectionable if the process was otherwise adequate. A cautionary note is sounded, however, by the Delaware Supreme Court's recent observation that: "History has demonstrated boards 'that have failed to exercise due care are frequently boards that have been rushed.' "[46]

Information and process. The central issue in *Van Gorkom* was the board's failure to make an informed decision. The legal standard that emerges from the decision is straightforward—directors must inform themselves of all material information reasonably available to them.[47] This standard seemingly requires an in-depth study of the problem. The board must be informed of the company's value to the bidder, the course of the negotiations, the terms of the offer and their fairness, and the like.

---

45. See, e.g., Park McGinty, The Twilight of Fiduciary Duties: On the Need For Shareholder Self–Help in an Age of Formalistic Proceduralism, 46 Emory L.J. 163, 193 n.42 (1997); see also William J. Carney, Fairness Opinions: How Fair Are They and Why We Should Do Nothing About It, 70 Wash. U. L.Q. 523, 527 (1992) (opining that *Van Gorkom* "could be called the Investment Bankers' Civil Relief Act of 1985").

46. McMullin v. Beran, 765 A.2d 910, 922 (Del.2000).

47. Smith v. Van Gorkom, 488 A.2d 858, 872 (Del.1985). See also Washington Bancorporation v. Said, 812 F.Supp. 1256, 1269 (D.D.C.1993); Estate of Detwiler v. Offenbecher, 728 F.Supp. 103, 150 (S.D.N.Y.1989). The Delaware supreme court subsequently defined the term "material" in this context as "relevant and of a magnitude to be important to directors in carrying out their fiduciary duty of care in decisionmaking." Brehm v. Eisner, 746 A.2d 244, 259 n. 49 (Del.2000).

This standard is too demanding. Information is costly and share-holders will only want managers to invest an additional dollar in gathering information where there is an additional dollar generated from better decision making. By requiring directors to have all information "reasonably available" to them the *Van Gorkom* court required the directors to over-invest in information.[48] In contrast, the ALI PRINCIPLES only require directors to be informed to the extent that they reasonably believe to be appropriate under the circumstances.[49] Unlike the Delaware standard, at least as read literally, the ALI standard permits directors to make decisions on less than all reasonable available information, provided they reasonably believe doing so is appropriate given the situation. The time available to make the decision may require that the directors take risks to secure what appears to be a good outcome, which includes the risk that they do not have all of the relevant facts. A decision to accept that risk in order to secure the benefits of a proposed transaction will be appropriate under some circumstances.

In practice, of course, there are significant limitations on the board's ability to gather primary sources of information. Nobody seriously expects boards to read merger agreements cover to cover—not even the *Van Gorkom* court.[50] Reading long and boring legal documents is what boards pay their lawyers and subordinates to do. Under the circumstances, however, Trans Union's directors had a duty of inquiry. Considering the haste and other circumstances surrounding the decision, they should have pressed Van Gorkom with regard to the details of the deal. Instead, the board blindly relied on Van Gorkom's assertion that the price was fair. Van Gorkom failed to disclose, and the board failed to make sufficient inquiry to discover, key facts suggesting that the deal was not as attractive as it might seem on first blush.[51]

Qualitative studies of board processes have found wide variances. Some boards simply go through the motions of showing up and voting, without having done their homework.[52] The Delaware Supreme Court

---

48. Cf. In re RJR Nabisco, Inc. Shareholders Litig., 1989 WL 7036 (Del.Ch.1989), in which Chancellor Allen observed that "information has costs." Id at *19. He further opined "that the amount of information that it is prudent to have before a decision is made is itself a business judgment of the very type that courts are institutionally poorly equipped to make." Id.

49. ALI Principles § 4.01(c)(2).

50. Smith v. Van Gorkom, 488 A.2d 858, 883 n. 25 (Del.1985) ("We do not suggest that a board must read *in haec verba* every contract or legal document which it approves...."). In its controversial *Omnicare* decision, a majority of the Delaware supreme court snidely "assumed arguendo" that the target's board of directors "exercised due care when it: ... executed a

merger agreement that was summarized but never completely read" by the board. Omnicare, Inc. v. NCS Healthcare, Inc., 818 A.2d 914, 929 (Del.2003).

51. In other words, the formal structure of the corporate governance system vests most decision-making power in the board of directors, especially with regard to major corporate changes such as a merger. Facts tending to suggest that senior officers are trying to railroad a decision through the board therefore are inconsistent with that model. Unfortunately for Trans Union's directors, the *Van Gorkom* record was rife with such facts.

52. Daniel P. Forbes & Frances J. Milliken, Cognition and Corporate Governance: Understanding Boards of Directors as Stra-

concluded that the Trans Union directors were just such a board—the board was "grossly negligent in approving the 'sale' of the Company upon two hours' consideration, without prior notice, and without the exigency of a crisis or emergency." Other boards, however, exhibit far greater diligence. Such boards research issues, participate actively in discussion, and exercise critical judgment.

How should corporate law encourage boards to exercise due diligence in the decision-making process? Should the corporate statute specify board procedures, for example? In general, corporation codes do not mandate detailed rules of board process or procedure. How the board sets its agenda, whether formal voting rules are observed, and other matters of parliamentary procedure are left to the board's discretion. This makes sense, as it is doubtful whether ex ante legislative solutions would be viable given the complexities and uncertainties of life. Ex post judicial review of board process may be beneficial, however.

Consistent with that hypothesis, *Van Gorkom* rests not on failure to comply with some judicially imposed decision-making model but on the absence of a sufficient record of any deliberative process. Put differently, if the decision-making process is adequate, the court will continue to defer to the decision that emerges from that process. The basic thrust of the opinion then is that the board must provide some credible, contemporary evidence that it knew what it was doing. If such evidence exists, the court will not impose liability—even if the decision proves to have been the wrong one.

By so focusing its opinion, the *Van Gorkom* court arguably created a set of incentives consistent with the teaching of the literature on group decision making. The decision disfavors agenda control by senior management. The decision penalizes boards that simply go through the motions. The decision encourages inquiry, deliberation, care, and process. The decision strongly encourages boards to seek outside counsel and financial advice, which is consistent with evidence groupthink can be prevented by outside expert advice and evaluations.[53] Even the court's criticism of the board's willingness to take action after a single meeting is consistent with suggestions that a "second-chance meeting" also helps prevent groupthink.

Summation. While the substantial criticism to which *Van Gorkom* has been subjected is not wholly unmerited, ultimately the decision is defensible. Even at the time *Van Gorkom* was decided, the more exaggerated fears of judicial intervention into board decision-making processes were clearly overstated. Strict adherence to the court's decision-making model likely is not a prerequisite for the business judgment rule to be applicable. On the facts of the case before it, however, the court conclud-

tegic Decision-making Groups, 24 Acad. Mgmt. Rev. 489, 494 (1999).

53. See generally Irving Janis, L. Groupthink (2d ed. 1982) (discussing solutions for groupthink).

ed that the board had abdicated its responsibility and allowed itself to be railroaded by management to so great an extent that deference became inappropriate. In addition, the decision at issue related to a major transaction having final period consequences. Under those circumstances, the board's process failures justified holding them to account.

In closing, however, it should be noted that *Van Gorkom* probably has resulted in many board decisions being over-processed. In many cases, even relatively minor board decisions are subjected to exhaustive review, with detailed presentations by experts. Why? The answer lies in the incentive structures of the relevant players. Who pays the bill if the director is found liable for breaching the duty of care? The director.[54] Who pays the bill for hiring lawyers and investment bankers to advise the board? The corporation and, ultimately, the shareholders. Suppose you were faced with potentially catastrophic losses, for which somebody offered to sell you an insurance policy. Better still, you don't have to pay the premiums, someone else will do so. Buying the policy therefore doesn't cost you anything. Would not you buy it?

It's also important to consider the incentives of the lawyers who advise corporations. Deciding how much time and effort to spend on making decisions is itself a business decision. Because that decision is driven by liability concerns, however, legal advice is usually critical to the making of the decision. Why might lawyers have an incentive to encourage boards to over-invest in the decision-making process? The cynical answer is that a more complicated decision-making process, which is driven by liability concerns, is likely to result in higher fees. A less cynical explanation is that the law is full of sports, mutants, and mistakes. Clients often lack the information or willingness to recognize that their situation was one of the exceptions that proves the rule. Instead, clients tend to blame the lawyer for an adverse outcome even if the lawyer did nothing wrong. Because the lawyers will be blamed even if losing the case was an act of god equivalent to a 100–year flood, lawyers are often conservative in giving advice. (The term conservative here is not used in its political sense, but rather in the sense of being cautious.) In economic terms, lawyers are risk averse. In a risky situation, the best thing for the lawyer to do is to point the client towards strategies whose outcome is certain.

In sum, the incentives of both sellers and buyers of legal advice are congruent. Lawyers have strong incentives to encourage clients to expend a lot of time, energy, and money on the decision-making process, while corporate boards of directors have strong incentives to take that advice. All of which goes to show that otherwise puzzling things become readily explicable if one understands the economic incentives at play.

---

54. Note that this assumes that neither indemnification nor insurance is available. Given the ready availability of indemnification under Delaware law and the reasonable availability of D & O insurance, the caution often seen in board decision making is truly puzzling.

§ 3.6   Disclosure of Merger Negotiations

Bidders typically seek to prevent disclosure of an impending acquisition at least until an agreement in principle has been reached. Among other things, deferral of disclosure helps prevent potential competing bidders from getting wind of the deal at an early stage. Where the target agrees to keep the negotiations confidential, it may expose itself to liability under the federal securities laws.

It will be helpful if you treat the disclosure inquiry as raising two distinct issues. First, when do the parties have an affirmative obligation to disclose the merger negotiations? In other words, at what stage of the process are they required to announce that a merger is in the works? Second, how may the target respond to inquiries? Assuming the target is not yet obliged to affirmatively disclose its plans, how should the target respond when a shareholder or analyst asks if negotiations are taking place? These questions should be treated separately due to the nature of liability for securities fraud. Where the claim is predicated on an omission, a failure to speak, liability can only arise if the defendant had a duty to disclose. Absent a duty to speak, there can be no liability for silence. If you speak, however, you have a duty to tell the truth and the whole truth.

In *Basic Inc. v. Levinson*, the U.S. Supreme Court held that a target may not make misrepresentations in connection with material preliminary merger negotiations, materiality being defined by "a highly fact-dependent probability/magnitude balancing approach."[55] *Basic*, however, did not impose an affirmative duty of disclosure in connection with material preliminary negotiations and, at least implicitly, permits a target to respond to inquiries with a "no comment" statement. It thus probably remains the case that the parties may keep the transaction secret during the negotiating process.[56]

One option in these settings, of course, is for the target to issue a "no comment" response to inquiries. But isn't a "no comment" response the equivalent of lying by omission? In *Basic*, the court noted that a "no comment" statement indeed is the functional equivalent of silence, but it also noted that silence is not unlawful, absent an affirmative duty to disclose. Accordingly, absent such a duty, the "no comment" response is not an unlawful omission. But isn't a no comment response a pretty clear cut signal that in fact merger negotiations are underway? In *Basic*, the court implicitly suggested that corporations adopt a policy of always saying "no comment" whenever inquiries about merger negotiations are received—regardless of whether negotiations are in fact underway. If they do so, a no comment response has no signaling effect.

---

55.   485 U.S. 224 (1988).

56.   Cf. Securities Act Release No. 6,835 (May 18, 1989) (management's discussion and analysis in annual reports need not disclose preliminary merger negotiations if doing so would jeopardize transaction, provided certain other conditions are satisfied).

§ 3.7   M & A Contracts

Whether the buyer or seller initiates negotiations, the preliminary discussions as to price, structure and other factors often will be concluded by the signing of a letter of intent (a.k.a. the agreement in principle) addressed by the acquiring corporation to the acquiring corporation. The negotiation process then shifts to preparation of a definitive merger agreement. At the same time, the parties will conduct due diligence, seek any necessary regulatory approvals, and begin preparing for the shareholder vote. If either of the constituent corporations is a reporting company under the Securities Exchange Act, that company will have to prepare proxy solicitation materials, most notably a proxy statement containing detailed financial information. Because the transaction will have to be approved by a majority of the outstanding shares, not just those present at the meeting, the services of a professional proxy solicitation firm will often be retained so as to help drum up shareholder support.

Once this process is completed, the parties will proceed to obtain requisite board and shareholder approvals. Assuming the necessary approvals are forthcoming, they will finally proceed to the closing.

One of the key issues in the negotiated acquisition context is whether the target is obliged or permitted to seek out competing bids. This is usually addressed in the acquisition agreement, although some provisions are sometimes broken off into separate side agreements. A voluntary auction can be initiated as part of a planned search for an acquirer by target management or simply by the announcement that the target has received an unsolicited takeover bid. In a planned search, the board of directors (or a board committee) typically retains an investment banking firm, which solicits bids from potential acquirers. The bidders are given an offering document describing the target and a proposed merger agreement, and may be offered a limited opportunity to meet with target management and conduct due diligence reviews before submitting their bid. Once the investment banking firm identifies several serious bidders, the surviving potential buyers are given an opportunity for more detailed due diligence review. At the same time, the seller's representatives will typically begin negotiating merger agreements with each of the bidders so that a more or less final agreement can be presented to the target's board when the time comes for the board to decide which bid to accept. One or more additional bidding and negotiating rounds are then likely. At the end of the winnowing process, the target's board will accept one of the bids and the transaction will go forward in much the same way as in the traditional single bidder format.

A.   The Letter of Intent

The letter of intent will set forth the proposed structure of the deal (e.g., merger or tender offer), the price, the form of consideration, and other key terms. Most letters of intent specifically state that they do not create a binding obligation. Instead, the letter of intent typically is intended to be merely a written proposal. One concern is that a binding letter of intent may trigger disclosure obligations. Another is that negotiating a binding letter of intent may take as long as negotiating the actual acquisition agreement. Lastly, of course, the parties may wish to preserve their rights to walk away from the deal until due diligence and negotiations are concluded.

Nevertheless, a non-binding letter of intent is still a useful document. First, it creates a sense of moral obligation during the lengthy process of negotiating a full agreement. Second, it provides a framework and context for further negotiations and due diligence. Third, negotiating the letter of intent may help potential deal breakers to surface at an early point. Finally, it may be useful in dealing with regulators and or sources of financing, who may wish to see a commitment by the parties before becoming engaged with the transaction.

The key legal issue in using a letter of intent thus is whether it will be deemed a binding contract. If so, seeking to renege on the deal will expose the reneging party to liability for breach of contract. If the target sought to renege so as to merge with a competing bidder, a binding letter of intent will also expose the competing bidder to liability for tortious interference with contract.[57] In *United Acquisition Corp. v. Banque Paribas*,[58] the court adopted a four factor test for determining whether a letter of intent is binding: (1) Does the document contain an express statement of intent to be bound only by a written agreement? (2) Has one party partially performed and has the other party accepted that performance? (3) Are there issues remaining to be negotiated? (4) Does the agreement involve complex issues in which definitive written contracts are the norm?[59]

B. The Acquisition Agreement

The contents of the typical acquisition agreement have become quite standardized. Indeed, most provisions of a merger agreement are essen-

---

57. The tort of intentional interference with contract imposes liability on an actor who intentionally and improperly interferes with the performance of an enforceable contract between plaintiff and a third party by inducing or otherwise causing the third party not to perform the contract, thereby giving rise to a pecuniary loss on the part of the plaintiff. See Restatement (Second) of Torts § 766 (1979); see generally Harvey Perlman, Interference with Contract and Other Economic Expectancies: A Clash of Tort and Contract Doctrine, 49 U. Chi. L. Rev. 61 (1982). The alternative tort of interference with prospective business advan-

tage will rarely be applicable to exclusive merger agreement litigation, since fair economic competition is typically a defense to such claims. See Belden Corp. v. Inter-North, Inc., 413 N.E.2d 98, 101–03 (Ill.App. 1980); see generally Mark Loewenstein, Tender Offer Litigation and State Law, 63 N.C.L. Rev. 493 (1985).

58. 631 F.Supp. 797 (S.D.N.Y.1985).

59. The test was derived from an earlier case involving a letter of intent to award a franchise. R.G. Group, Inc. v. Horn & Hardart Co., 751 F.2d 69, 75 (2d Cir.1984).

tially boilerplate. Most provisions deal with basic housekeeping details, such as who is responsible for getting regulatory approvals, restrictions on new borrowing or dividend payments, and the like. Counsel for the two sides may quibble about the details of some provisions, but generally everybody is working from the same basic set of forms.

1. Price and Form of Consideration Terms

The acquisition agreement provisions of greatest interest to the shareholders, of course, are those dealing with the consideration. Price and form of the consideration likewise will have been the focus of extended negotiations between the parties. Indeed, it is fair to say that everything else hinges on these terms.

Valuation is an inexact science, as we will discuss in Chapter 4. In the case of a publicly held target corporation, the market value tells you only what the equilibrium price of a single share of stock. As we have seen, however, the acquirer typically will pay a control premium in an acquisition. There is no single right answer to how much of a premium should be paid in any given case. Instead, there will be a range of values that a buyer would be willing to offer and a range that a seller would be willing to accept. Assuming the two ranges overlap, where the parties end up will be solely a matter of negotiation. Given the importance of that issue, of course, those negotiations typically will be undertaken by the respective companies' CEOs, with input from financial advisors, and supervision by the boards of directors.

Things become even more complex where the target is closely held, of course. In that case, there is no market price to serve as a base line for negotiations. Instead, each party will use various financial tools (such as those discussed in Chapter 4) to estimate their respective bid and offer prices.

Using earnout clauses to adjust the price ex post: Because valuation is such an inexact science, the parties may not be able to agree on a definitive price. In such cases, the deal may still be able to go forward if the parties include ex post price adjustments in the merger agreement.

Contingent earnout provisions typically arise in the context of merger negotiations when buyer and seller find themselves at a fundamental disagreement with respect to valuation of the seller. Fundamentally, these disagreements revolve around different views of the uncertain post-signing prospects of the seller. Such prospects may be technical or commercial in nature. Or, they may simply relate to future states of the world that are simply unknowable by either party. With respect to these uncertainties the seller is typically more optimistic than the acquirer. This may be because the seller has private information about the seller's future prospects that it cannot credibly convey to the buyer, or it may simply be because the buyer and seller just have very different expectations about future states of the world. This divergence in views about the seller's future results in differences in the question of valuation of the seller that if left unaddressed can prevent parties from reaching agreement.

The earnout provision is a contractual term that can help bridge these differences. It does so by creating a post-closing contingent payment obligation that becomes effective in the event the seller meets certain targets or exceeds predetermined thresholds with respect to revenue, profitability, market acceptance, technical achievements, or regulatory approvals.[60]

In *LaPoint v. AmerisourceBergen Corp.*,[61] for example, the merger agreement between acquirer AmerisourceBergen Corporation ("ABC") and target Bridge Medical, Inc. ("Bridge") included an earnout clause pursuant to which the former bridge shareholders would receive additional compensation in the event that Bridge met certain financial targets during the first two years after the merger closed. Specifically, the agreement contemplated "sliding scale of earnout payments depending upon the Adjusted EBITA achieved by Bridge in 2003 and 2004. EBITA was to be calculated according to GAAP and adjusted according to the provisions of the merger agreement. In 2003, former Bridge shareholders would receive no earnout payments if Adjusted EBITA fell below $2.31 million, and would receive a maximum earnout of $21 million if Adjusted EBITA exceeded $4.29 million. In 2004, former Bridge shareholders were to receive no earnout if Adjusted EBITA did not reach $5.46 million, and would receive a maximum of $34 million if Adjusted EBITA exceeded $11.83 million."[62]

The earnout clause presumably helped resolve differences between the parties about revenue expectations for Bridge's products by deferring the ultimate valuation of Bridge to a later point in time at which more information would be available. "Where the buyer and seller have differences over their respective expectations of the seller's future performance ... or differences over the relevant period in time over which value will be generated, these differences can lead to significant divergences in the valuation of the seller. By agreeing to defer resolution of these differences until the future after the seller's actual performance becomes known the earnout can help the buyer and seller align their time horizons, thereby permitting the parties to efficiently price the asset for sale."[63] Such differences might arise where the parties have asymmetric information or expectations about the future.

60. Brian J.M. Quinn, Putting Your Money Where Your Mouth Is: The Performance of Earnouts in Corporate Acquisitions, B.C. L. Sch. Res. Paper No. 251 (November 12, 2011).

61. 970 A.2d 185 (Del. 2009).

62. LaPoint v. AmerisourceBergen Corp., 2007 WL 2565709, at *2 n.3 (Del. Ch.

2007). EBITA is an acronym for the corporation's earnings before deductions are taken for interest, tax and amortization expenses.

63. Brian J.M. Quinn, Putting Your Money Where Your Mouth Is: The Performance of Earnouts in Corporate Acquisitions,

The trouble with these sort of ex post price adjustments, of course, is that they create an incentive for the acquirer to hold down earnings during the earnout period and only take full advantage of its newly acquired business once the earnout period ends. Typically, the agreement will contain certain provisions designed to prevent the acquirer from doing so. In *LaPoint*, for example, the agreement obliged ABC to "exclusively and actively promote [Bridge's] current line of products and services" and to refrain from "any products, services or companies that compete either directly or indirectly with [Bridge's] current line of products and services." In addition, ABC agreed to "act in good faith during the Earnout Period and" to "not undertake any actions during the Earnout Period any purpose of which is to impede the ability of the [Bridge] Stockholders to earn the Earnout Payments." When ABC allegedly violated those agreements, former Bridge shareholders successfully brought suit seeking damages.

The problem, of course, is ensuring that the target's former shareholders can effectively monitor the acquirer's compliance with its obligations. Earnout clauses thus are most effective in sales of closely held businesses in which the target's former shareholders remain affiliated with the company as officers, board members, or some other capacity.[64] The resulting access to inside information is invaluable in monitoring the acquirer's efforts.

The acquisition of closely held Advanced Bionics Corp. ("Bionics") by publicly held Boston Scientific Corp. provides a good example of the kinds of provisions that can be used to make an earnout clause more effective.

Under the merger agreement, Bionics shareholders received $742 million in cash at closing and the right to receive additional compensation through earnout payments contingent upon Bionics's sales growth. Approximately 800 former Bionics shareholders and option holders had a right to receive earnout payments with a projected value of $3.2 billion.

The merger agreement contained provisions outlining a system of joint control of Bionics designed to protect the interests of the earnout recipients. The officers of Bionics would be responsible to a six-person executive board comprised of three representatives appointed by Boston Scientific and three representatives appointed by the earnout recipients. A multi-step dispute resolution process was provided to deal with deadlock. The disputed matter would first be referred to Mann and the chief executive officer of Boston Scientific

B.C. L. Sch. Res. Paper No. 251 (November 12, 2011).

64. Earnout clauses are included in 29% of acquisitions of private companies. Brian J.M. Quinn, Putting Your Money Where Your Mouth Is: The Performance of Earn-

outs in Corporate Acquisitions, B.C. L. Sch. Res. Paper No. 251 (November 12, 2011). In contrast, earnout clauses appear in no more than 7% of acquisitions of public companies. Id.

(or their successors). If they were unable to resolve the dispute jointly, the chief executive officer of Boston Scientific was entitled to resolve it unilaterally, provided that if Mann or his successor disagreed with Boston Scientific's decision, Mann could refer the matter to a committee of three independent business people jointly selected by Mann and the Boston Scientific chief executive officer to propose a nonbinding resolution. Ultimately, if the Boston Scientific chief executive officer made a decision over the objection of Mann and the executive board, the Bionics stockholders' representative, acting on behalf of the earnout recipients, was entitled to challenge the decision in a court proceeding.

The merger agreement also specifically provided that: "for the benefit of the Earn Out Recipients, without the approval of the Executive Board," Boston Scientific was prohibited from replacing Mann or Jeffrey Grenier ("Grenier"), the co-chief executive officers of Bionics, and that if either ceased to be a co-chief executive officer, Mann and the Boston Scientific chief executive officer were required to agree jointly on the appointment of a successor.[65]

In effect, the merger agreement turned Mann and the earnout recipients' representatives on the executive board into monitors of Boston Scientific's compliance with the earnout clause. The case thus "illustrates the importance of addressing in detail in an acquisition agreement what corporate governance and other business restrictions will be imposed on the operation of the target company during the earnout period."[66]

Winshall v. Viacom International Inc. further illustrates the importance of contractual specificity in drafting earnout clauses.[67] Viacom effected a triangular merger with a company called Harmonix Music Systems, Inc., which manufactured two highly popular music video games, "Rock Band" and "Guitar Hero." As a result of the merger, Harmonix became a wholly owned Viacom subsidiary and the former Harmonix shareholders got a total of $175 million in cash and an earnout clause granting them contingent rights to additional payouts based on Harmonix's performance in 2007 and 2008. Prior the merger Harmonix had entered into a distribution agreement with Electronic Arts Inc. After the merger, EA asked to renegotiate the distribution contract so as to get broader distribution rights to Rock Band and its sequels. In return for granting EA the broader rights, Harmonix could have bargained for an immediate reduction in the distribution fees it paid EA, which would have increased the earnout payments to the

---

65. The M & A Jurisprudence Subcommittee, Negotiated Acquisitions Committee, American Bar Association Section of Business Law, Annual Survey of Judicial Developments Pertaining to Mergers and Acquisitions, Bus. Law. 531, 537–38 (2008) (footnotes omitted).

66. Id. at 538.

67. Winshall v. Viacom Int'l Inc., 2011 WL 5506084 (Del. Ch. 2011).

former shareholders. Instead, at Viacom's direction, Harmonix negotiated a reduction in those fees for future years, after the earnout period ended.

The selling Harmonix shareholders knew about the deal with EA and could have protected themselves contractually against the possibility that that deal might be improved during the earnout period. But the contract failed to do so.

The former Harmonix shareholders nevertheless sued, claiming a breach and the covenant of good faith and fair dealing. Delaware Chancellor Leo Strine dismissed, pithily opining that the "implied covenant of good faith and fair dealing is not a license for a court to make stuff up." Chancellor Strine elaborated that the covenant does not give the court "a license to rewrite contractual language just because the plaintiff failed to negotiate for protections that, in hindsight, would have made the contract a better deal." Rather, a party may only invoke the protections of the covenant when it is clear from the underlying contract that "the contracting parties would have agreed to proscribe the act later complained of ... had they thought to negotiate with respect to that matter."

All the implied covenant of good faith and fair dealing requires in the context of an earnout clause thus is that the buyer refrain from arbitrary or unreasonable conduct that deprives the former target shareholders of the fruits of its bargain. The buyer has no duty to give the former target shareholders the benefit of a better deal than the one for which they bargained. The take home lesson once again is for target shareholders to devote considerable attention to drafting an earnout clause that takes into account foreseeable future changes in this business that could affect the target's profitability.

Unfortunately, even a well-drafted earnout clause may not achieve the parties' goals. Recent research suggests that target companies' post-merger performance typically falls below the expectations of both buyers and sellers, even after those expectations are discounted for risk. The persistent high level of failures to meet earnout targets suggest that earnout clauses in practice are not proving to be an effective contracting tool for overcoming the problems of asymmetric information and moral hazard.[68] As a result, transactional lawyers ought to consider whether there are better ways for privately held sellers to credibly convey to buyers private information about their firm's future prospects.

Calculating the price in non–cash transactions: The price term can become quite complex if the form of consideration is anything other than cash. Suppose, for example, that the target's shareholders are to receive stock of the acquiring company. A ratio of acquiring company to target

---

68. Brian J.M. Quinn, Putting Your Money Where Your Mouth Is: The Performance of Earnouts in Corporate Acquisitions, B.C. L. Sch. Res. Paper No. 251 (November 12, 2011).

company shares must be established. A simple statement of the ratio at which the shares are to be exchanged, however, will not suffice. There is a lengthy delay between the signing of the merger agreement and the passing of the consideration at closing. During that period, the acquiring and target companies' stock will naturally fluctuate with stock market changes. Therefore, the ratio agreed today may not be favorable by the time the merger closes.

In theory, the prospect of market volatility should lead neither side to favor a fixed exchange rate. If the acquirer's stock price rises relative to that of the target, the target shareholders get a higher than expected price. If the acquirer's shareholders get a vote on the merger, they may therefore squelch the deal. Conversely, if the acquirer's stock price falls relative to that of the target, the buyer's shareholders will get less than they anticipated, and they may vote down the deal. In practice, the latter is the more common case. As we saw in Chapter 2, bidders often overpay for targets. Because investors are aware of this phenomenon, announcement of a takeover bid often results in downward pressure on the acquiring company's stock price as investors adjust to the overpayment risk.

The target corporation therefore will often insist on a floating exchange rate, perhaps with a collar that negates the deal with the seller's stock price either rises or falls beyond a certain amount. In this event, the parties first set a dollar price per share and then provide a formula for converting that price into the corresponding number of acquirer shares. A common conversion feature uses a formula like this one: The number of target shares owned by a shareholder is multiplied by a factor determined by dividing the agreed upon merger consideration per share in dollars by the average closing price of the acquirer's shares, as set forth in the Wall Street Journal, for the twenty trading days prior to the closing. The product is the number of acquirer shares received by the shareholder. The average price over a period of time rather than the price on the closing date itself is used so as to smooth out temporary market fluctuations.

The formula also typically sets upper and lower limits on the number of shares to be issued, so that if one company's price changes dramatically relative to the other's, there will still be some limit on how many shares change hands. Finally, the agreement typically will provide for payment of cash in lieu of fractional shares.[69]

Getting the money to the shareholders: The consideration and price provisions also will track the applicable merger statute by providing that shares of the target automatically become shares of the acquirer by

---

69. Alternatively, the target may opt for a walk away provision pursuant to which its board of directors may opt either to terminate the deal or, at least, to make a nega-tive recommendation to the shareholders on the merger vote. Acquirers who grant such a term typically will insist on a termination fee, as discussed below.

virtue of the merger. Of course, the shares still exist in a physical sense. So the agreement will provide a mechanism for physically exchanging the target's share certificates for comparable acquirer share certificates. In a cash merger, similar provision would be made for distribution of the cash consideration.

2. *Warranties and Representations*

Warranties, representations, and covenants make up the bulk of the acquisition agreement. Representations and warranties basically are fact statements the parties make about their respective businesses. According to Black's Law Dictionary, a representation is a statement of fact "made to induce someone to act, especially to enter into a contract." In contrast, a warranty in this context is defined the "seller's promise that the thing being sold is as represented or promised." According to other commentators, however, "representations are statements of past or existing facts, while warranties are promises that existing or future facts are or will be true."[70]

In theory, there are various differences between the two. A lawsuit claiming breach of a representation typically is a tort, while one claiming breach of a warranty sounds in contract. In turn, this distinction can affect such matters as the remedies available and the duration of statutes of limitation.

In practice, however, the difference between the two has proven unimportant. "Separating them explicitly in an acquisition agreement is a drafting nuisance, and the legal import of the separation has been all but eliminated."[71] As such, the phrase "representation and warranties" has become a unitary term of art in takeover parlance.

The goal is to paint a detailed picture of the respective firms— especially the target (whose representations and warranties are usually much more detailed than those of the acquirer). As such, "the representations and warranties serve as a safety net for the seller and buyer. If, prior to closing, either the seller or buyer discovers that a representation or warranty made by the other party is not true, they have grounds for backing out of the deal."[72]

In constructing such a safety net, however, there is an inherent tension between the target and acquirer's interests. The acquirer wants broad representations and warranties to ensure that it gets what it paid for. In contrast, the target will be loath to give the acquirer a blanket insurance policy against the myriad of things that can go wrong in a takeover. The target will want to limit representations to facts within its

---

70. Leigh Walton, Representing the Growing Business: Tax, Corporate, Securities, and Accounting Issues, SL054 ALI– ABA 897 (2005).

71. Id.

72. Western Filter Corp. v. Argan, Inc., 540 F.3d 947, 952 (9th Cir. 2008).

possession and known with certainty. Likewise, the target will want the warranties limited to conditions under its control.

One advantage of extensive representations and warranties is that they convert the parties' claims about their businesses into contract. If one side lied, accordingly, the other side need not sue for fraud but can simply sue for breach of contract. Because it is easier to prove breach of contract than fraud, since you need not prove things like scienter in the former case, using representations and warranties makes the parties' disclosures to one another more credible. Put in economic terms, representations and warranties address the agency costs created by the information asymmetries between targets and acquirers.

In addition to generic contract remedies, the representations and warranties provisions in the acquisition agreement typically also are given teeth by certain additional provisions within the agreement. For example, one usually sees a requirement that the target's lawyers and accountants give an opinion that the representations and warranties are true. This makes those advisors potentially liable for negligence if the representation or warranty turns out to be false.

The merger agreement also will usually provide that the falsehood of a representation or warranty is grounds for terminating the agreement. Such a provision, of course, is only useful if the misrepresentation is discovered before the deal closes. "Unless the parties agree to a survival clause—extending the representations and warranties past the closing date—the breaching party cannot be sued for damages post-closing for their later discovered breach."[73] In some merger agreements, you therefore see post-closing remedies. Some agreements, for example, create an escrow account in which part of the consideration is held back and forfeited if a representation or warranty turns out to be false. One also sometimes sees indemnification provisions by which the seller agrees to compensate the buyer for false statements.

As noted, survival clauses can extent the life of representations and warranties beyond closing. Where the agreement expressly states that representations and warranties terminate at closing, "the parties have made clear their intent that they can provide no basis for a post-closing suit seeking a remedy for an alleged misrepresentation. That is, when the representations and warranties terminate, so does any right to sue on them."[74] In the face of such an express term, of course, pre-closing due diligence takes on special importance.

In some cases, the survival clause will specify a limited time period during which representations and warranties remain binding post-clos-

---

73. Id.

74. GRT, Inc. v. Marathon GTF Technology, Ltd., 2011 WL 2682898, at *13 (Del. Ch. 2011). Where the agreement purports that representations and warranties survive indefinitely, courts assume that an action on them must be brought within the applicable statute of limitations in order to be timely. Id. at *15.

ing. In effect, such a time period acts as a contractual statute of limitations. Accordingly, "it is clear that a provision of an acquisition agreement that states, for example, that a representation and warranty survives for a year, means that any claim that such representation was false must be made prior to the end of the one-year period."[75] In California and New York, courts require "clear and explicit" language in the contract for the agreement to set a limitations period.[76] As a practical matter, however, setting a time period ought to be sufficiently clear evidence of the parties' intent.

Representations and warranties will frequently refer to so-called "schedules" that accompany the merger agreement. A representation might state that there are no related party transactions between the target corporation and any of its officers and directors except as set forth in "Schedule A." In turn, that schedule might contain a very lengthy list of related party transactions between officers and directors of the target and the target. An important question, which ought to be explicitly addressed in the merger agreement, is the extent to which the target may amend the schedules pre-closing without having to renegotiate the representation and warranty section of the agreement.

3. Covenants

Covenants are a series of promises about how the parties will behave during the interim (usually two to four months) between the time the agreement is signed and the closing. A key covenant is that governing the target's conduct of the business during the pendency of the merger agreement. Usually, the target is prohibited from doing anything other than engaging in ordinary course transactions that are consistent with past practice. Typically, certain major acts will be expressly forbidden, such as changes to the articles or by-laws, dividends, stock repurchases, and the like. Obviously, this covenant is intended to ensure that the acquirer gets the benefit of its bargain. Where the target's current management is being kept on, however, negotiations over this covenant often become obstreperous. If those managers are to continue running the business after the acquisition, they may well object to significant restrictions on their discretion. In addition, the target's managers may be concerned about foregoing valuable opportunities in the event the merger breaks down and does not go forward. Including a covenant that permits the target to undertake non ordinary course actions with the acquirer's consent can alleviate these concerns. Such provisions usually

---

75. Id. at *14 (quoting Professor Samuel C. Thompson, Jr.). As a result, "the presence (or absence) of a survival clause that expressly states that the covered representations and warranties will survive beyond the closing of the contract, although it may act to shorten the otherwise applicable stat-ute of limitations, never acts to lengthen the statute of limitations, at least in jurisdictions, like Delaware, whose statutes have been read to forbid such extensions." Id. at *15.

76. Id.

also require that the acquirer may not unreasonably withhold its consent.

A related covenant, which is also quite common, is a provision allowing the acquirer to terminate the agreement if there is a "material change" in the condition of the target's assets prior to closing. Courts have interpreted these so-called "no material change" covenants quite narrowly. A significant drop in value of the target's assets is not covered, for example, absent quite explicit contractual language. Instead, courts usually interpret these clauses as referring to a change in the physical condition of or title to the target's assets.[77] In addition, courts put the burden on the party seeking to invoke the clause to show that the allegedly material adverse effect will be significant and lasting. Accordingly, such a clause is treated as "a backstop protecting the acquirer from the occurrence of unknown events that substantially threaten the overall earnings potential of the target in a durationally-significant manner. A short-term hiccup in earnings should not suffice; rather the Material Adverse Effect should be material when viewed from the longer-term perspective of a reasonable acquiror."[78]

As a practical matter, judicial hostility to material adverse change clauses means that acquirers rarely can rely on them as a justification for walking away from the deal. In *Hexion Specialty Chemicals, Inc. v. Huntsman Corp.*,[79] for example, the Delaware Chancery Court emphasized that an acquirer has a "heavy burden" to establish the existence of a material adverse change. Indeed, that burden is so heavy, that "Delaware courts have never found a material adverse effect to have occurred in the context of a merger agreement."[80]

The target also usually must covenant that its board of directors and management will use their best efforts to obtain necessary regulatory and shareholder approvals. Courts readily enforce the former obligation.[81] As discussed below, however, courts are sharply divided as to the enforceability of provisions requiring the use of best efforts to obtain shareholder approval.

4. Conditions Precedent to the Closing

The merger agreement will contain a number of conditions precedent that must be satisfied before the parties are obliged to proceed to

---

77. See, e.g., Esplanade Oil & Gas, Inc. v. Templeton Energy Income Corp., 889 F.2d 621 (5th Cir.1989); John Borders v. KRLB, Inc., 727 S.W.2d 357 (Tex.App. 1987).

78. IBP, Inc. v. Tyson Foods, Inc. (In re IBP, Inc. S'holders Litig.), 789 A.2d 14, 68 (Del. Ch. 2001). See also Hexion Specialty Chemicals, Inc. v. Huntsman Corp., 965 A.2d 715, 738 (Del. Ch. 2008) ("The important consideration therefore is whether there has been an adverse change in the target's business that is consequential to the company's long-term earnings power over a commercially reasonable period, which one would expect to be measured in years rather than months.").

79. 965 A.2d 715 (Del. Ch. 2008).

80. Id. at 738.

81. See, e.g., US Airways Group, Inc. v. British Airways PLC, 989 F.Supp. 482 (S.D.N.Y.1997).

closing. Obviously, approval by the shareholders of the constituent corporations is an essential condition precedent to a merger. If stock or debt securities constitute the form of consideration, an effective registration statement under the Securities Act will be a required condition precedent (or, in the alternative, an opinion of counsel that an exemption from registration is available). All necessary regulatory approvals must have been obtained. There must be no litigation pending seeking to prevent the merger. Where the merger is intended to be a tax-free reorganization, an opinion from tax counsel that the merger so qualifies is required. The truth and accuracy of all representations and warranties and the fulfillment of all covenants is an essential condition precedent to closing. Various other conditions may be required to suit the particular facts of the transaction in question, as well.

5. Remedies for Breach

Assuming all conditions precedent have been satisfied, what remedies are available if one party refuses to go forward with closing the deal? Obviously, monetary damages calculated under standard contract law rules are one option. Indeed, many merger agreements include termination fees payable as liquidated damages in the event the deal fails to close.

The more interesting question is whether the recalcitrant party can be forced to go forward with the deal. In *Hexion Specialty Chemicals, Inc. v. Huntsman Corp.*,[82] after determining that there had been no material adverse change excusing the acquirer from its obligations, the Delaware Chancery Court held that the target was entitled to specific performance of the merger agreement.

Where the deal includes a termination fee, however, the parties will often include terms disavowing any entitlement to specific performance. Instead, upon payment of the fee, the breaching party is free to walk away. In general, courts should be liberal in enforcing such provisions. Not only should the basic normative principle ought to be freedom of contract, the law disfavors specific performance as a remedy. In *United Rentals, Inc. v. RAM Holdings, Inc.*,[83] for example, the court held that even though the relevant provisions of the merger agreement were ambiguous, the target was not entitled to specific performance. Instead, the target was only entitled to payment by the acquirer of the $100 million termination fee.

C. Due Diligence

Although drafting the acquisition agreement is a significant part of the lawyer's job in negotiated acquisitions, due diligence is probably the

---

82. 965 A.2d 715 (Del. Ch. 2008).   **83.** 937 A.2d 810 (Del. Ch. 2007).

most important (at least for young lawyers). Due diligence is relevant to two issues: (1) Assists the board in making an informed judgment as per state law duty of care requirements; (2) Assists with preparation of disclosure documents and acts as an insurance policy against securities law liabilities on the part of the firms and other signatories of relevant disclosure documents.

Unfortunately, there is no cookbook for due diligence. Generally, evaluation of the extent of due diligence required in a given case uses a sliding scale taking into account such factors as the nature of the liability at issue, the defendant's relationship with the firm, knowledge, expertise, and role in the process. And, of course, each individual company always presents different and unique problems. Having said all that, however, there are still some common practices that have been developed to guide counsel.

Due diligence is time-consuming. It is therefore expensive. It therefore tends to be dome by young associates. The first critical element in any due diligence review therefore is oversight by experienced lawyers. The second is standardization. You need checklists and the like to make sure that all of the bases get covered. The process described here is only one of many possible systems, but it is one many firms use.

The first step in the process is getting to know the company. The lawyers need to have general familiarity with the firm and the industry. Trade periodicals, prospectuses by companies in the same business, and any prior prospectuses of this firm are good sources of information.

The next step is preparation of the so-called "Company Questionnaire." The questionnaire is designed to elicit from the firm information that is required to be in disclosure documents, such as a proxy or registration statement. Where the company has previously made acquisitions, the questionnaire is often designed to up-date the old proxy and/or registration statements. In addition, much work is directed at following up on prior disclosures.

The next step is preparation of the so-called "Document List." Counsel must request a large number of documents from the firm. Many of these documents must be attached to the proxy or registration statement as exhibits. The others provide the factual basis for the statements made in those disclosure documents. The standard list is quite long, but still has to be expanded and particularized after the company questionnaire is completed because the answers to that questionnaire often kick up new documents that need to be examined. Some generally accepted items are on virtually every list, such as the firm's charter and by-laws, minutes of the board and committees, major contracts, compensation plans, lists of assets, financial statements, copies of any documents relating to pending litigation, and copies of all prior or pending SEC filings.

In any case, at about the same time as counsel begins the document review, counsel also should disseminate the so-called "D & O[84] Questionnaire." This questionnaire elicits personal information about senior management and the board of directors.

Finally comes the evaluation stage, which is known as the corporate examination. Counsel typically visits the firm. Counsel reviews the questionnaires and the produced documents. You're looking for holes and gaps. Are there missing documents or missing pages? Are there things that don't appear to be complete? Is there anything that doesn't pass the smell test? Is there anything you just don't understand? If anything jumps out at you, then you need to start asking questions. Counsel cannot blindly rely on the answers. You've got to ask to see the underlying documents or other proof of what the firm's people are saying. This requires the lawyer to walk a fine line. There are lots of horror stories about young associates who thought they were Perry Mason cross-examining the murderer. Lots of law firms have lost lots of clients because the lawyer pushed too hard or was too obnoxious in dealing with the client. How do you do it? Tact, dignity and, most of all, knowing when to let the partner be the one to ask the questions. In any case, as counsel goes through the due diligence process, counsel must keep good records. File memos should be prepared covering all conversations and all documents reviewed.

Once counsel is finally satisfied, a due diligence memorandum is prepared. The memorandum sets out what counsel did, what was found, what problems came up and how they were resolved. When a draft of the registration statement is ready, the draft and the due diligence memorandum are provided to senior management and the board.

What is the client's role in due diligence? Should clients do anything besides cooperate with and then rely upon their lawyers? Are there any affirmative steps they should take personally once they receive the due diligence memorandum? In short, yes. Each director and officer should attend all meetings at which the deal was discussed. They should review carefully any contracts or disclosure documents before signing them and, ideally, any documents incorporated into the disclosure statements by reference. Directors should have asked corporate managers and lawyers about the deal and the contents of any disclosure statements, especially anything that looks odd.

D.   Registration of Securities Issued in Acquisition

In a statutory transaction, approval of the transaction by the holders of the requisite number of shares is binding on all shareholders. In effect, the statute creates a species of private eminent domain under which a dissenting shareholder is forced to participate in the transaction

---

84. I.e., directors and officers.

unless appraisal rights are available. As such, statutory acquisitions lack the element of individual volition inherent in tender offers, stock acquisitions, and proxy contests. In 1951, the SEC pointed to this lack of individual volition in adopting Rule 133. Under that rule, mergers and asset sales effected pursuant to shareholder approval were excluded from the definition of sale. Although there was an exchange of one type of security for another, the absence of a sale meant that the registration requirements of the Securities Act were inapplicable to the transaction.

In 1973, the SEC repealed Rule 133 and replaced it with Rule 145. Under the new rule, a statutory acquisition is treated as a sale of a security for purposes of Securities Act § 5. Accordingly, absent an exemption from registration, the issuer must register the securities used as consideration in the transaction. As justification for this dramatic 180–degree reversal, the SEC argued that the prior focus on individual volition was "only correct in the formalistic sense" and "overlook[ed] the reality of the transaction." The SEC now argued that the "corporate action" inherent in a statutory acquisition in fact has a sufficient volitional element, in that it consists of "the aggregate effect of the voluntary decisions made by the individual stockholders."[85]

In a stock for stock merger or a stock for asset sale, the acquirer now must comply with both the Securities Act registration disclosures and procedures and the Securities exchange Act proxy rules. Although this may somewhat increase the burden on acquirers, it was the effect on controlling shareholders and other affiliates of the target that was especially important when the rule was first adopted. Under prior Rule 133, target affiliates such as controlling shareholders were free to immediately resell the securities received in the transaction. Under Rule 145, as originally adopted, in contrast, affiliates of a target company who received registered securities in the transaction were deemed presumptively to be "underwriters" and therefore subject to certain restrictions in connection with any resale of such registered securities. In 2008, however, the SEC amended Rule 145 to eliminate those restrictions. As such, target affiliates are now free to resell.[86]

§ 3.8   Ensuring Exclusivity

Announcement of a pending acquisition often leads other bidders to make competing unsolicited offers. Although it is difficult to gauge accurately the likelihood of a competing takeover proposal, conventional takeover wisdom treats competing bids as a serious risk for the initial bidder. The prospective acquirer incurs substantial up-front costs in making the offer, among which are: Search costs entailed in identifying an appropriate target, which can be significant in some circumstances.

---

85. 37 Fed.Reg. 23631, 23632 (Nov. 7, 1972).

86. If the target affiliate becomes an affiliate of the acquirer, however, he will be subject to the resale restrictions under Rule 144.

Once an appropriate target is identified, preparation of the offer typically requires the services of outside legal, accounting, and financial advisers. If all or part of the purchase price is to be paid from sources other than cash reserves, a likely scenario, the bidder incurs commitment and other financing fees. Finally, the bidder may pass up other acquisition opportunities while negotiating with the target. Unfortunately for the bidder, however, the emergence of a competing bid may reduce or eliminate the expected return on its sunk costs. Second bidders prevail in a substantial majority of competitive bidding contests. Even if the initial bidder prevails, the ultimate acquisition price is likely to be substantially higher than the initial bid.[87]

A. Exclusive Merger Agreements

Exclusivity provisions in corporate merger agreements are intended to prevent (or, at least, discourage) competing bids from interfering with the planned transaction. Such provisions may be conveniently divided into two basic categories: performance promises, wherein the target's board agrees to engage (or agrees not to engage) in certain types of conduct prior to the shareholder vote; and cancellation fees, typically a specified amount the target agrees to pay the favored bidder if the transaction does not go forward.

Performance promises can be further broken down into best efforts clauses and the various forms of no shop covenants. A best efforts clause requires both parties to use their "best efforts" to consummate the transaction.[88] It is intended to assure that the target's board of directors will not attempt to back out of the agreement. The best efforts clause also typically imposes corresponding obligations on the favored bidder's board with respect to its shareholders. Even in cases where approval by the bidder's shareholders is not required, such as in a triangular merger, the favored bidder may still agree to use its best efforts to assure that the transaction is consummated.

---

87. Richard S. Ruback, Assessing Competition in the Market for Corporate Acquisitions, 11 J. Fin. Econ. 141, 147 (1983) (second bidders prevailed in 75% of the 48 cases examined).

88. In this context, "best efforts" imposes "at a minimum a duty to act in good faith toward the party to whom it owes a 'best efforts' obligation." Jewel Cos., Inc. v. Pay Less Drug Stores Northwest, Inc., 741 F.2d 1555, 1564 n. 11 (9th Cir.1984). But see Great Western Producers Co-op. v. Great Western United Corp., 613 P.2d 873, 878 (Colo.1980) (holding, under Delaware law, that a best efforts clause merely imposed an obligation to "make a reasonable, diligent, and good faith effort"). *Jewel*'s interpretation is more consistent with the use of best efforts terminology in other contexts, where it often is defined to mean "maximizing the contractual benefits of the person to whom the duty is owed, even if the benefits to the one owing the duty have been depleted." See In re Heard, 6 Bankr. 876, 884 (Bankr.W.D.Ky.1980); see generally E. Allan Farnsworth, On Trying to Keep One's Promises: The Duty of Best Efforts in Contract Law, 46 U. Pitt. L. Rev. 1 (1984); Charles J. Goetz & Robert E. Scott, Principles of Relational Contracts, 67 Va. L. Rev. 1089, 1111–26 (1981).

No shop clauses prohibit the target corporation from soliciting a competing offer from any other prospective bidders, although they allow the target to consider an unsolicited bid and even negotiate with the competing bidder. In contrast, the no negotiation covenant prohibits such negotiations. An intermediary version, the no merger provision, permits the target to negotiate with a prospective competing offeror, but prohibits it from entering into a merger agreement with the competitor until the initial bid has been brought before the shareholders.

Provisions for monetary compensation of the favored bidder in the event the transaction fails to go forward are common in negotiated acquisitions.[89] Cancellation fees, the most widely used member of this category, essentially are liquidated damages payable if the acquirer fails to receive the expected benefits of its agreement. A variation of the cancellation fee arrangement, closely akin to stock lockups, involves giving an option to the acquirer pursuant to which the acquirer has the right to purchase a specified number of target shares and also a right to resell those shares to the target at a price higher than the exercise price in the event that an alternative bid is accepted. As such, the target is required to pay some specified dollar amount to the acquirer in the event that the transaction is not consummated, reimbursing the acquirer for out of pocket costs associated with making the offer and perhaps also including an increment reflecting the acquirer's lost time and opportunities.[90] Topping fees are another variation on the basic theme. Instead of specifying the dollar amount to be paid if the merger is not consummated, a topping fee requires that the target pay the defeated offeror a percentage of the victorious bidder's acquisition price.[91] In either case, the fee ordinarily falls in a range of 1 to 5% of the proposed acquisition price.[92] Payment of the fee is commonly triggered by the acquisition of a specified amount of target stock by a third party.[93] Variants include termination of the merger agreement by the target or shareholder rejection of the acquisition proposal.[94]

---

89. See, e.g., Cottle v. Storer Communication, Inc., 849 F.2d 570, 578 (11th Cir. 1988); Beebe v. Pacific Realty Trust, 578 F.Supp. 1128, 1150 n. 7 (D.Or.1984).

90. White knights proposing a leveraged buyout of the target in response to a hostile takeover bid also frequently require an engagement fee, requiring the target to pay a relatively small fee as consideration for the white knight's preparation and submission of its bid. See, e.g., Cottle v. Storer Communication, Inc., 849 F.2d 570, 572 (11th Cir. 1988); Hanson Trust PLC v. ML SCM Acquisition, Inc., 781 F.2d 264, 269 (2d Cir. 1986).

91. See, e.g., In re J.P. Stevens & Co., Inc., 542 A.2d 770, 777 (Del.Ch.1988).

92. See St. Jude Medical, Inc. v. Medtronic, Inc., 536 N.W.2d 24, 27 (Minn.App. 1995) (citing Stephen M. Bainbridge, Exclusive Merger Agreements and Lock–Ups in Negotiated Corporate Acquisitions, 75 Minn. L. Rev. 239, 246 (1990)).

93. See, e.g., Revlon, Inc. v. MacAndrews & Forbes Holdings, Inc., 506 A.2d 173, 178 (Del.1986); Hanson Trust PLC v. ML SCM Acquisition Inc., 781 F.2d 264, 269 (2d Cir.1986).

94. See, e.g., Cottle v. Storer Communication Inc., 849 F.2d 570, 572 (11th Cir. 1988); Beebe v. Pacific Realty Trust, 578 F.Supp. 1128, 1150 (D.Or.1984).

Courts are sharply divided as to the enforceability of exclusive merger agreements. In theory, these cases turn on "a delicate interplay of principles of both contract law and corporate law, neither wholly controlling the outcome."[95] The basic contract issue posed by exclusivity provisions is whether shareholder approval of the merger is a condition precedent to the formation of the agreement or merely to the target's duty to complete the transaction. Only in the latter case could the board make binding promises as to its own behavior prior to shareholder approval. The two modern decisions to treat this question in any detail reached opposing results, but the better view is that exclusivity provisions are enforceable as a matter of contract law during the interim before shareholder action.[96]

In practice, most courts have ignored or only paid lip service to contract law concerns, instead focusing on the corporate law aspects of exclusivity provisions. In so doing, the courts have received little direct statutory guidance. Modern corporation codes are generally silent on the effect of a merger agreement pending shareholder approval. The Model Act, for example, merely states that the merger agreement shall contain certain basic information and also "[m]ay set forth ... other provisions relating to the merger," without placing any limitations on the substantive content of such provisions.[97] Some courts therefore have sought inferential guidance from other statutory provisions. But this search has not produced consistent results. For example, many corporation codes permit the target's board to abandon a merger or asset sale that has received shareholder approval, subject to the contractual rights of any third parties, without the need for further shareholder action. The Colorado Supreme Court interpreted the abandonment clause of Delaware's asset sale provision as supporting its conclusion that a target board may not lawfully bind itself to a proposed merger by means of exclusivity provisions.[98] In contrast, the Ninth Circuit interpreted the comparable provision of California's corporate code as validating exclusive merger agreements. In addition to indirectly supporting the court's belief that directors have broad discretion to make binding promises respecting their own conduct, the abandonment provision directly sup-

---

95. ConAgra, Inc. v. Cargill, Inc., 382 N.W.2d 576, 586 (Neb.1986).

96. Compare ConAgra, Inc. v. Cargill, Inc., 382 N.W.2d 576, 588 (1986) ("The [target] board was without statutory power to bind the corporation to the proposed [favored bidder] merger absent shareholder approval."), with Jewel Cos., Inc. v. Pay Less Drug Stores Northwest, Inc., 741 F.2d 1555, 1560–61 (9th Cir.1984) (target board has power to enter into binding performance promises prior to shareholder approval). Cf. Texaco, Inc. v. Pennzoil Co., 729 S.W.2d 768, 788–96 (Tex.App.1987) (agree-

ment in principle binding on target); Scott v. Stanton Heights Corp., 131 A.2d 113 (Pa.1957) (asset sale agreement binding pending shareholder approval); Smith v. Good Music Station, Inc., 129 A.2d 242 (Del.Ch.1957) (asset sale agreement could not have "any ultimate binding" effect prior to shareholder action); Masonic Temple v. Ebert, 18 S.E.2d 584 (S.C.1942) (same).

97. MBCA § 11.01(c)(2).

98. Great Western Producers Co-op. v. Great Western United Corporation, 613 P.2d 873, 878 n. 6 (Colo.1980).

ported the legality of performance promises by recognizing that the acquirer possesses significant legal rights prior to shareholder approval.[99]

In general, however, the legal effect of an exclusive merger agreement has depended not on this or other debatable questions of statutory interpretation, but rather on equally debatable judicial interpretations of target directors' fiduciary duties. State corporate law has long recognized "the basic principle that corporate directors have a fiduciary duty to act in the best interests of the corporation's stockholders."[100] Directors cannot validly contract away this duty—a contract that purports to relieve directors of their fiduciary duties simply is not binding.[101]

In *Great Western Producers Co-op. v. Great Western United Corp.*,[102] the Colorado Supreme Court interpreted Delaware law as permitting a target board to renege on an exclusive merger agreement. Section 271(a) of the Delaware corporation statute requires target directors to determine that a proposed asset sale is in the best interests of the corporation. The Court interpreted this provision as imposing an ongoing responsibility to evaluate whether the terms and conditions of the transaction are in the shareholders' best interest. Once a competing bid is made, the target's directors are charged with investigating the new offer. If, in the exercise of their independent good faith judgment, the competing bid is deemed superior to the favored bidder's, the board is bound to recommend the better offer. Because the directors may not validly agree to abrogate that function, a best efforts clause will not bind the target to the favored bidder in the face of a higher competing offer or other changed circumstances that render the initial offer less attractive. Despite the presence of a performance promise, the target board retains both the power and the duty to recommend against shareholder approval of the favored bidder's proposal if the board concludes it is no longer in the shareholders' interest. As the *Great Western* court stated:

> The [best efforts] obligation ... must be viewed in the context of unanticipated events and the exigencies of continuing business development and cannot be construed to require that such events and exigencies be ignored or overcome at all costs.

As the best efforts clause at issue in *Great Western* did not specifically require the target's board to recommend the sale, the court did not need

---

99. Jewel Cos., Inc. v. Pay Less Drug Stores Northwest, Inc., 741 F.2d 1555, 1563 n. 10 (9th Cir.1984).

100. Unocal Corp. v. Mesa Petroleum Co., 493 A.2d 946, 955 (Del.1985).

101. See, e.g., Jewel Cos., Inc. v. Pay Less Drug Stores Northwest, Inc., 741 F.2d 1555, 1563 (9th Cir.1984); ConAgra, Inc. v. Cargill, Inc., 382 N.W.2d 576, 587–88 (Neb. 1986); Great Western Producers Co-op. v. Great Western United Corp., 613 P.2d 873,

878 (Colo.1980). This rule reflects the general proposition that contracts entered into by a fiduciary which involve a breach of duty by the fiduciary are unenforceable as contrary to public policy. See Restatement (Second) of Contracts § 194 (1981).

102. 613 P.2d 873 (Colo.1980). Accord R–G Denver v. First City Holdings of Colorado, Inc., 789 F.2d 1469 (10th Cir.1986); ConAgra, Inc. v. Cargill, Inc., 382 N.W.2d 576 (Neb.1986).

to decide whether such a clause could be binding. The court's imposition of a continuing duty to evaluate the fairness of the transaction's terms, however, may mandate that such clauses not be given effect; by definition, a contractual obligation to recommend the offer, irrespective of changed conditions, would conflict with the court's interpretation of a board's duties. In *ConAgra, Inc. v. Cargill, Inc.,*[103] the Nebraska Supreme Court so interpreted *Great Western* in the face of just such a provision.

So interpreting a best efforts clause would not be controversial where the agreement contains an appropriate fiduciary out. A fiduciary out may be simply a proviso stating that nothing contained in the merger agreement shall relieve the board of directors of its fiduciary duty to the shareholders.[104] Alternatively, the fiduciary out may expressly retain a right for the target's board to solicit other offers or to negotiate with other bidders if its fiduciary duties so require. The most potent version relieves the target board of its obligation to recommend the initial offer to the shareholders if a better offer is made or permits the target to terminate the merger agreement if a higher offer is received. Buyers typically resist inclusion of a fiduciary out, as it largely undermines the basic purpose of an exclusive merger agreement (especially in the latter variants), while there is a division of opinion among takeover practitioners as to whether targets should insist on such a provision.

ConAgra, Inc. v. Cargill, Inc.,[105] however, indicates that such provisos are unnecessary. The best efforts clause at issue there included a fiduciary out providing that the clause did not "relieve either Board of Directors of their continuing duties to their respective shareholders." That language could have been interpreted as waiving the obligation to recommend shareholder approval if the directors decided the offer was no longer in the shareholders' interest. However, the court merely noted: "it is clear that the parties recognized that there was a continuing fiduciary duty owed by each board of directors to its respective shareholders which could not be contracted away." The court evidently believed that the directors' fiduciary duty overrides the contractual best efforts obligation regardless of whether a fiduciary out is included in the agreement. This interpretation is further supported by the court's endorsement of the doctrine that target directors are subject to a duty to reevaluate the favored bidder's proposal in light of changing circumstances. By focusing on fiduciary rather than contractual duties, ConAgra permits a target board to freely renege on an exclusive merger agreement even in the absence of an explicit fiduciary out.

103. 382 N.W.2d 576 (Neb.1986). See also R–G Denver v. First City Holdings of Colorado, Inc., 789 F.2d 1469, 1474–75 (10th Cir.1986).

104. See, e.g., ConAgra, Inc. v. Cargill, Inc., 382 N.W.2d 576, 582 (Neb.1986); Smith v. Van Gorkom, 488 A.2d 858, 879 (Del.1985); see generally William T. Allen, Understanding Fiduciary Outs: The What and the Why of an Anomalous Concept, 55 Bus. Law. 653 (2000); R. Franklin Balotti and A. Gilchrist Sparks, III, Deal–Protection Measures and the Merger Recommendation, 96 Nw. U.L.Rev. 467 (2002).

105. 382 N.W.2d 576 (Neb.1986).

In contrast, the Ninth Circuit implicitly rejected the *Great Western/ConAgra* methodology in *Jewel Cos., Inc. v. Pay Less Drug Stores Northwest, Inc.*[106] The court defined the target directors' fiduciary duties as permitting the board "to decide that a proposed merger transaction is in the best interests of the shareholders at a given point in time" and to enter into an exclusive merger agreement reflecting that determination.[107] The exclusive merger agreement thus does not constitute a contracting away of the directors' duties, as target directors are still required to act in the shareholders' best interest. In contrast to *Great Western* and *ConAgra*, however, their compliance with that standard is determined (absent a fiduciary out providing to the contrary) as of the time the merger agreement is made rather than when a competing bidder subsequently comes forward. There is no requirement that the directors reevaluate the favored bidder's proposal in light of changed circumstances.

Jewel and *Belden Corp. v. InterNorth, Inc.*[108] found support for an affirmative answer to the question of whether the merger agreement can be exclusive in the basic structure of public corporations. Modern corporation statutes give considerable responsibility and latitude to target directors in negotiating a merger agreement. The target's board possesses broad authority to determine whether to merge the firm and to select a merger partner. If the target's board rejects the initial bidder, the merger process comes to a halt without shareholder involvement—a target's rejection does not require shareholder approval, the rejection decision being vested in the unilateral discretion of the board of directors. The initial decision to enter into a negotiated merger transaction is thus reserved to the board's collective business judgment, shareholders having no statutory power to initiate merger negotiations.[109] The

---

106. 741 F.2d 1555 (9th Cir.1984).

107. Id. at 1563. Accord ConAgra, Inc. v. Cargill, Inc., 382 N.W.2d 576, 589–95 (Neb.1986) (White, J., dissenting); see also Crouse–Hinds Co. v. InterNorth, Inc., 634 F.2d 690, 703 n. 22 (2d Cir.1980) ("We know of no support for the ... view ... that the [target's] directors were required to reconsider the merger agreement that had been entered into and that they were contractually bound to recommend to shareholders."); Texaco, Inc. v. Pennzoil, Co., 729 S.W.2d 768, 808–09 (Tex.App.1987) ("Once the agreement was made, [the target] could not evade it, citing fiduciary duty, just because a higher offer came along."); Scott v. Stanton Heights Corp., 131 A.2d 113 (Pa.1957) (board not liable to shareholder for adhering to asset sale agreement in face of subsequent higher offer).

108. 413 N.E.2d 98 (Ill.App.1980).

109. In a few instances, shareholders have attempted to use the federal shareholder proposal rule. SEC Rule 14a–8, as a means of inducing a fundamental corporate change such as a merger, sale of assets or liquidation. Although Rule 14a–8 requires that an issuer include in its proxy materials proposals made by eligible shareholders, the rule also permits the issuer to exclude those proposals that are "under the laws of the registrant's domicile, not a proper subject for action by security holders." This provision was intended to prevent shareholders from infringing on matters committed by state law to the authority or discretion of the board of directors. Exchange Act Release No. 20091, reprinted in [1983–84 Transfer Binder] Fed. Sec. L. Rep. ? 83,417 at 86,204. However, the SEC has generally required inclusion of shareholder proposals calling for a merger or acquisition of the issuer where the proposal is cast in the form of a recommendation to the issuer's

board also has sole power to negotiate the terms on which the merger will take place and to arrive at a definitive merger agreement embodying its decisions as to these matters. Shareholders have no statutory right to amend or veto specific provisions, their role being limited to approving or disapproving the merger agreement as a whole, with most statutes only requiring approval by a majority of the outstanding shares.

Jewel used this statutory division of responsibility between directors and shareholders to both validate and limit the target board's discretionary power to enter into a binding merger agreement pending submission of the agreement to the shareholders for approval. In order to assure that shareholders can exercise their role in the statutory scheme, *Jewel* prohibits target directors from taking any action which deprives the shareholders of their right to make the ultimate decision as to the corporation's future—the board may only preserve the status quo until the shareholders consider the offer. Of course, preserving the status quo between the signing of the merger agreement and the shareholder vote is precisely the purpose of exclusive merger agreements. *Jewel* specifically validated no shop clauses by permitting the target's board to "lawfully bind itself in a merger agreement to forbear from negotiating or accepting competing offers until the shareholders have had an opportunity to consider the initial proposal." Best efforts clauses should also generally pass muster under *Jewel* because they, at most, require the directors to recommend shareholder approval. While the board may thus agree that it will not renege on the transaction in light of changed circumstances, the agreement cannot affect the shareholders' right to do so. The shareholders remain free to accept or reject the merger proposal presented by the board, to respond to a merger proposal or a tender offer made by another firm subsequent to the board's execution of an exclusive merger agreement, or to hold out for a better offer.[110]

board of directors, rather than in the form of a direction that the board seek out an acquirer. See, e.g., Rorer Group, Inc., SEC No–Action Letter (Feb. 27, 1985); Richton International Corp., SEC No–Action Letter (July 21, 1983); Texaco, Inc., SEC No–Action Letter (Jan. 27, 1983); Harnischfeger Corp., SEC No–Action Letter (Dec. 15, 1981); Two B System, Inc., SEC No–Action Letter (Sept. 14, 1979).

110. *Jewel* and *Belden* also addressed the question of whether a competing bidder faces liability for tortious interference with contract if the exclusive merger agreement with the initial bidder is not consummated. They made clear that not all competing bids will constitute tortious interference with contract. Absent a fiduciary out, an enforceable exclusivity provision does give the favored bidder an unequivocal right to receive the performance promised by target man-

agement. Because the target board may only bind itself, however, the favored bidder does not have an unequivocal right for the merger to be consummated. Rather, it has only a mere expectancy in the merger. A best efforts clause, for example, only entitles the favored bidder to have the merger presented and recommended to the target shareholders. As noted, the shareholders are under no obligation to approve the merger. A target board is thus bound by its contractual obligations, but a competing bidder will have substantial freedom to provide target shareholders with an alternative. While the favored bidder's expectancy will receive judicial protection from unfair competition, the favored bidder is not protected from all types of competition. If the competing bidder does no more than to make a tender offer and identify the options open to target shareholders, the competing

Although both *ConAgra* and *Great Western* purported to interpret Delaware law, it long remained unclear which line of authority would prevail in the Delaware courts. The Delaware Supreme Court first touched on this question in *Smith v. Van Gorkom.*[111] The merger agreement at issue there included a fiduciary out in which prospective acquirer Pritzker acknowledged that Trans Union's directors "may have a competing fiduciary obligation to the shareholders under certain circumstances." The Court concluded that "this language on its face cannot be construed as incorporating . . . either the right to accept a better offer or the right to distribute proprietary information to third parties," at least suggesting that Trans Union's board would remain bound by its contractual obligation to recommend the merger to the shareholders even if a higher bid emerged. This implication is further supported by the Court's discussion of the board's options with respect to the shareholder vote on the merger: "the Board had but two options: (1) to proceed with the merger and the stockholder meeting, with the Board's recommendation of approval; or (2) to rescind its agreement with Pritzker, withdraw its approval of the merger, and notify the stockholders that the proposed shareholder meeting was cancelled. . . . But the second course of action would have clearly involved a substantial risk—that the Board would be faced with suit by Pritzker for breach of contract. . . . " By indicating that the breach of contract suit posed a "substantial risk," the court appeared to suggest that the target board could legally bind itself to an exclusive merger agreement. But the issue of the board's legal authority remained open to question, because the court focused on an entirely different matter: the board's duty of care.

Trans Union's directors were ultimately denied the protections of the business judgment rule because they failed "to act in an informed and deliberate manner in determining whether to approve an agreement of merger before submitting the proposal to the stockholders." Trans Union claimed that the directors' duty of care was satisfied in light of two conditions the board allegedly placed on its acceptance of the merger

bidder's conduct will not give rise to liability. Because the favored bidder must show that the contract was breached, or that a breach is imminent, liability should arise only where the competing bidder induces the target board to renege on the contract. Because the target in *Belden* was "firmly aligned" in opposition to the competing bid, the favored bidder's tort claims failed. Professor Gilson suggests that *Jewel* should be interpreted as being consistent with *Belden*: "There is at least an implication that the mere making of a competing offer would not constitute tortious interference." Ronald J. Gilson, The Law and Finance of Corporate Acquisitions 837 n.14 (1986). Cf. Texaco, Inc. v. Pennzoil, Co., 729 S.W.2d 768 (Tex.App.1987), in which Pennzoil received a judgment of approximately 8.5 billion dollars against Texaco for the latter's interference with Pennzoil's merger contract with Getty Oil. This decision is best regarded as an aberration that does not disprove the *Belden* rule. Setting aside any criticisms, which might be directed at the court's analysis, Texaco went beyond merely making a tender offer for Getty's shares. In particular, it entered into stock purchase contracts with major Getty shareholders who were parties to the agreement with Pennzoil and through them and other Getty representatives sought the support of Getty's board. See id. at 796–805.

111.   488 A.2d 858 (Del.1985).

agreement signed in September 1980: "(1) that Trans Union reserved the right to accept any better offer that was made during the market test period; and (2) that Trans Union could share its proprietary information with any other potential bidders." In early October, the merger agreement was amended to allow active solicitation of competing bids. Trans Union would be permitted to terminate the agreement with Pritzker if, prior to February 10, 1981, it either had consummated a merger or asset sale with a third party or had entered into a definitive acquisition agreement on more favorable terms. Trans Union hired an investment banker to solicit other bids, but no firm offer materialized. Trans Union's board attempted to justify their September 1980 decision to accept Pritzker's offer by arguing that the original agreement, and certainly the October amendments, allowed them to escape the merger agreement with Pritzker in the event a higher offer was made. In other words, any deficiencies in their original decision were cured by a subsequent search for competing bids—the so-called market test. The court rejected this rationale on several grounds. First, it concluded that the original merger agreement did not in fact permit the board to terminate the agreement with Pritzker if a higher offer was received. Second, in its view, the October amendments, especially in light of the surrounding circumstances, did not permit a meaningful market test. The board could no longer withdraw simply because a better offer was received. A requirement that Trans Union use its best efforts to mail a proxy statement relating to Pritzker's offer by early January effectively shortened the market test period. The announcement that Pritzker had exercised the lockup option and had completed financing may have deterred other bidders. Finally, the Court apparently believed that Van Gorkom's conduct during the market test period might have chilled the bidding process.

Van Gorkom, however, does not require target boards to shop the company among competing bidders in order to satisfy their duty of due care.[112] Rather, the court seems to be saying that target boards must have some credible basis for determining that a proposed merger is in the best interest of their shareholders. An unfettered market test is merely one means of satisfying the board's duties. A determination of the firm's "intrinsic value," preferably in the form of a fairness opinion by an independent financial expert, is another. A combination of both techniques is probably the safest approach, but the duty of due care should be satisfied even if only the latter device is utilized.[113]

112. *Van Gorkom*, however, was decided before the duty to auction control emerged in Revlon, Inc. v. MacAndrews & Forbes Holdings, Inc., 506 A.2d 173 (Del.1986). Subsequent Delaware decisions suggest that the *Revlon* auctioneering duty may apply where the merger would result in a change of control, such as where a publicly held corporation goes private by means of a merger. Omnicare, Inc. v. NCS Healthcare, Inc., 818 A.2d 914, 928 (Del.2003).

113. Cf. In re TW Services, Inc. Shareholders Litigation, [Current] Fed.Sec.L.Rep. (CCH) ¶ 94,334 at 92,179 n.8 (Del.Ch.1989) ("alternatives to an auction for collecting

Van Gorkom remains relevant to the analysis of deal protection devices under Delaware law. A target board that agrees to an exclusive merger agreement still must have made an informed decision to do so. As Delaware law evolved, however, the legitimacy of deal protection devices became bollixed up with the problem of target board defenses against hostile takeovers. Accordingly, we'll defer further consideration of this issue to Chapter 7.

B. Lockups

Given the relative weakness of exclusivity provisions as a bidding deterrent, an additional device was necessary to insure that the favored bidder's acquisition proposal would succeed—one that would more effectively deter competing bids. Transaction planners found the necessary device in the lockup. A lockup is any arrangement or transaction by which the target corporation gives the favored bidder a competitive advantage over other bidders. So defined the term includes such tactics as an unusually large cancellation fee or an agreement by the target to use takeover defenses to protect the favored bid from competition.[114] Lockup options refer more narrowly to agreements (usually separate from the merger agreement) granting the acquirer an option to buy shares or assets of the target. As with cancellation fees, the option commonly becomes exercisable upon the acquisition by some third party of a specified percentage of the target's outstanding shares.[115]

Stock lockup options give the favored bidder an option to purchase treasury or authorized but unissued target shares. If the option is exercised prior to the shareholder vote on the merger agreement, the favored bidder can vote the additional shares in favor of the merger, helping to assure that the requisite approval will be obtained. If a competing bidder prevails, the favored bidder can exercise the option and sell the additional shares on the open market or tender them to the successful bidder, thereby recouping some or all of its sunk costs. Finally, the risk that the option will be exercised, thereby driving up the

---

the information that directors need to make an informed choice may be appropriate"); In re Amsted Indus. Inc. Litigation, 1988 WL 92736 (Del.Ch.1988) (alternatives to auction procedures acceptable).

114. In so-called shareholder lockups, the favored bidder enters into a lockup arrangement, running from stock purchase agreements and options to purchase stock to agreements to tender to the bidder or not to tender to others and voting agreements, with a target shareholder or shareholder group. Shareholder lockups seem most likely to be successful in companies where a single shareholder or a cohesive shareholder group already owns a controlling (if not

majority) interest in the target. As discussed in the previous section, however, where the lockup presents minority shareholders with a *fait accompli*, they may be invalid under Delaware law, at least where the board of directors is a party to the agreement.

115. E.g., Hanson Trust PLC v. ML SCM Acquisition Inc., 781 F.2d 264, 267 (2d Cir.1986); Mobil Corp. v. Marathon Oil Co., 669 F.2d 366 (6th Cir.1981), cert. denied, 455 U.S. 982 (1982); DMG, Inc. v. Aegis Corp., No. 7619, slip op. (Del.Ch.1984), reprinted in 9 Del. J. Corp. L. 437, 439 (1984).

number of shares that must be acquired in order to obtain control and thus increasing the overall acquisition cost, may deter competing bids in the first instance.

Asset lockup options grant the favored bidder an option to purchase a significant target asset. While asset lockups often are used to entice a prospective bidder, they are principally intended to end or prevent competitive bidding for the target. Accordingly, the subject of the option is usually either the asset most desired by a competing bidder or those essential to the target's operations.[116] Asset lockups thus are sometimes referred to as "crown jewel options," the name coming from the notion that the asset subject to the option is the target's crown jewel, i.e., its most valuable or desirable asset.

The validity of lockup arrangements largely turns on whether deterring competing bids is a legitimate part of the negotiated acquisition process. As with exclusive merger agreements, this question has gotten completely bollixed up with the broader issue of target board resistance to unsolicited tender offers. Hence, discussion of the lockup's validity also is deferred to Chapter 7.

§ 3.9 The Appraisal Remedy

Mergers and sales of all or substantially all corporate assets can be likened to a form of private eminent domain. If the requisite statutory number of shares approves the transaction, dissenting shareholders have no statutory basis for preventing the merger. Granted, some of the minority shareholders may believe that the merger that is being forced upon them is unfair. They may want to retain their investment in the target or they may believe that the price is unfair. Corporate statutes give hold-out shareholders no remedy where they simply want to keep their target shares—the statutes permit majority shareholders to effect a freeze-out merger to eliminate the minority. All the statute gives disgruntled shareholders is a right to complain about the fairness of the price being paid for their shares; namely, the appraisal remedy.

In theory, appraisal rights are quite straightforward. Briefly, they give shareholders who dissent from a merger the right to have the fair value of their shares determined and paid to them in cash, provided the shareholders comply with the convoluted statutory procedures. Unfortunately, putting this simple theory into practice has proven surprisingly difficult. Indeed, the current status of the appraisal doctrine is best described as "tattered."[117]

---

116. See, e.g., Hanson Trust PLC v. ML SCM Acquisition Inc., 781 F.2d 264, 267 (2d Cir.1986); Mobil Corp. v. Marathon Oil Co., 669 F.2d 366 (6th Cir.1981), cert. denied, 455 U.S. 982 (1982).

117. The fiduciary duties of controlling shareholders have laid a significant gloss on the appraisal remedy. The result has been most unfortunate, at least insofar as doctrinal clarity is concerned.

A. Mechanics

1. *Availability of Appraisal*

All appraisal statutes authorize appraisal rights in statutory mergers of close corporations. Beyond that, however, it is impossible to generalize. Whether appraisal rights are available for any other type of transaction depends on which state's law governs. In many states, appraisal is available in connection with a wide range of fundamental transactions, including mergers, sales of all or substantially all corporate assets, and even certain amendments to the articles of incorporation. For example, MBCA § 13.02(a)(4) provides appraisal rights in connection with article amendments effecting a reverse stock split.

In contrast, under DGCL § 262, Delaware law provides appraisal rights only in connection with statutory mergers. But not even all mergers are covered. Section 262(b)(1) provides that appraisal rights shall not be available for companies whose stock is listed on a national securities exchange or which has more than 2,000 record shareholders.[118] However, § 262(b)(2) then restores appraisal rights for such firms' shareholders if the consideration paid in the merger is anything other than stock of the surviving corporation, stock of another corporation that is listed on a national securities exchange or held by more than 2,000 record shareholders,[119] and/or cash in lieu of fractional shares.[120]

2. *Eligibility for Appraisal*

In order to be eligible to make use of the appraisal remedy, Delaware § 262(a) requires that a stockholder: (1) hold shares continuously through the effective date of the merger; (2) perfect his appraisal rights by complying with the provisions of Delaware § 262(d) by sending written notice to the corporation, prior to the shareholder vote, that he intends to exercise his appraisal rights (it is not sufficient to merely vote against the merger at the meeting); and (3) neither vote in favor of nor consent in writing to the merger. MBCA § 13.21 is substantially similar.

3. *Exclusivity of Appraisal*

A key question is whether appraisal is the exclusive remedy by which a shareholder may challenge a merger. The Delaware Supreme Court's *Weinberger* decision indicated appraisal would be exclusive except in cases of fraud, misrepresentation, self-dealing, deliberate waste of

---

118. As used here, national securities exchange includes the NASDAQ inter-dealer automated quotation system.

119. This provision would come into play in a triangular merger, in which the surviving corporation ends up as a wholly owned subsidiary of the acquirer. This pro-

vision allows the use of acquiring company stock as consideration.

120. The Model Act provides a similar market out, although its version is far more complex by virtue of various exceptions for conflicted interest transactions. MBCA § 13.02(b).

corporate assets or gross and palpable over-reaching.[121] The subsequent *Rabkin* decision, however, allows plaintiffs to bring a class action for damages whenever the plaintiffs can prove a breach of the duty of fair dealing.[122] Consequently, appraisal is exclusive only in cases in which plaintiff's claims go solely to the adequacy of the price.

B. Valuation in Appraisal Proceedings

In theory, the value of a share of common stock is the present discounted value of all future dividends to be paid by the corporation.[123] This proposition seems counter-intuitive, because many corporations pay no dividends. As the theory goes, however, in the long run all corporations run out of investment opportunities and begin paying profits out to the shareholders as dividends. It is the expectation of those future dividends that determines the present value of the stock.

The foregoing proposition presents two analytical problems. First, how does one know what dividends are going to be paid in the future? Obviously one cannot project future dividends with certainty and even projecting estimated dividends is a very difficult task to which the full art and science of valuation is devoted. Second, how does one discount the stream of future dividends to present value? This is a far simpler task, involving basic principles arising out of the time value of money.

1. Valuation Basics: The Time Value of Money and Discounting to Present Value

Even in a world without risk, most people would rather be paid a dollar today than be paid a dollar one year from today. This is why money is said to have a time value: people place a higher value on money to be received today than on money to be received later. The time value of money, along with risk, explains why lenders charge interest and depositors receive interest. Interest on a bank account, just as interest on a loan, is partially compensation for foregoing current consumption.

Suppose Jane deposits one dollar at the First National Bank. The Bank will pay Jane interest to compensate her for giving up the opportunity to spend the dollar today. Assume the Bank pays simple annual interest of 6%. At the end of one year, Jane will receive 6 cents in interest, and the value of her account will grow to $1.06. The formula by which one calculates the future value of a deposit is:

---

121. Weinberger v. UOP, Inc., 457 A.2d 701 (Del.1983).

122. Rabkin v. Philip A. Hunt Chemical Corp., 498 A.2d 1099 (Del.1985).

123. Accessible introductions to valuation include Jay W. Eisenhofer & John L.

Reed, Valuation Litigation, 22 Del. J. Corp. L. 37 (1997); Samuel C. Thompson, A Lawyer's Guide to Modern Valuation Techniques in Mergers & Acquisitions, 21 J. Corp. L. 459 (1996).

$$FV = A_i(1+\frac{r}{m})^{mn}$$

where FV stands for the value of the deposit at some time in the future; A_i is the amount of the initial deposit; r is the interest rate; m is how many times per year interest compounds; n is the number of years the deposit is left in the account.

Suppose Jill deposits $1 today at a bank that pays 6% interest compounding quarterly. At the end of three years the value of Jill's account is $1.20, which is calculated from the foregoing equation as follows:

$$FV = \$1(1+\frac{0.06}{4})^{12} = \$1x1.05^{12} = \$1x1.20$$

The concept of present value, which is critical to corporate valuation, depends on the time value of money. If I promise to pay you $1 in one year, how much is that promise worth to you today? We answer that question by calculating the promise's present value (a.k.a. present discounted value). Instead of asking how much a dollar will be worth in one year, we ask how much one must invest today to receive a dollar in one year. As such, calculating present value simply flips the future value equation around. Put another way, the present value calculation is the inverse of the future value calculation:

$$PV = \frac{A_n}{(1+k)^n}$$

where PV is the present value; A_k is the amount to be received; k is the applicable interest rate, which is now referred to as a discount rate; and n is the number of years before the amount is to be received. Suppose Anita promises to pay Carol $1 in five years. The present value of that promise is 75 cents, which is calculated as follows:

$$PV = \frac{\$1}{(1+0.06)^5} = \frac{\$1}{(1.06)^5} = \frac{\$1}{1.34}$$

The discount rate is simply the opportunity cost of capital, adjusted for risk. This is a very easy concept to articulate, but a very complex one to actually calculate.[124] Opportunity cost is deceptively simple—it is simply the rate of return on the next best comparable investment. Unfortunately, it can be very hard to identify the next best comparable investment. Likewise, the question of how much to adjust for risk is a highly subjective question.

   2.   *Valuation Methods Based on the Present Value of Future Dividends*

   As already noted, the theoretical value of a share of stock is the present value of all future dividends. Because the future is uncertain, however, attempting to estimate future dividends obviously is a project fraught with peril. Although a few highly technical and complex valuation methods undertake that project, they are rarely used in legal settings. Instead, far simpler methods are typically used both in planning and litigation. Two such methods use current dividends as a proxy for future dividends. These methods assume that there will be a perpetual dividend stream emanating from the corporation and therefore value the stock using the formula for discounting perpetuity to present value.

   A perpetuity is a stream of income that will be paid perpetually (i.e., indefinitely). The present value of a constant perpetuity is calculated by dividing the value of each installment by the discount rate:

$$PV = \frac{A_i}{k}$$

where PV is the present value of the perpetuity; A_i is the amount of each installment; k is the discount rate. Suppose Ann agrees to pay Barbara $1 per year in perpetuity. Assume the applicable discount rate is 10 percent. The present value of the perpetuity is $1 divided by 0.10, which equals $10.

   The zero growth in dividends valuation method assumes that dividends will remain constant in the future. The value of a share of stock is therefore determined by dividing the current per share dividend by an appropriate discount rate:

$$V = \frac{D}{k}$$

where V is the value of the firm; D is the annual dividend; k is the discount rate. Suppose Acme, Inc., pays an annual dividend of one dollar

---

124. The CAPM formula is often used to estimate the discount rate. See, e.g., Cede & Co. v. Technicolor, 1990 WL 161084 (Del.Ch.1990); see generally Samuel Thompson, A Lawyer's Guide to Modern Valuation Techniques in Mergers & Acquisitions, 21 J. Corp. L. 459 (1996).

on its common stock. Assuming an 8% discount rate, the value of each share of common stock is $1 divided by 0.08, which equals $12.50.

The preceding method has only limited utility in connection with a rapidly growing company that is retaining all or almost all of its earnings. In such a case, using historical dividend data significantly understates the corporation's value. One solution to that problem is switching the valuation method to the formula used to calculate the present discounted value of a growing perpetuity:

$$V = \frac{D}{k-g}$$

where g is a "growth factor." The most commonly accepted growth factor is return on equity (ROE) times the firm's retention rate. ROE is calculated by dividing earnings by shareholders equity. The retention rate is the percentage of earnings retained by the corporation (i.e., 1 minus the dividend pay out rate). If the dividend and discount rate are held constant, this constant growth formula will produce a higher valuation than the zero growth formula, because the denominator will be smaller. Suppose Acme, Inc., currently pays a $1 dividend per share. Acme's return on equity is 0.05, while its retention rate is 80%. Assuming an 8% discount rate, the value of a share of Acme common stock is $25:

$$V = \frac{\$1}{\left(0.08 - \left[0.05x0.80\right]\right)} = \frac{\$1}{0.08 - 0.04} = \frac{\$1}{0.04}$$

3.   The Delaware Block Method

The so-called Delaware block method takes various forms in different states, but generally requires one to take the weighted average of three different valuation measures: net asset value, capitalized earnings, and market value. Net asset value is a variant of the basic book value methodology. Book value is a balance sheet-based valuation method. A corporation's book value is simply its net assets (total assets minus total liabilities). Suppose Acme has total assets of $73,000 and total liabilities of $60,500. Acme's book value is the difference—i.e., $12,500. To determine a per share book value, simply divide the firm's book value by the number of shares of common stock outstanding.

Book value has only one advantage as a valuation methodology, albeit an important one: almost every corporation has a balance sheet no matter how financially unsophisticated the corporation's shareholders may be. Accordingly, the book value of virtually all corporations can be determined quickly and easily. Unfortunately, the valuation obtained by the book value method usually is quite unreliable. Because it is based solely on the balance sheet, book value fails to account for intangible assets that do not appear on the balance sheet, such as goodwill. Book value is also unreliable because assets generally are carried on the balance sheet at their historical cost, which may be wholly unrelated to their current fair market value. Finally, because book value simply involves totaling up assets and liabilities, it fails to account for any synergy resulting from the use of these particular assets by this particular corporation. In other words, book value is based on liquidation value rather than the firm's value as a going concern.[125]

Net asset value tries to correct for these failings. As the Pennsylvania courts have defined the term, for example, it includes "every kind of property and value, whether realty or personalty, tangible or intangible, including good will and the corporation's value as a going concern."[126] Properly understood, net asset valuation thus requires an appraisal of the current fair market value of the corporation's assets on a going concern basis. The Pennsylvania courts nevertheless have cautioned against giving net asset value much weight.[127] In doing so, however, they have confused book value and net asset value. The courts express concern, for example, that net asset value is based on historical cost and excludes going concern values.[128] But net asset value in fact measures both tangible and intangible assets at their current going concern value. The Pennsylvania precedents thus reflect a misunderstanding of their own terminology.

Capitalized earnings are incorporated into all variants of the Delaware block, albeit in subtly different ways. In all its forms, the capitalized earnings valuation method tries to overcome the problems associated with book value by relying on the corporation's income statement rather than on its balance sheet. Value is determined under this method by dividing the corporation's earnings per share by an appropriately chosen capitalization rate.[129] The chief difficulty with this method is

---

125. Going concern valuation values the company as though it will remain in business after the transaction giving rise to the need for valuation. In other words, the going concern value asks what price the company would command if it were sold as an entity. Liquidation valuation assumes the company will be broken up and all of its assets sold off individually. Generally speaking, going concern values will be higher. If the business is successful, there should be some synergistic effect from the combination of assets, and the whole should be worth more than the sum of the parts. But poor management can accumulate assets that subtract value.

126. In re Watt & Shand, 304 A.2d 694, 698 n. 7 (Pa.1973).

127. See, e.g., In re Watt & Shand, 304 A.2d 694 (Pa.1973); In re Spang Indus., Inc., 535 A.2d 86 (Pa.Super.Ct.1987).

128. In re Watt & Shand, 304 A.2d 694, 700 (Pa.1973).

129. Suppose, for example, that Acme Corporation's earnings last year were $2.10/share. The average price/earnings ratio for comparable corporations is 16. An approximate capitalization rate is estimated by taking the reciprocal of the average price/earnings ratio, which is 0.0625. Acme's earnings per share figure is then divided by the

determining an appropriate capitalization rate. In theory, the capitalization rate is the reciprocal of the multiplier, which is also known as the price/earnings ratio. The problem, of course, is that one must know the price of the corporation's stock in order to determine the capitalization rate. Yet, this method nevertheless is frequently used to value close corporations, as to which no market price exists. An approximate capitalization rate is chosen by comparing the corporation to similar corporations with known price/earnings ratios.[130]

The Pennsylvania and Massachusetts precedents illustrate some of the subtle differences in how courts capitalize earnings under the Delaware block method. Massachusetts uses a version known as "earnings value," which is defined as the average corporate earnings for the preceding five years, excluding extraordinary gains and losses.[131] In contrast, Pennsylvania uses a version called "investment value," which requires one to capitalize a representative earnings figure.[132] Investment value thus requires a greater degree of subjective judgment by the appraiser, who must decide what constitutes the requisite representative figure.

Finally, the Delaware Block includes market value. The Delaware block method assumes that no one of the three factors is itself the fair value of the company, but that a weighted average of the three factors is the fair value. Yet, if the company has a market value, how could the fair value and the market value be different? Presumably the answer is either that market value does not reflect a control premium or that the market in which the stock is traded is not efficient. In any event, what does one do if the corporation has no market value, as will be the case for close corporations? Some older Delaware cases suggest that in such cases it may be appropriate to "reconstruct" a market value.[133] The process of doing so is an arcane one, somewhat analogous to determining how many angels can dance on the head of a pin. In practice, it typically involves some variant of either book value or capitalized earnings, thereby giving that element double impact.

None of the three methods is particularly reliable. Net asset value becomes less reliable as it becomes more subjective. To the extent the

---

capitalization rate, which equals $33.60/ share.

130. See, e.g., Universal City Studios, Inc. v. Francis I. duPont & Co., 334 A.2d 216, 219 (Del.1975) (averaging price-earnings ratios of nine other motion picture companies as of date of merger); Gibbons v. Schenley Indus., Inc., 339 A.2d 460, 471 (Del.Ch.1975) (using price-earnings ratio of the Standard & Poor's Distiller's Index as of date of merger); Felder v. Anderson, Clayton & Co., 159 A.2d 278, 285 (Del.Ch. 1960) (averaging price-earnings ratios of

representative stocks over the preceding five-year period).

131. See, e.g., Piemonte v. New Boston Garden Corp., 387 N.E.2d 1145, 1150 (Mass.1979).

132. See, e.g., In re Spang Indus., Inc., 535 A.2d 86, 89–90 (Pa.Super.Ct.1987).

133. Compare In re Delaware Racing Ass'n, 213 A.2d 203, 211–12 (Del.1965) with Universal City Studios, Inc. v. Francis I. duPont & Co., 334 A.2d 216, 222 (Del. 1975).

firm's going concern value diverges from its book value, accordingly, net asset value ought to receive lower weight. Capitalized earnings become less reliable as earnings become more volatile. At one extreme, in a well-established noncyclical firm, earnings should be relatively stable and capitalized earnings should be given a relatively high weight. At the other extreme, in a start-up venture with no earnings history, earnings-based values should get almost no weight. Finally, the weight given market value ought to depend mainly on the thickness of the market for the firm's stock.

In any event, having separately determined the three valuations, one then takes their weighted average. The trial court's assignment of weights to each factor is subject to appellate review under an abuse of discretion standard,[134] which is ironic because the whole process is highly arbitrary. In the oft-cited *Spang Industries* decision, for example, the Pennsylvania appeals court opined that net asset value should receive little weight for the reasons discussed above. The court then proceeded to affirm the trial court's assignment of a weight of 80% to net asset value, which in turn the trial court had determined by taking the equally weighted average of three widely divergent expert opinions.[135]

4. Weinberger and its Discounted Cash Flow Progeny

The Delaware block method compares apples and oranges. The three factors have very little to do with each other, are based on radically different assumptions and methodologies, and thus can lead to widely divergent results. Courts then blithely proceed to compound the problem by assigning largely arbitrary weights to each factor. The method's sole justification is that the calculations are simple and relevant expert testimony is easy to understand. Accordingly, the block method is easy for nonexpert judges and juries to apply.

As a determiner of value, the Delaware chancery court has significant advantages over courts of other states. As a specialist court, the Delaware chancellors obtain considerable experience with valuation issues. As a court of equity, the expert judge need not fear jury confusion. Accordingly, we might expect that Delaware courts can be more concerned with precision than with ease of calculation.

In *Weinberger*, the Delaware Supreme Court officially abandoned the block method. (The method's retention of the Delaware name thus is a misnomer.) The court acknowledged that the block method makes little sense from a finance theory perspective. The court therefore set out to up-date Delaware law. Curiously, it did so by throwing open the courthouse door to virtually anything short of the valuation equivalent of junk science: "We believe that a more liberal approach must include proof of

---

134. See, e.g., Piemonte v. New Boston Garden Corp., 387 N.E.2d 1145, 1153 (Mass.1979).

135. In re Spang Indus., Inc., 535 A.2d 86, 90–91 (Pa.Super.Ct.1987).

value by any techniques or methods which are generally considered acceptable in the financial community and otherwise admissible in court...."[136] Consequently, the court explained, "market value, asset value, dividends, earning prospects, the nature of the enterprise and any other facts which were known or which could be ascertained as of the date of merger and which throw any light on future prospects of the merged corporation are not only pertinent to an inquiry as to the value of the dissenting stockholders' interest, but must be considered...."

In the years following *Weinberger*, the Delaware chancery court has come to rely mainly on the discounted cash flow (DCF) valuation method. DCF has several basic steps:

- Estimate cash flows that the firm will generate over some period of time (the "projection period"). By convention, it is assumed that all cash flows are booked at the end of the fiscal year.[137]

- Determine the terminal value (TV), which is the present discounted value, as of the end of the projection period, of the firm's cash flows beyond the projection period. TV can be calculated in one of two ways:

- Discounting dividends using either the zero growth or constant growth method as appropriate to the company in question.

- Capitalizing earnings.

- Determine an appropriate discount rate, which is usually set at the firm's estimated cost of capital. The capital asset pricing model (CAPM) is a commonly used means of estimating an appropriate discount rate.

- Discount to present value both the projected cash flows and the TV. This process is represented algebraically as follows:

$$V_f = \left[\sum_0^n \frac{C_n}{(1+k)^n} \right] + \frac{TV}{(1+k)^n}$$

where: V_f is the value of the firm; C_n are the cash flows in each year n; k is the discount rate; n are the years from the present to the end of the projection period; and TV is the terminal value.

---

136. Weinberger v. UOP, Inc., 457 A.2d 701, 713 (Del.1983).

137. In Cede & Co. v. JRC Acquisition Corp., 2004 WL 286963 (Del. Ch. 2004), the court observed that it "prefers valuations based on management projections available as of the date of the merger and holds a healthy skepticism for post-merger adjust-ments to management projections or the creation of new projections entirely. Expert valuations that disregard contemporaneous management projections are sometimes completely discounted." Id. at *2. A plain-tiff's expert who disregards management projections in favor of his own estimates thus receives little credence.

An example may be helpful. Assume the appraiser has chosen a four-year projection period and has projected cash flows, dividends, and earnings as follows:

Table 1:

Year	Cash Flow	Dividend	Earnings
1	$100	$10	$75
2	$110	$12	$80
3	$125	$12	$85
4	$140	$13	$90

Further assume that the appraiser has used CAPM to estimate a 10% discount rate. A growth rate of 3% has been calculated using the common method of multiplying the return on equity by the retention rate. The appraiser is using a capitalization rate of 15%. Under these assumptions, the DCF value of the firm, using the capitalized earnings method to determine a terminal value, equals $726.52.

$$V = \left[\frac{\$100}{(1+0.10)}\right] + \left[\frac{\$110}{(1+0.10)^2}\right] + \left[\frac{\$125}{(1+0.10)^3}\right] + \left[\frac{\$90/_{0.15}}{(1+0.10)^3}\right]$$

The first three sums are the discounted cash flows for each of the first three years in the projection period. The final sum is the terminal value calculated using capitalized earnings. Notice, as is typical, that the terminal value ($450.79) contributed over 60% of the total value of the firm.

The DCF value of the firm, using the constant growth dividend method to calculate the terminal value is the same, except for the final sum. Using the constant growth dividend formula, the terminal value here is calculated by dividing the dividend by the difference of the discount rate and the growth factor:

$$V = \left[\frac{\$100}{(1+0.10)}\right] + \left[\frac{\$110}{(1+0.10)^2}\right] + \left[\frac{\$125}{(1+0.10)^3}\right] + \left[\frac{\$13/_{(0.10-0.03)}}{(1+0.10)^3}\right]$$

The fact that this method results in a lower terminal value ($415.24) than the capitalized earnings method is purely an artifact of the way the problem is set up.

5. *Recent Developments*

In recent cases, the Delaware Chancery Court has departed from exclusively focusing on DCF analysis. As one Chancellor explained, where "a discounted cash flow analysis reveals a valuation similar to a comparable companies or comparable transactions analysis, I have more confidence that both analyses are accurately valuing a company."[138] The comparable companies approach asks what stock price (or earnings multiple) is commanded by similar publicly traded companies. The comparable transactions approach looks at prices recently paid in acquisitions of similar companies.

Although this new multi-factor test does not amount to a return to the Delaware block method, it does introduce more uncertainty into the valuation process as the court tries to triangulate a valuation using all three approaches.[139] Valuation thus remains more an art than a science. It also thus remains a playing field for a battle of very expensive experts.

6. *Elements of Value Arising from the Merger*

DGCL § 262(h) provides that shareholders who succeed in an appraisal proceeding are entitled to the "fair value" of their shares "exclusive of any element of value arising from the accomplishment or expectation of the merger." Query whether that language makes control premia irrelevant? In *Armstrong v. Marathon Oil*, Marathon merged with U.S. Steel on March 11, 1982. U.S. Steel previously had acquired a majority of Marathon's stock in a cash tender offer at $125 per share. In the merger, U.S. Steel paid $100 per share in the form of newly issued U.S. Steel bonds. In a subsequent appraisal proceeding, the Ohio Supreme Court held that the $125 paid in the cash tender offer was irrelevant to determining the fair value of the shares subject to the appraisal proceeding.[140] Applying the Ohio appraisal statute, which was substantially similar to that of Delaware, the court deemed control premia to be irrelevant to the value of shares by a stockholder who already had control of the company. Instead, the value of plaintiffs' shares was to be determined by their market value on March 10, 1982, which was about $75, adjusted downward to the extent that the market price anticipated the pending merger.

In *Weinberger*, by way of contrast, the Delaware Supreme Court held that only "speculative elements of value that may arise from the 'accom-

---

138. In re Hanover Direct, Inc. S'holders Litig., 2010 WL 3959399 at *3 (Del. Ch. 2010).

139. Niso Abuaf, Valuing Illiquid Equity Securities in Light of the Financial Crisis of 2007–2009, 20 Journal of Applied Finance 110, 113 (2010) ("Most practitioners triangulate among the three approaches. Triangulation shows scientific humility and legal prudence. That is, if we do not know what the truly correct approach is, we might as well be non-dogmatic and consider all the reasonable approaches, cross-check them against each other, and estimate the final result by quoting a range and not a point estimate.").

140. Armstrong v. Marathon Oil Co., 513 N.E.2d 776 (Ohio 1987).

plishment or expectation' of the merger are excluded" from the determination of fair value under DGCL § 262(h). The word speculative nowhere appears in the statutory text, of course. The court nevertheless went on to describe the disallowance of "speculative elements of value" as "a very narrow exception to the appraisal process, designed to eliminate use of pro forma data and projections of a speculative variety relating to the completion of a merger." The chancery court thus may consider "elements of future value, including the nature of the enterprise, which are known or susceptible of proof as of the date of the merger and not the product of speculation...."[141] As such, evidence of control premia paid in this and comparable acquisitions typically will be relevant.

Despite the Delaware Supreme Court's departure from the plain language of the statutory text, the court's approach makes substantial policy sense. As we've seen, if the Delaware courts followed the plain language of the statute, they ought to start with the pre-merger market price and adjust it downward to eliminate any appreciation resulting from the merger. One perhaps could justify such a result by the history of the appraisal statute and its supposed purpose of giving dissenting shareholders the same value they would have received had the business remained in existence as a going concern without the merger taking place. Starting with the pre-merger price and working down from there, however, makes little practical sense. Given the universality of control premia, who would invoke the appraisal statute if such a rule were followed? The real issue, moreover, is whether the dissenting shareholders received a fair premium over market. In order to answer that question, one must start with the price paid in the merger and, if appropriate, work up from there.

Suppose there is a significant lapse of time between the initial acquisition and the subsequent freeze-out merger, during which the acquirer makes changes in the corporation's business plans that add new value. Suppose plaintiff sought to admit evidence relating to synergistic effects the merger would have, making the combined entity more valuable than the separate companies, such as might be the case if the merger created a vertically integrated company that achieves great economies of scale. What relevance would such information have to valuation in an appraisal proceeding brought in connection with the eventual freeze-out merger? In one of its many *Technicolor* decisions, the Delaware Supreme Court held that in a two-step acquisition value added by the acquiring corporation subsequent to its initial purchase of a controlling block of shares was properly to be considered part of going concern value that dissenting shareholders who sought appraisal were entitled to share. The Chancery Court had refused to consider such elements of value on grounds that doing so "would be tantamount to

---

141. Weinberger v. UOP, Inc., 457 A.2d
701, 713 (Del.1983).

awarding [the dissenting shareholder] a proportionate share of a control premium, which the Court of Chancery deemed to be both economically undesirable and contrary" to precedent. The Supreme Court disagreed, opining that "[t]he underlying assumption in an appraisal valuation is that the dissenting shareholders would [have been] willing to maintain their investment position had the merger not occurred."[142] Note that making such an assumption seemingly leads to the *Marathon* result, as no control premia would have been paid if the merger had not occurred. It seems doubtful, however, that the Delaware Supreme Court intended that result.

C. Marketability and Minority Discounts

Minority discounts are at issue when one is valuing the stock of a minority shareholder in a corporation—public or close—that has a controlling shareholder. Minority discounts reduce the appraised value of the minority shareholders' stock to reflect the fact that someone else controls the company. Marketability discounts are at issue when valuing stock that lacks a trading market. Marketability discounts reflect the generally lower value carried by illiquid investments. All else being equal, the lack of a market exit makes such stocks more risky, which causes shareholders to demand a higher return.

Whether one thinks a minority or marketability discount is appropriate in an appraisal proceeding depends in the first instance on what one believes to be the purpose of such a proceeding. In *Cavalier Oil*, the Delaware Supreme Court stated that appraisal is intended to value the corporate entity, not the shares held by a particular shareholder.[143] If so, this understanding of appraisal's purpose argues against a minority discount, because the question of whether the shares are held by a minority or majority shareholder is irrelevant to the value of the entity as a whole. In contrast, the court's analysis should permit a marketability discount, because the entity as a whole is worth less because the illiquidity of its securities raises its cost of capital and thus reduces its value as a going concern. Curiously, however, the court disallowed both discounts. The opinion treats marketability and minority discounts as though they were one and the same, reflecting a lack of understanding of

---

142. Cede & Co. v. Technicolor, Inc., 684 A.2d 289, 298 (Del.1996).

143. Cavalier Oil Corp. v. Harnett, 564 A.2d 1137, 1144–45 (Del.1989). The court's conclusion seems clearly contrary to the plain text of the statute, which speaks of the fair value of "the shares." Specifically, DGCL § 262(g) requires the court to determine which shareholders are entitled to appraisal. Section 262(g) further provides that the court may order such shareholders to surrender their shares, if held as certifi-

cates, to "the Register in Chancery for notation thereon of the pendency of the appraisal proceedings." DGCL § 262(h) then provides: "After determining the stockholders entitled to an appraisal, the Court shall appraise the shares ... together with a fair rate of interest, if any, to be paid upon the amount determined to be the fair value." The reference to "the shares" clearly refers not to the entity as a whole but rather to the shares held by those stockholders who have perfected their appraisal rights.

the conceptual difference between the two types of discounts. In effect, the court mixed apples and oranges.

In slight contrast to the Delaware view, the American Law Institute Principles of Corporate Governance contend that, in an appraisal proceeding, the corporation's value should be determined "without any discount for minority status or, absent extraordinary circumstances, lack of marketability."[144] The comments to that section define extraordinary circumstances to include "more than the absence of a trading market in the shares; rather, the court should apply this exception only when it finds that the dissenting shareholder has held out in order exploit the transaction giving rise to appraisal so as to divert value to itself that could not be made available proportionately to the other shareholders." The New Jersey Supreme Court recently adopted the ALI position, holding that extraordinary circumstances could not be found where "the company instigated the restrictions [placed on transfer of the stock] and restructuring; [while] the dissenters merely pursued their lawful options" to, inter alia, institute an appraisal proceeding.[145]

A better approach would focus on case-by-case analysis rather than trying to impose a rule of general applicability. The underlying transaction at issue in *Cavalier Oil*, for example, was a freeze-out merger effected by a controlling shareholder who had allegedly usurped a corporate opportunity. The court opined that "to fail to accord to a minority shareholder the full proportionate value of his shares imposes a penalty for lack of control, and unfairly enriches the majority shareholders who may reap a windfall from the appraisal process by cashing out a dissenting shareholder, a clearly undesirable result."[146] In the freeze-out merger setting, the desire to prevent the controlling shareholder from reaping a windfall would justify disallowing a minority discount. A marketability discount would be appropriate in such cases, however, because lack of liquidity equally affects the value of both minority and control shares.

Given this analysis, would either a marketability or a minority discount be appropriate in a court-supervised buy back in lieu of dissolution? In this context, a minority shareholder of a close corporation typically invokes the statutory dissolution procedure as a remedy for oppression by the majority shareholders. In many states, the court can allow the majority to buy back the minority's shares in lieu of dissolution. If the court does so, it must appraise the shares to determine their fair value. In such a proceeding, a marketability discount again seems appropriate because illiquidity drives down the value of all shares. In contrast, a minority discount seems even less appropriate in this setting.

144. ALI Principles § 7.22 (a).
145. Lawson Mardon Wheaton, Inc. v. Smith, 734 A.2d 738, 749–50 (N.J.1999).

146. Cavalier Oil Corp. v. Harnett, 564 A.2d 1137, 1145 (Del.1989).

A minority discount on such facts serves only to reward those whose misconduct gave rise to the finding of oppression in the first place.[147]

§ 3.10   De Facto Mergers

A.   Shareholder Litigation

We have seen that transaction planners often structure deals so as to eliminate shareholder voting and appraisal rights. Transaction planning does not take place in a vacuum, however. Shareholders denied voting and/or appraisal rights by virtue of the deal's structure may seek to reclaim those rights by invoking the de facto merger doctrine. This doctrine is based on the principle of equivalence—like things ought to be treated alike. Put another way, the de facto merger elevates substance over form.

Assume that Buyer Corporation and Target Inc. agree that Buyer will acquire Target via a reverse triangular merger. As a result, Buyer's shareholders will not be entitled to vote on the merger nor will they be eligible for appraisal rights. Disgruntled Buyer shareholders sue, arguing that the reverse triangular merger is a de facto merger. If the court agrees, the court will ignore the form of the transaction, treat the deal as a standard two-party merger, and grant both Buyer and Target shareholders the right to vote and the right to dissent.

In *Hariton v. Arco Electronics*, the Delaware Supreme Court emphatically rejected the de facto merger doctrine.[148] Arco agreed to sell all of its assets to Loral Electronics in return for 283,000 Loral shares. Arco then planned to dissolve, distributing the Loral shares to its shareholders as a final liquidating dividend. An Arco shareholder sued, claiming that the nominal asset sale was, in substance, a merger. The court agreed "that this sale has achieved the same result as a merger," but held that form was to be elevated over substance. The de facto merger doctrine offended the equal dignity of the merger and asset sale provisions of the corporation code. Put another way, the legislature has provided multiple vehicles by which to achieve the same substantive outcome. Each statutory acquisition method had "independent legal significance," and the court could not gainsay the legislative decisions to provide different acquisition forms carrying different levels of shareholder protection.

In contrast, the Pennsylvania courts long tried to preserve the doctrine. In 1957, the Pennsylvania legislature amended the state's corporation code with the self-evident intent of eliminating the de facto merger doctrine. Despite clear legislative history indicating such intent,

---

147.   See, e.g., Brown v. Allied Corrugated Box Co., 154 Cal.Rptr. 170, 176 (Cal.App. 1979).

148.   Hariton v. Arco Elec., Inc., 188 A.2d 123 (Del.1963).

the Pennsylvania Supreme Court in *Farris v. Glen Alden Corp.* held that the de facto merger doctrine survived the amendment.[149] In 1959, the legislature again amended the statute, this time explicitly entitling the act as "abolishing the doctrine of de facto mergers or consolidation." The Pennsylvania courts subsequently ignored the de facto merger doctrine, leaving it for the Third Circuit sitting in a diversity proceeding to pronounce the doctrine's demise.[150]

In states where the de facto merger doctrine remains good law, courts support the doctrine mainly by platitudes: form should not be elevated over substance, like transactions should be treated alike, and so on. The problem is deciding when two transactions are alike, such that they should be treated alike. The general rule is to ask whether a transaction so fundamentally changes the nature of the business as to cause the shareholder to give up his shares in one company and against his will accept shares in a different enterprise. A relatively standard laundry list of factors to be considered has evolved, including: distribution of consideration to the shareholders; change in board composition; change in shareholder composition; significant changes in share value; and significant changes in the company's lines of business.[151]

Turning to policy concerns, does the de facto merger doctrine make sense? Put another way, why did the Delaware courts and the Pennsylvania legislature reject the de facto merger doctrine? Is it simply that

---

149. Farris v. Glen Alden Corp., 143 A.2d 25 (Pa.1958).

150. Terry v. Penn Central Corp., 668 F.2d 188, 192 (3d Cir.1981). Although the de facto merger doctrine apparently is no longer good law in Pennsylvania, the *Glen Alden* decision remains worthy of study. It involved an interestingly structured transaction, which resulted from the planner's imaginative exercise in statutory construction. A company called List owned 38.5% of Glen Alden and wanted to combine the two companies. In order to do so, List sold its assets to Glen Alden in return for Glen Alden stock. List then liquidated and distributed the Glen Alden stock to its shareholders. Because List was much larger than Glen Alden, the List shareholders wound up owning 76.5% of the Glen Alden stock. The plaintiff, a Glen Alden shareholder, claimed that he was entitled to appraisal rights.

The transaction was structured to fall between the cracks of Delaware and Pennsylvania law. Under Delaware law, shareholders in a merging corporation had appraisal rights, but shareholders in a corporation selling all of its assets did not. Under Pennsylvania law, appraisal rights were available to both constituent

parties to a merger, the selling company's shareholders in an asset sale, but not to the purchasing corporation's shareholders in an asset sale. Glen Alden was a Pennsylvania corporation. List was a Delaware corporation. Consequently, if the two companies had merged, both companies' shareholders would get appraisal rights. If Glen Alden sold its assets to List, the Glen Alden shareholders would have appraisal rights under Pennsylvania law. If List sold its assets to Glen Alden, however, neither firm's shareholders would be entitled to appraisal.

Ordinarily, the Glen Alden board alone would have approved the purchase. In this case, however, Glen Alden apparently had insufficient authorized but unissued shares of stock to distribute to List. Accordingly, the shareholders of Glen Alden were allowed to indirectly vote on the transaction, as their approval of an amendment to the articles of incorporation was necessary to authorize more shares.

151. See, e.g., Pratt v. Ballman–Cummings Furniture Co., 495 S.W.2d 509, 511 (Ark.1973); Good v. Lackawanna Leather Co., 233 A.2d 201, 207–08 (N.J.Super.Ch.1967).

they prefer corporate interests to shareholder interests? No. The statute provides various ways of accomplishing an acquisition. It does so because no one acquisition technique is always appropriate. If we let courts recharacterize the statutory alternatives, we increase uncertainty and we eliminate the wealth-creating advantages of having multiple acquisition formats.

Another useful way of looking at the problem is to compare the de facto merger doctrine to the definition of a sale of substantially all corporate assets. On their face, the two issues seem quite different. In a de facto merger doctrine case, the question is whether the court will recharacterize the transaction. In a sale of substantially all assets case, the transaction remains an asset sale. Note, however, that the remedy is effectively the same. A transaction that was to be effected without shareholder approval now must obtain approval. At a deeper level, there may be a connection between the two problems. Shareholder approval is a way of ensuring accountability. After a successful takeover, the incumbents no longer are subject to either shareholder or market penalties for self-dealing. We might therefore predict that courts will use the de facto merger doctrine in situations where the target is going out of business and management will no longer be subject to the risk of shareholder or market penalties.

B. Successor Liability Litigation

In a merger, the acquirer succeeds by operation of law to all of the obligations and liabilities of all the constituent corporations to the merger. In a two-party merger of equals, the surviving company thus is liable to the creditors of both acquirer and target. Other deal structures, however, can lead to different results.

In a triangular merger, the acquiring company is not one of the constituent parties to the transaction. Instead, they are the target and the acquirer subsidiary with which the target is merged. As such, only the resulting subsidiary is automatically liable to the target's preexisting creditors. If the subsidiary were unable to pay their claims, those creditors would have persuade a court to pierce the subsidiary's corporate veil in order to reach the assets of the acquiring company. In most states, this requires a showing that the corporation was the controlling shareholder's alter ego and that adherence to the limited liability rule would "sanction a fraud or promote injustice."[152] Because veil piercing is beyond the scope of this text, suffice it to say that the prospects of successfully doing so as not good.[153]

---

152. Van Dorn Co. v. Future Chemical and Oil Corp., 753 F.2d 565, 570 (7th Cir. 1985); Minifie v. Rowley, 202 P. 673, 676 (Cal. 1921).

153. For a discussion of the law governing piercing the corporate veil, see Stephen M. Bainbridge, Corporate Law 48–71 (2d ed. 2009).

Veil piercing also can come into play where the transaction is effected as a purchase of the target's shares. In such a transaction, the acquirer ends up as the target's controlling shareholder. The merger statute's provisions for transferring liability by operation of law are inapplicable. Instead, unpaid creditors of the newly acquired target would have to pierce the target's corporate veil to reach the acquiring company's assets.

Even that remedy will be unavailable where the acquirer effects the acquisition by purchasing all or substantially all of the target's assets. Instead, subject to a few exceptions, the seller's liabilities remain exclusively the responsibility of the seller. As the Third Circuit explained:

> Under the well-settled rule of corporate law, where one company sells or transfers all of its assets to another, the second entity does not become liable for the debts and liabilities, including torts, of the transferor.
>
> Four generally recognized exceptions qualify this principle of successor nonliability. The purchaser may be liable where: (1) it assumes liability; (2) the transaction amounts to a consolidation or merger; (3) the transaction is fraudulent and intended to provide an escape from liability; or (4) the purchasing corporation is a mere continuation of the selling company.
>
> The successor rule was designed for the corporate contractual world where it functions well. It protects creditors and dissenting shareholders, and facilitates determination of tax responsibilities, while promoting free alienability of business assets. The doctrine reflects the general policy that liabilities adhere to and follow the corporate entity. However, when the form of the transfer does not accurately portray substance, the courts will not refrain from deciding that the new organization is simply the older one in another guise.[154]

The "de facto merger and mere continuation" exceptions "are generally treated identically."[155] "Much the same evidence is relevant to each determination," and the same factors are used to determine "whether either of these exceptions applies."[156]

> In determining whether either of these exceptions applies, the fact finder must consider whether stock was part of the purchase price for the assets; whether there was a continuity of business, control or management between the two corporations; and whether the alleged successor corporation assumed the debts of the predecessor corporation. Not all of these factors need be present for a de

---

154. Polius v. Clark Equipment Co., 802 F.2d 75, 77–78 (3d Cir. 1986) (citations omitted).

155. Berg Chilling Systems, Inc. v. Hull Corp., 435 F.3d 455, 464 (3d Cir. 2006).

156. Luxliner P.L. Export Co. v. RDI/Luxliner, Inc., 13 F.3d 69, 73 (3d Cir. 1993).

facto merger or continuation to have occurred. The crucial inquiry is whether there was an "intent on the part of the contracting parties to effectuate a merger or consolidation rather than a sale of assets."[157]

In Philadelphia Electric Co. v. Hercules, Inc.,[158] for example, the court imposed successor liability on Hercules in connection with its acquisition of substantially all the assets of the Pennsylvania Industrial Chemical Corporation ("PICCO"). Hercules paid for PICCO's assets with shares of Hercules common stock. The agreement had numerous provisions suggesting a substantial continuity of PUCCO's enterprise by Hercules. The agreement, for example, required PICCO to use its best efforts to keep its business organization intact, to keep available to Hercules the service of its present employees and to maintain its relationship with its customers and suppliers for Hercules' benefit.[159] Hercules employed PICCO's management and personnel. PICCO transferred to Hercules the right to use its corporate name. PICCO was required by the agreement to dissolve as soon as practicable after the sale. Finally, "Hercules continued to operate the PICCO plants, produce the same PICCO products and represented to PICCO's customers that PICCO resins had became a part of Hercules' Organics Department."[160]

In contrast, many cases have found that there was no de facto merger where the purchaser paid for the assets with cash rather than stock.[161] Likewise, courts have declined to find a de facto merger even in stock for asset deals where there were no common officers, directors, and principal shareholders after the transaction.[162] Further, "at least two courts have concluded that there was no de facto merger when the seller corporation continued to exist but did not engage in any business operations."[163]

There has been some erosion of the successor liability rules in specific contexts. In particular, several states have adopted more liberal successor liability rules for products liability claims. In California, for example, a buyer that continues to manufacture the same type of article as the seller of the assets used in the manufacturing process becomes liable "for defects in units of the same product line previously manufactured" by the seller.[164] New Jersey and Pennsylvania courts have followed suit, as have a few other states.[165]

157. Id.

158. 587 F.Supp. 144 (E.D.Pa. 1984), aff'd, 762 F.2d 303 (3d Cir. 1985).

159. Id. at 152.

160. Id.

161. See Gehin–Scott v. Newson, Inc., 1994 WL 2530, at *3 (E.D. Pa. 1994) (citing cases).

162. See, e.g., East Prairie R–2 School Dist. v. U.S. Gypsum Co., 813 F.Supp. 1396, 1401 (E.D. Mo. 1993).

163. Village Builders 96, L.P. v. U.S. Laboratories, Inc., 112 P.3d 1082, 1089–90 (Nev. 2005).

164. Ray v. Alad Corp., 560 P.2d 3, 11 (Cal. 1977).

165. Ramirez v. Amsted Industries, Inc., 86 N.J. 332, 431 A.2d 811 (1981);

In Turner v. Bituminous Casualty Co.,[166] the Michigan Supreme Court promulgated what has come to be known as the substantial continuation exception for products liability cases. Under it, the buyer of all or substantially all another company's assets succeeds to the product liability claims arising out of the use of such assets where there has been a substantial "continuity of enterprise." The court looks to determine whether the buyer had retained key personnel, assets, and general business operations as well as the company name, and had assumed liabilities and obligations of the seller ordinarily necessary for normal business operations.

In federal labor law, a test very much like the substantial continuation standard is used to determine whether the purchaser of all or substantially all another company's assets is obliged to recognize the union that represented the seller's employees as continuing to represent the employees of the acquired facilities. Under the federal standard, if the purchaser is deemed to be the seller's successor, the union certified as the collective bargaining representative of the seller's employees presumptively retains its certification, provided at least a majority of the employees after the change in control had worked for the predecessor seller.[167] In order for the purchaser to be deemed a successor, there must be "substantial continuity" between the purchaser and seller's enterprises.[168] In turn, the requisite substantial continuity exists when the purchaser "acquired substantial assets of its predecessor and continued, without interruption or substantial change, the predecessor's business operations."[169] The focus of the analysis is on whether the acquired "operations, as they impinge on union members, remain essentially the same after the transfer of ownership."[170]

Dawejko v. Jorgensen Steel Co., 290 Pa.Super. 15, 434 A.2d 106 (1981). See generally Lefever v. K.P. Hovnanian Enterprises, Inc., 734 A.2d 290, 294–295 (N.J. 1999) (noting that while only 13 states have adopted the product line exception or a similar rule, these states encompass approximately 43% of the U.S. population).

166. 244 N.W.2d 873 (Mich. 1976).

167. NLRB v. Burns Int'l Sec. Servs., Inc., 406 U.S. 272, 279 (1972).

168. Fall River Dyeing & Finishing Corp. v. NLRB, 482 U.S. 27, 43 (1987).

169. Golden State Bottling Co., Inc. v. NLRB, 414 U.S. 168, 184 (1973).

170. International Union of Elec., Radio & Mach. Workers (IUEW) v. NLRB, 604 F.2d 689, 694 (D.C.Cir.1979).

Chapter 4

FREEZE-OUT MERGERS, SALES OF CONTROL, AND SIMILAR CONTROLLING SHAREHOLDER TRANSACTIONS

§ 4.1 Fiduciary Duties of Controlling Shareholders

At early common law, it was well-settled that a shareholder acting as a shareholder was entitled to vote his shares without regard to the interests of other shareholders.[1] As a general matter, it remains the law that shareholders qua shareholders are allowed to act selfishly in deciding how to vote their shares.[2] Where the shareholder has voting control of the corporation, however, liability for self-dealing may arise.

Absent cumulative voting, a controlling shareholder's voting power will suffice to elect the entire board of directors. Recognizing that such a board may not act independently of the controlling shareholder, courts early began to extend the board's fiduciary duties to the controlling shareholder.[3] Agency concepts provide a useful way of looking at the problem. Under familiar principles of vicarious liability, the controlling shareholder can be held liable (as principal) for the acts of the directors (as its agents). In other words, it is not necessary to disturb the notion that shareholders as such are independent of the corporation and of each other. Instead, the controlling shareholder is derivatively liable for the misconduct of its agents.[4] To be sure, courts do not require proof of an agency relationship between the controlling shareholder and the board. Instead, they ask whether the shareholder controlled the corporation and whether the board lacked independence.

---

1. See, e.g., Haldeman v. Haldeman, 197 S.W. 376, 381 (Ky.1917) ("A stockholder may in a stockholders' meeting vote with the view of his own benefit; he represents himself only.").

2. See, e.g., Thorpe v. CERBCO, Inc., 1993 WL 443406 at *5 (Del.Ch.1993); Gabhart v. Gabhart, 370 N.E.2d 345, 355 (Ind. 1977).

3. See, e.g., Southern Pac. Co. v. Bogert, 250 U.S. 483, 487–88 (1919) ("The majority [shareholder] has the right to control; but when it does so, it occupies a fiduciary relation toward the minority, as much so as

the corporation itself or its officers and directors."). The standard citation for this proposition remains Pepper v. Litton, 308 U.S. 295 (1939), in which Justice Douglas famously opined: "A director is a fiduciary. So is a dominant or controlling stockholder or group of stockholders." Id. at 306 (citations omitted).

4. Cf. Summa Corp. v. Trans World Airlines, Inc., 540 A.2d 403 (Del.1988) (imposing liability on controlling shareholder where "no independent board" would have taken the challenged action).

§ 4.2 Identifying Controlling Shareholders

In the federal securities laws, there is a presumption that a shareholder who owns ten percent or more of the voting stock has control.[5] ALI PRINCIPLES § 1.10(b) likewise presumes a shareholder who owns more than 25 percent of the voting stock has control. It is certainly true that a shareholder who owns relatively small amounts of stock nevertheless can exercise effective control. John D. Rockefeller, for example, succeeded in his famous struggle to oust the chairman of the board of Standard Oil of Indiana despite controlling only 14.9 percent of Standard Oil's stock. A bright-line presumption of control, however, is inappropriate in this setting. The basis for imposing fiduciary obligations on a controlling shareholder is not mere ownership of a specified amount of stock, but rather the creation of a de facto agency relationship between the shareholder and the board of directors. In other words, the question is whether a majority of the board lacks independence from the allegedly controlling shareholder.[6] Determining whether such a relationship exists necessarily must be done on a case-by-case basis. Any bright-line rule inevitably will be set arbitrarily and therefore prove simultaneously over- and under-inclusive.

Under Delaware law, a shareholder is deemed to have control if the shareholder either owns a majority of the voting stock or exercises control over corporate decision making.[7] If the shareholder owns less than 50 percent of the voting stock, plaintiff must show evidence of actual control of corporate conduct.[8] Consequently, for example, the

---

5. A.A. Sommer, Jr., Who's "In Control"?—SEC, 21 Bus. Law. 559, 568 (1966).

6. See Odyssey Partners, L.P. v. Fleming Companies, Inc., 735 A.2d 386, 407 (Del.Ch.1999) ("A party alleging domination and control of the majority of a company's board of directors, and thus the company itself, bears the burden of proving such control by showing a lack of independence on the part of a majority of the directors."). Put another way, as Delaware Vice Chancellor Jack Jacobs accurately observed, the concern in this context is "the potential for process manipulation by the controlling stockholder, and the concern that the controlling stockholder's continued presence might influence even a fully informed shareholder vote." In re Wheelabrator Technologies, Inc. Shareholders Litigation, 663 A.2d 1194, 1205 (Del.Ch.1995). If the shareholder lacks the power to so manipulate the process, there is no justification for departing from the traditional view that shareholders are entitled to act in their own self-interest.

7. See, e.g., Ivanhoe Partners v. Newmont Mining Corp., 535 A.2d 1334, 1344 (Del.1987) ("a shareholder owes a fiduciary duty only if it owns a majority interest in or exercises control over the business affairs of the corporation"); Solomon v. Armstrong, 747 A.2d 1098, 1116 n. 53 (Del.Ch.1999) ("Under Delaware law, the notion of a 'controlling' stockholder includes both *de jure* control and *de facto* control."). Conversely, where corporate action requires a supermajority shareholder vote and the majority shareholder's holdings are below the supermajority threshold, actual control may not exist. Cf. Gould v. Ruefenacht, 471 U.S. 701, 705 (1985) (federal securities law opinion noting that control may not exist where a supermajority clause is present).

8. See, e.g., Emerald Partners v. Berlin, 726 A.2d 1215, 1221 n. 8 (Del.1999); Kahn v. Lynch Communication Sys., 638 A.2d 1110 (Del.1994); Citron v. Fairchild Camera & Instrument Corp., 569 A.2d 53, 70 (Del. 1989). Similar standards have been adopted in other jurisdictions, as well. See, e.g., Locati v. Johnson, 980 P.2d 173, 176 (Or.App. 1999) ("In order to be a controlling shareholder who owes fiduciary duties a shareholder must either be (1) an individual who owns a majority of the shares or who, for other reasons, has domination or control of

Delaware Supreme Court in *Kahn v. Lynch Communication Systems, Inc.,*[9] held that a 43.3 percent shareholder exercised control, not based on the number of shares it owned, but because the board of directors deferred to the shareholder's wishes.[10] In contrast, the Delaware Chancery Court concluded in *Western National* that a 46% shareholder did not have sufficient control to be subjected to fiduciary duties to the other shareholders where "the record not only illustrates arm's length bargaining but also demonstrates that American General never improperly forced a merger transaction, one way or another, onto the Special Committee. Indeed, to the extent that Western National felt pressured to do a deal, that pressure emanated from regulatory constraints and product and capital markets, not from American General."[11]

§ 4.3 The Background: Parent–Subsidiary Transactions

One of corporation law's central legal fictions is the idea that a corporation is a legal person possessing most of the rights and powers of a natural person. One of the resulting powers with which corporations are endowed is that of owning stock in another corporation. Consequently, one corporation may own all or part of the stock of a second corporation. If Corporation A owns 100 percent of the stock of Corporation B, for example, we refer to Corporation A as the parent and Corporation B as a wholly-owned subsidiary. If Corporation A owns only 51 percent of Corporation B's voting stock, Corporation A still would be called the parent, but Corporation B now would be called a majority-owned subsidiary. This nomenclature change reflects an important change in the ownership structure of Corporation B. Corporation A is still the principal stockholder, but now there are outsiders who own a minority interest in the firm. Logically enough, these outsiders are termed minority shareholders. (If Corporation A controls Corporation B, while owning less than a majority of the stock, Corporation B would be referred to as a minority-controlled subsidiary.)

the corporation or (2) a member of a small group of shareholders who collectively own a majority of shares or otherwise have that domination or control."); cf. Essex Universal Corp. v. Yates, 305 F.2d 572 (2d Cir. 1962) (putting burden on 28.3% stockholder to rebut presumption of control by showing that another block could out-vote the 38.3% stockholder or other circumstances would lead shareholders to band together to oppose the 28.3% stockholder).

9. 638 A.2d 1110 (Del.1994).

10. *Kahn's* emphasis on board domination carried over into the standard of review applicable to alleged misconduct by a controlling shareholder. In *Kahn*, the con-

trolling shareholder attempted to freeze-out the minority shareholders via a merger. In such a transaction, the controlling shareholder bears the burden or proving the transaction's "entire fairness." If the transaction has been approved by a committee of independent directors or by a fully informed majority of the minority shareholders, however, the burden of proof shifts to the plaintiff on the issue of fairness. In general, disinterested director approval of a controlling shareholder transaction thus will provide a significant layer of protection against challenges by minority shareholders.

11. In re Western Nat. Corp. S'holders Litig., 2000 WL 710192, at *23 (Del. Ch. 2000).

Transactions between parent companies and wholly-owned subsidiaries rarely raise corporate law concerns, beyond whatever ministerial requirements the statutes may impose. In contrast, transactions between parent corporations and their majority-owned or minority-controlled subsidiaries have been a fertile field for litigation. Understandably, minority shareholders often feel that the parent company is using its voting control of the subsidiary to benefit itself at their expense. In such cases, the minority asserts that the parent company should owe them a duty of loyalty comparable to that owed by directors.

The canonical parent-subsidiary case remains the Delaware Supreme Court's opinion in *Sinclair Oil v. Levien*.[12] Sinclair Oil owned 97 percent of the stock of a subsidiary, the Sinclair Venezuelan Oil Company (Sinven), with the remaining 3 percent being held by minority shareholders. A minority shareholder challenged three transactions between Sinclair Oil and Sinven: (1) Payment of large cash dividends by Sinven; (2) Sinclair Oil's use of other (wholly-owned) subsidiaries to develop oil fields located outside of Venezuela; and (3) Sinclair Oil's actions with respect to a contract between Sinven and another Sinclair Oil subsidiary.

What standard of review should a court apply to such disputes? The Delaware Supreme Court identified two standards potentially applicable in such situations: the business judgment rule and the intrinsic fairness rule. Under the business judgment rule, the directors of Sinven get the benefit of a rebuttable presumption of good faith. Under the intrinsic fairness test, the burden of proof is on the directors to show, subject to close scrutiny, that the transactions were objectively fair to Sinven. In this case, as in most, it mattered quite a lot which standard applied. As is often the case, the party bearing the burden of proof on a given dispute lost.

Under *Sinclair Oil*, a court will apply the intrinsic fairness standard, as opposed to the business judgment rule, when the parent has received a benefit "to the exclusion and at the expense of the subsidiary."[13] In other words, the fiduciary obligations owed by a parent corporation are limited to self-dealing. The more exacting intrinsic fairness standard comes into play only when the parent is on both sides of the transaction and, moreover, used its position to extract non-pro rata benefits from a transaction to the minority shareholders' detriment.

The *Sinclair Oil* opinion began with a summary of the court's prior decision in *Getty Oil Co. v. Skelly Oil Co.*[14] In that case, a regulatory agency overseeing oil imports concluded that Getty controlled Skelly. As

12. Sinclair Oil Corp. v. Levien, 280 A.2d 717 (Del.1971).

13. Sinclair Oil Corp. v. Levien, 280 A.2d 717, 720 (Del.1971). See also Case v. New York Central Railroad Co., 204 N.E.2d 643 (N.Y.1965) (applying business judgment rule because parent had not benefited at minority's expense).

14. 267 A.2d 883 (Del.1970).

a result, the agency further determined that Skelly was no longer entitled to a separate allocation of imported crude oil. Skelly sued Getty, contending that it was entitled to a share of Getty's allocation. The court upheld Getty's refusal to share its allocation with Skelly, applying the business judgment rule. Intrinsic fairness was inapplicable, because Getty had not received a benefit at the expense of Skelly. Getty gained nothing to which it was not already entitled. Accordingly, there was no self-dealing, as result of which there was no intrinsic fairness review, and therefore no liability.

The *Sinclair Oil* opinion then turned to whether Sinven's dividend payment policy violated Sinclair's fiduciary duties. Sinven had paid out large amounts of dividends during the applicable period—dividends that in fact exceeded its earnings. Plaintiff contended that the dividends resulted from an improper motive; namely, Sinclair's need for cash. The court applied the business judgment rule to this dispute. Because the minority shareholders had received a pro rata share of the dividends, Sinclair did not receive a non-pro rata benefit at their expense. The dividends were within the limits proscribed by the relevant legal capital statute and were not so large as to amount to a waste of corporate assets. Accordingly, plaintiff was unable to rebut the business judgment rule's presumption of good faith. In dicta, the court suggested that the intrinsic fairness test would be applied to dividend decisions in which there are two classes of stock and dividends are paid on the class owned by the parent but not on the class owned by the minority. This example implicates the conflict of classes discussed in the next section.

The court next took up plaintiff's claim that Sinclair Oil had prevented Sinven from expanding. The Chancellor had applied the intrinsic fairness standard to this issue, concluding that Sinclair had improperly and unfairly denied Sinven opportunities to expand its operations outside of Venezuela. On appeal, the Delaware Supreme Court reversed, identifying the business judgment rule as the proper standard of review. Plaintiff could point to no opportunities that Sinclair had usurped from Sinven. Absent the taking of a corporate opportunity properly belonging to Sinven, the decision of which subsidiary would be allowed to act outside of Venezuela was a business judgment for Sinclair Oil to make.[15] Again, the key consideration was that Sinclair Oil did not take anything away from Sinven that belonged to Sinven.

Finally, the court turned to a contract between another Sinclair Oil subsidiary and Sinven. Sinclair Oil had used its power to cause Sinven to enter into a contract to exclusively sell oil to a wholly-owned Sinclair Oil subsidiary. When that subsidiary breached the contract, Sinclair Oil prevented Sinven from suing to enforce its contract rights. According to

---

15. See David J. Greene & Co. v. Dunhill Int'l, Inc., 249 A.2d 427 (Del.Ch.1968) (invoking corporate opportunity doctrine to hold parent liable for usurping an opportunity from a majority-owned subsidiary).

the court, this issue properly was reviewed under the intrinsic fairness standard. Forcing Sinven to contract with a Sinclair Oil entity was itself self-dealing. Because the contract was breached and not enforced, moreover, Sinclair Oil had gotten a non-pro rata benefit from the contract at the expense of the minority. Accordingly, Sinclair Oil had to show that its failure to enforce the contract was intrinsically fair to Sinven, which it could not do.

§ 4.4   Sales of Control

Suppose a parent corporation or other controlling shareholder wishes to sell its stock in the subsidiary to an outsider. In all probability, this "control block" will sell at a price substantially higher than the market price for the stock. Or, in the case of a close corporation without an active market for its stock, at a price higher than that which minority shares would command. Can the selling shareholder be held liable for failing to share the control premium with the minority?

We can imagine at least 3 possible standards that might be applied to such transactions: (1) A sharing rule, under which every holder of the class of stock in question is entitled to an equal opportunity to sell the holder's shares on a pro rata basis. (2) A no sharing rule, pursuant to which the controlling shareholder is free to sell at the highest price offered by a willing buyer. (3) A fiduciary duty-based rule, which asks whether the sale harms the minority shareholders.

Does our choice of standard depend on the reason the buyer is willing to pay a control premium? Recall that stock consists of two rights: economic and voting. A single share of stock gives the owner little control over the company. The market price of a share of stock thus reflects nothing more than the estimated present value of the future stream of dividends payable on that share. Someone buying a control block of stock, however, obtains significant control through the ability to elect the board of directors. Such control might be valuable if the purchaser believes it can use its position to extract non-pro rata special benefits from the corporation, such as generous salaries, perquisites, and the like. Note that such a sale does not necessarily leave the minority shareholders any worse off. The selling shareholder may well have been doing the same thing. Alternatively, the purchaser may believe that the shares will be worth more in its hands than in those of the incumbent. Perhaps the incumbent is a poor manager. If the stock price is depressed due to poor management, replacing the incumbents with more competent managers should raise the stock price and enable the purchaser to profit.[16] The problem, of course, is that motive can be difficult to

---

16. If so, of course, one must wonder why the purchaser did not attempt to acquire all of the outstanding shares by making an any-and-all offer—i.e., one open to all shareholders pursuant to which the buyer will purchase any and all shares tendered to it. Assume, for example, that the corporation has 100 outstanding shares, current-

determine and, moreover, mixed motives often will be present. At the very least, however, the potential for improper motives suggests a need to police sales of control.

A.   The General Rule

As a general rule, shareholders—controlling or not—are free to dispose of their stock as they see fit and on such terms as a willing buyer offers.[17] One of the risks incident to owning a minority interest in a corporation is that the majority may decide to sell—or decide not to sell—without consulting the minority. The cases setting out the general rule, however, typically go on to identify a number of exceptions. The laundry list usually includes such misconduct as a sale under circumstances indicating that the purchasers intend to loot or mismanage the corporation, the sale involves fraud or misuse of confidential information, the sale amounts to a wrongful appropriation of corporate assets that properly belong to the corporation, or the sale includes a premium for the sale of office.

B.   Sale to a Looter

Suppose that Susan Stockholder, the controlling shareholder of Acme Inc., sells her control block to Lorraine Looter. Looter then proceeds to loot Acme—she liquidates all the assets, steals the cash from the bank account, and absconds to some Pacific island where she sets up a satellite dish and spends her ill-gotten gains in general debauchery. Looter then dies from one of those nasty diseases to which debauchery so often leads. After casting about for a deep pocket to sue, the minority shareholders sue Susan Stockholder. Liability?

ly trading at $10 per share, of which the present controlling shareholder owns 40. The prospective buyer correctly believes that under its management the firm's shares would be worth $20. If the buyer successfully purchases the control block for $19 per share, its stock will produce a $40 profit when the stock price rises to reflect the company's value under its management. All the other shareholders, however, will also automatically receive a pro rata share of those gains. There is nothing the buyer lawfully can do to capture a non-pro rata share of the gains. As a result, the buyer confers a $600 benefit on the other shareholders. In contrast, if the buyer is able to purchase all the outstanding shares, at any price below $19 per share, its profit will exceed $100. To do so, moreover, it need not persuade all of the other shareholders

to sell. As long as the holders of at least 51 shares are willing to sell at a price below $19 per share, our hypothetical buyer will obtain voting control. It may then freeze out the remaining minority shareholders in a subsequent merger at approximately the same price. The most plausible good faith reason a buyer might be unwilling to make an any-and-all offer are risk aversion—a reluctance to put too many of the buyer's eggs into one basket—or a shortage of funds.

17.   For statements of the general rule, see Treadway Companies, Inc. v. Care Corp., 638 F.2d 357, 375 (2d Cir.1980); Clagett v. Hutchison, 583 F.2d 1259, 1262 (4th Cir.1978); Zetlin v. Hanson Holdings, Inc., 397 N.E.2d 387, 388 (N.Y.1979); Tryon v. Smith, 229 P.2d 251, 254 (Or.1951); Glass v. Glass, 321 S.E.2d 69, 74 (Va.1984).

There are not a lot of true sale to looter cases. In the leading *DeBaun v. First Western Bank and Trust Co.* decision, the controlling shareholder was aware of considerable information that should have alerted it to potential problems. A credit report on the prospective buyer indicated a large number of business failures. The purchase price was so high that the buyer would have to tap corporate assets in order to make the required payments. The selling shareholder had obtained but not collected a fraud judgment against the buyer. "Armed with knowledge of these facts," the seller knew or should have known that a sale would be detrimental to the minority shareholders' interests.[18] So, as a general rule, there is no duty to investigate. Where the controlling shareholder is presented with a suspicious character and/or a suspiciously high price, however, the controlling shareholder has a duty to reasonably investigate the buyer's plans.[19]

C. Sale of Office

Suppose Lorraine Looter agrees to purchase a control block of stock from Susan Stockholder. As part of their agreement, Stockholder promises to transfer control of the board to new directors of Looter's choosing. They effect the transfer through sequential resignations. Assume there are three directors: Stockholder, Frank Flunky, and Corrine Crony. Flunky resigns, which he may do at any time under DGCL § 141(b). Per DGCL § 223(a)(1), vacancies may be filled by a majority of the remaining directors. Acting pursuant to that statutory grant of authority, Stockholder and Crony then appoint Looter to the board. Crony then resigns, creating a vacancy to be filled by Stockholder and Looter. And so on, until Looter and her nominees hold all board spots. The new board then appoints Looter and her cronies as officers and day-to-day control has changed hands without a formal shareholder vote. Liability?

As a general rule, sales of corporate office are voidable as contrary to public policy. Any portion of the control premium attributable to the sale of office must be forfeited to the minority shareholders.[20] But suppose the buyer acquired a majority of the voting stock. The buyer then waits until the next annual meeting of the shareholders. Absent cumulative

---

18. DeBaun v. First Western Bank and Trust Co., 120 Cal.Rptr. 354, 360 (Cal.App. 1975).

19. See, e.g., Harris v. Carter, 582 A.2d 222, 235 (Del.Ch.1990) (although the seller is "not a surety for his buyer, when the circumstances would alert a reasonably prudent person to a risk that his buyer is dishonest or in some material respect not truthful, a duty devolves upon the seller to make such inquiry as a reasonably prudent person would make"); see also Gerdes v. Reynolds, 28 N.Y.S.2d 622 (Sup.Ct.1941)

(gross inadequacy of price could put seller on inquiry notice); but see Clagett v. Hutchison, 583 F.2d 1259, 1262 (4th Cir.1978) ($34.75 per share price for stock trading at $7.50 to $10 "cannot be said to be so unreasonable as to place [the seller] on notice of the likelihood of fraud on the corporation or the remaining shareholders").

20. See, e.g., Brecher v. Gregg, 392 N.Y.S.2d 776 (Sup.Ct.1975); Gerdes v. Reynolds, 28 N.Y.S.2d 622 (Sup.Ct.1941).

voting, the buyer's holdings suffice to elect the entire board. Yet, the minority shareholders would have no cause for complaint. Alternatively, the shareholder could call a special meeting to remove the existing board and elect replacements. Assuming the board may be removed without cause, or is willing to resign en masse, the minority again would have no cause for complaint. Imposing liability on a majority block seller and/or buyer who accomplish the same result by sequential resignations simply elevates form over substance and thus makes little policy sense. But what if the control block is less than a majority of the shares? At least in theory, if the issue were put before them at a meeting, the other shareholders could do something silly—like voting for other directors. In that case, perhaps liability should be imposed where sequential resignations are used to transfer control without a shareholder vote.

In the leading decision, *Essex Universal Corp. v. Yates,*[21] a high-powered three-judge panel of the Second Circuit splintered three different ways on this question. Chief Judge Lumbard said there should be no liability if the buyer purchased more than 50 percent of the voting stock, because the buyer would eventually get control of the board anyway. If the buyer purchased less than 50 percent, however, liability for sale of office should be imposed unless the buyer "would as a practical certainty have been guaranteed of the stock voting power to choose a majority of the directors." Because the 28.3 percent block acquired by the purchaser is "usually tantamount to majority control" Chief Judge Lumbard would put the burden of proof on the challenger. In contrast, Judge Friendly would hold a sequential resignation plan voidable as contrary to public policy except "when it was entirely plain that a new election would be a mere formality—i.e., when the seller owned more than 50% of the stock." Where the buyer purchases less than 50 percent of the shares, after all, it is not certain that its slate would in fact be elected. Finally, Judge Clark thought such arrangements are not per se unlawful. Instead, their legality was a question of fact to be determined at trial. Query: How?

D. Usurping a Corporate Opportunity

We come at last to one of corporate law's hoariest chestnuts: *Perlman v. Feldmann.*[22] Newport Steel Corporation, as its name suggests, was a steel manufacturer. During the Korean War demand for steel was very high relative to the available supply of steel. Basic economics tells us that the price of steel should have risen substantially. It did not, however, because the Truman administration had imposed price controls on steel. Newport Steel's dominant shareholder, one C. Russell Feldmann, devised the so-called Feldmann plan, pursuant to which steel purchasers were obliged to extend interest free loans to

---

21.   305 F.2d 572 (2d Cir.1962).   **22.**   219 F.2d 173 (2d Cir.1955).

Newport Steel. The effective price Newport Steel received thus included both the nominal purchase price and the present value of the interest charges it avoided. This was a legal—but somewhat shady—way of getting around the price controls on steel.

A consortium of manufacturers decided to ensure their access to steel by purchasing a steel company. One way to do so, of course, would be to acquire a steel company by means of a merger or tender offer in which all shareholders of the target steel manufacturer would share equally in any premium the consortium was willing to pay. Instead, the consortium formed the Wilport Company, a Delaware corporation, which then purchased Feldman's controlling block of Newport Steel shares at a substantial premium over market. The minority shareholders got nothing and sued. On those facts, the court held for the minority, opining that "siphoning off for personal gain corporate advantages to be derived from a favorable market situation" violated Feldmann's fiduciary duties to the minority.

A simplified example may be helpful. Assume there are 10 Newport Steel shares outstanding, of which Feldmann owns 3. Each year for the next ten years Newport Steel is expecting to sell $120 worth of steel. Ignoring expenses, assume projected annual earnings of $120 or $12 per share, $10 per share of which represents the sale of steel at the controlled price, and $2 per share of which represents cash flows generated by the Feldmann Plan. How much is one share of stock worth? In the real world, we would have to take into account the time value of money and risk by projecting the cash flow into the future and discounting the anticipated cash flows back to present value. To keep the problem simple, we will ignore that complication and assume each share of stock is worth $120 ($12 earnings per year per shore times ten years). If Wilport obtains control by purchasing Feldman's stock, it will get to decide who may purchase Newport Steel's output. Presumably, Wilport will force Newport Steel to sell all of its output to Wilport, a fact of which the court made much. But so what? As long as Newport is operating at full capacity and Wilport pays the maximum controlled price, the minority are no worse off under Wilport than they were under Feldmann. The kicker therefore is that Wilport also gets to decide whether or not to keep the Feldmann plan in place. If Wilport buys Newport and keeps the plan in place, it will pay $120 per year for steel. If Wilport buys Newport and cancels the plan, it will only pay $100 per year for Steel. Suppose Wilport pays Feldmann $150 per share ($450) for his stock and then cancels the Feldmann plan. Feldmann received $30 more than the stock is worth on a per share basis—a control premium. Everybody else now has stock that is worth only $100 ($10 earnings per year per shore, reflecting loss of Feldmann plan revenues, times ten years). Wilport thus paid $450 for stock that is only worth $300, but Wilport will save $20 per year on the price it pays for Steel, which translates into $200 over the teA year period for which we are projecting earnings. So Wilport is better off by a net of $50. The decline of $150 in the value of its Newport shares is off-set by the $200 it saves in costs.

Perlman v. Feldmann thus presented a very unique set of facts: (1) A unique profit making opportunity was available to the corporation only because of the government price controls. (2) The value of that profit making opportunity could be capitalized and divided between the purchaser and seller of the control block. (3) The minority shareholders thus lost significant sums that otherwise would have come to them in the ordinary course. So understood, *Perlman* is a very simple case. *Perlman* does not stand for the proposition that a controlling shareholder must give all other shareholders an equal opportunity to sell their stock on a pro rata basis. Instead, it simply stands for the proposition that a controlling shareholder may not usurp an opportunity that should be available to all shareholders. One could have reached the very same result under a *Sinclair Oil*-style analysis. The controlling shareholder received a benefit "to the exclusion and at the expense" of the minority. Not only were the minority excluded from the opportunity to sell at a premium, they were left worse off as a result.

Beyond *Perlman*'s unique facts, where are corporate opportunity issues most likely to arise? Probably in connection with structuring of acquisitions. Suppose Lorraine Looter approaches Susan Stockholder with an offer to buy Stockholder's control block at a premium. Should there be liability? Not if we adopt the *Sinclair Oil* analogy. The majority shareholder can do whatever she wants as long as she does not deprive the minority shareholders of something to which they are entitled. On these facts, there is no corporate opportunity to be usurped. But suppose Looter approached Stockholder with a slightly different proposal, under which Acme would be merged into a corporation owned by Looter. Stockholder rejects the merger proposal, but offers to sell Looter her control block at a premium. On these facts, the *Perlman* court likely would impose liability. The *Perlman* court found that Feldmann breached his fiduciary duty to the minority shareholders by arranging the transaction so that only Feldmann and his cronies shared in the premium. Susan Stockholder has done essentially the same thing. The original offer was a merger in which all shareholders would have a chance to participate. But the controlling shareholder refused to go along, effectively saying: "if you don't buy me out at a premium over what everybody else gets—no deal." Looter had no choice but to go along, thereby denying the minority shareholders an opportunity to share in the control premium. Stockholder abused her position to usurp an opportunity available to all shareholders.

E. Building a Better Approach to Sales of Control

Courts have not imposed a general obligation for controlling shareholders to share a control premium with the minority. The conventional explanation given by the courts is that it is not per se wrong for a controlling shareholder to sell at a price significantly higher than that available to non-controlling shareholders. It becomes wrong only under special circumstances, such as sale to a looter, sale of office, or taking of a corporate opportunity. In contrast, many scholars have argued for some sort of sharing or equal opportunity rule.[23] Should we adopt such a rule? In short, no.

One of the risks minority shareholders assume when they acquire stock in a corporation with a controlling shareholder is that the latter may sell at a premium without giving the minority an opportunity to participate. If the control block existed when the minority shareholder invested, the minority shareholder presumably paid a lower per share price than he would have paid in the absence of a controlling sharehold- er. In other words, assuming full disclosure, the minority became share- holders having accepted as adequate whatever trade-off was offered in recompense. Even if the control block was assembled after the minority shareholder invested, moreover, the possibility that such a block would be assembled is one of those risks of which a rational shareholder should be aware in making pricing decisions.

Bounded rationality and other transaction cost obstacles to complete contracting, of course, somewhat weaken the foregoing argument's force. Even if the pricing mechanism does not adequately protect minority shareholders, however, there are still efficiency arguments in favor of a no sharing rule. If we believe corporate takeovers promote economic efficiency by displacing inefficient incumbent managers, for example, controlling shareholders generally should be allowed to keep their premi- ums. Unequal distribution lowers the cost of doing takeovers, because the new controlling shareholder only needs to buy the control block, which should result in more takeovers. Giving the controlling sharehold- ers a special premium, moreover, essentially bribes them to quit. Conse- quently, a no sharing rule should facilitate replacement of inefficient incumbents.

The *Sinclair Oil* analogy provides the right default rule. As long as the controlling shareholder does nothing to leave the minority worse off, it should be allowed to sell on whatever terms the market will bear. Doing so is consistent with the reasonable expectations of minority shareholders and promotes efficient changes in control. If controlling shareholders could engage in transactions that affirmatively injure the minority, however, the latter doubtless would take precautions to pre-

---

23. Compare William D. Andrews, The Stockholder's Right to Equal Opportunity in the Sale of Shares, 78 Harv. L. Rev. 505, 506 (1965) (shareholders should have an "equal opportunity to participate ratably" on substantially the same terms) with Frank Easterbrook & Daniel Fischel, Cor- porate Control Transactions, 91 Yale L.J. 698 (1982) ("those who produce a gain should be allowed to keep it, subject to the constraint that other parties to the transac- tion be at least as well off as before the transaction").

vent such transactions. By providing a coercive backstop preventing such transactions, the *Sinclair Oil*-based default rule minimizes bargaining and enforcement costs.

§ 4.5   Refusals to Sell

Courts make cases like *Sinclair Oil* or *Perlman* unnecessarily difficult by blurring the distinction between director and shareholder fiduciary duties. Consider the sale of office cases: The real problem in these cases is not the sale of a control block, but rather the directors' abdication of their duty to make an informed business judgment. Instead of exercising their best individual business judgment, they mindlessly followed a contractual obligation.

Only rarely do you get cases that starkly present the question of shareholder duties qua shareholder duties without any intervening issue of director duties. Delaware Chancellor Allen's decision in *Mendel v. Carroll* is about as clear an example of such a case as one can ever expect to get. The Carroll Family collectively controlled Katy Industries, Inc., owning at various times 48 to 52% of the stock. Even when they did not have an outright majority, their status as the largest shareholder ensured that they had effective control.

The Carroll family proposed a freeze-out merger that would have cashed out the minority shareholders at about $26 per share. The board set up a special committee comprised of independent directors to consider the offer. A competing offer was made by a group organized by a fellow named Sanford Pensler at about $28 per share. The Carroll Family withdrew their merger proposal, but also announced they had no interest in selling their shares.[24] Their opposition to the Pensler proposal effectively precluded it from going forward. Minority shareholders sued, alleging both that the Carroll Family violated its fiduciary duties and that the board of directors violated its fiduciary duties.

If Carroll Family directors had voted on the proposal, the Carroll Family would have been on both sides of the deal. Because the board used a special committee of independent directors to make the decision, however, thereby keeping the Carroll Family out of the board's decision-making process, there are no complicating issues of whether any member of the Carroll Family had director duties. Instead, we have two distinct issues: (1) did the directors violate their fiduciary duties by failing to act against the majority shareholders' interests; (2) did the majority shareholders violate their fiduciary duty to the minority?

As to the board's duties, plaintiff argued that the originally proposed freeze-out merger amounted to a shift in control. Under Delaware law

---

24. As a business matter, why was the Carroll Family so adamant about not selling their shares? We can only speculate, of course, but one suspects the company had substantial free cash flow. The company was said to be "awash in capital." The board had enough money laying around to propose a $14 per share dividend.

governing corporate takeovers, where such a shift in control occurs the board of directors has a fiduciary duty to maximize immediate shareholder value.[25] The Carroll Family proposal was only $26; Pensler offered $28. The Pensler deal therefore was the better deal and the board had a duty to take it. The board responded by arguing that the Carroll Family would not sell their shares. If the family will not go along, a deal cannot be done. Consequently, the board's duty to the shareholders is limited to getting the best deal possible given the Carroll Family's intransigence. Plaintiff replied that the board was obligated under these circumstances to act against the majority shareholders' interest. Plaintiff suggested the board sell additional shares to the Pensler group, thereby diluting the Carroll Family holdings to the point at which they no longer had control.

Chancellor Allen left open the possibility that a board might sometimes be required to act against the majority's interest. Because the board also owes fiduciary duties to the majority, however, he limited this possibility to cases in which the majority shareholder is overreaching and trying to injure the minority. On the facts, this was not such a case. Allen pointed out that the plaintiff's argument broke down at several points. First, because the Carroll Family already had effective control at all relevant times, nothing they did amounted to a shift of control, and the takeover precedents were irrelevant. Second, Allen also took issue with the proposition that $28 was a better deal for the shareholders than $26. The Carroll Family already had control. Their offer thus would not include a control premium. The Pensler group was trying to buy control. The fact that they were only willing to pay a $2 control premium suggests that they might be low-balling the shareholders. Of course, Allen did not need to decide whether $28 from Pensler was in fact better or worse for the shareholders than $26 from the Carroll Family. In the absence of a showing that the board acted from conflicted interests, he properly left that issue to the board.

Turning to the fiduciary duties of controlling shareholders, the majority opinion in *Perlman v. Feldmann* had analogized shareholders to partners, drawing special attention to the broad dicta Judge Cardozo's famous *Meinhard v. Salmon* opinion. If we take Cardozo literally, partners may not behave selfishly towards one another. If we take *Perlman* literally, neither may "corporate fiduciaries." If we apply *Meinhard* and *Perlman* to the facts of *Mendel*, surely we conclude that the Carroll Family was acting selfishly, probably motivated by their desire to retain control over the firm's free cash flow.

Allen touched on the sale of control cases in passing. On the one hand, he recognized the legitimacy of sales of control at a premium. At the same time, however, he noted that liability for sale of control at a

---

25. See Revlon, Inc. v. MacAndrews & Forbes Holdings, Inc., 506 A.2d 173 (Del.   1986).

premium over market could be imposed in the canonical cases of sale to looters, sale of office, or usurpation of corporate opportunity. But *Mendel* involved the reverse situation: where the controlling shareholder refused to sell and, by that refusal, prevented a takeover. In that context, Allen held that self-sacrifice is not required. The family had no obligation to sell.

In connection with the sale of control cases, we suggested that liability should be imposed where the minority shareholders are worse off after the transaction than before. Why should that rule not be extended to cases in which the controlling shareholder refuses to sell? One answer may be the well-established distinction in tort between action and inaction. Another is that such a rule would amount to a species of private eminent domain—the would-be buyer can effectively condemn the majority shareholders' interest and force them to sell. Finally, on the facts, it was not clear the minority was injured. The price they paid for their shares presumably impounded the risk of intransigence by the Carrolls.

§ 4.6   Freeze-out Mergers and Variants

In a freeze-out transaction, the controlling shareholder buys out the minority shareholders, even if the minority object. The transaction typically is effected using a triangular merger in which the corporation is merged with a wholly owned subsidiary of the controlling shareholder. A merger combines two corporations to form a single firm. After a merger, only one of the two companies will survive, but that survivor succeeds by operation of law to all of the assets, liabilities, rights, and obligations of the two constituent corporations. In addition, a merger also converts the shares of each constituent corporation into whatever consideration was specified in the merger agreement. Suppose the merger agreement provided that minority shareholders were to receive $50 per share in cash. After the merger takes place, their shares are transformed by operation of law into a mere IOU for the promised cash payment.

Corporate law originally required unanimous shareholder approval of mergers. The unanimity requirement created serious holdout problems, allowing dissenting minorities to block Kaldor–Hicks efficient transactions. In the 1800s, the necessary vote was reduced in most states to a majority of the outstanding shares. A few states have slightly higher vote requirements, such as two-thirds, but none retains the old unanimity requirement.

Taken together, these rules provide the controlling shareholder with a form of private eminent domain. Its shares standing alone may suffice to approve the merger, even if every other shareholder votes against it. Assuming the merger is approved, the minority shareholders will be forced to accept the consideration specified in the merger agreement.

Although minority shareholders have no power to block a freeze-out merger, they are not wholly lacking in remedies. When states began moving away from the unanimity requirement, they also created the statutory appraisal proceeding. Recall that appraisal rights give dissenting shareholders the right to have the fair value of their shares determined and paid to them in cash, provided that the dissenting shareholder complies with specified procedures. In practice, however, appraisal is not a very attractive remedy. Getting a shareholder to the point where the statutes permit exercise of the appraisal rights tends to be like working one's way through a labyrinth. There are many traps for the unwary—the most significant of which is the requirement that a shareholder perfect his appraisal rights by giving the corporation written notice of his intent to do so before the shareholder vote on the merger. Facts tending to show that the price was unfair often will not be discovered until after the shareholder vote. In addition, many jurisdictions do not permit the use of class actions in appraisal proceedings. Accordingly, it can be very expensive to exercise appraisal rights because each dissenting shareholder must hire his own lawyer. In contrast, if he can bring a fraud or fiduciary duty claim outside the appraisal statute he can do so via a class or derivative action. Finally, it also is possible that he will get greater relief in a cause of action for damages than under appraisal.

Because of the advantages class and derivative actions possess over appraisal proceedings, the exclusivity of such proceedings is the critical issue. Should appraisal be regarded as the exclusive remedy or should unhappy shareholders be allowed to challenge the merger even if they were not eligible to make use of the appraisal remedy? This issue tends to come up most often in going private or freeze-out transactions where the buyer is either management and/or a controlling shareholder. Plaintiffs claim that there has been a breach of fiduciary duty or fraud or what have you. The question then becomes whether they are entitled to a remedy outside the appraisal process.

Current Delaware law on these issues originated with the Supreme Court's decision in *Weinberger v. UOP.*[26] A conglomerate named The Signal Companies purchased 50.5% of UOP's stock. Sometime thereafter Signal decided to acquire the remaining 49.5% of UOP's shares at $21 per share through a freeze-out merger between a wholly owned Signal subsidiary and UOP. Plaintiff challenged the fairness of the merger on a variety of grounds. In a far-reaching opinion, the court laid out a number of important principles. Although some of its pronouncements have undergone substantial subsequent modification, *Weinberger* remains the starting point for any discussion of freeze-out mergers.

26. Weinberger v. UOP, Inc., 457 A.2d 701 (Del.1983).

A. The Business Context: Why Freeze–Out the Minority?

After acquiring a majority block of UOP shares, Signal faced the same problem created by any successful tender offer. Where the acquirer obtains control of the target through a tender offer there will almost always be some holdout shareholders. Some target shareholders simply won't tender into the offer, either due to opposition or mere cluelessness, even if the offer is structured as a cash bid for any and all outstanding shares. Getting rid of the minority is fairly straight-forward—a triangular merger between the target corporation and a wholly owned subsidiary of the acquirer will do the trick.

The question remains however: why get rid of the minority? What is the cost-benefit analysis? On the cost side of the ledger, the principal factor is the price the controlling shareholder will have to pay minority shareholders in the freeze-out merger. The main planning issue on this side of the ledger therefore is the extent to which the law precludes the controlling shareholder from paying a low-ball price.

On the benefit side of the ledger, there are costs that can be eliminated through a freeze-out merger. If the target is a public company, taking it private eliminates all of the costs associated with the proxy rules and the periodic disclosure filings required of public firms. Sole ownership also may give the controlling shareholder more flexibility to transfer assets from one subsidiary to another or to dispose of assets.

To what extent do the fiduciary duties owed to the minority justify effecting a freeze-out merger? In other words, does complying with the rules set forth in the preceding section sufficiently complicate the controlling shareholder's life so as to justify the costs associated with eliminating the minority? To be sure, transactions between parent companies and their majority-owned subsidiaries are a fertile field for litigation. On balance, however, the controlling shareholder's liability exposure generally will not justify the expense (and litigation risk) associated with freeze-out mergers.

Recall from *Sinclair Oil* that the Delaware Supreme Court identified two legal standards potentially applicable to transactions between the target and the controlling shareholder: (1) the business judgment rule and (2) the intrinsic fairness standard.[27] A court will apply the intrinsic fairness test, as opposed to the business judgment rule, when the parent has received a benefit to the exclusion and at the expense of the minority shareholders of the subsidiary. The choice of which standard to apply matters because the burden of proof shifts depending on which standard is applied. Under the business judgment rule, the directors get the presumption of good faith and plaintiff must rebut that presumption. Under the intrinsic fairness test, the burden of proof is on the directors to show, subject to close scrutiny, that the transactions were objectively fair to the firm.

---

27. Sinclair Oil Corp. v. Levien, 280 A.2d 717 (Del.1971).

Although the fiduciary duties of a controlling shareholder seem like a significant limitation on its freedom to run the company, in practice they are not all that important. The situations in which majority shareholders have been held liable are fairly limited. Liability usually arises only where the minority shareholders have an expectancy in the challenged benefit and then fail to receive their pro rata share. As long as the controlling shareholder is willing to give the minority their pro rata share of any benefits, there should not be major liability concerns.[28]

Why then do controlling shareholders so frequently insist on freezing out the minority? Two answers suggest themselves. On the one hand, perhaps the controlling shareholder plans to extract more than its pro rata share of some corporate benefit. On the other hand, perhaps the controlling shareholder is simply risk averse and wishes to avoid the potential for aberrational litigation outcomes. The extent to which one thinks courts should scrutinize these transactions depends in large part on which answer seems more plausible.

B. The Business Purpose Test

In *Singer v. Magnavox*, shareholders of Magnavox challenged the corporation's agreement to be acquired by North American Philips in a reverse triangular merger.[29] Because North American indirectly owned 84.1% of Magnavox's outstanding shares by virtue of a prior tender offer, the outcome of the shareholder vote on the merger proposal was a foregone conclusion. After the merger became effective, plaintiff shareholders sought an order nullifying the merger and awarding compensatory damages on the grounds that the merger was fraudulent and constituted a breach of duty by the defendant directors and by North American as the controlling shareholder.

In *Singer*, the challenged freeze-out merger fully complied with the relevant Delaware merger statutes. The Supreme Court, however, held that compliance with the form of the statute did not end the inquiry: "inequitable action does not become permissible simply because it is legally possible." Accordingly, the court imposed certain limitations on the acquiring company's ability to freeze-out minority shareholders. Among these was the so-called business purpose test, which held that a merger could not be effected for the "sole purpose of freezing out minority shareholders."

If the business purpose test is based solely on the target corporation's interests, effecting a freeze-out merger becomes quite difficult. In many cases, the advantages of a going private transaction accrue mainly to the controlling shareholder. In subsequent decisions, however, the

---

28. For a good discussion of these issues, see Ronald J. Gilson and Bernard S. Black, The Law and Finance of Corporate Acquisitions 1237–52 (2d ed. 1995).

29. Singer v. Magnavox Co., 380 A.2d 969 (Del.1977).

Delaware Supreme Court effectively eviscerated the business purpose test by requiring only that the merger serve some bona fide purpose of the parent corporation.[30] Because competent transaction planners easily could create a paper trail showing the merger promoted some business interest of the parent, the test was left as mere formalism. Recognizing that the business purpose test afforded minority shareholders no meaningful protections, the Delaware Supreme Court abandoned it in *Weinberger*.[31]

C. Freeze-outs and Fairness

Weinberger is an annoyingly difficult decision to parse. It reminds one of trying to finish a jigsaw puzzle when some of the pieces are missing and others came from an entirely different puzzle. The court overruled a number of precedents, creating an entirely new remedy for freeze-out mergers, but declined to do so retrospectively. Portions of the opinion thus applied only to future cases, while other portions applied only to cases then pending. Worse yet, some of the prospective rules announced by *Weinberger* have undergone significant subsequent modifications.

According to *Weinberger*, a freeze-out merger must satisfy an "entire fairness" standard.[32] In turn, entire fairness has two components:

---

30. See, e.g., Tanzer v. International General Industries, Inc., 379 A.2d 1121 (Del.1977).

31. Weinberger v. UOP, Inc., 457 A.2d 701, 715 (Del.1983). In Coggins v. New England Patriots Football Club, Inc., 492 N.E.2d 1112 (Mass.1986), the Massachusetts court declined to follow *Weinberger* in this regard. The Massachusetts court both retained the business purpose test and interpreted that test to require the merger serve some legitimate business interest of the target subsidiary. As is often the case, the challenged merger's benefits flowed to the controlling shareholder, which the court deemed improper. Even in *Coggins*-like jurisdictions, however, careful transaction planning often can create the requisite paper trail showing a purported interest of the target subsidiary served by the freeze-out merger. See, e.g., Dower v. Mosser Industries, 648 F.2d 183 (3d Cir.1981) (merger enabled subsidiary to obtain a loan for expansion of its business); Grimes v. Donaldson, Lufkin and Jenrette, Inc., 392 F.Supp. 1393 (N.D.Fla.1974), aff'd, 521 F.2d 812 (5th Cir.1975) (merger permitted transactions between related corporations that otherwise would have been deemed a conflict of interest); Teschner v. Chicago Title & Trust Co., 322 N.E.2d 54 (Ill.1974)

(merger intended to reduce corporate expenses and simplify internal procedures); Alpert v. 28 Williams Street Corp., 483 N.Y.S.2d 667, 473 N.E.2d 19 (1984) (merger allowed firm to obtain additional capital from an investor who would not invest without elimination of minority interests); cf. Leader v. Hycor, Inc., 479 N.E.2d 173 (Mass.1985) (reverse stock split effected to take company private because costs of a public market for the stock was not justified by the poor market for that stock). Consequently, *Coggins* simply raises transaction costs, creates traps for the unwary, and provides employment for transactional lawyers.

32. The entire fairness standard applies only where the majority shareholder seeks to freeze-out the minority via a merger. According to the Delaware Supreme Court, "Delaware law does not impose a duty of entire fairness on controlling stockholders making a non-coercive tender or exchange offer to acquire shares directly from the minority holders." Solomon v. Pathe Communications Corp., 672 A.2d 35, 39 (Del. 1996) (citations and quotations omitted). In place of an entire fairness standard, the Delaware courts examine both the structure of the transaction to insure that it is volun-

fair price and fair dealing. The controlling shareholder's obligation to pay a fair price raises valuation issues discussed in § 3.9. Here we focus on the controlling shareholder's duty to deal fairly with the minority.

Even after acquiring a majority position in UOP, Signal still was sitting on a pile of excess cash for which it had been unable to find profitable uses. Illustrating the agency costs inherent in free cash flow, Signal's board failed to pay out the cash to the shareholders via a dividend or stock repurchase. Instead, after considering and rejecting many options, Signal turned its attention back to UOP. Signal's board ordered that a feasibility study be prepared relating to the possible acquisition by Signal of the remaining minority UOP shares. Messrs. Arledge and Chitiea prepared the study. They were both officers of Signal and also directors of both UOP and Signal. Using confidential UOP information, Arledge and Chitiea concluded that buying the remaining 49.5% of UOP's stock at any price up to $24 per share would be a good investment for Signal. After the feasibility study was completed, Signal's executive committee decided to effect a freeze-out merger at $21 per share, which the committee purportedly believed would be a fair price.

Negotiations between Signal and UOP were conducted on the latter's behalf by one Crawford, who was UOP's president but also had been a long-time Signal employee. Indeed, the court described Crawford as "Signal's man at UOP." When the matter was laid before UOP's board, the UOP board members who had been nominated by Signal were present at the meeting in person or by telephone conference call. They left the meeting to permit free discussion by the non-Signal directors, but returned before the final vote. Although they did not vote, the record showed that they would have voted affirmatively.

The court concluded that this course of conduct violated the duty of fair dealing in at least three respects. First, the Arledge–Chitiea report was prepared using confidential UOP information. It is perfectly permissible for someone to be a director of two corporations simultaneously, even if those corporations are related as parent and subsidiary.[33] "But such common directors owe the same fidelity to both corporations."[34] Consequently, Arledge and Chitiea could not use their positions as UOP directors to benefit Signal.

---

tary in nature and information disclosed to insure its adequacy and completeness. Where an offer is found to be both structurally non-coercive and fully disclosed, the court will leave the decision whether to tender or not up to the stockholders. See, e.g., In re Pure Resources S'holders Litig., 808 A.2d 421, 433–46 (Del.Ch.2002); In re Aquila Inc. S'holders Litig., 805 A.2d 184 (Del.Ch.2002); In re Siliconix Inc. S'holders Litig., 2001 WL 716787 (Del.Ch. 2001).

33. See, e.g., Roberts v. Prisk, 284 P. 984, 987 (Cal.App.1930) ("There must be either fraud or a lack of good faith, or some breach of trust shown in addition to the fact of interlocking directorates" for liability to be imposed or to avoid a conflicted interest transaction).

34. San Diego, Old Town, and Pacific Beach R.R. Co. v. Pacific Beach Co., 44 P. 333, 334 (Cal.1896).

Second, there was a lack of candor. As a controlling shareholder seeking to effect a freeze-out transaction, Signal's fiduciary duties to the minority included an obligation to fully disclose all material facts.[35] The Arledge–Chitiea report was clearly material—the reasonable investor would consider both the information therein and the manner in which it was prepared to be important in deciding how to vote—but the report was not disclosed either to the independent UOP directors or to the minority shareholders.

Finally, there was a lack of arms-length bargaining. As a prudential matter, Crawford and the Signal-affiliated board members should have recused themselves from the negotiations. A special committee of UOP's independent directors then should have been appointed to study the offer and conduct any negotiations. As the court explained: "Although perfection is not possible, or expected, the result here could have been entirely different if UOP had appointed an independent negotiating committee of its outside directors to deal with Signal at arm's length."[36] Instructively, the court went on to equate "fairness in this context" to the conduct that might be expected from "a theoretical, wholly independent, board of directors acting upon the matter before them." Notice how this expectation squares with the authority/accountability dichotomy we have developed in connection with judicial oversight of board decision making. Only where there is evidence of possible self-dealing do accountability concerns trump the null hypothesis of preserving the board's discretionary authority from judicial review. If independent and disinterested directors have conducted the transaction, accountability concerns are minimized, and the court appropriately will give more deference to the board's decisions.

Unlike some duty of loyalty settings, however, approval of a freeze-out merger by the disinterested directors (or shareholders for that matter) does not change the applicable standard of review to, say, the business judgment rule. As the Delaware court explained in *Kahn v. Lynch Communication Systems*,[37] "approval of the transaction by an independent committee of directors or an informed majority of minority shareholders shifts the burden of proof on the issue of fairness from the controlling or dominating shareholder to the challenging shareholder-plaintiff. Nevertheless, even when an interested cash-out merger transaction receives the informed approval of a majority of minority stockholders or an independent committee of disinterested directors, an entire fairness analysis is the only proper standard of judicial review." The court went on to emphasize that the burden shifts to plaintiff only if the

35. Cf. In re Wheelabrator Technologies, Inc. Shareholders Litigation, 663 A.2d 1194, 1198 (Del.Ch.1995) ("Delaware law imposes upon a board of directors the fiduciary duty to disclose fully and fairly all material facts within its control that would have a significant effect upon a stockholder vote.").

36. Weinberger v. UOP, Inc., 457 A.2d 701, 709 n. 7 (Del.1983).

37. 638 A.2d 1110, 1117 (Del.1994).

majority shareholder does not dictate the terms of the merger and the independent committee has "real bargaining power that it can exercise with the majority shareholder on an arm length basis."

D. Freeze-outs, Fiduciary Duties, and Appraisal

Weinberger's basic requirement of entire fairness was not a novel development, although the emphasis on fair dealing constituted an important refinement of the standard.[38] What good is a fairness requirement, however, if there is no effective remedy? Under *Singer* and its pre-*Weinberger* progeny, the statutory appraisal proceeding was not the sole remedy available for mergers failing to satisfy the entire fairness test. Instead, aggrieved shareholders could bring a class action for money damages, even if they were not eligible for appraisal. This had the significant advantage of permitting shareholders who voted for the merger to change their minds and seek damages if they subsequently decided the merger was unfair.

In contrast, the *Weinberger* court ruled that any future challenges to a merger's fairness generally must be made by means of an appraisal proceeding. (Cases then pending were allowed to proceed as class actions.) As the court explained, "a plaintiff's monetary remedy ordinarily should be confined to the more liberalized appraisal proceeding herein established." The court acknowledged that appraisal might not be "adequate in certain cases, particularly where fraud, misrepresentation, self-dealing, deliberate waste of corporate assets, or gross and palpable overreaching are involved." But while the Chancery Court was authorized to provide alternative measures of damages in those cases, such as by granting rescissory damages,[39] the court was to do so within the confines of the appraisal process.[40]

---

38. See, e.g., Singer v. Magnavox Co., 380 A.2d 969, 980 (Del.1977) (requiring that freeze-out mergers satisfy an "entire fairness" standard).

39. Rescissory damages give shareholders the value of their stock measured at the time of judgment, thereby giving the shareholders a share of the gains from the merger. This, at least in theory, was supposed to deter the practice of "low-balling," in which the bidder offered a price less than that which likely would be available in an appraisal proceeding on the theory that few if any shareholders would exercise their appraisal rights. In practice, however, it gives shareholders a put option. In other words, the dissenter can elect to be treated as though he had been a shareholder in the firm all along. This allows the dissenter to free ride on the majority shareholder's efforts to enhance share value. If the firm does worse than the market, however, he'll probably get at least the appraisal price plus interest. As a result, the availability of rescissory damages makes appraisal a no-risk proposition.

40. In light of the court's subsequent retreat from this position, it is worth quoting the relevant passage in full: "the provisions of 8 Del.C. § 262, as herein construed, respecting the scope of an appraisal and the means for perfecting the same, shall govern the financial remedy available to minority shareholders in a cash-out merger. Thus, we return to the well established principles of Stauffer v. Standard Brands, Inc., 187 A.2d 78 (Del.Supr.1962) and David J. Greene & Co. v. Schenley Industries, Inc., 281 A.2d 30 (Del.Ch.1971), mandating a stockholder's recourse to the basic remedy of an appraisal." Weinberger v. UOP, Inc., 457 A.2d 701, 715 (Del.1983).

Weinberger appeared to unequivocally leave appraisal as the exclusive remedy in freeze-out mergers. If a minority shareholder thought a merger was unfair, his remedy was to bring an appraisal proceeding, which meant there would be no class action and the shareholder would have to perfect his appraisal rights. In its subsequent *Rabkin* opinion, however, the Delaware Supreme Court took it all back—or, at least, most of it.

On March 1, 1983, the Olin Corporation bought 63 percent of the outstanding stock of the Philip A. Hunt Chemical Corporation from a company called Turner & Newall. Olin paid Turner & Newall $25 per share. The parties agreed that, if Olin bought the remainder of Hunt stock within one year, Olin would pay the minority shareholders $25 as well. At the time, Olin stated it had "no present intention" to buy the remaining shares. The court observed, however, that "it is clear that Olin always anticipated owing 100 percent of Hunt." In any case, just over one year later, on March 23, 1984, Olin met with its investment banking firm to plan its purchase of the remaining stock at $20 per share. Within a short time, it had engineered a freeze-out merger at $20.

Disgruntled shareholders plaintiffs rejected an appraisal and brought a class action challenging the merger as unfair. The defendants moved to dismiss on grounds that appraisal is the exclusive remedy. The Chancery Court agreed with the defendants and dismissed. The Delaware Supreme Court reversed, however, holding that the Chancery Court's view "render[ed] meaningless our extensive discussion of fair dealing" in *Weinberger*.[41] To be sure, *Weinberger* contemplated that the Chancery Court could take into account breaches of fiduciary duty when valuing stock in an appraisal proceeding. Ultimately, however, appraisal is concerned mainly with the adequacy of the price. If there is to be a successful collateral attack on the manner in which the controlling shareholder dealt with the minority, a class action for damages provides a far more effective tool. *Rabkin* implicitly recognized this truth, leaving

---

41. Rabkin v. Philip A. Hunt Chemical Corp., 498 A.2d 1099, 1104 (Del.1985). There is something of a puzzle in the court's apparent belief that Olin had dealt unfairly with the minority shareholders of Hunt. Suppose that at the time Olin bought its majority stake in Hunt, Olin anticipated buying the minority interest at $20 per share as soon as possible. The law is that paying a premium for control, without more, is unobjectionable. All that is added here Turner & Newall's insistence that Olin wait at least a year before cashing out the minority at a price below $25. The court seems to interpret the one-year rule as some sort of effort by Turner & Newall to encourage Olin to pay $25 per share to the minority shareholders, and some sort of agreement by Olin to do so, when in fact it probably was just an attempt by Turner & Newall to avoid sale of control litigation. To be sure, *Rabkin* was an appeal from a grant of a motion to dismiss on the pleadings. Yet, by giving plaintiffs an opportunity to prove a contractual right to the $25, the court implicitly acknowledges at least the potential that such a contract right exists. If so, however, where did it come from? Is the court saying that the plaintiffs were third party beneficiaries of the contract between Turner & Newall and Olin? Admittedly, the court noted some possible defalcations by Hunt directors, but it also squarely stated that plaintiffs sought "to enforce a contractual right to receive $25 per share."

appraisal a very limited scope of action. After *Rabkin*, appraisal apparently is exclusive only when plaintiff's claims go solely to the fairness of the price.[42] Although the court did not say so expressly, this conclusion follows inexorably from three aspects of the decision: (1) the Supreme Court's rejection of the Chancery Court's "narrow" interpretation of *Weinberger*; (2) the Supreme Court's emphasis that the case involved charges of "unfair dealing"; (3) the fact that plaintiff's allegation of unfair dealing was enough to defeat dismissal of the class action. In other words, Delaware has come full circle. In order to ensure that minority shareholders have an effective remedy in freeze-out mergers, the court has reopened the courthouse door to class and derivative actions.

In contrast, the Model Act has moved in just the opposite direction. Subject to two exceptions, MBCA § 13.02(d) states that a shareholder entitled to appraisal rights "may not challenge" a completed merger. One exception authorizes suit to remedy serious procedural errors in the decision making process, such as a failure to obtain the required votes. The other permits a class action outside of appraisal where shareholder approval of the merger was procured by fraud. Note also the implicit exception for equitable relief sought prior to the merger's completion. Finally, the exclusivity principle does not preclude a class action for damages brought against directors for violating their duties of care and loyalty. Hence, a *Van Gorkom*-type suit is not barred.[43]

E.   Effect of Shareholder Approval

As with other duty of loyalty claims, shareholder approval and/or ratification is not claim preclusive. Instead, valid shareholder action shifts the burden of proof from defendants to plaintiffs. Given the outcome determinative potential of assigning the burden of proof, of course, this is a nontrivial benefit for the defendants.

In a freeze-out merger, the controlling shareholder's conflict of interest is imputed to the target subsidiary's board. Accordingly, such a merger is treated as a type of self-dealing transaction and the burden of proof is on the defendant controlling shareholder and/or the controlled directors to prove that the transaction was fair to the minority. If a freeze-out merger is approved by a majority of the disinterested shareholders—the so-called "majority of the minority," however, the burden of proof shifts to the plaintiff to show that the merger was unfair. The standard of review remains entire fairness, with its integral fair price and fair dealing components, but the burden is now on plaintiff to show lack of fairness on one or both grounds.[44]

---

42.   See Cede & Co. v. Technicolor, Inc., 542 A.2d 1182 (Del.1988).

43.   Smith v. Van Gorkom, 488 A.2d 858 (Del.1985).

44.   See In re Wheelabrator Technolo-

F. Freeze-outs Via a Short-form Merger

The short-form merger is a statutory acquisition technique available only when the acquiring corporation owns some very high percentage—in most states, at least 90%—of the shares of the target corporation. Because the directors of such a thoroughly dominated subsidiary are unlikely to be truly independent of the parent corporation and the outcome of a shareholder vote would be a foregone conclusion, neither the subsidiary's board of directors nor its shareholders get a vote on the merger. Instead, in most cases, the decision to effect a short-form merger is vested solely in the discretion of the parent corporation's board of directors.

Subsidiary shareholders frozen out via a short-form merger do get appraisal rights under Delaware law. The parent corporation is required to notify the minority shareholders both that the merger will be effected and that appraisal rights are available. Unlike a freeze-out merger effected via the standard merger statute, however, Delaware courts do not apply the *Weinberger* entire fairness standard to short-form mergers.

In *Glassman v. Unocal Exploration Corp.*,[45] a subsidiary's minority shareholders filed a class action against the parent corporation and its directors, claiming that the latter had breached their fiduciary duties under *Weinberger* of entire fairness and full disclosure. the claims were presented as to the legitimacy of a controlling shareholder merger. In rejecting that claim, the Delaware Supreme Court acknowledged that "a parent corporation and its directors undertaking a short-form merger are self-dealing fiduciaries." Yet, the court also recognized that the short-form merger statute inherently contemplated "a summary procedure that is inconsistent with any reasonable notion of fair dealing."

> The equitable claim plainly conflicts with the statute. If a corporate fiduciary follows the truncated process authorized by § 253, it will not be able to establish the fair dealing prong of entire fairness. If, instead, the corporate fiduciary sets up negotiating committees, hires independent financial and legal experts, etc., then it will have lost the very benefit provided by the statute—a simple, fast and inexpensive process for accomplishing a merger. We resolve this conflict by giving effect the intent of the General Assembly. In order to serve its purpose, § 253 must be construed to obviate the requirement to establish entire fairness.

Accordingly, the court held, "absent fraud or illegality, appraisal is the exclusive remedy available to a minority stockholder who objects to a short-form merger."

gies, Inc. Shareholders Litigation, 663 A.2d 1194, 1203 (Del.Ch.1995); see also Kahn v. Lynch Communication Sys., 638 A.2d 1110 (Del.1994); Rosenblatt v. Getty Oil Co., 493 A.2d 929 (Del.1985).

45. 777 A.2d 242 (Del. 2001).

In doing so, we also reaffirm Weinberger's statements about the scope of appraisal. The determination of fair value must be based on all relevant factors, including damages and elements of future value, where appropriate. So, for example, if the merger was timed to take advantage of a depressed market, or a low point in the company's cyclical earnings, or to precede an anticipated positive development, the appraised value may be adjusted to account for those factors.

While the monetary relief available in an appraisal proceeding arising out of a short-form merger thus may differ but little from that available in a class action for breach of fiduciary duty, the procedural hurdles inherent in the appraisal action mean that shareholders often will have no practicable remedy.

Delaware Chancellor Leo Strine has remarked upon the apparent inconsistency between this line of cases and those applicable to freeze-outs effected by a standard merger:

> When a transaction to buy out the minority is proposed, is it more important to the development of strong capital markets to hold controlling stockholders and target boards to very strict (and litigation-intensive) standards of fiduciary conduct? Or is more stockholder wealth generated if less rigorous protections are adopted, which permit acquisitions to proceed so long as the majority has not misled or strong-armed the minority? Is such flexibility in fact beneficial to minority stockholders because it encourages liquidity-generating tender offers to them and provides incentives for acquirers to pay hefty premiums to buy control, knowing that control will be accompanied by legal rules that permit a later "going private" transaction to occur in a relatively non-litigious manner?

> At present, the Delaware case law has two strands of authority that answer these questions differently. In one strand, which deals with situations in which controlling stockholders negotiate a merger agreement with the target board to buy out the minority, our decisional law emphasizes the protection of minority stockholders against unfairness. In the other strand, which deals with situations when a controlling stockholder seeks to acquire the rest of the company's shares through a tender offer followed by a short-form merger under 8 Del.C. § 253, Delaware case precedent facilitates the free flow of capital between willing buyers and willing sellers of shares, so long as the consent of the sellers is not procured by inadequate or misleading information or by wrongful compulsion.

> These strands appear to treat economically similar transactions as categorically different simply because the method by which the controlling stockholder proceeds varies. This disparity in treatment persists even though the two basic methods (negotiated merger versus tender offer/short-form merger) pose similar threats to minority stockholders. Indeed, it can be argued that the distinction in

approach subjects the transaction that is more protective of minority stockholders when implemented with appropriate protective devices—a merger negotiated by an independent committee with the power to say no and conditioned on a majority of the minority vote—to more stringent review than the more dangerous form of a going private deal—an unnegotiated tender offer made by a majority stockholder. The latter transaction is arguably less protective than a merger of the kind described, because the majority stockholder-offeror has access to inside information, and the offer requires disaggregated stockholders to decide whether to tender quickly, pressured by the risk of being squeezed out in a short-form merger at a different price later or being left as part of a much smaller public minority. This disparity creates a possible incoherence in our law.[46]

As yet, however, the disparity remains unresolved.

This disparity in treatment has had the practical effect of encouraging controlling shareholders to structure freeze-out transactions as either a so-called "unilateral two-step freeze-out" or a "negotiated two-step freeze-out" The former "refers to a going-private transaction in which a controller unilaterally launches a first-step tender offer and commits to eliminate any remaining stockholders through a second-step short-form merger."[47] The latter "refers to the same transactional structure when effected pursuant to an agreement between the controller and the subsidiary."[48] In some such transactions, the subsidiary's board of directors will agree to a so-called "top up option" pursuant to which, if the tender offer does not put the controlling shareholder over the 90% threshold necessary to effect a short-form merger, the subsidiary will issue sufficient new shares to the controlling shareholder to put the latter over the 90% line.

The so-called *Siliconix* line of cases holds that because neither the tender offer nor the short form merger involves the controlled board, other than that board's federal law obligation to issue a Schedule 14D–9 statement stating its' position on the proposal, fiduciary duty analysis simply does not apply to a tender offer even one followed by a short form merger.[49] As a result, the *Glassman* rule on short form mergers is extended to the situation in which that merger followed a tender offer that put the controlling shareholder over the 90% threshold. The *Siliconix* approach makes sense because, for entire fairness to apply, a controlling stockholder must stand on both sides of the transaction. In a

---

46. In re Pure Resources, Inc., S'holders Litig., 808 A.2d 421, 434–35 (Del. Ch. 2002).

47. In re CNX Gas Corp. S'holders Litig., 2010 WL 2705147 at *1 n.1 (Del. Ch. 2010).

48. Id.

49. See, e.g., In re Pure Resources S'holders Litig., 808 A.2d 421 (Del.Ch. 2002); In re Aquila Inc. S'holders Litig., 805 A.2d 184 (Del.Ch.2002); In re Siliconix Inc. S'holders Litig., 2001 WL 716787 (Del.Ch. 2001).

tender offer, however, the controlling shareholder stands on only one side of the transaction, with the minority shareholders standing on the other.

Although such a transaction will not be subjected to *Weinberger* entire fairness review that does not necessarily mean it is entirely immune from judicial review. One line of "Court of Chancery decisions holds that a unilateral two-step freeze-out will not be reviewed substantively if: (i) it is subject to a non-waivable majority of the minority tender condition; (ii) the controlling stockholder promises to consummate a prompt short-form merger at the same price if it obtains more than 90% of the shares; (iii) the controlling stockholder has made no retributive threats; and (iv) the independent directors on the target board have free rein and adequate time to react to the tender offer."[50] Another line of Chancery cases, however, simply holds that "a unilateral two-step freeze-out will not be reviewed for entire fairness unless the offer is structurally coercive."[51] One is left to hope that the Delaware Supreme Court will eventually sort all of this out.

G. Freeze-outs Via a Reverse Stock Split

1. *Stock splits*

In colloquial speech, the term "stock split" is often used to describe a stock dividend in which the number of shares issued equals or exceeds the number of shares outstanding. In legal capital terms, however, this is a misuse of terminology. A stock dividend is an issuance of authorized but unissued stock to the shareholders and may be effected by the board of directors acting alone. A stock split, in contrast, is effected by amending the articles of incorporation to reduce the par value.

Suppose ABC's board wanted to effect a 2:1 split, in which each shareholder will end up owning 2 "new" shares post-split for every one pre-split share. ABC's board would recommend that the shareholders approve an amendment to the articles of incorporation reducing the par value from $5 to $2.50 per share. Each shareholder will then receive two "new" shares of common stock for each "old" share they previously owned. Because a stock split is effected via a reduction in the par value, it has no impact on the corporation's balance sheet. Accordingly, the board need not redesignate surplus "as capital . . . if shares are being

---

50. *CNX Gas Corp. S'holders Litig.,* 2010 WL 2705147 at *4.

51. Id. The court noted a third line of cases potentially applying an entire fairness standard, but those older cases are inconsistent with Delaware Supreme Court precedents holding that a controlling shareholder is "free to make a tender offer [for the remaining shares] at whatever price it chooses so long as it does not: i) 'structurally coerce' the [target] minority by suggesting explicitly or implicitly that injurious events will occur to those stockholders who fail to tender; or ii) mislead the [target] minority into tendering by concealing or misstating the material facts." In re Pure Resources, Inc., S'holders Litig., 808 A.2d 421, 433 (Del. Ch. 2002).

distributed by a corporation pursuant to a split-up or division of its stock rather than as payment of a dividend declared payable in stock of the corporation."[52] This is so because the capital is the aggregate par value of all outstanding shares. Here the number of outstanding shares went up by 2 but the par value is ½ its former value, so capital is unchanged.

2. Reverse Stock Splits and Freeze–Outs

An interesting wrinkle on this class of transactions is provided by the so-called "reverse stock split," which is often used as a vehicle for freezing out minority shareholders with small share holdings. Consider *Leader v. Hycor, Inc.*,[53] for example, in which the corporation's shareholders approved an amendment to the articles of incorporation changing the par value from one cent to $40 per share. As with a regular stock split, the transaction had no impact on Hycor's balance sheet.

Hycor shareholders, however, received one new post-split share for every 4,000 "old" shares they owned pre-split. What happened, you may ask, to shareholders who owned less than 4,000 shares? If you owned 1,000 shares, would you receive a quarter share? Like most states, Massachusetts allows but does not require a corporation to issue fractional shares. Where a corporate transaction would leave some shareholders with fractional shares, the corporation may cash out the holders of such shares by paying them the fair value of their shares. The effect (and presumably the intent) of Hycor's reverse stock split thus was to squeeze-out the firm's minority shareholders, all of whom owned less than 4,000 shares. Curiously, however, whether such transactions are thus subject to review under the fiduciary duty standards applicable to freeze-out mergers or close corporation squeeze-outs remains uncertain.

Hycor involved a going private transaction by a Massachusetts corporation. Without deciding whether Hycor should be treated as a close corporation and thus be subjected to the exacting fiduciary duties applied by Massachusetts to such firms, the court concluded that Hycor had met that standard. Eliminating the costs associated with being a public corporation was a legitimate business purpose and that the objecting minority could show no less harmful alternative.[54]

The Delaware Chancery Court has held that if "a controlling stockholder uses a reverse split to freeze out minority stockholders without any procedural protections, the transaction will be reviewed for entire

---

52. DGCL § 173.

53. 479 N.E.2d 173 (Mass. 1985).

54. Id. at 177–78. See also Goldman v. Union Bank and Trust, 765 P.2d 638 (Colo. Ct. App. 1988) (courts reviewing freeze-outs effected by a reverse stock split usually require defendants to show a legitimate business purpose for the transaction); Teschner v. Chicago Title & Trust Co., 322 N.E.2d 54 (Ill. 1974) (plaintiff not entitled to relief in connection with a freeze-out effected by reverse stock split where plaintiff failed to show that the transaction was fraudulent, unfair, or had an improper purpose); Lerner v. Lerner, 511 A.2d 501 (Md. 1986) (freeze-out by reverse stock split enjoined on fiduciary duty grounds).

fairness with the burden of proof on the defendant fiduciaries."[55] This is so, the court explained, because a reverse stock split is the functional equivalent of a freeze-out merger.

> If the controlling stockholder permits the board to form a duly empowered and properly functioning special committee, or if the transaction is conditioned on a correctly formulated majority-of-the-minority vote, then the burden could shift to the plaintiff to prove that the transaction was unfair. If the controlling stockholder permits the use of both protective devices, then the transaction could avoid entire fairness review.[56]

Note that this holding thus creates the same dichotomy vis-à-vis short form mergers as exists with respect to standard mergers.

In any case, the use of reverse stock splits to squeeze-out minority shareholders is also mitigated somewhat by the fact that such transactions require an amendment to the articles of incorporation. Indeed, under the MBCA, a reverse stock split triggers both group voting and appraisal rights.[57]

§ 4.7   Conducting a Sale of the Corporation in the Presence of a Controlling Shareholder

In *McMullin v. Beran*,[58] Atlantic Richfield Company ("ARCO") was the majority shareholder (at 80+%) of ARCO Chemical Company ("Chemical"). In the spring of 1998, ARCO received an unsolicited inquiry from Lyondell Petrochemical Company ("Lyondell"), in which Lyondell expressed interest in acquiring Chemical. ARCO notified Chemical's board, which (oddly enough) authorized ARCO to explore a sale of Chemical. Negotiations between ARCO and Lyondell eventually Supreme Court culminated in a $57.75 cash tender offer for any and all Chemical shares, to be followed by the usual cleanup freeze-out merger at the same price.[59] Chemical's board approved the deal, which a Merrill Lynch fairness opinion had blessed. Minority shareholders sued, alleging that Chemical's board made an uninformed decision, that the Chemical board was beholden to ARCO and approved the deal because ARCO needed quick cash, that Chemical's board improperly delegated the responsibility to conduct negotiations to ARCO, and that the tender offer document failed to disclose material facts. The Chancery Court dismissed for failure to state a claim. The Supreme Court reversed and remanded.

The Supreme Court (per Justice Holland) emphasized that Chemical's directors (allegedly) were in ARCO's pocket. Chemical's directors

---

55. Reis v. Hazelett Strip–Casting Corp., 2011 WL 4346913 (Del. Ch. 2011).

56. Id. at *10 (citation omitted).

57. See MBCA § 10.04(a)(4) (group voting); MBCA § 13.02(a)(4) (appraisal rights).

58. 765 A.2d 910 (Del.Sup.2000).

59. It is puzzling that ARCO didn't simply sell its 80.1% to Lyondell, which then could have effected a freeze-out merger. Were they worried about Perlman v. Feldman issues?

hastily approved a deal for ARCO's benefit, without determining whether this was a good deal for the minority. But, on the other hand, what could Chemical's board do under the circumstances? The court opined that Chemical's directors had a duty to maximize shareholder wealth, even though a majority shareholder was present, but also acknowledged that the majority shareholder's presence precludes the board from affirmatively seeking alternative deals opposed by the majority.

The court thus gave little shrift to the very real problem facing the independent board members. Any deal supported by ARCO will pass a shareholder vote and any deal opposed by ARCO will fail such a vote. In theory, if the independent directors concluded the ARCO favored deal was a bad one, they have several options, none of which are likely to prove palatable in the real world.

The independent directors could vote against the deal, but ARCO and its favored buyer could end run the board by structuring the deal as a tender offer or stock acquisition.[60] The independent board members could contacted the minority shareholders to encourage the minority shareholders to exercise their appraisal rights in the event of a freeze-out merger, as the court suggests, but the ineffectiveness of the appraisal remedy leaves one skeptical of the merits of that option.

At the extreme, the board could authorize Chemical to issue enough stock to dilute ARCO's holdings to the point at which they no longer have control. Once ARCO no longer has control, an alternative deal could go forward. In view of ARCO's domination of the board, of course, such a decision is most unlikely. As a doctrinal matter, moreover, Chancellor Allen indicated in *Mendel v. Carroll*,[61] that such measures rarely would be required of a board faced with a majority shareholder.

It may be doubted that many directors have enough independence to take such drastic steps. On the other hand, the very presence of independent directors to whom decisions must be presented for approval and who must be persuaded to give their approval should go a long way towards encouraging managers to make better decisions. Indeed, that supposition is the justification for giving independent directors such a prominent role in this setting.

The real puzzler is why the ARCO/Chemical lawyers failed to do a better job of sanitizing the deal with appropriate independent action by the Chemical board. It is almost as though ARCO set out to create a textbook example of how not to structure such a deal. What should they have done? Appoint a committee of independent directors to haggle with Lyondell. Give the committee outside legal counsel and financial advis-

---

60. If ARCO pressed forward with such an approach, of course, the Schedule 14D–9 would have to disclose the independent directors' objections.

61. 651 A.2d 297 (Del.Ch.1994).

ors. Order those financial advisors to do a valuation study. Make full disclosure of all material information. And so on.[62]

62. The question of whether the *Unocal* enhanced scrutiny standard applies to sales where there is a controlling shareholder is taken up in Chapter 7.

Chapter 5

SHAREHOLDER VOTING IN ACQUISITIONS AND ACQUISITIONS BY SHAREHOLDER VOTE

Because a merger or asset sale requires shareholder approval, the state laws governing shareholder voting obviously are highly relevant to negotiated acquisitions. Likewise, because public corporations generally need to solicit proxies in order to conduct a shareholder vote, the federal proxy rules also come into play in a negotiated deal. Because state law allows a dissident shareholder to contest the election of the board of directors by putting forward an alternative slate of candidates and federal law allows the dissident to solicit proxies in support of that slate, the voting rules also create an alternative vehicle for acquiring control of a corporation; namely, the proxy contest.

Historically, proxy contests were not a very important vehicle for effecting a change in corporate control. To be sure, they are the most direct means of doing so. As we shall see, however, proxy insurgents face significant barriers. In the face of target board resistance, a tender offer or other form of stock purchase usually was a far more effective tool for the hostile acquirer.

The rise of effective takeover defenses and state antitakeover legislation, however, gave the proxy contest a new lease on life. The emergence of the poison pill as the premier takeover defense was an especially significant factor. A standard poison pill typically contains a provision for redemption by the board of directors, which makes the pill vulnerable to a pre-offer proxy contest in which the hostile bidder seeks to elect to a new slate of directors committed to redeeming the pill.[1] As a result, proxy contests and takeover battles have become closely intertwined. Indeed, most recent proxy contests have been ancillary to a hostile tender offer.

§ 5.1 Shareholder Voting: State Law

A. Overview

Shareholders normally vote only at meetings,[2] of which there must be at least one per year (called, logically enough, the annual meeting of

---

1. See § 7.1.B.

2. A majority of states allow shareholders to act without a meeting by unanimous

shareholders). In addition, all statutes have some provision for so-called special meetings—i.e., meetings held between annual meetings to consider some extraordinary matter that cannot wait. Who is entitled to call a special meeting varies from state to state. Almost all state corporation laws allow the board to call a special meeting. Most allow a specified percentage of the shareholders acting together to call a special meeting. A few allow a specified corporate officer, such as the president or chairman of the board, to call a special meeting. MBCA § 7.02(a)(1) empowers the board of directors and any other person authorized by the articles or bylaws to call a special meeting. MBCA § 7.02(a)(2) empowers the holders of at least 10% of the voting shares to call a special meeting. The articles may specify a lower or higher percentage, but not to exceed, 25% of the voting power. In contrast, per DGCL § 211(d), only the board of directors and any other person authorized by the articles or bylaws may call special meetings.

Whether it is an annual or special meeting, most shareholders will not show up. Large corporations with thousands of shareholders frequently hold their shareholder meetings in small halls or even just very large conference rooms. Most shareholders vote by proxy. (In a sense, proxy voting is the corporate law equivalent of absentee voting.) Since the 1930s, the federal securities laws have extensively regulated proxy voting. Hence, federal rather than state law governs many of the mechanics of shareholder voting. Generally speaking, state law governs substantive aspects of shareholder voting, such as how many votes a shareholder gets, when they get to vote, and the types of questions on which they get to vote. Federal law governs the procedures by which shareholders vote and the disclosures to which shareholders are entitled.

B. Notice and Quorum

Whether shareholders will vote in person or by proxy, statutory notice and quorum requirements must be satisfied if their action is to be valid. MBCA § 7.05(a), for example, requires no less than 10 but no more than 60 days notice for both annual and special meetings. Under MBCA § 7.05(b), notice of an annual meeting need not state the purposes for which the meeting is called, although the federal proxy rules mandate such notice. Under MBCA § 7.05(c), by contrast, only those matters specified in the notice may be taken up at a special meeting.

The Model Act's default quorum is a majority of the shares entitled to vote, although the articles of incorporation can specify either a higher or lower figure.[3] Although there is some case law to the contrary, the

written consent. See, e.g., MBCA § 7.04. A substantial minority, including Delaware, permit shareholders to act by written consent even if the shareholders are not unanimous. See, e.g., DGCL § 228.

3. MBCA § 7.25(a). Delaware law is similar, except it forbids the articles from setting a quorum of less than one-third the shares entitled to vote. DGCL § 216.

Model Act effectively precludes a shareholder from "breaking the quorum" by leaving the meeting. If a shareholder's stock is represented at the meeting in person or by proxy, that shareholder's stock is deemed to be present for quorum purposes for the remainder of the meeting.[4]

C.   Vote Required for Proposal to be Approved

Subject to the special rules governing election of directors and those governing acquisitions, discussed below, MBCA § 7.25(c) provides that "action on a matter ... is approved if the votes cast ... favoring the action exceed the votes cast opposing the action." In contrast, DGCL § 216 states that "the affirmative vote of the majority of shares present in person or represented by proxy at the meeting and entitled to vote on the subject matter shall be the act of the stockholders." The distinction between the two formulations is subtle but significant. Suppose there are 1000 shares entitled to vote, 800 of which are represented at the meeting either in person or by proxy, and which are voted as follows:

In Favor	399
Opposed	398
Abstain	3

Under the MBCA, the motion carries, as more shares were voted in favor of the motion than against it. Under the Delaware statute, however, a majority of the shares present at the meeting—401—must be voted in favor of the motion for it to carry, and this motion therefore fails. In effect, Delaware treats abstentions as no votes, while the MBCA ignores them.[5]

D.   Election of Directors

1.   *Majority Voting*

As just discussed, in most cases, state corporate law contemplates that shareholder action requires the affirmative votes of a majority of

---

4. See MBCA § 7.25(b); but see, e.g., Levisa Oil Corp. v. Quigley, 234 S.E.2d 257 (Va.1977) (shareholder may break quorum by departing meeting); see also Textron, Inc. v. American Woolen Co., 122 F.Supp. 305 (D.Mass.1954) (shareholder present before a quorum is established may depart and, if so, may not be counted towards a quorum).

5. The articles of incorporation may require a higher vote than the default statutory minimum, either across the board or on specified issues. State corporation laws also typically provide that certain extraordi-

nary actions require approval by a higher vote. MBCA § 10.03 requires, for example, that amendments to the articles of incorporation be approved by a majority of the shares entitled to vote. Again, suppose there are 1000 shares entitled to vote, 800 of which are represented at the meeting either in person or by proxy. In order for the amendment to be adopted, 501 shares must be voted in favor. The same vote is required for approval of a merger (per § 11.04) or sale of all or substantially all the corporation's assets (per § 12.02). Delaware law is similar.

the shareholders present at a meeting at which there is a quorum. When it comes to electing directors, however, state law until recently merely required a plurality shareholder vote. Delaware General Corporation Law § 216(3) formerly provided, for example, that "Directors shall be elected by a plurality of the votes of the shares present in person or represented by proxy at the meeting and entitled to vote on the election of directors." The comments to MBCA § 7.28(a), which also used a plurality standard, defined that term to mean "that the individuals with the largest number of votes are elected as directors up to the maximum number of directors to be chosen at the election."

The federal proxy rules accommodated state law by providing, in former SEC Rule 14a–4(b), that the issuer must give shareholders three options on the proxy card with respect to electing directors. A shareholder could vote for all of the nominees for director, withhold support for all of them, or withhold support from specified directors by striking out their names.

The net effect of these rules was that the corporate electoral system did not provide for a straight up or down vote for directors. Instead, one either granted authority to the proxy agent to vote for the specified candidates or one withheld authority for the agent to do so. Absent a contested election, because only a plurality vote was required, so long as the holder of at least a single share granted authority for his share to be cast in favor of the nominees, the slate of directors nominated by the incumbent board therefore would be elected even if every other shareholder withheld authority for their shares to be voted.

The origins of the plurality rule are somewhat obscure. It presumably arose to deal with situations in which there are more nominees than vacant director positions, which is most commonly the case in contested elections. In a close race, abstentions and spoiled ballots might mean that fewer nominees than the number of vacancies would receive a majority of the votes cast. In the worst case, which is made more likely by the use of slate voting, the election might fail completely as no directors would receive a majority. Plurality voting avoided that risk and the adverse consequences that might follow.

Over time, withholding authority to vote for some or all of the nominees put forward by the incumbent board became a common protest tactic by shareholder activists. In the 2004 shareholder revolt at The Walt Disney Company, for example, shareholder activists opposed the election of CEO Michael Eisner and certain other candidates. Under the then-existing plurality standard, Eisner would have been reelected even if holders of a majority of the shares had withheld authority for their shares to be voted for him. In the event, holders of 43% of Disney shares withheld such authority. Although Eisner was reelected, the high vote was seen as a powerful protest. Shortly thereafter, he initiated a succession process.

State law developments: The Disney episode triggered considerable interest in changing the traditional plurality standard so as to transform the process from a mere opportunity to send a protest signal into a real election. In 2006, Delaware responded to considerable pressure from activists and others by amending the statutory provisions on director election to accommodate various forms of majority voting.

A number of Delaware corporations had responded to post-Disney pressure from shareholder activists by voluntarily adopting so-called Pfizer policies—named after the first prominent corporation to adopt one—pursuant to which directors who receive a majority of withhold "votes" are required to submit their resignation to the board. Section 141(b) of the Delaware General Corporation Law was amended to accommodate such bylaws. It does so by providing that: "A resignation [of a director] is effective when the resignation is delivered unless the resignation specifies a later effective date or an effective date determined upon the happening of an event or events. A resignation which is conditioned upon the director failing to receive a specified vote for reelection as a director may provide that it is irrevocable."

The trouble with these so-called Pfizer or plurality-plus policies, at least from the perspective of shareholder activists, is that the board retains authority to turn down the resignation of a director who fails to get the requisite majority vote. In *City of Westland Police & Fire Retirement System v. Axcelis Technologies, Inc.*,[6] the Delaware Supreme Court confirmed that the board has substantial discretion to do just that. Axcelis Technologies had a seven-member board staggered into three classes. In 2008, all three of the incumbent directors up for reelection failed to receive a majority of the votes cast. Pursuant to the company's plurality-plus policy, all three submitted their resignations. The board rejected all three resignations. A shareholder initiated a § 220 request to inspect the relevant books and records of the company preparatory to filing a derivative suit challenging the board's decision. In order to prevent shareholders from conducting fishing expeditions, Delaware courts will grant such inspection requests only where there is a credible basis from which to infer that some wrongdoing may have occurred. In acknowledging that § 220 requests sometimes can be meritorious in this context, the Court observed that "the question arises whether the directors, as fiduciaries, made a disinterested, informed business judgment that the best interests of the corporation require the continued service of these directors, or whether the Board had some different, ulterior motivation."[7] It thus seems fair to infer that the business judgment rule will be the standard by which courts evaluate board decisions under such policies.

---

6. 1 A.3d 281 (Del. 2010).   **7.** Id. at 291.

Activists also objected to the Pfizer-style approach because it typically was effected by changing board of directors corporate governance policies rather than by amending the bylaws or articles. As such, continuation of the policy was subject to the discretion of the directors.

Shareholder activists therefore began using Rule 14a–8 to put forward bylaw amendments mandating true majority voting. A bylaw voluntarily adopted by Intel received wide activist support as a model for bylaw amendments at other issuers. Under it, a director who fails to receive a majority of the votes cast is not elected. In the case of an incumbent director who fails to receive a majority vote in favor of his reelection, there is the complication that, under DGCL § 141(b), a director's term continues until his successor is elected. The Intel (a.k.a. majority-plus) model requires resignation of such a director.

Shareholder activists preferred a bylaw approach to one based on the articles of incorporation because of the latter's board approval requirement. In most states, however, a shareholder-adopted bylaw would be vulnerable to subsequent board amendment or even repeal. Recall that DGCL § 109(a) provides that the articles of incorporation may confer the power to amend the bylaws on the board of directors, but that such a provision does not divest the shareholders of their residual power to amend the bylaws.

The resulting concurrent power of both shareholders and boards to amend the bylaws raises the prospect of cycling amendments and counter-amendments. Suppose the shareholders adopt a majority vote bylaw. The board then repeals the new bylaw provision using its concurrent power to amend the bylaws. The MBCA allows the shareholders to forestall such an event. MBCA § 10.20(b)(2) authorizes the board to adopt, amend, and repeal bylaws unless "the shareholders in amending, repealing, or adopting a bylaw expressly provide that the board of directors may not amend, repeal, or reinstate that bylaw." In the absence of such a restriction, however, the board apparently retains its power to amend or even repeal the bylaw. If the board does so, the shareholders' remedies presumably are limited to readopting the term limit amendment, this time incorporating the necessary restriction, and/or electing a more compliant board.

Delaware § 109 lacks any comparable grant of power to the shareholders. Worse yet, because the board only has power to adopt or amend bylaws if that power is granted to it in the articles of incorporation, a bylaw prohibiting board amendment arguably would be inconsistent with the articles and, therefore, invalid.

In *American Int'l Rent a Car, Inc. v. Cross*,[8] the Delaware Chancery Court suggested that, as part of a bylaw amendment, the shareholders "could remove from the Board the power to further amend the provision

8. 1984 WL 8204 (Del. Ch. 1984).

in question." Dicta in several other Delaware precedents, however, was to the contrary. In *General DataComm Industries, Inc. v. State of Wisconsin Investment Board*,[9] for example, Vice Chancellor Strine noted the "significant legal uncertainty" as to "whether, in the absence of an explicitly controlling statute, a stockholder-adopted bylaw can be made immune from repeal or modification by the board of directors." In *Centaur Partners, IV v. National Intergroup, Inc.*,[10] the Delaware Supreme Court addressed a shareholder-proposed bylaw limiting the number of directors. As proposed, the bylaw contained a provision prohibiting the board from amending or repealing it. Noting that the corporation's articles gave the board authority to fix the number of directors through adoption of bylaws, the Supreme Court opined that the proposed bylaw "would be a nullity if adopted." Consequently, it seemed doubtful that restrictions on the board's power over the bylaws would pass muster in Delaware or other states likewise lacking a MBCA-style provision.

In response to activist shareholder pressure, however, Delaware amended § 216 by adding the following sentence: "A bylaw amendment adopted by stockholders which specifies the votes that shall be necessary for the election of directors shall not be further amended or repealed by the board of directors." It is curious that the legislature did not adopt a more explicit validation of bylaw provisions requiring that a director receive a majority vote in order to be elected. Section 216, however, clearly seems to imply their validity and, if so, ensures that such bylaws could not be undercut by subsequent unilateral board action.

Congress punts: An early Senate version of the legislation that became the Dodd–Frank Act of 2010 included a majority-voting mandate. Under it, public corporations would have been required to accept the resignation of any director who receives less than a majority vote in an uncontested election, unless the board unanimously declined to accept the resignation. In the face of the state developments and the reality that majority voting is now the norm, however, Congress opted to omit any version of majority voting.

Assessment: Critics of majority voting schemes contend that failed elections can have a destabilizing effect on the corporation. Selecting and vetting a director candidate is a long and expensive process, which has become even more complicated by the new stock exchange listing standards defining director independence. Suppose, for example, that the shareholders voted out the only qualified financial expert sitting on the audit committee. The corporation immediately would be in violation of its obligations under those standards.

Critics also complain that qualified individuals will be deterred from service. The enhanced liability and increased workload imposed by Sarbanes–Oxley and related regulatory and legal developments has made

---

9. 731 A.2d 818, 821 n.1 (Del. Ch. 1999).   **10.** 582 A.2d 923, 929 (Del. 1990).

it much harder for firms to recruit qualified outside directors. The risk of being singled out by shareholders for a no vote presumably will make board service even less attractive, especially in light of the concern board members demonstrate for their reputations.

Finally, critics claim that, at least as it is being implemented so far, majority voting is "little more than smoke and mirrors."[11] William Sjostrom and Young Sang Kim conducted an event study of firms adopting some form of majority vote bylaw. They found no statistically significant market reaction to the adoption.[12] The implication is that the campaign for majority voting has created little shareholder value.

2. Cumulative Voting

Under standard voting rules, a majority shareholder can elect the entire board of directors. This is why prospective buyers place a higher value on control blocks vis-à-vis shares owned by noncontrolling shareholders. Cumulative voting provides an alternative mechanism for electing the board of directors that can assure board representation for the minority. An example will be helpful.

Assume ABC Corporation has 3 shareholders: A, who owns 250 shares; B, who owns 300 shares; C, who owns 650.[13] The bylaws specify a four member board of directors. Under standard voting procedures, directors are elected by a plurality of the votes cast at the meeting on a one share-one vote basis.[14] Suppose, for example, that each of A, B and C are supporting four different candidates for director. The following will result:

A–1: 250 for	B–1: 300 for	C–1: 650 for; elected
A–2: 250 for	B–2: 300 for	C–2: 650 for; elected
A–3: 250 for	B–3: 300 for	C–3: 650 for; elected
A–4: 250 for	B–4: 300 for	C–4: 650 for; elected

Consequently, C elects the entire board of directors. This is of vital importance, because directors make most corporate decisions. In this example, the board will be composed entirely of people nominated by C.

In cumulative voting, by contrast, the number of votes each shareholder may cast is determined by multiplying the number of shares owned by the number of director positions up for election. Each share-

---

11. William K. Sjostrom Jr. & Young Sang Kim, Majority Voting for the Election of Directors, 40 Conn. L. Rev. 459 (2007)

12. Id.

13. The example is taken from Michael P. Dooley, Fundamentals of Corporation Law 376 (1995).

14. See, e.g., MBCA § 7.28 (a). It might help if you think of director balloting as voting for a slate: Each share entitles its owner to cast one vote towards determining which slate will be elected. Alternatively, you can think of each director position as a seat that can be filled by only one person. Each share entitles its owner to cast one vote towards determining the occupant of that seat.

holder then may concentrate his votes by casting all of his votes for one candidate (or distributing his votes among two or more candidates).[15] The directors receiving the highest number of votes will be elected. In this example, A has 1000 votes available to be cast; B has 1200 votes; and C has 2600 votes. A and B each nominate themselves and cast all of their votes for themselves on their respective ballots. A receives 1000 votes. B receives 1200 votes. C nominates herself and her friends C–1, C–2, and C–3. But C cannot cast her votes so as to elect all four of her nominees. C might, for example, cast 1100 votes for herself and 1000 votes for C–1. Both C and C–1 will be elected. Unfortunately for C, however, she has only 500 votes left to divide between C–2 and C–3. Accordingly, they cannot be elected.

The following formula is used to determine the number of directors a given shareholder may elect under cumulative voting:

$$X = \frac{Y \times N_1}{N+1} + 1$$

where N is the total number of directors to be elected; N_1 is the number of directors a shareholder wishes to elect; Y is the total number of shares outstanding; and X is the number of shares needed to elect the desired number of directors (N_1). If you solve this equation for directors $N_1 = 4$; you will find that C needs 961 shares in order to elect all 4 directors. Notice that even if B and C cumulated their votes together, they could not prevent A from electing at least one director. If you work out all the permutations, you will find that in this hypothetical A can elect one director, B can elect one, and C can elect two. Unless all three agree, no combination of shareholders can elect all four directors.

Cumulative voting was very much in vogue in the late 1800s. A number of states adopted mandatory cumulative voting as part of their state constitutions. Others did the same by statute. During the last few decades, however, cumulative voting in public corporations has increasingly fallen out of favor. Opponents of cumulative voting argue it produces an adversarial board and results in critical decisions being made in private meetings held by the majority faction before the formal board meeting. Today, only 8 states have mandatory cumulative voting.[16]

---

15. See, e.g., MBCA § 7.28 (c).

16. MBCA § 7.28 stat. comp. (listing Arizona, California, Hawaii, Kentucky, Nebraska, North Dakota, South Dakota, and West Virginia). The California Corporations Code provides for application of various code provisions to a foreign corporation if the firm does a majority of its business in California and if a majority of the record holders of their shares are California residents. In Wilson v. Louisiana–Pacific Res., Inc., 187 Cal.Rptr. 852 (App.1982), applica- tion of California's cumulative voting provisions to a Utah corporation meeting the foregoing test was upheld against a dormant commerce clause challenge. The court opined: "A corporation can do a majority of its business in only one state at a time; and it can have a majority of its shareholders resident in only one state at a time. If a corporation meets those requirements in this state, no other state is in a position to regulate the method of voting by shareholders on the basis of the same or similar criteria. It might also be said that no state

The MBCA, Delaware, and most other states allow cumulative voting on an opt-in basis.[17] In other words, standard voting is the default rule in these states but the corporation may provide for cumulative voting in its articles of incorporation. In all states, of course, cumulative voting is limited to the election of directors—shareholders are not allowed to cumulate votes as to other types of shareholder decisions.

3. Classified Boards

Typically, the entire board of directors is elected annually, whether by standard or cumulative voting, to a one-year term.[18] Alternatively, however, the articles of incorporation or bylaws may provide for a classified or staggered board of directors.[19] In this model, the board is divided into two or three classes. In a board with two classes of directors, the members serve two-year terms so that only half the board is up for election in any given year. In a board with three classes, directors serve three year terms and only a third of the board is up for election annually.

Classified boards have significant change of control implications and are often used as a defense against proxy contests and corporate take-overs. Under a staggered board with three classes, for example, the shareholders must wait two annual meeting cycles before they can replace a majority of the board. In order for the classified board to actually delay a change of control, of course, the classification scheme must be protected from the possibility that the shareholders will remove the directors without cause or pack the board with new appointments. Classified board provisions in articles of incorporation therefore typically are coupled with additional terms reserving to the board the sole right to determine the number of directors and to fill any vacancies. If permitted by state law, drafters of a classified board scheme also limit or abolish the right of shareholders to call a special shareholders meeting or to remove directors without cause.

could claim as great an interest in doing so." Id. at 860.

17. See DGCL § 214; MBCA § 7.28(b); see generally MBCA § 7.28 stat. comp. (listing 30 states with opt-in cumulative voting and 12 with opt-out cumulative voting).

18. Under MBCA § 8.05(b), the directors' term in office technically expires at the next annual shareholders' meeting following their election. Under DGCL § 141(b), a director's term continues until his successor is elected.

19. See, e.g., DGCL § 141(d). Curiously, MBCA § 8.06 permits staggered boards only if there are nine or more directors.

E. Approving Acquisitions

1. Mergers

At early common law, a merger required unanimous shareholder approval. The unanimity requirement created the potential for hold up problems, as a dissenting minority could block a transaction in hopes of being assuaged by side-payments. Unanimity gradually gave way to supermajority voting requirements, which in Delaware and further eroded into a mere majority of the outstanding shares. The Model Act has gone even further. If a quorum is present, the merger will be approved if more votes are cast in favor of the plan of merger than against it.[20] About one-third of the states retain some form of supermajority voting requirement, however, typically two-thirds of the shares entitled to vote.[21]

In most states, a shareholder vote is not required if the transaction qualifies as a so-called short-form merger. The short-form merger statute is a special provision for a merger between a parent corporation and one of its subsidiaries. The statute may be invoked only if the parent corporation owns a high percentage—typically 90%—of the subsidiary's outstanding stock.[22] Early short-form merger statutes typically required the transaction to be approved by the board of directors of each corporation. Neither corporation's shareholders were allowed to vote. MBCA § 11.05(a) and DGCL § 253(a), however, reflect a modern trend towards even more liberal short-form mergers. Both statutes authorize a short-form merger when the parent owns at least 90% of the subsidiary's stock. If that threshold is met, only the parent corporation's board need approve the merger.[23] Neither the subsidiary's board nor its minority shareholders have any say. The assumption seems to be that both votes would be foregone conclusions.

Under Delaware law, shareholder voting rights also may be eliminated for certain transactions that do not qualify for treatment as short-form mergers if three conditions are met: (1) the agreement of merger does not amend the surviving corporation's articles of incorporation; (2) the outstanding shares of the surviving corporation are unaffected by the transaction;[24] and (3) the transaction does not increase the number of

---

20. MBCA § 11.04(e).

21. The most prominent supermajority holdout, New York, amended its statute in 1998 to require approval by a majority of the shares entitled to vote with respect to subsequently formed corporations. N.Y. Bus. Corp. L. § 903. In addition, the New York statute allows pre-existing corporations to opt for a majority vote rule by amending their articles. Id. Given New York's long prominence as a holdout jurisdiction, this action may presage a gradual further erosion of supermajority vote requirements in the remaining holdouts.

22. The statutory elimination of shareholder voting rights makes sense in this context because the outcome of any vote by the subsidiary's shareholders would be a foregone conclusion and because how a parent corporation votes shares of a subsidiary is a business decision for the parent's board rather than the parent's shareholders.

23. If the parent will not survive or the articles of merger will effect a change in the parent's articles of incorporation, however, the parent's shareholders must approve the transaction. DGCL § 253(c); MBCA § 11.05(c).

24. Specifically, DGCL § 251(f) provides that "each share of stock of such constituent corporation outstanding immediately prior to the effective date of the merger is

outstanding shares by more than 20%. If all three conditions are satisfied, approval by the surviving corporation's shareholders is not required. Approval by any other constituent corporation's shareholders is still required, however.[25]

2. Sales of All or Substantially All Assets

Recall that the board of directors has essentially unconstrained authority to dispose of corporate assets without shareholder approval. Where the board attempts to dispose of all or substantially all corporate assets, shareholder approval is required.[26] Under DGCL § 271(a), the required vote is a majority of the outstanding voting shares. Under MBCA § 12.02(e), by contrast, the requisite vote is only a majority of those present and voting. In both cases, only the selling corporation's shareholders are entitled to vote.[27]

3. Stock Exchange Listing Standards

As we saw in Chapter 3, transaction planners often structure transactions so as to deny shareholders a vote on a proposed acquisition. Although this is difficult to do with respect to target shareholders, simple deal structures—such as asset purchases, triangular mergers, or tender offers—can eliminate voting rights for the acquiring company's shareholders. Although state law provides such shareholders with no recourse, excepting only the handful of states in which the de facto merger doctrine has any real teeth, stock exchange listing standards may step in to fill this perceived gap in shareholder rights.

NYSE Listed Company Manual § 312.03, for example, provides in pertinent part that:

to be an identical outstanding or treasury share of the surviving corporation after the effective date of the merger." This curious language was intended to preclude the use of § 251(f) in so-called reverse triangular mergers. In such a transaction, the target corporation is merged with a subsidiary of the acquiring corporation, with the target surviving. Absent the quoted language, § 251(f) could be invoked to prevent the target corporation's shareholders from voting, provided the other two conditions were satisfied.

25. DGCL § 251(f). Under DGCL § 262, shareholders of the surviving company are denied appraisal rights in such transactions.

26. DGCL § 271. In 1999, the Model Act adopted amendments incorporating a new terminology. Under revised MBCA § 12.02(a), shareholder approval is required if the transaction "would leave the corpora-

tion without a significant continuing business activity."

27. Note that we are discussing only dispositions of assets in this section. The decision to purchase assets is vested solely in the board, although shareholder action may be required indirectly by ancillary legal regimes. This is especially likely to be true if the acquiring corporation will issue a substantial amount of stock in connection with the transaction. Under MBCA § 6.21(f)(1)(ii), for example, shareholders must approve an issuance of stock for consideration other than cash if the shares to be issued "will comprise more than 20 percent of the voting power of the shares of the corporation that were outstanding immediately before the transaction." The major stock exchanges impose similar requirements in their listing standards.

(c) Shareholder approval is required prior to the issuance of common stock, or of securities convertible into or exercisable for common stock, in any transaction or series of related transactions if:

(1) the common stock has, or will have upon issuance, voting power equal to or in excess of 20 percent of the voting power outstanding before the issuance of such stock or of securities convertible into or exercisable for common stock; or

(2) the number of shares of common stock to be issued is, or will be upon issuance, equal to or in excess of 20 percent of the number of shares of common stock outstanding before the issuance of the common stock or of securities convertible into or exercisable for common stock.

However, shareholder approval will not be required for any such issuance involving:

-any public offering for cash;

-any bona fide private financing, if such financing involves a sale of:

-common stock, for cash, at a price at least as great as each of the book and market value of the issuer's common stock; or

-securities convertible into or exercisable for common stock, for cash, if the conversion or exercise price is at least as great as each of the book and market value of the issuer's common stock.

The American Stock Exchange and NASDAQ have comparable rules.

As a result, if an acquirer uses its own common stock or securities convertible into common stock as the consideration in an acquisition, and the effect of the transaction is to increase the number of outstanding acquirer shares by an amount equal to 20% of the previously outstanding shares, the acquirer must obtain approval from its shareholders. As a result, a number of transactions that would not require a vote of the acquiring company shareholders under state law must obtain shareholder approval by virtue of the listing standard, including:

- A triangular merger in which a wholly owned subsidiary of the acquirer is merged with the target. Because under state law only shareholders of the constituent corporations to the merger get a vote, in this deal structure only the shareholders of the target and the acquirer's subsidiary get to vote. The acquirers subsidiary, of course, has only one shareholder; namely, the acquiring company itself. The acquiring company's board of directors rather than its shareholders will determine how the acquirer will vote its shares of the subsidiary.

- A purchase of all or substantially all of another company's assets.

- A tender offer or other purchase of the target company's stock.

Technically, of course, the stock exchange rule does not require approval of the underlying transaction. Instead, it only requires approval of the stock issuance. As a practical matter, however, the acquiring company must disclose the purpose for the issuance. As a result, the required vote becomes a de facto referendum on the acquisition.

F. Group Voting

Ordinarily all shares with voting rights vote as a single group. In some circumstances, however, the shareholders may be divided into two or more voting groups with each group consisting of one or more classes or series of stock. For example, where an amendment to the articles of incorporation or a proposed reorganization affects a particular class or series of stock, that class or series likely will have the right to vote on the proposed amendment as a separate group. Indeed, the group may be entitled to vote even if the class or series otherwise has no voting rights.

MBCA § 11.04 requires group voting on a merger in several situations. First, a class or series of stock is entitled to vote as a separate group if the plan of merger contemplates converting that class or series of stock into other securities, cash, or other rights. Second, a class or series is entitled to vote as a separate group if the plan of merger includes a provision that would trigger group voting if effected as an amendment to the articles of incorporation. In turn, MBCA § 10.04 details eight distinct changes to the articles that trigger group voting: (1) an exchange or reclassification of all or part of the shares of the class into shares of another class; (2) an exchange or reclassification of all or part of the shares of another class into shares of the class; (3) a change in the rights, preferences, or limitations of all or part of the shares of the class; (4) changing the shares of all or part of the class into a different number of shares of the same class; (5) creating a new class of shares having rights or preferences with respect to distributions or to dissolution that are prior or superior to the shares of the class; (6) increasing the rights, preferences, or number of authorized shares of any class that, after giving effect to the amendment, will have rights or preferences with respect to distributions or to dissolution that are prior or superior to the shares of the class; (7) limiting or denying an existing preemptive right of all or part of the shares of the class; or (8) canceling or otherwise affecting rights to distributions that have accumulated but not yet been authorized on all or part of the shares of the class. Per § 10.04(b), if the amendment would affect a series of stock in one of the specified ways, the series is entitled to vote as a separate group. Conversely, per subsection (c), if an amendment that effects two or more classes or series in substantially similar ways, the affected classes or series must vote as a single group. Finally, subsection (d) grants voting rights to affected classes even though the articles of incorporation provide that the shares are nonvoting.

In contrast, DGCL § 251 on its face does not contemplate voting by groups on a merger. Likewise, § 251 does not contemplate non-voting stock being granted the right to vote on a merger.

Per DGCL § 242(b)(2), group voting is triggered under Delaware law only in the event of an amendment to the articles of incorporation by which a class or series of stock is affected adversely. Specifically, the statute provides for group voting on an amendment to the articles "if the amendment would increase or decrease the aggregate number of authorized shares of such class, increase or decrease the par value of the shares of such class, or alter or change the powers, preferences, or special rights of the shares of such class so as to affect them adversely." The analysis does not change if the class lacks voting rights, as is often the case with preferred stock, because § 242(b) confers group voting rights even if the group is otherwise denied voting rights by the articles.

Delaware's "adversely affect" language is less determinate than the more specific MBCA formulations and, hence, more likely to produce litigation. In *Dalton v. American Investment Co.*,[28] for example, AIC was acquired by Leucadia, Inc. in a triangular merger between AIC and a wholly owned Leucadia subsidiary. AIC was the surviving entity. AIC's common shareholders were cashed out, but AIC's preferred shareholders were left in place. Certain of AIC preferred's holders sued. Because the plan of merger would amend AIC's articles of incorporation, the preferred claimed a right to vote on the plan of merger as a separate group. The pre-merger articles contained two relevant provisions: (1) The board was authorized to redeem—but not to call—the preferred. (2) If the board offered to buy back some (but not all) of the preferred shares, and the offer was over-subscribed, the shares to be redeemed were to be determined by lot. The plan of merger replaced these provisions with a sinking fund coupled with a call provision. Under the sinking fund provision, the board would retire 5% of the preferred annually for 20 years. To the extent that board repurchased preferred shares on the open market during a given year, those shares would count as a credit against the redemption obligation. The Chancellor determined that the amendment did not adversely affect the preferred and, accordingly, they were not entitled to vote as a separate group. To be sure, if the market price of the preferred was below the redemption price specified in the articles, the board could satisfy its obligation under the sinking fund by buying stock on the market. As a result, the apparent opportunity to get cashed out at a premium proved illusory. Yet, as the Chancellor pointed out, the amendment did not deprive the preferred of any rights they had previously possessed.

How then would the "adversely affect" phraseology impact other cases? Suppose the corporation's board of directors proposed an amendment that would cut the preferred stock's dividend from 8% to 5%. The

---

28. 490 A.2d 574 (Del. Ch.), aff'd, 501 A.2d 1238 (Del. 1985).

amendment doubtless adversely affects the preferred and that class' holders would be entitled to vote as a separate group. Assume the requisite majority of the class of common stock votes yes, but that the proposed amendment is not approved by the requisite majority of the class of preferred. What happens? The amendment is not approved. Approval of this amendment requires approval by both classes.

Now suppose the corporation's board of directors proposed an amendment to create a new class of preferred stock with rights superior to those of the existing class of preferred. This amendment adversely affects the interests of the existing class of preferred, whose claims have been subordinated to a prior claimant, but the amendment does not "alter or change the powers, preferences, or special rights of the pre-ferred." Although creation of a class with superior rights may redound to the economic detriment of both the existing common and the existing preferred, it does not "alter or change" the rights of either class. As an old Delaware case explained, "the relative position of one class of shares in the scheme of capitalization is not to be confused with rights incident to that class as compared with other classes of shares."[29] The amend-ment in question affects the former, rather than the latter, but only the latter is covered by the statute.

G. Shareholder Inspection Rights

An insurgent shareholder conducting a proxy contest typically wants to communicate directly with his fellow shareholders. In addition, the shareholder may want access to other corporate books and records, so as to gain information that might bolster his arguments. The federal proxy rules provide limited mailing rights for an insurgent, but no other inspection rights. Consequently, the insurgent must look to state law inspection rights.

State shareholder inspection rights statutes must balance two com-peting concerns. On the one hand, shareholders have a legitimate interest in using the proxy system to hold the board accountable. On the other hand, nobody wants a junk mail distributor to get access to the shareholder list or a competitor to get access to the corporation's trade secrets and other proprietary information.[30] DGCL § 220(b) balances these concerns by requiring a shareholder asserting inspection rights to make a written demand setting forth a "proper purpose" for the request. The statute further defines a "proper purpose" as one "reasonably

29. Hartford Accident & Indemnity Co. v. W. S. Dickey Clay Mfg. Co., 24 A.2d 315, 318 (Del. 1942).

30. Cf. Cooke v. Outland, 144 S.E.2d 835, 842 (N.C.1965) ("Considering the huge size of many modern corporations and the necessarily complicated nature of their bookkeeping, it is plain that to permit their thousands of stockholders to roam at will through their records would render impos-sible not only any attempt to keep their records efficiently, but the proper carrying on of their businesses.").

related to such person's interest as a stockholder." If the corporation denies the shareholder access to its records, the shareholder may sue in the Chancery Court. Under subsection (c), where the shareholder only seeks access to the shareholder list or stock ledger, the burden of proof is on the corporation to show that the shareholder is doing so for an improper reason. Where the shareholder seeks access to other corporate records, however, the shareholder must prove that he is doing so for the requisite proper purpose.

The statutory framework poses several questions. First, what reasons for seeking access to a shareholder list constitute proper purposes? Attempts to investigate alleged corporate mismanagement are usually deemed proper, although the shareholder must have some factual basis for making the request and is not allowed to conduct a fishing expedition.[31] Collecting information relevant to valuing shares is a proper purpose.[32] A tender offeror stated a proper purpose in desiring to inform other shareholders of the pending offer and soliciting tenders from them.[33] Most pertinently for purposes of this Chapter, communicating with fellow shareholders in connection with a planned proxy contest is a proper purpose.[34] Improper purposes include attempting to discover proprietary business information for the benefit of a competitor, to secure prospects for personal business, to institute strike suits, and to pursue one's own social or political goals.[35]

The latter improper purpose—pursuit of noneconomic social or political goals—has proven an especially problematic subject for Delaware courts. In the well-known *State ex rel. Pillsbury v. Honeywell, Inc.* decision,[36] plaintiff belonged to an antiwar group trying to stop Honeywell from producing anti-personnel fragmentation bombs for the military. After buying some Honeywell stock, plaintiff requested access to Honeywell's shareholder list and to corporate records relating to production of such bombs. In denying plaintiff access to those records, the court emphasized that plaintiff's stated reasons were based on his pre-existing social and political views rather than any economic interest. Accordingly, the court carefully limited its holdings to the facts at bar: "We do not

31. See, e.g., Nodana Petroleum Corp. v. State, 123 A.2d 243, 246 (Del.1956); Helmsman Mgmt. Servs., Inc. v. A & S Consultants, Inc., 525 A.2d 160, 165 (Del.Ch. 1987); Skouras v. Admiralty Enters., Inc., 386 A.2d 674, 678 (Del.Ch.1978).

32. See, e.g., State ex rel. Nat'l Bank of Del. v. Jessup & Moore Paper Co., 88 A. 449 (Del.Super.Ct.1913).

33. Crane Co. v. Anaconda Co., 382 N.Y.S.2d 707, 346 N.E.2d 507 (1976).

34. See, e.g., Hatleigh Corp. v. Lane Bryant, Inc., 428 A.2d 350 (Del.Ch.1981).

35. Tatko v. Tatko Bros. Slate Co., 569 N.Y.S.2d 783 (App.Div.1991). Once the shareholder has demonstrated a proper purpose, the shareholder is entitled to "all of the documents in the corporation's possession, custody, or control, that are necessary to satisfy that proper purpose." Saito v. McKesson HBOC, Inc., 806 A.2d 113 (Del. 2002). Consequently, a shareholder may not be denied access to "necessary documents solely because the documents were prepared by third parties or because the documents predate the stockholder's first investment in the corporation." Id.

36. 191 N.W.2d 406 (Minn.1971) (interpreting Delaware law).

mean to imply that a shareholder with a bona fide investment interest could not bring this suit if motivated by concern with the long- or short-term economic effects on Honeywell resulting from the production of war munitions." The court further noted that the "suit might be appropriate when a shareholder has a bona fide concern about the adverse effects of abstention from profitable war contracts on his investment in Honeywell." As such, *Honeywell* puts more emphasis on proper phrasing of one's statement of purpose than on the validity of the purpose itself. So long as one's social agenda can be dressed up in the language of economic consequences, one gets access to the list.[37] Does this formalistic approach make sense? The Delaware chancery court seems to think not, as at least one chancery decision opines that Delaware law has de facto rejected *Honeywell's* requirement that the shareholder's purpose must relate to the "enhancement of the economic value of the corporation."[38]

Second, to what extent will the court scrutinize the shareholder's stated reasons? On the one hand, Delaware courts expressly retain the right to scrutinize the shareholder's stated purpose to determine whether it is the real reason for which he seeks access. On the other hand, Delaware courts have made clear that the existence of an improper secondary purpose is not enough to deny the shareholder access. Because "a shareholder will often have more than one purpose, [§ 220(b)] has been construed to mean that the shareholder's *primary* purpose must be proper; any *secondary* purpose, whether proper or not, is irrelevant."[39]

Finally, to which shareholder list is the plaintiff entitled? All corporations maintain a list of shareholders of record. When investors buy stock of public corporations through a broker, however, their shares typically are registered in so-called "street name." The broker places shares in the custody of depository firms, such as Depository Trust Co., which then uses a so-called "nominee" to register the shares with the issuer. The broker, of course, retains records identifying the beneficial owner of the shares. As a result, a public corporation's list of record shareholders will consists mostly of street names—i.e., the names of the nominees used by the various depository firms—not the names of the actual beneficial owners. A so-called CEDE list identifies the brokerage firms on whose behalf the depository institution's nominee holds

37. See, e.g., Conservative Caucus Research, Analysis & Education Foundation, Inc. v. Chevron Corp., 525 A.2d 569 (Del. Ch.1987) (a political group successfully sought access to Chevron's shareholder list for the stated purpose of warning its fellow "stockholders about the allegedly dire economic consequences which will fall upon Chevron if it continues to do business in Angola").

38. Food & Allied Serv. Trades Dep't, AFL–CIO v. Wal–Mart Stores, Inc., 1992 WL 111285 at *4 (Del.Ch.1992).

39. BBC Acquisition v. Durr–Fillauer Medical, 623 A.2d 85, 88 (Del.Ch.1992). On yet another hand, however, where the corporation is able to show an improper secondary purpose, the court may circumscribe the shareholder's access so as to protect legitimate corporate interests. Safecard Servs., Inc. v. Credit Card Serv. Corp., 1984 WL 8265 (Del.Ch.1984).

shares.[40] A nonobjecting beneficial owner (NOBO) list pierces the street name by providing a list of the names and addresses of beneficial owners who have not objected to being identified as such.[41] Under New York state law, a shareholder is entitled to both the CEDE and NOBO lists. Indeed, if the corporation has not already compiled such lists, New York law entitles a shareholder to demand that the corporation do so.[42] In contrast, while Delaware law grants the shareholder access to pre-existing lists of both types, it does not require the issuer to compile a NOBO list on shareholder request.[43]

§ 5.2   Federal Regulation of Proxies

A.   Origins

Most shareholders attend neither the corporation's annual meeting nor any special meetings. Instead, they are represented—and vote—by proxy. Shareholders send in a card (called a proxy card) on which they have marked their vote. The card authorizes a proxy agent to vote the shareholder's stock as directed on the card. The proxy card may specify how the shares are to be voted or may simply give the proxy agent discretion to decide how the shares are to be voted. (Confusingly, older materials sometimes refer to both the proxy card and the proxy agent as a proxy without explanatory qualification.)

In 1934, when the federal Securities Exchange Act was first adopted, state corporate law was largely silent on the issue of corporate communications with shareholders. Typical state statutes required only that the corporation send shareholders notice of a shareholders meeting, stating where and when the meeting would be held. Under most state laws, the notice merely was required to briefly identify the issues to be voted on— and some states did not even require that minimal disclosure in connection with annual meetings. (In most states, the corporation statute still does not require much more than this minimal notice.)

---

40. The list's name comes from the fact that the largest depository firm, Depository Trust Co., uses Cede & Co. as its nominee name.

41. SEC Exchange Act Rule 14b–1 requires brokers to assemble a NOBO list at the issuer's request. The question of whether a shareholder is entitled to demand that the issuer request the creation of such a list or to access to a pre-existing NOBO list, however, is left to state corporate law.

42. Sadler v. NCR Corp., 928 F.2d 48 (2d Cir.1991).

43. RB Assocs. of N.J., L.P. v. Gillette Co., 1988 WL 27731 (Del.Ch.1988). See also Luxottica Group S.p.A. v. U.S. Shoe Corp.,

919 F.Supp. 1091, 1093 (S.D.Ohio 1995) (because Ohio statute only authorized inspection of records, "if any, on file with the corporation," the court declined to order issuer to compile a NOBO list for shareholder to inspect); Cenergy Corp. v. Bryson Oil & Gas P.L.C., 662 F.Supp. 1144 (D.Nev. 1987) (corporation is not obliged to produce information it did not possess). The Delaware supreme court has made clear that shareholders are entitled to inspect books and records prepared before the shareholder's first investment in the firm. Saito v. McKesson HBOC, Inc., 806 A.2d 113 (Del. 2002).

By 1934, however, we had already seen the development of large public corporations having thousands of shareholders and using the proxy system of voting. Congressional hearings on the Exchange Act presented numerous allegations that incumbent managers used the corporate shareholder list and corporate funds to solicit proxies in connection with a shareholder meeting. Obviously, because the incumbents were the ones asking for proxies, the proxy cards and soliciting materials were designed to encourage shareholders to vote as the incumbents desired. The proxy system thus allegedly helped incumbent directors and managers to perpetuate themselves in office.

Congress ultimately settled on disclosure as the principal vehicle by which the proxy system was to be regulated at the federal level. Incumbent corporate managers and directors were not to solicit proxies from shareholders without giving the shareholders enough information on which to make an informed voting decision. Comparable disclosures were to be required from insurgents soliciting proxies in opposition to the incumbents, as well.

After several legislative false starts, the Congress dumped the job of creating a disclosure-based proxy regime in the SEC's lap. As adopted, Exchange Act § 14(a) provides:

> It shall be unlawful for any person, by use of the mails or by any means or instrumentality of interstate commerce or of any facility of a national securities exchange or otherwise, in contravention of such rules and regulations as the Commission may prescribe as necessary or appropriate in the public interest or for the protection of investors, to solicit or to permit the use of his name to solicit any proxy or consent or authorization in respect of any security (other than an exempted security) registered pursuant to Section 12 of this title.

Notice that § 14(a) is not self-executing. It proscribed nothing until the SEC adopted implementing rules and regulations. Pursuant to this broad grant of authority, the SEC has created a complex regulatory scheme governing the manner in which proxies are solicited and, therefore, the manner in which shareholder decisions are made.

B. The Regulatory Framework

Per Exchange Act § 14(a), federal proxy regulation extends only to corporations registered with the SEC under § 12 of that Act. Accordingly, virtually all public corporations are regulated by the proxy rules, while most close corporations are exempt. Because § 14(a) simply states that it shall be unlawful to solicit proxies in contravention of such rules as the SEC may proscribe, however, the rest of the regulatory framework is provided not by statute but entirely by SEC rules.

1. What is a Solicitation of Proxies?

Given the wording of Exchange Act § 14(a), the definition of "solicit" is the linchpin of the entire regulatory structure. The standard judicial definition of "solicit" includes not only "direct requests to furnish, revoke or withhold proxies, but also ... communications which may indirectly accomplish such a result or constitute a step in a chain of communications designed ultimately to accomplish such a result."[44] The basic question is whether a communication is reasonably calculated to influence a shareholder's vote. If so, it is a proxy solicitation.

The expansive definition of solicitation long created major obstacles for prospective insurgents. In *Studebaker Corporation v. Gittlin*,[45] for example, defendant Gittlin was a disgruntled shareholder of plaintiff Studebaker. Gittlin and his associates requested changes in the board of directors and announced their intention of conducting a proxy contest if their demands were not met. When talks with the incumbent board broke down, Gittlin filed an action in New York state court seeking to inspect the corporation's shareholder list and other books and records. Under the applicable New York statute, only shareholders holding 5% or more of the corporation's stock are entitled to inspect such records. Because Gittlin owned only 5,000 shares, he gathered written authorizations from 42 other shareholders collectively holding an aggregate of more than 5% of the stock. Studebaker's incumbent board sued Gittlin under § 14(a), claiming that the process of gathering written authorizations was itself a solicitation of proxies.

Gittlin first argued that Studebaker lacked standing to sue for an alleged proxy violation. The court rejected this argument. As the court read the legislative history, Congress did not intend for incumbent directors to be a passive observer of proxy contests. In addition, the U.S. Supreme Court had characterized the individual shareholder's cause of action for violations of the proxy rules as being derivative in nature.[46] Accordingly, the *Gittlin* court reasoned, the cause of action really belongs to the firm, which therefore may bring actions in its own name.[47]

---

44. Long Island Lighting Co. v. Barbash, 779 F.2d 793, 796 (2d Cir.1985). In *LILCO*, an environmentalist group ran newspaper and radio ads critical of the defendant electrical utility's management. The utility managers alleged that the group was acting in conjunction with an insurgent shareholder conducting a proxy contest. The incumbent managers sued the environmentalists, alleging that their ads constituted a proxy solicitation. Over a strong dissent by Judge Ralph Winter (a former professor of corporate law at Yale), the court declined to reach the obvious First Amendment issues posed by the case. Instead, having adopted the definition of a solicitation quoted in the text, the court remanded for a determination of whether the defendants had solicited proxies under that definition.

45. 360 F.2d 692 (2d Cir.1966).

46. See, e.g., J. I. Case Co. v. Borak, 377 U.S. 426 (1964).

47. But cf. Diceon Elec., Inc. v. Calvary Partners, L.P., 772 F.Supp. 859 (D.Del. 1991) (holding that the issuer does not have standing to sue under § 14(a) for damages). As a practical matter, *Gittlin* thus gives incumbent directors yet another weapon with which to fend off insurgent shareholders.

Turning to the definitional issue, the court noted § 14(a)'s broad application to solicitation of a "proxy, consent or authorization." Accordingly, the court opined, any communication with shareholders will be deemed a solicitation subject to the proxy rules if it is part of a continuous plan intended to end in a solicitation of proxies and to prepare the way for success in a proxy contest. Because gathering authorizations was part of such a plan, it therefore was a solicitation subject to the proxy rules, and Gittlin had violated the regulatory requirement to prepare and disseminate a proxy statement prior to soliciting proxies. Gittlin therefore had to start over by distributing a proxy statement to the 42 shareholders and resoliciting their authorizations.

The court rather summarily dismissed the "inconvenience to Gittlin in having to start over again." Consider, however, the decision's impact on Gittlin. Under SEC rules at the time, communications with up to 10 people were exempted from the definition of solicitation. In other words, Gittlin did not need to prepare, file, and distribute a proxy statement if he only talked to ten people. If Gittlin could access the shareholder list, he could use it to identify large holders. He could then communicate with the ten largest holders without having to give them a proxy statement. As a result of those communications, he could determine whether he could expect support in his proxy contest. This would assist him in determining whether it was worthwhile to go to the expense of a proxy contest. But the court required Gittlin to prepare a proxy statement just to get access to the list, because his talks with the group of 42 shareholders were part of a continuous plan intended to lead to a solicitation of proxies and, of course, he had to exceed the ten shareholder limit just to satisfy the statutory 5% threshold. The opinion thus required Gittlin to incur much of the expense of a proxy contest before he could determine whether it was worthwhile to conduct such a contest.

Fortunately for insurgents, subsequent regulatory developments have lessened *Gittlin*'s negative impact. SEC rules under Exchange Act § 13(d) now require that persons owning more than 5% of a public firm's stock must file reports of their holdings with the SEC. In addition, under § 13(f), most institutional investors (such as pension and mutual funds) must report all of their stock holdings, no matter how small. Because these reports are publicly available, shareholders in Gittlin's situation less often require early access to the shareholder list. Instead, the shareholders can now use the reports to identify large shareholders and then approach up to ten large shareholders to feel them out as to the merits of a proxy contest.

Additionally, the SEC in 1992 liberalized the proxy rules to encourage greater communication between shareholders, in large part by exempting numerous communications from the definition of solicitation. Among the more important exemptions of general application are:

- Rule 14a–8(a)(1)(*l*) exempts public statements of how the shareholder intends to vote and its reasons for doing so.

- Rule 14a–8(b)(1), subject to numerous exceptions, exempts persons who do not seek "the power to act as proxy for a security holder" and do not furnish or solicit "a form of revocation, abstention, consent or authorization." Consequently, for example, a newspaper editorial advising a vote against incumbent managers is now definitively exempted.[48] Note that the Rule thus addresses—although hardly eliminates—the obvious First Amendment concerns implicated by regulating speech in connection with shareholder voting.

- Rule 14a–8(b)(2) preserves the long-standing exemption for solicitations of 10 or fewer persons.

- Rule 14a–8(b)(3) exempts the furnishing of proxy voting advice by someone with whom the shareholder has a business relationship. (A number of firms now provide such voting advice to institutional investors.)

Finally, Rule 14a–12 later was amended to allow "test the waters" proxy solicitations, which reverses the *Gittlin* holding. Coupled with the availability of on-line communication via e-mail and the internet, this rule change will enhance shareholder communication and make proxy contests easier. On the other hand, the amendments also leveled the playing field by, for the first time, allowing managers to contact shareholders about matters that will be on future proxy statements without having to comply with the proxy solicitation process.

2. *The Proxy Rules*

Under SEC Rule 14a–3, the incumbent board of directors' first step in soliciting proxies must be the distribution to shareholders of the firm's annual report.[49] The annual report contains detailed financial statements and a discussion by management of the firm's business. It is intended to give shareholders up-to-date information about what the firm is doing and to give shareholders a basis on which to assess how well management is performing.

---

48. Note that all of the exemptions under Rule 14a8–2(b) are limited in that they do not exempt the communication from Rule14a–9's prohibition of fraudulent and misleading proxy solicitations.

49. The annual report may be sent to the shareholders before proxies are solicited or may be sent in the same package as the proxy solicitation materials. The main point is that the annual report must be in the shareholder's hands when they make voting decisions.

Once the annual report is in the shareholders' hands, the proxy solicitation process can begin. The solicitor's goal is to get the shareholder to sign and date a proxy card, voting his shares in the manner the solicitor desires. Because the end goal of this process is the proxy card, it may be helpful to focus initially on a simplified example of a proxy card that complies with the applicable rules. (See Figures 1 and 2. Obviously, the figures are not to scale.)

Figure 1. Simplified sample proxy card conforming to Rule 14a–4 (front)

THIS PROXY IS SOLICITED ON BEHALF OF THE BOARD OF DIRECTORS.

Alice Able, Bill Black, and Candice Charles and each of them, each with the power of substitution, are hereby authorized to represent and to vote the stock of the undersigned in ACME CORPORATION at the Annual Meeting of its stockholders to be held on April 29, 200X and any adjournments thereof.

MANAGEMENT RECOMMENDS AND WILL VOTE FOR THE ELEC-TION OF THE FOLLOWING AS DIRECTORS (UNLESS OTHERWISE DIRECTED):

1. Alice Able, Bill Black, Candice Charles, Delta Dawn, Eddie Eagle, and Fred MacFred.

To vote for all nominees, check this box. []

To withhold authority to vote for all nominees, check this box. []

To withhold authority to vote for any individual nominee while voting for the remainder, write this nominee's name in the space following:

MANAGEMENT RECOMMENDS AND WILL VOTE FOR THE FOL-LOWING (UNLESS OTHERWISE DIRECTED):

2. Appointment of Dewey Cheatem & Howe LLP as Independent Public Accountants.

FOR [] AGAINST [] ABSTAIN []

MANAGEMENT DOES NOT RECOMMEND AND WILL VOTE AGAINST THE FOLLOWING STOCKHOLDER PROPOSAL (UNLESS OTHERWISE DIRECTED):

3. Provide information about toxic chemicals.

FOR [] AGAINST [] ABSTAIN []

(OVER)

Figure 2. Simplified sample proxy card conforming to Rule 14a–4 (back)

4. In their discretion, the Proxies are authorized to vote upon such other business as may properly come before the meeting.

You are encouraged to specify your choices by marking the appropriate boxes on the reverse side, but you need not mark any boxes. If you wish to vote in accordance with the board of directors recommendations, simply sign and date this form in the space below. The proxies cannot vote your shares unless you sign and return this card.

Signature: _____

Date: _____

The sample card has been designed to comply with the requirements of SEC Rule 14a–4, which governs the form of the proxy card. The first item of interest can be found at the top of Figure 1 (the card's front), where the card identifies the party soliciting the shareholder's proxy. In this case, it is the incumbent board of directors. This statement is mandated by SEC Rule 14a–4(a)(1), which requires that the proxy card clearly state whether or not is being solicited by the current board of directors.[50]

The second point to be noticed can be found in the paragraph just below that line. By signing the card, the shareholder appoints three people—Able, Black, and Charles—as proxies (i.e., proxy agents) and authorizes them to vote the shareholder's stock in accordance with the instructions on the card. Note that this proxy card is not a permanent delegation of authority—the proxy agents only have authority to vote the shares at the specified shareholder meeting.

Now look at the portion of the card relating to the election of directors (i.e., the first numbered paragraph in Figure 1). Under SEC Rule 14a–4(b), the solicitor must give shareholders three options: vote for all of the nominees for director, vote against all of them, and vote against certain of the directors by striking out their names. Note that provision need not be made for write-in candidates.

Next look at the next two numbered paragraphs. With respect to any other matters to be voted on at the meeting, the solicitor again must give shareholders three options. But this time the options are: vote for, vote against, or abstain.

Turn to Figure 2 (the back of the card). The first paragraph (numbered 4) gives the proxy agents authority to use their discretion to vote on any other business to come before the meeting. Under SEC Rule 14a–4(c), unless the proxy card contains an express statement like the one in this card, the shareholder's stock may not be voted on any matters other than the specific matters enumerated on the card. Discretionary authority can be very important. Suppose an insurgent shows up at the meeting and makes a motion to which the incumbent board objects. If the board has been granted the discretionary authority conveyed in numbered paragraph 4 of this card, all of the shares represented by those cards can be voted against the motion. If not, the board may have to scrounge up votes from those shareholders who attended in person. (If the party soliciting the proxies knew in advance that a particular issue would come before the meeting, however, the grant of discretionary authority will not be valid.)

The statement in the next paragraph tells shareholders how their stock will be voted if they return a signed card containing no instruc-

---

50. In addition, SEC Rule 14a–9 provides that failure to clearly distinguish one party's proxy card from that of another party constitutes fraud. When a proxy contest occurs, for example, the two sides typically use different colored cards.

tions. This is to deal with the common problem of apathetic shareholders who simply sign the card and mail it back in, without ever indicating how their shares are to be voted. In such cases, a statement of this sort gives the proxy agents authority under SEC Rule 14a–4(e) to vote the shares in the indicated manner.

The signature block may seem purely ministerial, but even it has a substantive component. Proxies of the sort at issue here are revocable. Shareholders are free to change their minds and revoke previously granted proxies at any time up to the moment of the election. In practice, there are two ways shareholders revoke prior proxies: (1) by showing up at the shareholders' meeting and voting the shares in person; or (2) by giving a later dated proxy. Where the shareholder signs more than one proxy card, only the most recent card counts—all earlier cards are thereupon revoked. Hence, the significance of the date.

Along with the proxy card, the SEC requires that the solicitor provide solicited shareholders with a proxy statement containing mandated disclosures relating to the matters to be acted upon. The cover page of the proxy statement typically includes the state law-required notice of where and when the meeting is to be held, and will also state what issues are to be decided at the meeting. A proxy statement relating to an annual meeting, at which directors are being elected, will typically open with biographical information about the candidates. The proxy statement will also include disclosures about board of director committees, board and executive compensation (see the next section), relationships between the firm and its directors and senior officers, and a description of any other matters to come before the shareholders.

Per Rule 14a–6, a preliminary proxy card and statement must be filed with the SEC at least 10 calendar days before proxies are first solicited. Filing of preliminary materials is not required, however, with respect to an uncontested annual meeting at which only basic matters such as election of directors and appointment of an independent auditor are to be decided. In either case, definitive copies of the proxy card, proxy statement, and any other soliciting materials (such as letters to shareholders) must be filed with the SEC no later than the day they are first used.

In a proxy contest, a key factor will be the insurgent's ability to communicate directly with the shareholders. Towards that end, the insurgent will want access to the corporation's list of shareholders. SEC Rule 14a–7, however, does not require the incumbent board to provide a copy of the shareholder list to the insurgent. The incumbents are given an alternative: they can provide the shareholder list to the insurgent or they can require that the insurgent provide its proxy materials to the corporation, which is obligated to promptly mail those materials to the shareholders (at the insurgent's expense). The incumbents usually prefer the latter route, as it gives them greater control over the process by which proxies are solicited. Commonly, however, insurgents are able to circumvent this restriction by seeking access to the shareholder list under state law.

C. Proxy Contests

Law and economics scholar Henry Manne famously described proxy contests as "the most expensive, the most uncertain, and the least used of the various techniques" for acquiring corporate control.[51] Until the last few years, no one questioned his assessment. Insurgents contemplating a proxy battle face a host of legal and economic disincentives. Various state statutes permit corporations to adopt measures—so-called shark repellents—making it more difficult for an insurgent to gain control of the board of directors via a proxy contest. Among the more important of these are classified boards, the elimination of cumulative voting, and dual class stock plans. Other impediments include management's informational advantages and investor perceptions that proxy insurgents are not serious contenders for control. The two most common obstacles for a would-be insurgent, however, are the rules governing reimbursement of expenses and shareholder apathy. Despite these disincentives, however, in recent years proxy contests have become somewhat more common as a new set of countervailing incentives favoring proxy contests have emerged. In particular, as noted at the beginning of this chapter, the emergence of the poison pill as a takeover defense encouraged hostile bidders to launch a proxy content concurrently with a tender offer.

1. Reimbursement of Expenses

Proxy contests are enormously expensive. Any serious contest requires the services of lawyers, accountants, financial advisers, printers, and proxy solicitors.[52] None of these folks come cheap. Even incidental costs, such as mailing expenses, mount up very quickly when one must communicate (usually several times) with the thousands of shareholders in the typical public corporation. As it is always more pleasant to spend someone else's money than it is to spend one's own, both incumbents and insurgents will want the corporation to pay their expenses.

In theory, incumbent directors do not have unbridled access to the corporate treasury. In practice, however, incumbents rarely pay their own expenses. Under state law, the board of directors may use corporate funds to pay for expenses incurred in opposing the insurgent, provided the amounts are reasonable and the contest involves policy questions

---

51. Henry G. Manne, Mergers and the Market for Corporate Control, 73 J. Pol. Econ. 110, 114 (1965).

52. See generally Randall S. Thomas & Catherine T. Dixon, Aranow & Einhorn on Proxy Contests for Corporate Control § 2.03[C][1] (1998) (listing potential expenses).

rather than just a "purely personal power struggle."[53] Only the most poorly advised of incumbents find it difficult to meet this standard. The board merely needs have its lawyers parse the insurgent's proxy materials for policy questions on which they differ. Such a search is bound to be successful: if the insurgent agrees with all of management's policies, why is it trying to oust them?

In contrast, insurgents initially must bear their own costs. Insurgents have no right to reimbursement out of corporate funds. Rather, an insurgent will be reimbursed only if an appropriate resolution is approved by a majority of both the board of directors and the shareholders.[54] If the incumbents prevail, of course, they are unlikely to look kindly on an insurgent's request for reimbursement of expenses. In effect, the insurgent must win to have any hope of getting reimbursed.

The rules on reimbursement of expenses take on considerable importance when coupled with the rules on standing in proxy litigation. In *J. I. Case Co. v. Borak*,[55] the Supreme Court held that proxy claims under § 14(a) are both direct and derivative in nature. Consequently, *Borak* gives management standing to sue the insurgent in the corporation's name.[56] As a practical matter, the incumbent board thus has another weapon with which to fend off insurgent shareholders. If the Supreme Court had treated proxy litigation as direct in nature, only shareholders would have standing to sue for violations of the proxy rules. Although the board still could bring suit against the insurgent, it would have to do so in the directors' individual capacity as shareholders. As such, they could not use firm resources to finance the litigation. Because the firm is permitted to sue in its own name for violations of the proxy rules, however, the board can use the firm's deep pocket to pay for legal expenses incurred in such suits. In contrast, because of the rules on reimbursement of expenses, the insurgent's litigation costs come out of its own pocket.

A potentially important development in this area took place in 2008, when the Delaware Supreme Court ruled on a shareholder-proposed bylaw governing reimbursement of proxy expenses. AFSCME's pension fund invoked SEC Rule 14a–8 to propose an amendment to CA's bylaws pursuant to which a shareholder who successfully conducted a short slate proxy contest would be entitled to reimbursement of its reasonable expenses. CA objected to inclusion in the proxy statement of the proposal and asked the SEC for a no-action letter supporting exclusion.[57]

---

53. E.g., Rosenfeld v. Fairchild Engine & Airplane Corp., 128 N.E.2d 291 (1955), reh'g denied, 130 N.E.2d 610 (1955).

54. E.g., Steinberg v. Adams, 90 F.Supp. 604 (S.D.N.Y.1950); Grodetsky v. McCrory Corp., 267 N.Y.S.2d 356 (Sup.Ct.1966).

55. 377 U.S. 426 (1964).

56. E.g., Studebaker Corp. v. Gittlin, 360 F.2d 692 (2d Cir.1966).

57. CA, Inc. v. AFSCME Employees Pension Plan, 953 A.2d 227 (Del. 2008). Under SEC Rule 14a–8, shareholders meeting specified eligibility requirements may a proposal and accompanying supporting statement not exceeding 500 words in

Before answering CA's request, the SEC invoked Delaware's new constitutional provision allowing the SEC to certify questions of law to the Delaware Supreme Court. The SEC certified two questions: (1) Was AFSCME's proposal a proper subject for shareholder action under Delaware law and (2) would the proposal, if adopted, cause CA to violate any Delaware law?

The Delaware Supreme Court held that the proposal is a proper subject of shareholder action. The Court recognized that there is a recursive loop between DGCL § 109 and 141(a). The former empowers both directors (so long as the articles of incorporation so provide, as CA's did) and shareholders of a Delaware corporation to adopt, amend, or repeal bylaws. The latter vests the board of directors with exclusive authority to manage the business and affairs of the corporation. The conflict arises because § 109(b) imposes an important limitation on the otherwise sweeping scope of permissible bylaws: "The bylaws may contain any provision, not inconsistent with law or with the certificate of incorporation, relating to the business of the corporation, the conduct of its affairs, and its rights or powers or the rights or powers of its stockholders, directors, officers or employees." Clear conflicts between the statute or articles and the bylaws present little difficulty. But what if the bylaw nominally complies with the letter of the law, but conflicts with its spirit?

The circularity arises here because, on the one hand, § 141(a) provides that "[t]he business and affairs of every corporation organized under this chapter shall be managed by or under the direction of a board of directors." A bylaw that restricts the board's managerial authority thus seems to run afoul of § 109(b)'s prohibition of bylaws that are "inconsistent with law." On the other hand, § 141(a) also provides that the board's management powers are plenary "except as may be otherwise provided in this chapter." Does an otherwise valid bylaw adopted pursuant to § 109 squeeze through that loophole?

The Supreme Court declined to "articulate with doctrinal exactitude a bright line" that would divide those bylaws that shareholders may permissibly adopt from those that go too far in infringing upon the directors' right to manage the corporation. Bylaws that relate to the process for electing directors, however, go to "a subject in which shareholders of Delaware corporations have a legitimate and protected interest." Accordingly, the AFSCME proposal was a proper subject for stockholder action.

On the other hand, the court also noted that, if adopted, the proposal would cause CA to violate Delaware law in some cases. The proposal could require the board to reimburse a successful short slate

length for inclusion in the company's proxy statement and on the company's proxy card. An included proposal must then be brought up at the shareholder meeting for a vote.

proxy contestant even if a proper application of fiduciary principles would preclude the board from doing so. As examples of such cases, the Court pointed to a proxy contest undertaken for "personal or petty concerns, or to promote interests that do not further, or are adverse to, those of the corporation." In order not to violate the board's fiduciary duties under Delaware law, the proposal therefore would have to include a fiduciary out pursuant to which the board may refuse to reimburse an insurgent when doing so would violate the board's fiduciary duties.

In response to *CA*, the Delaware legislature adopted DGCL § 113, which expressly authorizes proxy expense reimbursement bylaws. The bylaw must be adopted prior to the record date of the meeting at which the insurgent solicited proxies, thereby preventing an insurgent from seeking to simultaneously elect directors and amend the bylaws. Section 113 also permits the bylaw to impose a number of conditions on reimbursement. The bylaw may condition reimbursement on the insurgent seeking to elect a short slate rather than to replace the entire board. The amount to be reimbursed can be determined based on the proportion of votes received by the insurgent's candidate(s). The list of conditions is non-exclusive.

Although § 113 mostly codifies the *CA* decision, the statute does not expressly require a fiduciary out. Whether courts will follow the *CA* decision and continue to require that a bylaw include a fiduciary out in order to be valid remains uncertain. A precedent for doing so is provided by the Delaware Supreme Court's treatment of Delaware's force-the-vote statute. In *Smith v. Van Gorkom*,[58] the Delaware Supreme Court held that directors could not submit a merger to shareholders without making a recommendation that it be approved. The Delaware legislature later overturned that result by adopting DGCL § 251(c), which provides: "The terms of the agreement may require that the agreement be submitted to the stockholders whether or not the board of directors determines at any time subsequent to declaring its advisability that the agreement is no longer advisable and recommends that the stockholders reject it." In *Omnicare, Inc. v. NCS Healthcare, Inc.*,[59] the court held that § 251 did not trump the fiduciary duties of directors. "Taking action that is otherwise legally possible, however, does not ipso facto comport with the fiduciary responsibilities of directors in all circumstances. . . . Section 251 provisions . . . are 'presumptively valid in the abstract.' Such provisions in a merger agreement may not, however, 'validly define or limit the directors' fiduciary duties under Delaware law or prevent the [NCS] directors from carrying out their fiduciary duties under Delaware law.'"[60] If so, however, what is the point of § 251? In any case, *Omnicare* thus stands as a clear precedent for a judicial mandate that § 113 bylaws include a fiduciary out despite the statute's silence on the point.

58. 488 A.2d 858 (Del.1985).   **60.** Id. at 937–38.
59. 818 A.2d 914 (Del.2003).

2. Shareholder Apathy and Related Problems

The insurgent's problems are said to be compounded by the other shareholders' rational apathy. As the theory goes, a rational shareholder will expend the effort to make an informed decision only if the expected benefits of doing so outweigh its costs. Given the length and complexity of proxy statements, especially in a proxy contest where the shareholder is receiving multiple communications from the contending parties, the opportunity cost entailed in reading the proxy statements before voting is quite high and very apparent. Shareholders also probably do not expect to discover grounds for opposing management from the proxy statements. Finally, most shareholders' holdings are too small to have any significant effect on the vote's outcome. Accordingly, shareholders can be expected to assign a relatively low value to the expected benefits of careful consideration. Shareholders are thus rationally apathetic. For the average shareholder, the necessary investment of time and effort in making informed voting decisions simply is not worthwhile.[61]

Instead of carefully considering the contending parties' arguments, shareholders typically adopt the so-called Wall Street Rule: it's easier to switch than fight. To the extent the shareholders are satisfied, they will vote for management. Disgruntled shareholders, in contrast, will have long since sold out. As a result, shareholders are likely to vote for management even where that is not the decision an informed shareholder would reach. The insurgent thus risks laying out considerable funds for no return on that investment.

3. The Proxy Contest's (Slight) Resurgence

Starting in the 1990s, various factors combined to make hostile tender offers a much less attractive, and proxy contests a much more attractive, acquisition technique than they had been up to that point. Perhaps the most important factors in the proxy contest's resurgence were two supreme court decisions. *Paramount Communications, Inc. v. Time Inc.*,[62] by the Delaware Supreme Court, significantly weakened the standards by which target takeover defenses are measured. Under Delaware law, incumbent directors must show that the hostile offer poses a threat to corporate policy and that their response was reasonable in relation to the threat.[63] *Time* both recognized a much broader class of cognizable threats and weakened the proportionality requirement. As a result, effective management takeover defenses should pass muster more easily. Not only does this trend make hostile tender offers more difficult,

---

61. Frank H. Easterbrook and Daniel R. Fischel, Voting in Corporate Law, 26 J. L. & Econ. 395, 402 (1983); Martin Lipton, Corporate Governance in the Age of Finance Corporatism, 136 U. Penn. L. Rev. 1, 66–67 (1987). The problem is compounded by the likelihood that a substantial number of shareholders will attempt to freeride on the efforts of the few informed shareholders.

62. 571 A.2d 1140 (Del.1989).

63. See Unocal Corp. v. Mesa Petroleum Co., 493 A.2d 946 (Del.1985).

it also encourages bidders to conduct a proxy contest before making a tender offer. If elected, the bidder's nominees often can lower the target's defenses and thereby permit the tender offer to go forward.

In *CTS Corp. v. Dynamics Corp.*,[64] the U.S. Supreme Court for the first time upheld a state takeover law against constitutional challenge. Since *CTS*, state takeover laws have routinely withstood constitutional scrutiny. By erecting new barriers to hostile tender offerors, they make tender offers less attractive. Because most permit the target's board of directors to waive their application to a particular bid, they also encourage pre-offer proxy contests.

Proxy contests probably will never become commonplace. They remain expensive and risky. Yet, they are an essential part of the market for corporate control. So long as outsiders want to buy companies whose incumbent directors and officers want to remain independent, proxy contests will be part of the buyer's toolkit.

D. The Proxy Access Debate

In 2003, the SEC proposed a dramatic shakeup in the process by which corporate directors are elected. Under both state and federal law, the director nomination machinery is under the control of the incumbent board of directors. When it is time to elect directors, the incumbent board nominates a slate, which it puts forward on the company's proxy statement. There is no mechanism for a shareholder to put a nominee on the ballot. Instead, a shareholder who wishes to nominate directors is obliged to incur the considerable expense of conducting a proxy contest to elect a slate in opposition to that put forward by the incumbents.

If adopted, proposed Rule 14a–11 would have permitted shareholders, upon the occurrence of certain specified events and subject to various restrictions,[65] to have their nominees placed on the company's proxy statement and ballot. A shareholder-nominated director thus could be elected to the board in a fashion quite similar to the way shareholder-sponsored proposals are now put to a shareholder vote.

As proposed, Rule 14a–11 contemplated a two-step process stretching over two election cycles. Under the rule, a shareholder could place his or her nominee on the corporation's proxy card and statement if one of two triggering events occurs. First, a Rule 14a–8 proposal to authorize shareholder nominations had been approved by the holders of a majority of the outstanding shares at a meeting of the shareholders. Second, shareholders representing at least 35 percent of the votes withheld authority on their proxy cards for their shares to be voted in favor of any

---

64.   481 U.S. 69 (1987).

65.   For a detailed description and critique of the proposal, see Stephen M. Bain-

bridge, A Comment on the SEC's Shareholder Access Proposal, Engage, April 2004, at 18.

director nominated by the incumbent board of directors. In either case, at the next annual meeting of the shareholders, shareholder nominees would be included in the company's proxy statement and ballot.

The SEC failed to act on the proposal, neither adopting nor withdrawing it. In lieu of SEC action, some activist investors began putting forward Rule 14a–8 proposals to amend the bylaws to permit shareholder access to the company proxy. In response, corporate boards argued that such proposals could be excluded under Rule 14a–8(i)(8), which permits the issue to exclude a proposal that "relates to an election for membership on the company's board of directors or analogous governing body."

When the SEC agreed that proxy access bylaw proposals could be excluded under Rule 14a–8(i)(8), the American Federation of State, County & Municipal Employees' pension plan (AFSCME) indirectly challenged that decision by seeking an injunction requiring American Insurance Group (AIG) to include an AFSCME proxy access proposal in AIG's proxy statement. The Second Circuit held that AIG could not exclude the proposal.[66] The pertinent legal question should have been whether Rule 14a–8(i)(8) allows firms to exclude all proposals concerning corporate elections or only proposals relating to a particular seat in a particular election. The court did not reach that issue, however, instead basing its opinion on a quirk of administrative law.

In 1976, the SEC had issued a statement asserting that "the election exclusion is limited to shareholder proposals used to oppose solicitations dealing with an identified board seat in an upcoming election" and rejecting "the somewhat broader interpretation that the election exclusion applies to shareholder proposals that would institute procedures making such election contests more likely."[67] Around 1990, the SEC reversed its position to take the latter view, "although at first in an ad hoc and inconsistent manner."[68] The SEC did so informally through issuing no action letters in response to issuer requests to exclude such proposals. Only in an amicus brief in the AFSCME litigation did the SEC formally announce the new policy.

The court acknowledged that there might be good policy reasons for the SEC's shift in position. It also recognized that the SEC is entitled to change its mind. Where the rule is ambiguous, as was the case with the 14a–8(i)(8) exclusion, however, the SEC may not change its interpretation without giving reasons. Instead, it has a "duty to explain its departure from prior norms."[69] Accordingly, the court held that it would defer to the 1976 statement as the authoritative agency pronouncement.

In the wake of the *AIG* decision, the SEC began a rulemaking process to determine whether Rule 14a–8(i)(8) should be amended to

---

66. AFSCME v. AIG, Inc., 462 F.3d 121 (2d Cir. 2006).

67. Id. at 128.

68. Id. at 123.

69. Id. at 129.

permit or deny shareholder access to the corporate ballot. On November 28, 2007, the SEC announced an amendment to Rule 14a–8(i)(8), pursuant to which the Rule would now read:

(i) Question 9: If I have complied with the procedural requirements, on what other bases may a company rely to exclude my proposal?
. . .

(8) Relates to election: If the proposal relates to a nomination or an election for membership on the company's board of directors or analogous governing body or a procedure for such nomination or election.

The amendment thus reversed the 1976 statement and effectively overturned the substantive result of the *AIG* case. At the same time, however, the SEC announced its intention to continue studying the issue.

The 2008 election of President Barack Obama shifted control of the SEC from Republican to Democratic hands. The new Democratic SEC Chairman, Mary Shapiro, promptly announced that the Commission would revisit the proxy access question. In response, a coalition of business interests announced their intent to challenge the SEC's authority to regulate proxy access.

Proponents of proxy access therefore persuaded Congress to include a provision in the Dodd–Frank financial reform legislation of 2010 affirming that the SEC has authority to adopt proxy access rules.[70] Section 971 of the Act did not require that the SEC do so.[71] On the other hand, if the SEC chose to do so, § 971 expressed Congress' intent that the SEC "should have wide latitude in setting the terms of such proxy access."[72] In particular, § 971 expressly authorizes the SEC to exempt "an issuer or class of issuers" from any proxy access rule and specifically requires the SEC to "take into account, among other considerations, whether" proxy access "disproportionately burdens small issuers."[73]

Section 971 probably was unnecessary. As noted, an SEC rulemaking proceeding on proxy access was well advanced long before Dodd–Frank was adopted, so a shove from Congress was superfluous. As to the question of SEC authority, proxy access almost certainly fell within the disclosure and process sphere over which the SEC has unquestioned authority.[74] By adopting § 971, however, Congress did preempt an expected challenge to any forthcoming SEC regulation.

---

70. Dodd–Frank § 971.

71. S. Rep. No. 111–176, at 146 (2010) (discussing proxy access provision then numbered § 972).

72. Id.

73. Dodd–Frank § 971(c).

74. See Stephen M. Bainbridge, The Scope of the SEC's Authority Over Shareholder Voting Rights, Engage, June 2007, at 25 (analyzing relevant case law and legislative history).

In any case, the ink was hardly dry on Dodd–Frank when the SEC announced final adoption of new Rule 14a–11.[75] The rule would have required companies to include in their proxy materials, alongside the nominees of the incumbent board, the nominees of shareholder rs who own at least 3 percent of the company's shares and have done so continuously for at least the prior three years.[76] A shareholder could only put forward a short slate, consisting of at least 1 nominee or up to 25% of the company's board of directors whichever was greater.[77] Oddly, this entitlement applied even to minority shareholders of a corporation that had a controlling shareholder with sufficient voting power to elect the entire board. Application of the rule to small companies was to be deferred for three years, while the SEC studied its impact.[78]

As was the case with the 2003 proposal, in order for an individual to be eligible to be nominated under Rule 14a–11, that individual would have had to satisfy the applicable stock exchange listing standard definition of independence from the company. The 2003 proposal also contemplated that the nominee must satisfy a number of independence criteria (e.g., no family or employment relationships) vis-à-vis the nominating shareholder or group. The SEC at that time clearly was concerned that the proposal would be used to put forward special interest directors who would not broadly represent the shareholders as a whole but rather only the narrow interests of those who nominated them. In contrast, as adopted, Rule 14a–11 contained no such requirement. Accordingly, there was a very real risk shareholder nominated directors would perceive themselves as representatives of their electoral constituency rather than all shareholders.[79]

Insurgents, however, could not use the rule to bypass a proxy contest for control. Shareholders whose disclosed intent was to seek control of the company could not use the rule to nominate directors. Likewise, shareholders whose disclosed intent was to elect more directors than the number authorized by the rule could not use the rule to nominate directors. In either case, such shareholders would have had to run a traditional proxy contest.

Concurrently, the SEC amended Rule 14a–8(i)(8). As amended, the new rule stated that a proposal may be excluded if it:

(i) Would disqualify a nominee who is standing for election; (ii) Would remove a director from office before his or her term expired;

---

75. Facilitating Shareholder Director Nominations, Exchange Act Rel. No. 62,764 (Aug. 25, 2010).

76. Id. at 108. On the other hand, the rule allows groups of shareholders to aggregate their holdings for purposes of meeting the 3% threshold. Id. at 14.

77. Id. at 26.

78. Id. at 70–71.

79. A nominating shareholder must file a Schedule 14N providing notice of its intention to nominate a candidate under the rule. The disclosure statement must include information about the relationship, if any, between the nominating shareholder and the nominee. 17 C.F.R. § 240.14n–101. Disclosure will at least allow other shareholders to consider possible conflicts of interest.

(iii) Questions the competence, business judgment, or character of one or more nominees or directors; (iv) Seeks to include a specific individual in the company's proxy materials for election to the board of directors; or (v) Otherwise could affect the outcome of the upcoming election of directors.

In adopting these amendments, the SEC explained that proxy access bylaws no longer were automatically excludable. To the contrary, bylaws that expand proxy access rights to a broader group of shareholders or create alternative proxy access rights were expressly authorized. A shareholder proposal to eliminate or restrict proxy access rights, however, was impermissible.

In *Business Roundtable v. S.E.C.*,[80] however, the U.S. Court of Appeals for the District of Columbia struck down Rule 14a–11 in a lawsuit brought by the Business Roundtable and the U.S. Chamber of Commerce. Even though the SEC clearly had authority to adopt the rule, the court found that the SEC had:

> [A]cted arbitrarily and capriciously for having failed ... adequately to assess the economic effects of [the] new rule. Here the Commission inconsistently and opportunistically framed the costs and benefits of the rule; failed adequately to quantify the certain costs or to explain why those costs could not be quantified; neglected to support its predictive judgments; contradicted itself; and failed to respond to substantial problems raised by commenters.

The court agreed with those who argue that, if proxy access were validly adopted, a board often would have not just the right—but the duty—to oppose shareholder nominees:

> [T]he American Bar Association Committee on Federal Regulation of Securities commented: "If the [shareholder] nominee is determined [by the board] not to be as appropriate a candidate as those to be nominated by the board's independent nominating committee ..., then the board will be compelled by its fiduciary duty to make an appropriate effort to oppose the nominee, as boards now do in traditional proxy contests."

The court also decisively rejected the SEC's claim that shareholder activism is beneficial for corporate performance:

> The petitioners also maintain, and we agree, the Commission relied upon insufficient empirical data when it concluded that Rule 14a–11 will improve board performance and increase shareholder value by facilitating the election of dissident shareholder nominees. ... The Commission acknowledged the numerous studies submitted by commenters that reached the opposite result. ... One commenter, for example, submitted an empirical study showing that "when dissi-

---

80. 647 F.3d 1144 (D.C. Cir. 2011).

dent directors win board seats, those firms underperform peers by 19 to 40% over the two years following the proxy contest." .... The Commission completely discounted those studies "because of questions raised by subsequent studies, limitations acknowledged by the studies' authors, or [its] own concerns about the studies' methodology or scope."

The Commission instead relied exclusively and heavily upon two relatively unpersuasive studies, one concerning the effect of "hybrid boards" (which include some dissident directors) and the other concerning the effect of proxy contests in general, upon shareholder value. ... Indeed, the Commission "recognize[d] the limitations of the Cernich (2009) study," and noted "its long-term findings on shareholder value creation are difficult to interpret." ... In view of the admittedly (and at best) "mixed" empirical evidence, ... we think the Commission has not sufficiently supported its conclusion that increasing the potential for election of directors nominated by shareholders will result in improved board and company performance and shareholder value....

Likewise, the Court agreed with those who argue that certain institutional investors—most notably union pension funds and state and local government pension funds—would use proxy access as leverage to extract private gains at the expense of other investors:

Notwithstanding the ownership and holding requirements, there is good reason to believe institutional investors with special interests will be able to use the rule and, as more than one commenter noted, "public and union pension funds" are the institutional investors "most likely to make use of proxy access." ... Nonetheless, the Commission failed to respond to comments arguing that investors with a special interest, such as unions and state and local governments whose interests in jobs may well be greater than their interest in share value, can be expected to pursue self-interested objectives rather than the goal of maximizing shareholder value, and will likely cause companies to incur costs even when their nominee is unlikely to be elected.

The D.C. Circuit opinion is not the end of the story. As this book went to print, it was unclear what next steps—if any—the SEC would take. The SEC could go back to the rule-making process and try again. Alternatively, the SEC could leave the problem to private ordering. After the D.C. Circuit decision, the SEC put its planned amendments to Rule 14a–8 into effect. Accordingly, shareholders who want proxy access now can put forward proposals under that rule to amend the issuer's bylaws so as to permit shareholder nominees to be included on the proxy card.

E. Proxy Litigation

There are many ways to violate the proxy rules, because there are so many technical rules that must be complied with, but the likeliest source of liability is an illegal proxy solicitation. It is illegal to solicit proxies until the solicitor has delivered a proxy statement to the shareholders. It also is illegal to solicit proxies using materials that have not been filed with the SEC. Finally, it is illegal to solicit proxies using false or misleading soliciting materials. In examining these issues, we focus on several questions: (1) Does a cause of action exist for violations of the proxy rules and, if so, who has standing to bring such an action? (2) What must the plaintiff show in order to prevail in such a cause of action? (3) What remedies are available to injured parties?

1. The Implied Private Right of Action

No matter how closely one scrutinizes Securities Exchange Act § 14(a), one will not find anything relating to a private party cause of action under the statute or rules. In *J. I. Case Co. v. Borak*,[81] however, the Supreme Court implied a private right of action from the statute. Case proposed to merge with American Tractor Co. Borak owned around 2000 shares of Case stock and sought to enjoin the merger on the grounds, inter alia, that the company's proxy materials were false and misleading. Borak claimed that the merger was approved by a small margin and would not have been approved but for the false and misleading statements. Case argued that Borak had no standing to sue, as the federal proxy rules provided no private party cause of action.

Despite the lack of any statutory authorization for a private party cause of action, Justice Clark's opinion for the Court found that such an action in fact existed. As a fig leaf to cover the otherwise naked exercise of judicial activism, Justice Clark purported to find a statutory basis for the cause of action in Exchange Act § 27. Noting that § 27 gives district courts jurisdiction over "all suits in equity and actions at law brought to enforce any liability or duty" under the Act, Justice Clark contended that "[t] he power to enforce implies the power to make effective the right of recovery afforded by the Act. And the power to make the right of recovery effective implies the power to utilize any of the procedures or actions normally available to the litigant...." His argument, however, is spurious. Section 27 speaks of liabilities imposed by the Act, but nothing in § 14(a) or the rules thereunder creates such liabilities vis-à-vis shareholders.

Borak is better understood as an exercise of judicial fiat. A private right of action exists not because Congress intended it, but because a majority of the Supreme Court said so. The general legitimacy of implied

---

81. 377 U.S. 426 (1964).

private rights of action is beyond our purview, however.[82] Instead, we are concerned solely with Justice Clark's policy justification for this particular cause of action.

Justice Clark was quite above-board as to his motivation—he wanted to deter fraud and other proxy violations. According to Justice Clark, private enforcement provides "a necessary supplement" to SEC efforts. He implied that shareholders are in a better position than the SEC to detect proxy violations—they have fewer proxy statements to review and presumably are better informed about the company. Again, however, the argument is spurious. Most shareholders do not carefully review proxy materials. Instead, they are rationally apathetic. They lack both the desire and the incentive to closely monitor the firm. Justice Clark doubtless knew that individual shareholders were unlikely to emerge as champions of corporate truth and justice. Instead, it seems probable that he was trying to provide incentives for the plaintiffs' bar to become more active in proxy litigation.

At this point, we must digress briefly to discuss the economics of deterrence. Following Jeremy Bentham, many modern deterrence theorists assume that man is a rational calculator of costs and benefits. A rational calculator will not violate the law if the costs of illegal activity exceed the benefits to be derived from it. To be sure, the idea that criminals are rational calculators seems improbable, but there is some evidence that criminals behave as though they were rational calculators, especially with respect to economic crimes like securities fraud.[83] The economic theory of deterrence therefore argues that the number of offenses reflects the expected benefits and sanctions associated with crime. Where potential offenders perceive that the potential gains from the activity are greater than the potential penalties, offenses will increase. In contrast, offenses will be reduced when the expected sanction exceeds the expected benefit. The expected benefit depends on the probability of success and the likely gain. Similarly, the expected sanction is a function of the nominal penalty and the probability of conviction or settlement.[84]

---

82. For analyses with application to securities law, see Joseph A. Grundfest, Disimplying Private Rights of Action Under the Federal Securities Laws: The Commission's Authority, 107 Harv. L. Rev. 963 (1994); Michael J. Kaufman, A Little "Right" *Musick*: The Unconstitutional Judicial Creation of Private Rights of Action Under Section 10(b) of the Securities Exchange Act, 72 Wash. U. L.Q. 287 (1994); Marc I. Steinberg and William A. Reece, The Supreme Court, Implied Rights of Action, and Proxy Regulation, 54 Ohio St. L.J. 67 (1993). Noting that the Supreme Court's standards for creating implied private rights of action have stiffened in recent

years, some lower courts have questioned whether *Borak* would be decided the same way today and even whether its reasoning remains valid. See, e.g., Reschini v. First Fed. Sav. & Loan Ass'n of Ind., 46 F.3d 246, 255 (3d Cir.1995) (opining that *Borak* "is still good law as a construction of the 1934 Act and Rule 14a–9. However, it is not clear that *Borak*, if it arose for the first time today, would be decided the same way.").

83. Richard A. Posner, Economic Analysis of Law 223–224 (4th ed. 1992).

84. Put more precisely, deterrence seeks to minimize the social loss associated with crime, which can be viewed as a func-

The express nominal sanctions for violations of the proxy rules are fairly severe. Violations can be referred to the Justice Department for criminal prosecutions, the SEC can bring an action to enjoin violations or to enjoin actions taken because of the violations (such as a merger based on false proxy materials), and the SEC can institute administrative proceedings to require compliance with its rules. However, as Justice Clark pointed out, the SEC has limited resources. The chances that the SEC will detect and successfully prosecute proxy violations are rather small. Because the expected sanction is a multiple of the nominal sanction and the probability of conviction, the expected sanction for violations of the proxy rules is relatively low. Accordingly, we would not expect SEC enforcement to provide an adequate level of deterrence.

The various forms of equitable and monetary relief made available by creating a private right action would increase the level of the nominal sanction. More important, however, if the plaintiffs' bar could be encouraged to act as so-called "private attorneys general," the probability of detection and conviction would increase substantially.

That Justice Clark was concerned with creating incentives for the plaintiffs' bar is suggested by his characterization of the implied private right of action as being both direct and derivative in nature. (Strikingly, he did so over *Borak*'s strong argument that the suit was only direct in nature.) At the time *Borak* was decided, the modern federal class action procedure had not yet been adopted. If proxy actions were allowed to proceed only directly, and plaintiffs' lawyers were limited to representing individual shareholders, the contingent fees generated by proxy litigation would be insufficient to attract quality lawyers. (The situation would be even worse in cases like *Borak*, where plaintiff sought only equitable relief.) Because the implied cause of action had a derivative element, however, a plaintiffs' lawyer could effectively sue on behalf of all shareholders, by nominally suing in the corporation's name, generating larger damage claims and bigger contingent fees.

tion of the loss created by the activity itself (activity loss), the cost of enforcing a prohibition against the activity (enforcement loss), and the cost of imposing sanctions against the activity (penalty loss). Activity loss is a function of the number of offenses and of the loss resulting from each offense. Enforcement and penalty losses are distinguished primarily by the stage of the deterrence process where they occur. Enforcement loss is the cost to society of detecting and convicting wrongdoers. Penalty loss is the cost of subsequent punishment. The sum of the costs to society and to the individual resulting from the imposition of the sanction and from any externalities created is the net penalty loss to society. Any attempt to minimize social loss must attempt to minimize the sum of all three factors, and not merely activity losses. If activity losses were the only factor in determining social loss, the social loss could be minimized simply by increasing the nominal sanction or the probability of conviction until the expected sanctions far outweigh the expected benefits. An increase in enforcement activity, however, requires increased enforcement expenditures and increases the enforcement loss to society. Similarly, an increase in nominal sanctions increases the externalities associated with imposing the sanction—such as deterrence of beneficial activities—thereby increasing the penalty loss to society. See generally Gary S. Becker, Crime and Punishment: An Economic Approach, 76 J. Pol. Econ. 169 (1968).

The Supreme Court's emphasis on promoting private attorneys general became even more pronounced in its next major proxy decision, *Mills v. Electric Auto–Lite Co.*[85] Mergenthaler Linotype Company owned over 50% of Auto–Lite's stock. About one-third of Mergenthaler's voting stock, in turn, was owned by American Manufacturing Co. American had voting control of Mergenthaler and through it Auto–Lite. Auto–Lite and Mergenthaler agreed to merge. The merger agreement required approval by two-thirds of Auto–Lite's outstanding shares, which therefore required affirmative votes from at least some of the minority shareholders. Plaintiffs alleged that the proxy materials used to solicit those votes were false and misleading and sued to enjoin the shareholder vote.

In the portion of its opinion dealing with remedies, the Supreme Court created a strong incentive for members of the plaintiffs' bar to act as private attorneys general. The Court opined that shareholder-plaintiffs "who have established a violation of the securities laws by their corporation and its officials, should be reimbursed by the corporation or its survivor for the costs of establishing the violation." Note carefully that plaintiffs' counsel was entitled to attorney's fees simply for finding a violation—there was no requirement that the plaintiff ultimately prevail in the sense of recovering damages. Indeed, in *Mills*, the shareholders ultimately recovered nothing, but the plaintiffs' attorneys' fees were still paid by the corporation.[86] *Mills* thus created a powerful economic incentive for lawyers to sue even in cases where it was clear that no injury had been caused by the violation.

The sweeping mandate in *Mills* to plaintiff's attorneys to go forth and uncover proxy rule violations was somewhat pared back by later Supreme Court decisions.[87] Today, the case law requires that the plaintiff's cause of action must create either a common fund from recovered damages or some substantial nonmonetary benefit in order for fees to be awarded.[88] Because injunctive relief likely satisfies the "substantial benefit" standard, however, there is still an incentive to sue even where it seems unlikely that monetary damages ultimately will be forthcoming.

2. Key Elements of the Proxy Cause of Action

When proxy litigation is grounded on an allegation of fraud, four key elements must be considered: (1) the materiality of the alleged misrepresentation or omission; (2) causation; (3) reliance; and (4) the defendant's

---

85. 396 U.S. 375 (1970).

86. Mills v. Eltra Corp., 663 F.2d 760 (7th Cir.1981); Mills v. Electric Auto–Lite Co., 552 F.2d 1239 (7th Cir.1977).

87. See, e.g., Alyeska Pipeline Service Co. v. Wilderness Society, 421 U.S. 240 (1975) (holding that absent statutory authorization, courts should not award attorneys fees to a plaintiff simply because plaintiff he served as a private attorney general).

88. See, e.g., Goldberger v. Integrated Resources, Inc., 209 F.3d 43 (2d Cir.2000); Amalgamated Clothing and Textile Workers Union v. Wal–Mart Stores, Inc., 54 F.3d 69 (2d Cir.1995); Smillie v. Park Chemical Co., 710 F.2d 271 (6th Cir.1983).

state of mind. We consider these elements seriatim in the sections that follow.

Materiality. Recall that in *Mills v. Electric Auto–Lite Co.*,[89] the plaintiffs were shareholders of Auto–Lite, which was controlled by Mergenthaler Linotype Company, which in turn was controlled by American Manufacturing Co. Plaintiffs alleged that the proxy materials used in connection with the shareholder vote on a proposed merger between Auto–Lite and Mergenthaler were false and misleading because they failed to disclose that all of Auto–Lite's directors were Mergenthaler nominees.

Under *Mills*, a statement or omission is material when "it might have been considered important by a reasonable shareholder who was in the process of deciding how to vote." In other words, the statement or omission must have "a significant propensity to affect the voting process." Today, it is still the case that materiality is an essential element of the cause of action, but the definition of materiality has changed. In the *TSC Industries* case, the Supreme Court adopted a uniform standard of materiality under the securities laws: whether "there is a substantial likelihood that a reasonable shareholder would consider it important in deciding how to vote."[90]

Query whether the *Mills* omission would have been material under today's standard? On the one hand, the proxy statement did inform shareholders that Mergenthaler owned over 50% of Auto–Lite and that the boards of both companies had approved the merger. Arguably, reasonable shareholders should have been able to figure out for themselves that Mergenthaler elected all of Auto–Lite's directors. On the other hand, facts tending to show that the merger was approved by a board subject to a conflict of interest likely would be considered important by a reasonable shareholder. If the proxy statement had highlighted the fact that all of Auto–Lite's directors were Mergenthaler nominees, the conflict of interest would have been flagged, and the shareholders might have assessed the merger more carefully. (Note that in assessing materiality of disclosures, courts ignore the fact that most shareholders are rationally apathetic.)

In *Virginia Bankshares, Inc. v. Sandberg*,[91] the Supreme Court further refined the materiality standard by addressing its application to statements of belief or opinion. First American Bancshares (FABI) owned 100 percent of Virginia Bankshares (VBI). In turn, VBI owned 85 percent of First American Bank of Virginia (Bank). VBI merged Bank into itself, and paid Bank shareholders $42 per share. Under Virginia law (the applicable standard), the merger required a two-thirds vote. Because VBI owned 85 percent of the voting stock, a proxy solicitation

89. 396 U.S. 375 (1970).

90. TSC Indus., Inc. v. Northway, Inc., 426 U.S. 438, 449 (1976).

91. 501 U.S. 1083 (1991).

was unnecessary to effect the transaction. Nevertheless, VBI solicited proxies from the other shareholders. In pertinent part, the proxy statement opined: "The Plan of Merger has been approved by the Board of Directors because it provides an opportunity for the Bank's public shareholders to achieve a high value for their shares." Plaintiff Sandberg (a minority shareholder) claimed that the shares were worth $60, that the directors knew $42 was a low price, and that the directors nevertheless went along with a low-priced merger because they hoped not to lose their seats on the board. Justice Souter's majority opinion concluded that the statement was material, but only after an astonishingly tortuous analysis. Justice Scalia's concurring opinion summed up the resulting rule of law far more succinctly:

> As I understand the Court's opinion, the statement "In the opinion of the Directors, this is a high value for the shares" would produce liability if in fact it was not a high value and the directors knew that. It would not produce liability if in fact it was not a high value but the directors honestly believed otherwise. The statement "The Directors voted to accept the proposal because they believe it offers a high value" would not produce liability if in fact the directors' genuine motive was quite different—except that it would produce liability if the proposal in fact did not offer a high value and the Directors knew that.

Judge Scalia went on to caution, however:

> [N]ot every sentence that has the word "opinion" in it, or that refers to motivation for directors' actions, leads us into this psychic thicket. Sometimes such a sentence actually represents facts as facts rather than opinions—and in that event no more need be done than apply the normal rules for § 14(a) liability. I think that is the situation here. In my view, the statement at issue in this case is most fairly read as affirming *separately* both the fact of the Directors' opinion *and* the accuracy of the facts upon which the opinion was assertedly based.

Causation. The law is well-settled that a proxy litigation plaintiff seeking monetary damages must show that the violation caused an injury to the shareholders—but it is a funny kind of causation. In *Mills*, the Supreme Court held that a plaintiff proves causation by showing that the proxy solicitation itself (as opposed to the defect) was an "essential link" in the accomplishment of the transaction.[92] Note that under this standard almost any violation "causes" an injury. In most transactions requiring shareholder approval, the proxy solicitation will be an essential link in accomplishing the transaction, because the solicitation was necessary to obtain the requisite shareholder vote.

---

92. Mills v. Electric Auto–Lite Co., 396 U.S. 375, 385 (1970).

In *Mills*, the Supreme Court left open the question of "whether causation could be shown where the management controls a sufficient number of shares to approve the transaction without any votes from the minority." In *Virginia Bankshares*, whose facts were recounted in the preceding section, the Supreme Court concluded that the requisite causation could not be shown in that situation.[93] Plaintiff advanced two explanations for VBI's decision to solicit proxies, both of which plaintiff argued supported a finding of causation. First, plaintiff argued that FABI wanted minority shareholder approval for reasons of goodwill, an explanation the court deemed too speculative to provide the requisite causation. Second, and far more significantly, plaintiff argued that VBI sought shareholder ratification to insulate the transaction from challenge under state law fiduciary duty rules. On the facts at bar, the Court also rejected this argument. Under Virginia law, VBI would be immunized from breach of fiduciary duty claims only if the transaction was approved by a majority of the minority shareholders after full disclosure. If VBI lied in the proxy material, there could be no valid approval. Absent valid approval, VBI gets no protection from the shareholder vote, and the proxy solicitation could not have been an essential step in the merger. Absent that showing, plaintiff cannot prove causation.[94]

Reliance. According to the prevailing view, reliance is not an essential element of the plaintiff's cause of action under the proxy rules.[95] At one time, however, the Ninth Circuit held that "shareholders who do not rely on allegedly misleading or deceptive proxy solicitations lack standing to assert direct (as opposed to derivative) equitable actions under § 14(a)."[96] The court subsequently qualified that rule, granting standing to sue directly to a shareholder who did not rely on the alleged misrepresentations, provided suit was brought before the shareholder vote occurred. The court explained that otherwise "a shareholder who learns of a material omission in a proxy statement before an election could never sue directly, because a shareholder aware of the omission will not rely on the proxy statement when voting. Further, no shareholder could sue before the election, because those shareholders satisfying [the reliance] requirement ... would be precisely those who were ignorant of the information necessary to sue until after they voted."[97]

93. Virginia Bankshares, Inc. v. Sandberg, 501 U.S. 1083 (1991).

94. If VBI had been honest, there might have been ratification and the proxy might have been an essential step, but because there would not have been a misleading statement, the plaintiff would still lose. Cf. Howing Co. v. Nationwide Corp., 972 F.2d 700 (6th Cir.1992) (upon remand by the Supreme Court for reconsideration in light of *Virginia Bankshares*, holding that loss of a state law appraisal remedy in a freezeout merger satisfies the causation requirement).

95. See, e.g., Cowin v. Bresler, 741 F.2d 410 (D.C.Cir.1984).

96. Gaines v. Haughton, 645 F.2d 761, 774 (9th Cir.1981).

97. Western Dist. Council v. Louisiana Pac. Corp., 892 F.2d 1412, 1415–16 (9th Cir.1989).

In *Stahl v. Gibraltar Financial Corp.*,[98] the Ninth Circuit disavowed any remaining reliance requirement. Gibraltar Financial's board of directors proposed an amendment to the articles of incorporation to immunize its directors from monetary liability for certain breach of fiduciary duty claims. In the proxy solicitation materials, the board stated that it was unaware of any relevant pending litigation. Shareholder Stahl, however, was personally involved in just such a lawsuit. Knowing the solicitation material was false, he sued to enjoin the vote, but failed to obtain a preliminary injunction. At the meeting, Stahl voted against the amendment. After the amendment nevertheless passed, Stahl filed an amended complaint seeking to overturn the result. The district court held that Stahl lacked standing to sue, because he obviously could not have relied on the misleading statement. Believing "it is somewhat incongruous to deny standing to those shareholders who ferret out the misstatements but grant it to those who were beguiled," the Ninth Circuit reversed. Accordingly, even those "who do not vote their proxies in reliance on the alleged misstatements have standing to sue under section 14(a)—both before and after the vote is taken."

Although the court's policy analysis seems sensible at first blush, it proves misguided on closer examination. The Ninth Circuit's pre-*Stahl* regime was problematic only when viewed ex post. From an ex ante perspective, however, that regime did a better job of setting the right incentives. If a shareholder received proxy solicitation material that he knew to be misleading, the old regime required the shareholder to act immediately. If the shareholder promptly sued, the court had a chance to resolve the matter before the shareholder vote. If the court found material misrepresentations or omissions, the court could order corrective disclosures. As such, shareholders have an opportunity to make an informed decision. If the shareholder waits until after the meeting, however, much greater cost and difficulty may be incurred in undoing the corporate action. As a way to give shareholders an incentive to sue while the annual meeting can still resolve the questions at issue, the old rule thus made eminently good sense.

In addition its misunderstanding of the policies at stake, the Ninth Circuit also botched its analysis of precedent. In deciding that plaintiff had standing, the court relied on the Supreme Court's decision in *Virginia Bankshares*. Reliance was not an issue in *Virginia Bankshares*. On the facts of *Virginia Bankshares*, however, it is clear that the plaintiff had not been misled. Hence, plaintiff could not have satisfied the reliance requirement. The Ninth Circuit opined: "Because standing to sue is jurisdictional . . . we take the Supreme Court's consideration of Sandberg's § 14(a) action to mean that a plaintiff may bring a direct

---

98.   967 F.2d 335 (9th Cir.1992).

action after the complained-of proxy vote even where he has not himself relied on the challenged misstatements." But this is error.[99]

Although standing and merits issues are often intertwined, the issue of standing mainly has to do with questions such as that of "injury in fact." We can plausibly assume that Stahl was injured, probably by a decrease in the value of his stock. The proper issue thus is not whether Stahl has standing, but whether reliance is an element of the 14(a) cause of action. Why then did the Ninth Circuit treat this as a standing issue? If reliance is an element of the cause of action, Stahl might have standing but (a) would not be an adequate representative of the class of shareholders and (b) would not himself have a cause of action because he cannot prove an essential element of the claim. If reliance is an element of the cause of action, moreover, the fact that Sandberg did not rely on the misrepresentation at issue in *Virginia Bankshares* loses jurisprudential significance. Unlike issues of standing, which courts are supposed to consider *sua sponte*, failure to plead and prove an element of the cause of action and the Supreme Court's subsequent failure to address Sandberg's lack of reliance would not have any precedential implications. If one had a policy goal of encouraging private attorneys general, however, Stahl is exactly the sort of person one would want to encourage. He knows the company lied and is motivated to litigate the issue. Accordingly, one would structure the issue to ensure that Stahl is able to bring the cause of action. Which is exactly what the Ninth Circuit did. The curious thing is that the Supreme Court, led in large part by its more conservative justices, has been hacking away at the private attorneys general concept for many years. Yet, here we have an opinion by one of the most conservative 9th Circuit judges (Kozinski) that makes sense only as being intended to promote the use of private attorneys general. It is all quite odd.

State of mind. In both *Virginia Bankshares* and *TSC Industries*, the Supreme Court declined to decide whether the defendant must have acted with scienter or merely negligently in order to be held liable for fraud in a § 14(a) action.[100] As to issuer liability, and that of officers and directors, courts generally hold that negligence suffices.[101] As to collateral

---

99. In addition, the Ninth Circuit gave the Supreme Court far too much credit. One doubts that anyone on the Supreme Court even thought about this issue when deciding *Virginia Bankshares*. In applying Supreme Court decisions in the securities arena, one generally should not assume that the justices knew what they were doing. See Stephen M. Bainbridge & Mitu Gulati, How do Judges Maximize? (The Same Way Everybody Else Does—Boundedly): Rules of Thumb in Securities Fraud Opinions, 51 Emory L.J. 83 (2002).

100. Note that the *Virginia Bankshares* approach to opinions and statements of belief makes the state of mind issue—why the board voted in favor of the merger—irrelevant with respect to such opinions. The question in such cases becomes simply: did the board knowingly misstate the underlying facts? If VBI's stock is worth $60 and the board members announce that it is worth $42 when they know it is worth $60, the plaintiff can sue.

101. See, e.g., Wilson v. Great American Indus., Inc., 855 F.2d 987 (2d Cir.1988); Gerstle v. Gamble—Skogmo, 478 F.2d 1281

participants, such as accountants who certify financial statements contained in a proxy statement (as is done when a merger is to be voted on), at least one court has held that plaintiff must prove scienter.[102]

Remedies. Probably the most common remedy in proxy litigation is some form of prospective relief, such as an ex ante injunction against the shareholder vote. The court typically forbids the company from going forward with the shareholder meeting until the party soliciting proxies provides a new proxy statement, correcting whatever violation has been identified, and resolicits the proxies. Retrospective monetary relief, however, is available in appropriate cases. Damages must be shown, which means that plaintiff must establish a monetary injury. Because the violation itself is not an injury, plaintiff must show some sort of actual loss or harm resulting from the violation.

The most drastic option, at least from the firm's perspective, is a setting aside of the transaction. In *Mills*, for example, the merger could be undone and the two firms restored to their prior position as separate entities. This option is chosen very rarely. Courts tend to look at mergers and similar transactions the way a cook looks at an omelet: once the eggs have been scrambled, you can't put them back in the shells. When a merger takes place, all sorts of commingling takes place. Employees are fired or transferred, assets (such as bank accounts) are mixed up and reallocated, operating procedures are changed, and the like. The courts are very aware of this commingling process and therefore will set aside a merger only where it is possible to do so without harming the overall value of the firms and no other remedy can make the injured parties whole.

(2d Cir.1973); see also Shidler v. All American Life & Fin. Corp., 775 F.2d 917 (8th Cir.1985) (rejecting an argument that strict liability was the standard).

102. Adams v. Standard Knitting Mills, 623 F.2d 422 (6th Cir.1980).

Chapter 6

TENDER OFFERS AND OTHER STOCK PURCHASES

§ 6.1 The Forms of Nonstatutory Acquisitions

As we have seen, the target corporation's board of directors serves as a gatekeeper in all of the statutory acquisition forms. Target board approval is a condition precedent to putting the transaction to a shareholder vote and, of course, to ultimately closing the transaction to occur. If the board disapproves of a prospective acquisition, an outsider must resort to one of the three nonstatutory acquisitions devices: proxy contests, share purchases, or tender offers.

A. Share Purchases v. Tender Offers

Absent cumulative voting, ownership of 50.1% of the outstanding voting stock guarantees one the right to elect the entire board of directors. Once the acquirer replaces the incumbent board with new members, the old board's opposition is moot. The acquirer could obtain the necessary shares through purchases on the open market or privately negotiated block transactions. These techniques have significant disadvantages. They are time consuming. The acquisition program eventually must be disclosed, as SEC regulations require disclosure by holders of more than 5% of a company's stock, and may leak even earlier. In either case, news of an acquisition program typically drives up the stock price. Search and other transaction costs may be significant. Privately negotiated block transactions at a premium over market raise fiduciary duty concerns. And so on.

The tender offer was devised as a shortcut to bypass such concerns. A tender offer is a public offer to shareholders of the target corporation in which the prospective acquirer offers to purchase target company shares at a specified price and upon specified terms. The offer is made during a fixed period of time. The offer may be for all or only a portion of a class or classes of securities of the target corporation. Shareholders wishing to accept the offer "tender" their shares to the bidder, which are then held in escrow until the offer ends. At that time, the bidder may—but need not—"take down" the tendered shares. If the bidder does so, the escrow agent releases the promised consideration to the shareholders. Otherwise, the escrow agent returns the tendered shares to the owners.

B. Tender Offers v. Proxy Contests

Proxy contests long have been "the most expensive, the most uncertain, and the least used of the various techniques" for acquiring corporate control.[1] As we saw in Chapter 5, insurgents contemplating a proxy battle face a host of legal and economic disincentives, including: (1) the incumbents' informational advantages; (2) long-standing investor perception that proxy insurgents are not serious contenders for control; (3) classified boards of directors, which mean that even a successful proxy contest can only unseat a minority of the board; (4) restrictions on reimbursement of the insurgent's expenses, while the incumbent board is allowed essentially unfettered access to the corporate treasury; (5) rational shareholder apathy.

During the 1960s, the cash tender offer emerged as a potent alternative that suffered from relatively few of these disadvantages. At the time, a principal advantage was the almost total absence of regulation. Since the 1930s, proxy contests have been subject to numerous federal rules imposing substantial disclosure obligations on prospective acquirers. The expensive process of preparing and vetting the requisite disclosure documents directly increases the transaction costs associated with such acquisitions. More subtly, mandatory disclosure rules decrease an insurgent's profit margin by forcing it to reveal the anticipated sources of gain to be had from a change of control. Prior to the 1968 adoption of the Williams Act, in contrast, cash tender offers were essentially unregulated. Accordingly, offers slightly over market could succeed and bidders thus reaped a non-pro rata share of the gains.

After passage of the Williams Act, tender offerors faced disclosure obligations (and thus transaction costs) comparable to those under the proxy rules. Tender offers nevertheless still remained more profitable than proxy contests. Although the Williams Act undoubtedly reduced offerors' profit margins, the tender offeror is still able to reap a non-pro rata share of the gains from a change in control. The changes made by the Williams Act thus reduced, but did not eliminate, the cash tender offer's advantages.

Assume, for example, that the target company has 110 outstanding shares, currently trading at $10 per share, of which the bidder owns ten. The bidder correctly believes that under its management the firm's shares would be worth $20. If the bidder successfully gains control through a proxy contest, its ten shares will produce a $100 profit when the stock price rises to reflect the company's value under its management. All the other shareholders, however, will also automatically re-

---

1. Henry G. Manne, Mergers and the   Econ. 110, 114 (1965).
Market for Corporate Control, 73 J. Pol.

ceive a pro rata share of those gains. There is nothing the bidder lawfully can do to capture a non-pro rata share of the gains. As a result, the bidder confers a $1,000 benefit on the other shareholders (many of whom undoubtedly voted for management).

In contrast, if the tender offeror is able to purchase all the outstanding shares it does not already own at a price below $19 per share, its profit will exceed the $100 figure available from a successful proxy contest. To do so, of course, it need not persuade all of the other shareholders to sell. As long as the holders of at least 46 shares are willing to tender at a price below $19 per share, our hypothetical bidder will obtain voting control. It may then freeze out the remaining minority shareholders in a subsequent merger at approximately the same price.

How likely is this scenario? Quite likely. Unlike the proxy contest, the tender offer does not automatically confer a pro rata share of the gains from a change of control on the target's shareholders. Instead, their share of the gains is now determined by the size of the premium paid by the bidder. No rule requires that the premium constitute a pro rata share of the gains. Instead, the premium will be no larger than necessary to obtain a controlling block of target stock. Granted, the disclosures mandated by the Williams Act may enable shareholders to estimate the gains anticipated by the bidder. It is unlikely, however, that shareholders will obtain all of those gains. For one thing, collective action problems preclude the hard bargaining needed to extract a full share of the gains. Absent competing bids or successful management resistance, there is no mechanism for the shareholders to demand a bigger piece of the pie. Rational shareholders thus can be expected to accept a premium reflecting a less than pro rata sharing of the gains, reasoning that some profit is better than none.

In addition to enabling the bidder to obtain a greater share of the gains from a change of control, the tender offer (if followed by a freeze-out merger) enables the bidder to eliminate the complications caused by controlling a company with minority shareholders. With minority shareholders remaining in place after a proxy contest, the firm's directors may not benefit the controlling shareholder to the exclusion or at the expense of the minority. With the minority eliminated by a tender offer and freeze-out merger, the bidder may do with the target as it will.

In sum, these factors predict that tender offers should succeed far more often than proxy contests. The data confirm this prediction. Proxy contests tend to succeed less than half the time. In contrast, tender offers succeed in the majority of cases. When the tender offer's greater probability of success is coupled with its higher profitability, one would expect bidders to prefer it to proxy contests. Again the data confirm this expectation, both on an absolute scale and when compared to the frequency of tender offers. Although there was an up-tick in proxy contest activity during the 1990s, much of that activity was attributable to the general rise in takeover activity. Indeed, as we saw in Chapter 5, many proxy contests during that period were made in conjunction with tender offers.

§ 6.2   A Brief History of Federal Regulation of Tender Offers

Prior to the 1968 passage of the Williams Act, neither federal securities nor state corporate law regulated tender offers. As already noted, this absence of regulation was one of the intrinsic advantages the tender offer possessed over other acquisition forms and thus led to the enormous growth in the volume of tender offers during the early and middle part of that decade. In 1965, Senator Harrison Williams of New Jersey proposed federal legislation to protect target companies from what he called "industrial sabotage" of hostile corporate raids on "proud old companies."[2] Although the 1965 legislation was not adopted, a second bill was introduced in 1967. The 1967 bill was considerably more balanced and focused primarily on disclosure and antifraud. As Senator Williams and others emphasized, the bill attempted to favor neither the target nor the offeror. As subsequently amended, the Williams Act has four components of principal interest for our purposes:

1. Securities Exchange Act § 13(d) regulates beachhead acquisitions of target stock. (The term beachhead acquisition refers to purchases of an initial block of target stock, either on the open market or privately, before the bidder announces its intent to conduct a tender offer.)

2. Securities Exchange Act § 13(e) regulates self-tender offers by issuers. Among the powers of a corporation is the right to buy its own stock. Stock redemptions and repurchases are subject to the legal capital statute of the state of incorporation. Where effected by means of a tender offer, however, they must also comply with § 13(e).

3. Securities Exchange Act § 14(d) regulates tender offers generally. The statute and the SEC regulations thereunder impose both disclosure and procedural requirements on the offer.

4. Securities Exchange Act § 14(e) prohibits fraud in connection with a tender offer.

There is no doubt that the Williams Act dramatically changed the takeover game. It eliminated such favorite raider tactics as the "Saturday night special"—the surprise offer made over a weekend. It significantly increased the amount of information available to target shareholders, predictably driving up the average control premium paid in

---

2. Corporate raider is a pejorative dating from the 1960s to describe bidders, especially those who do not actually acquire target companies but rather use the tender offer process to make quick profits through greenmail or by selling blocks of target stocks to other bidders.

takeovers. Finally, it significantly expanded the federal government's role in corporate governance.

§ 6.3   Beachhead Acquisitions and Other Stock Purchases

For the would be acquirer, keeping its interest in the target and takeover plans secret for as long as possible is crucial. As soon as a possible bid is disclosed, the target's stock price jumps. Target management may begin erecting defenses against the bid or seeking alternative transactions. Other potential acquirers may begin looking at the target with the idea of making a competing bid, such that the initial bidder's disclosures may simply serve to identify the target and publicize its vulnerability. In pre-Williams Act days, it was common for a prospective acquirer to quietly buy up substantial amounts of target stock before initiating its public offer. In some cases, bidders managed to acquire de facto control before going public. Today, however, Securities Exchange Act § 13(d) and the SEC rules thereunder form an early warning system effectively mandating early disclosure of impending control contests.

A.   The Obligation to Disclose

Securities Exchange Act § 13(d) requires that any person who acquires beneficial ownership of more than 5% of the outstanding shares of any class of voting equity securities registered under Securities Exchange Act § 12 must file a Schedule 13D disclosure statement within 10 days of such acquisition with the SEC, the issuer, and the exchanges on which the stock is traded.[3] Amendments must be filed within 10 days of any material change in the information in the prior filing. Let's break this requirement down into its component pieces:

Any person: Suppose two corporations or individuals are working together to acquire the target corporation. Each plans to buy just under 5% of the target's stock, thinking that they will thereby get almost 10% without having to file a Schedule 13D disclosure statement. This plan will not work. Section 13(d)(3) provides that when two or more persons act as a group for the purpose of acquiring, holding or disposing of shares of the issuer they will collectively be deemed a "person" under the statute. Accordingly, such a group must file a Schedule 13D report if the members' aggregate holdings exceed the 5% threshold.

---

3. The § 13(d) reporting requirement also applies to acquisitions of more than 5% of the outstanding shares of any class of voting equity securities of a closed-end investment company registered under the Investment Company Act of 1940 or of an insurance company exempted from registration by Securities Exchange § 12(a)(2)(G).

Certain institutional investors who hold shares with no intent of affecting the control of the issuer may file a short form Schedule 13G, which essentially requires disclosure only of the amount of shares held and the nature of the holder. Rule 13d–1(b). All other 5% holders must file the longer Schedule 13D. Schedule 13D requires substantially greater disclosure (including the purpose of the holding) and must be amended more frequently. (Schedule 13G typically is filed on an annual basis.)

Generally speaking, some kind of agreement is necessary before it can be said that a group exists. Not only must there be an agreement, but the agreement must go to certain types of conduct. The relevant statutory provision, Securities Exchange Act § 13(d)(3) identifies "acquiring, holding, or disposing" of stock as the requisite purposes. Shortly after the Williams Act was adopted, the question arose whether two or more persons acting together for the purpose of voting shares, as when they cooperate in conducting a proxy contest, form a group for purposes of this provision. The courts split on that question.[4] The SEC subsequently adopted Rule 13d–5(b)(1), which expanded the statutory list of purposes to include voting. Consequently, a group is formed when two or more shareholders agree to act together for the purposes of voting their shares, even if they do not intend to buy any additional shares. The rule's adoption seems to have resolved the controversy, even if the SEC's authority to effectively amend the statute remains somewhat obscure.

Proving the existence of the requisite agreement is a complex and potentially difficult question of fact. On the one hand, "Section 13(d) allows individuals broad freedom to discuss the possibilities of future agreements without filing under securities laws."[5] On the other hand, an agreement to act in concert need not be formal or written.[6] The existence of such an agreement may be proven by circumstantial evidence.[7] Taken together, these factors create substantial uncertainty for putative group members. Given the minimal penalties for violating § 13(d), one suspects many groups err on the side of not filing.

Who acquires: In cases where a group is at issue, the meaning of the statutory term "acquires" takes on particular import. Suppose the group members' aggregate holdings exceed five percent when they enter into the agreement by which the group is formed for § 13(d) purposes. None of the group members, however, buy any additional shares. Do they have an immediate filing obligation or is their filing obligation only triggered

---

4. Compare GAF Corp. v. Milstein, 453 F.2d 709 (2d Cir.1971) (group exists) with Bath Indus., Inc. v. Blot, 427 F.2d 97 (7th Cir.1970) (no group).

5. Pantry Pride, Inc. v. Rooney, 598 F.Supp. 891, 900 (S.D.N.Y.1984). See also Lane Bryant, Inc. v. Hatleigh Corp., 1980 WL 1412 at *1 (S.D.N.Y.1980) ("Section 13(d) seems carefully drawn to permit parties seeking to acquire large amounts of shares in a public company to obtain information with relative freedom, to discuss preliminarily the possibility of entering into agreements and to operate with relative freedom until they get to the point where they do in fact decide to make arrangements which they must record under the securities laws"). Hence, for example, merely showing the existence of a relationship or

the sharing of information or advice between the alleged group members, will not suffice absent some additional evidence that indicates an intention to act in concert. Similarly, investment analysts who follow one another's trades without any agreement so to do, tacit or otherwise, will not be held to be a group. See, e.g., K–N Energy, Inc. v. Gulf Interstate Co., 607 F.Supp. 756 (D.Colo.1983).

6. Morales v. Quintel Entertainment, Inc., 249 F.3d 115, 124 (2d Cir.2001); Wellman v. Dickinson, 682 F.2d 355, 362–63 (2d Cir.1982).

7. Morales v. Quintel Entertainment, Inc., 249 F.3d 115, 124 (2d Cir.2001); SEC v. Savoy Indus., 587 F.2d 1149, 1163 (D.C.Cir.1978).

by further acquisitions of additional shares? The Seventh Circuit early held that the group must acquire additional shares, over and above the shares they own at the time the agreement is made, before the filing obligation is triggered.[8] In contrast, the Second Circuit held that the group acquires stock, and thus triggers the filing obligation, at the moment they enter into an agreement to act in concert, even if the members do not intend to acquire additional shares.[9] In promulgating Rule 13d–5(b), the SEC adopted the Second Circuit position by providing that a group is formed "when two or more persons agree to act together for the purpose of acquiring, holding, voting or disposing of" stock.

Beneficial ownership of more than 5% of any equity security registered under Exchange Act § 12: Rule 13d–3(a) deems a person to be the beneficial owner of stock if he has the power (by contract, understanding, arrangement, relationship or otherwise) to vote or dispose of (or to direct the voting or disposition of) the securities in question. Rule 13d–3(d) further provides that a person shall be deemed the beneficial owner of a security if he has the right to acquire ownership of the security within 60 days (e.g., by exercise of an option, conversion of a convertible security, or revocation or termination of a trust) or acquires such a right (whether or not exercisable within 60 days) with a purpose of affecting control of the issuer. Brokers, pledgees and underwriters are not deemed the beneficial owners of securities when they hold them in the ordinary course of their business. Finally, the SEC long has taken the position that a holding company is the indirect beneficial owner of the securities held by its subsidiaries, so that if the holding company and its subsidiaries hold an aggregate of more than 5% of the outstanding shares of the class in question, they must report. All of the statutory jargon boils down to a very simple point: Beneficial ownership is a broader concept than having title to the securities. Someone can be the beneficial owner of securities even if somebody else actually has title to them. If someone has or shares the power to vote or dispose of the shares, he is their beneficial owner.

Within 10 days after such person crosses the five percent threshold: Under § 13(d), the acquirer has 10 days before it must file a Schedule 13D disclosure statement. The 10–day window begins to run on the day the acquiring person makes an acquisition that puts his holdings over the five percent threshold. Where a group is formed, the 10–day window begins to run on the day they enter into the requisite agreement to act in concert, provided their aggregate holdings exceed 5% on that date.

The statutory framework had a predictable timing effect. A bidder who intends or expects to make a hostile takeover will buy up to 4.9% as quietly as possible. It will not cross the 5% threshold until all its preparations are completed. Once it crosses that threshold, it will begin

8. Bath Indus., Inc. v. Blot, 427 F.2d 97, 109 (7th Cir.1970).

9. GAF Corp. v. Milstein, 453 F.2d 709, 715 (2d Cir.1971).

actively buying stock, attempting to acquire as many shares as possible without alerting the target during the 10–day window. Pre-filing acquisitions of 10% of the issuer's stock are common and there are anecdotal accounts of pre-filing acquisitions of as much as 25% or more of the stock.

Amending the disclosure statement: Rule 13d–2(a) requires reporting parties to file an amendment to their Schedule 13D promptly in the event of any material change in the facts set forth in the statement. "Material" is defined to include (but is not limited to) any acquisition or disposition of at least 1% or more of the class of securities in question. "Promptly" is not the most precise term the drafters might have chosen, of course, as it creates a question of fact to be determined on a case-by-case basis.[10] As a rule of thumb, most practitioners assume that "promptly" means no more than a couple of days.[11]

B.　The Content of a Schedule 13D Disclosure Statement

As with other SEC forms, Schedule 13D does not follow the "fill in the box" format familiar from tax returns. Instead, its various items identify topics that must be addressed in a narrative form. Three of the required disclosure narratives are significant for our purposes: Item 2 on disclosure of identity; Item 4 on disclosure of intent; and Item 6 on disclosure of agreements or understandings.

Item 2—Identity: For individuals, Item 2 disclosure presents no real problem. The individual must disclose such basic items as name, business address, occupation, and whether the individual has ever been found in violation of specified laws. As to the latter point, Item 2 specifically requires disclosure of whether the filer, during the preceding five years, has been convicted in any criminal proceeding, excluding traffic violations or similar misdemeanors. If so, the filer must provide disclosure of the nature and date of the conviction, the name and location of the court, and any penalty imposed. Item 2 also requires disclosure of whether the filer, during the preceding five years, was the subject of a judgment or consent decree enjoining the filer from violating the securities laws in the future or finding a past of such laws.

For corporate parties things get more complicated. In addition to such basic items as identifying the state of incorporation and the like, Instruction C requires Item 2 disclosures with respect to each executive officer and director, and each controlling person. If the controlling person is itself a corporation, Item 2 disclosures are required with

---

10. Scott v. Multi–Amp Corp., 386 F.Supp. 44, 61 (D.N.J.1974); SEC v. GSC Enterprises, 469 F.Supp. 907, 914 (N.D.Ill. 1979).

11. See, e.g., Kamerman v. Steinberg, 123 F.R.D. 66, 72–73 (S.D.N.Y.1988) (denying motion for summary judgment on ground that a jury reasonably could find that weekend events should have been disclosed at the start of business on the following Monday).

respect to each intermediary corporation and each officer and director of the ultimate parent controlling corporation. Surprisingly, it is not clear whether Item 2 disclosures are required with respect to executive officer and director of intermediary corporations.

Item 4—Intent: Item 4 is the heart of any Schedule 13D and, along with deciding who is a member of the group, the source of most § 13(d) litigation. The instructions require disclosure of "any plans or proposals which the reporting persons may have which relate to or would result in" any of 9 specified actions or, in a tenth catch-all provision, any "action similar to any of those enumerated above." Among the enumerated actions are: (1) acquisition or disposition of the target's securities; (2) a merger or other extraordinary transaction involving the target or any of its subsidiaries; (3) a sale or transfer of a material amount of the target's assets; (4) changes in the composition of the target's board of directors or management; and so on. In addition to the numerous specifics required by the instructions to Item 4, courts have held that the reporting person must explicitly state whether it intends to seek or is considering seeking control of the issuer.[12]

In practice, Item 4 disclosures tend to be boilerplate and to throw in every possible purpose except the proverbial kitchen sink. The reporting person discloses what options it is considering, but buries its true intent in a lengthy statement of everything it might conceivably do someday. Although courts have occasionally criticized the kitchen sink approach, it remains the safest and most common form of Item 4 disclosure.

Item 6—Contracts and understandings: Item 6 requires disclosure of any contracts, arrangements, understandings, or relationships with respect to the securities of the issuer. At a minimum, Item 6 requires disclosure of the terms of an agreement or understanding among the members of a reporting group. If such an agreement has been reduced to writing, a copy of the agreement must be attached to the disclosure statement as an exhibit pursuant to Item 7.

C. Section 13(d) Litigation

Nobody likes to be fired, so it is hardly surprising that target directors and managers frequently resist unsolicited takeover bids. Among the most common takeover defenses is litigation under § 13(d), typically alleging some form of nondisclosure. Suppose Bidder filed a Schedule 13D disclosure document containing the following Item 4 disclosure: "Bidder has determined to make a large equity investment in Target. From time to time, as market conditions warrant in its view, Bidder may purchase or sell shares of Target's common stock on the

---

12. See, e.g., Dan River, Inc. v. Unitex Ltd., 624 F.2d 1216, 1226 n. 9 (4th Cir. 1980); Chromalloy American Corp. v. Sun Chem. Corp., 611 F.2d 240, 247 (8th Cir. 1979); SEC v. Amster & Co., 762 F.Supp. 604, 613–14 (S.D.N.Y.1991).

open market." Shortly before filing the initial schedule 13D, Bidder entered into a brokerage contract with a well known brokerage firm specializing in takeover stocks. The contract provides: (1) the broker will purchase up to 4.9% of Target's outstanding common stock; (2) Bidder will reimburse the broker for any losses suffered in connection with those acquisitions; and (3) the broker will pay over to Bidder any profits realized in connection with those acquisitions, less its usual brokerage fee plus an additional 5%, including any profits realized by tendering or otherwise selling the shares to Bidder. This so-called "parking" agreement was not disclosed in any of Bidder's filings. The target sues, alleging that Bidder violated § 13(d) by not disclosing the parking arrangement and by not adequately disclosing whether it intended to seek control of Target.

Obviously, the SEC has standing to prosecute violations of the tender offers rules. In a civil proceeding, the SEC may seek a variety of sanctions ranging from disgorgement of profits to corrective disclosures. To be sure, the SEC cannot conduct a criminal prosecution, but the SEC can refer cases to the Justice Department for criminal prosecution, as it frequently did in connection with the insider trading scandals of the 1980s.

Targets of an unsolicited offer frequently inform the SEC of alleged violations and ask that the SEC bring charges against the bidder. This is largely a pro forma act, as the SEC only rarely takes an aggressive posture in prosecuting § 13(d) violations. Instead, the target brings most § 13(d) litigation.

Standing presents the initial hurdle for private party litigation under § 13(d). More precisely, there are two distinct issues here, which all too often get bollixed up: (1) Is there an implied private right of action under § 13(d), at all? (2) Assuming that there is an implied private right of action under § 13(d), does this plaintiff have standing to assert that right of action in this case? As to the former question, most courts have found that there is an implied private right of action under § 13(d). As to the latter, we must bifurcate the inquiry. Do shareholders of the target corporation have standing under § 13(d)? Does the target corporation have standing under § 13(d)?

As for shareholder standing, most courts hold that shareholders have standing to seek injunctive but not monetary relief under § 13(d). As a result, shareholders generally cannot receive damages for § 13(d) violations.[13] Shareholders who wish to sue for false or misleading § 13(d) reports thus are relegated to the damage remedies provided by Securities Exchange Act § 18(a) and/or Rule 10b–5. Section 18(a) usually is of

---

13. See, e.g., Sanders v. Thrall Car Mfg. Co., 582 F.Supp. 945, 960–61 (S.D.N.Y. 1983), aff'd, 730 F.2d 910 (2d Cir.1984); Rosenbaum v. Klein, 547 F.Supp. 586, 591 (E.D.Pa.1982); Issen v. GSC Enterprises, Inc., 508 F.Supp. 1278, 1295 (N.D.Ill.1981); Myers v. American Leisure Time Enterprises, Inc., 402 F.Supp. 213, 214 (S.D.N.Y. 1975), aff'd mem., 538 F.2d 312 (2d Cir. 1976).

limited utility to investors. To recover under Section 18(a), an investor must show actual "eyeball" reliance on the false or misleading report, namely that the investor actually saw the report and relied on it.[14] This requirement has precluded the enforcement of claims under § 18(a) by class action, the only efficient means of litigating such claims. In addition, it can be difficult to show damages under § 18(a), because that section requires the misstatement to have affected the price of the securities (i.e., a causal nexus must be proven between the misrepresentation and the loss or diminishment of the plaintiff's investment).[15] Rule 10b–5 is also potentially available, but is of limited utility in this context because the investor must prove scienter and must be a purchaser or seller of the security.[16]

As for target corporations, they too lack standing to seek damages for § 13(d) violations.[17] Initially, federal courts almost uniformly granted issuers standing to seek injunctive relief under § 13(d).[18] In the oft-cited *Liberty National* case, however, the standing issue got bollixed up with the issue of allowable remedies. A bit of background on the latter issue is necessary. In *Rondeau v. Mosinee Paper Corp.*, the issuer brought suit for the defendant's failure to file a Schedule 13D. The Seventh Circuit granted an injunction that for a period of 5 years would have prevented the defendant from voting any shares purchased between the date when a Schedule 13D should have been filed and the date on which it was in fact filed. The Supreme Court reversed, on the grounds that the plaintiff had not shown such irreparable harm that a sterilizing injunction was appropriate. The Court suggested that less severe remedies might be available under appropriate fact settings, such as enjoining the defendant from voting, acquiring additional shares or commencing a takeover bid pending compliance.[19] Since *Rondeau*, however, courts finding a § 13(d) violation generally have been quite conservative in fashioning a remedy. Typically, they merely issue an order directing that the violation be cured, either by amending the filing or by filing a Schedule 13D not previously filed. Courts have been unwilling, in the belief that they are unauthorized, to grant more effective relief.[20]

14. See, e.g., Gross v. Diversified Mortgage Investors, 438 F.Supp. 190, 195 (S.D.N.Y.1977).

15. Cramer v. General Telephone & Elec., 443 F.Supp. 516, 525 (E.D.Pa.1977), aff'd, 582 F.2d 259 (3d Cir.1978).

16. See Ernst & Ernst v. Hochfelder, 425 U.S. 185, 193 (1976).

17. See, e.g., Hallwood Realty Partners, L.P. v. Gotham Partners, L.P., 286 F.3d 613 (2d Cir.2002) (holding that a target has no private cause of action for damages under § 13(d)).

18. See, e.g., Florida Commercial Banks v. Culverhouse, 772 F.2d 1513, 1519 n. 2

(11th Cir.1985) (citing cases in 1st, 2d, 4th, 7th, 8th and 9th Circuits); Portsmouth Square, Inc. v. Shareholders Protective Comm., 770 F.2d 866, 871 n. 8 (9th Cir. 1985); Gearhart Indus., Inc. v. Smith Int'l, Inc., 741 F.2d 707, 714 (5th Cir.1984).

19. Rondeau v. Mosinee Paper Corp., 422 U.S. 49 (1975).

20. See, e.g., Dan River, Inc. v. Icahn, 701 F.2d 278, 287 (4th Cir.1983) (court would not order "sterilization" of shares due to the prior insufficient disclosure); Treadway Companies, Inc. v. Care Corp., 638 F.2d 357, 380 (2d Cir.1980) (refusing an injunction where defective filing was

In *Liberty National*, the target corporation sought an aggressive equitable remedy ordering the bidder to divest all of its target stock holdings. In broad language, which lay extensive emphasis on the conflict of interest between target corporation managers and shareholders in the hostile takeover setting, the Eleventh Circuit held that "no cause of action under section 13(d) exists *for the relief Liberty requests*."[21] Notice how the court blurred three distinct inquiries: the existence of a cause of action; standing of the party at bar; and the remedy being sought. Instructively, a subsequent Eleventh Circuit decision limited *Liberty National* to the relief being sought. Where the target corporation sought only corrective disclosure, the target corporation had standing.[22]

§ 6.4 Tender Offer Disclosure and Procedural Rules

The Williams Act's announced goal is protection of target shareholders.[23] Disclosure provided the principal vehicle by which this goal was to be achieved; consequently, the Act imposes substantial disclosure requirements on both target management and the bidder.[24] To be sure, the Williams Act also provides a number of procedural protections for shareholders. In general, however, the Act's procedural requirements mainly serve to make the disclosure requirements more effective, as they generally "require or prohibit certain acts so that investors will possess additional time within which to take advantage of the disclosed information."[25]

Accordingly, the bidder must disseminate a Schedule 14D–1 disclosure statement containing, among other things, information relating to the bidder's identity, the source of its funds and any plans to merge with or otherwise make material changes in the target if the bid is successful.

---

cured and "shareholders had ample time to digest th[e] information"); Chromalloy American Corp. v. Sun Chemical Corp., 611 F.2d 240, 248–49 (8th Cir.1979) (court would not require "cooling-off" period after submission of corrected Schedule 13D); Energy Ventures, Inc. v. Appalachian Co., 587 F.Supp. 734, 743–44 (D.Del.1984) (interim injunctive relief deemed inappropriate where corrective filing had been made); University Bank & Trust Co. v. Gladstone, 574 F.Supp. 1006, 1010 (D.Mass.1983) (injunction denied where purchaser had made curative disclosure). A rare exception authorized disgorgement in a parking case brought by the SEC. SEC v. First City Fin. Corp., Ltd., 890 F.2d 1215 (D.C.Cir.1989).

21. Liberty Nat'l Ins. Holding Co. v. Charter Co., 734 F.2d 545, 567 (11th Cir. 1984) (emphasis supplied).

22. Florida Commercial Banks v. Culverhouse, 772 F.2d 1513, 1519 (11th Cir. 1985).

23. S. Rep. No. 550, 90th Cong., 1st Sess. 3 (1967); H.R. Rep. No. 1711, 90th Cong., 2d Sess. 3 (1968). See also Rondeau v. Mosinee Paper Corp., 422 U.S. 49, 58 (1975). The extent to which the Williams Act's requirements actually protect target shareholders has been a matter of considerable debate. See, e.g., Daniel R. Fischel, Efficient Capital Market Theory, the Market for Corporate Control, and the Regulation of Cash Tender Offers, 57 Tex. L. Rev. 1 (1978).

24. See Schreiber v. Burlington Northern, Inc., 472 U.S. 1, 8 (1985) ("It is clear that Congress relied primarily on disclosure to implement the purpose of the Williams Act."); see also Piper v. Chris–Craft Indus., 430 U.S. 1, 28 (1977).

25. Schreiber v. Burlington Northern, Inc., 472 U.S. 1, 9 (1985).

If all or part of the tender offer price is to be paid in the form of securities, rather than purely in cash, the bidder likely also will be required to incorporate a Securities Act registration statement in its offering materials and to generally comply with the Securities Act and state blue sky laws on offering securities. Similarly, if the company makes a tender offer for its own shares, it is subject to a series of SEC rules under Exchange Act § 13(e) that basically track the disclosure and procedural rules applicable to third-party tender offers under §§ 14(d) and 14(e).

A. Definition of Tender Offer

Although the Williams Act establishes an extensive regulatory scheme governing tender offers, the Act never actually defines what constitutes a tender offer subject to the statute and the rules thereunder. The obvious rationale for this failure was a desire on the part of Congress and the SEC to retain regulatory flexibility to deal with novel transactions that might fall outside the scope of a statutory definition, while still raising the same regulatory concerns as covered transactions.

Nobody doubts that the Williams Act applies to "conventional" tender offers, which might be defined as: A public offer to purchase at a specified price and terms during a specified period of time all or part of a class or classes of securities of a publicly held corporation. But what about privately negotiated block purchases or secondary market purchases, as well as other "unconventional" acquisition techniques?

The issue arose during the 1970s and 1980s in connection with two stock purchase techniques: the creeping tender offer and the street sweep. The term "creeping tender offer" is actually a misnomer. The bidder never makes a conventional tender offer. Rather, the bidder directly purchases a sufficient number shares on the open market to give it effective control over the target. Once the bidder has working control over the target, it then effects a merger with the target in order to solidify its control and to eliminate remaining minority shareholders.

In contrast, a street sweep begins with a conventional tender offer that is subsequently withdrawn. The tactic was devised to take advantage of the takeover arbitrageur phenomenon. Arbitrageurs seek profit by buying target company stock on the open market and subsequently tendering the stock to the bidder at the higher tender offer price. Risk averse target shareholders commonly are prompted to sell by the price increase that generally follows announcement of a tender offer. Arbitrageurs, who are willing to take the risk that the deal will not go forward, therefore can acquire substantial blocks of the target's stock. In a street sweep, the nominal bidder withdraws the tender offer and purchases a controlling block of target shares directly from arbitrageurs through open market or privately negotiated transactions. In *Hanson Trust PLC v. SCM Corp.*,[26] for example, Hanson (and affiliated companies) launched a tender offer for all outstanding shares of SCM. After Hanson terminated the tender offer in response to defensive moves by SCM, Hanson made five privately negotiated and one open market purchase from arbitrageurs, totaling 25% of SCM's outstanding common stock.

To determine whether these types of transactions should be deemed tender offers—and thereby subject to § 14(d) and the underlying rules— courts have frequently looked to the eight factors of the so-called *Wellman* test:

> (1) active and widespread solicitation of public shareholders; (2) for a substantial percentage of the issuer's stock; (3) at a premium over the prevailing market price; (4) offer terms fixed, rather than negotiable; (5) offer contingent on the tender of a fixed minimum or limited to a maximum number of shares to be purchased; (6) offer open for only a limited time period; (7) offeree subjected to pressure to sell; and (8) public announcement of a purchasing program preceding or accompanying a rapid accumulation of a large amount of the target's securities.[27]

Not all factors need be present for a transaction to be deemed a tender offer. Indeed, one may not even need a majority to be present, as the court emphasized that identifying the determinative factors is to be done on a case-by-case basis. Having said that, however, the factors that usually seem most important are publicity and pressure to sell. These

---

26. Hanson Trust PLC v. SCM Corp., 774 F.2d 47 (2d Cir.1985).

27. Wellman v. Dickinson, 475 F.Supp. 783, 823 (S.D.N.Y.1979), aff'd on other grounds, 682 F.2d 355 (2d Cir.1982). Note that Rule 10b–13 prohibits a bidder from making open market or private purchases of target stock during the pendency of a tender offer. Under the rule, a bidder may purchase target stock prior to commencing the tender offer. See, e.g., Heine v. Signal Companies, Inc., [1976–77 Transfer Binder] Fed.Sec.L.Rep. (CCH) ¶ 95,898, 1977 WL 930 (S.D.N.Y.1977) (delaying announcement of a self-tender offer in order to purchase a block of its shares in a privately negotiated transaction did not violate the rule; inter alia, because Signal had obtained a no-action letter from the SEC staff in connection with the proposed series of transactions). Likewise, entering into option agreements to purchase target shares prior to the commencement of a tender offer should not violate the rule, provided the option period does not extend into the tender offer period, since the rule does not prohibit such arrangements until the ten-

der offer period begins to run. Rule 10b–13 obviously will not affect a bidder's ability to conduct a creeping tender offer; it is simply inapplicable to acquisition contests not involving a tender offer. In contrast, the rule will somewhat affect street sweeps: while the initial tender offer is pending, it will prohibit a bidder from entering into arrangements for the private post-offer purchases from arbitrageurs and other shareholders of the target. Its impact on street sweeps, however, is likely to be minimal. In the first instance, it may be difficult to detect and prove the existence of such arrangements. More importantly, bidders and arbitrageurs have demonstrated an ability to come to terms very quickly following the conclusion of a tender offer. For example, in six transactions over a two hour period on the same day that its tender offer was withdrawn Hanson Trust was able to acquire 3.1 million SCM shares (representing approximately 25% of those outstanding). As long as bidders and arbitrageurs are able to move that rapidly, the strictures of Rule 10b–13 will not significantly impede them.

are the factors that make a purchase program most look like a tender offer.

The ambiguity inherent in the *Wellman* test has not precluded its widespread use. Although the SEC has not formally adopted the *Wellman* test, the SEC enforcement staff developed the test for use in litigation and the SEC staff has often urged its adoption by the courts on a case-by-case basis.[28] The Ninth Circuit, for example, relied on the *Wellman* test in determining that a creeping tender offer by Carter Hawley Hale was not a tender offer within the meaning of the Act.[29]

In *Hanson Trust*, however, the Second Circuit called the validity of the *Wellman* test into question, arguing that a "mandatory 'litmus test'" appears to be both unwise and unnecessary."[30] The issue at bar was whether a street sweep constituted a tender offer subject to the disclosure and procedural mandates of the Williams Act. After Hanson's rapid block purchases following the termination of its tender offer, SCM sought injunctive relief, including enjoining Hanson from acquiring additional shares or voting the shares it held, alleging that Hanson's block purchases were a tender offer in violation of § 14. In lieu of the *Wellman* factors, the Second Circuit invoked the guidelines used to determine whether an offering of securities is eligible for the private placement exemption under Securities Act § 4(1). As such, the main issue is whether the offerees are sophisticated investors who do not need the Williams Act's protections. Applying that standard, the court determined that Hanson Trust's street sweep was neither a new tender offer nor a "de facto" continuation of the withdrawn tender offer. The offerees from whom Hanson Trust bought were all professional investors fully capable of looking out for themselves.

B. Commencement of a Tender Offer

Determining when a tender offer commences is critical for several reasons. For one thing, it tells the bidder when its disclosure obligation triggers. For another, many tender offer rules contain time periods that run from the commencement date. Rule 14d–2 governs the commencement of a tender offer. It identifies two basic events that may constitute the commencement of a tender offer; whichever event takes place first in a particular offer will be the commencement date for that offer. Under Rule 14d–2(a), publishing or transmitting offering materials to the shareholders commences the offer. Under Rule 14a–2(b), subject to a

28. David J. Segre, Open–Market and Privately Negotiated Purchase Programs and the Market for Corporate Control, 42 Bus. Law. 715, 727 (1987).

29. The offer in question actually was a defensive stock purchase program effected on the secondary market by the target company for its own stock—a creeping self-tender offer, if you will. SEC v. Carter Hawley Hale Stores, Inc., 760 F.2d 945 (9th Cir.1985).

30. Hanson Trust PLC v. SCM Corp., 774 F.2d 47, 57 (2d Cir.1985).

limited exception, any public announcement of takeover plans commences the offer. Hence, if the bidder discloses such information as its identity, the target's identity, the amount of securities it will offer to buy, and the price it is willing to pay—the bidder has just commenced the tender offer. Pre-offer communications are exempted if they (1) do not identify the means by which target shareholders may tender their stock and (2) all written communications are filed with the SEC and issuer.

C. Content of Required Disclosure

On the day the offer commences, the bidder must file a disclosure document on Schedule 14D–1 with the SEC. Most of the information contained in the Schedule 14D–1 also must be disseminated to the target's shareholders, but the Williams Act gives the offeror two options as to how to effect that distribution. The first, and least used option, is so-called long-form publication of the offer in a newspaper. Typically one prepares an advertisement containing all the necessary disclosures and then runs the ad in the Wall Street Journal, New York Times and perhaps one or two other papers of national distribution. This option is unpopular because it is extremely expensive to buy the necessary ad space and, more important, because there is no guarantee that a substantial number of target shareholders will notice the ad or pay much attention to it.

Alternatively, and more commonly, the offeror publishes a summary of the proposal in a newspaper advertisement and then mails a more detailed disclosure statement directly to the shareholders. Although this option is probably at least as expensive as the first, if not more so, there is a fair degree of certainty that all target shareholders will receive notice of the proposal by this means. As with a proxy statement, the issuer must either provide the bidder with a copy of the shareholder list or agree to mail the tender offer materials on behalf of the offeror and at his or her expense.

Most of the disclosures in a tender offer are similar to those required in a Schedule 13D, albeit more detailed, and are fairly mechanical. Counsel just follows the instructions, inserting the usual boilerplate. The most technically difficult issue is the question of soft information disclosure. Consider two companies: Target Corp. and Acquirer Co. Suppose that Target's stock currently is trading at $15 per share. Acquirer does an extensive evaluation of Target. Acquirer prepares business plans for incorporating Target into the existing company, it commissions appraisals of Target's assets, it prepares projections of future income and operating results, and the like. At the end of this process, Acquirer determines on a reservation price of $25 per share. In other words, Acquirer concludes that an acquisition of Target would be profitable at any price up to $25 per share. Clearly, Acquirer is not obliged to disclose its actual reservation price. But what about the appraisals and forecasts from which that price was determined? Must they be disclosed?

Historically, disclosure of soft information was disfavored. In recent years, the SEC has adopted safe harbor rules permitting disclosure of certain soft information, such as appraisals and projections.[31] Because that rule does not mandate disclosure, however, it does not resolve the question at hand. Note that the issue here is different from the run of the mill omissions case under the securities laws, where the initial issue is whether the defendant had a duty to speak. In this context, the bidder has an affirmative obligation to file a Schedule 14D–1 containing significant disclosures. The question here therefore is whether the soft information in question is material, such that it also must be disclosed. Before the Third Circuit's decision in *Flynn v. Bass Brothers*,[32] most courts held that there is no affirmative duty to disclose soft information. In other words, the failure to disclose soft information was not regarded as a material omission. In *Flynn*, however, the Third Circuit held that courts must make a case-by-case determination of whether soft information, such as asset appraisals and projections of future earnings are material. The standard to be applied is whether the benefits to the shareholders will outweigh the harm to the shareholders. The factors the court will consider include: the qualifications of those who prepared the information; the purpose for which it was intended; its relevance to the decision; the degree of subjectivity in its preparation; the degree to which the information is unique; and the availability of other more reliable sources of information.

What rule would a diversified investor prefer? Returning to the hypothetical developed above, assume the pre-announcement market price for Target's stock was $15. Assume that Acquirer's appraisal predicts that the deal will be profitable at any price up to $25. The total gain from this transaction is $10 per share: the difference between what the stock is currently trading at and the maximum price Acquirer is willing to pay. Obviously Acquirer doesn't want to pay more than $25 per share. It should be equally obvious that Acquirer would like to pay less than $25 per share. The issue then is how we will divide up the gain from the transaction between the Target shareholders and Acquirer. If Acquirer is forced to disclose the soft information on which its reservation price is premised, several bad things happen: Target shareholders will have a better sense of the company is worth to Acquirer and therefore will demand a higher price. Target might itself adopt any value-enhancing ideas disclosed by Acquirer or use the disclosures as a means of persuading competing bidders to enter the picture.

31. The relevant Securities Exchange Act rule is Rule 3b–6.

32. Flynn v. Bass Bros. Enterprises, Inc., 744 F.2d 978, 988 (3d Cir.1984).

Disclosure thus forces the bidder to share information its worked to acquire, resulting in a transfer of wealth from the first bidder to target shareholders and/or subsequent bidders. This wealth transfer discourages prospective bidders from investing in takeover activity, reducing the overall number of takeovers. Put another way, the lower the bidder's return, the lower the level of investment. Mandatory disclosure thus results in fewer deals but higher prices in those that take place. Once again, we are required to determine whether diversified investors are better off with a rule that maximizes the control premium in a given case or a rule that maximizes the number of takeovers. As before, some scholars argue that, because a diversified investor is as likely to be a shareholder of Acquirer as of Target, such an investor should be indifferent to how takeover gains are distributed. Instead, such an investor should prefer a rule maximizing the number of deals, which in this context is a rule permitting acquirers to withhold soft information.

This analysis depends in the first instance on an assumption that the rules of the takeover game ought to be drafted without regard for their effect on nondiversified investors. This assumption is admittedly controversial,[33] but seems a logical extension of portfolio theory. The risk of being on the "wrong" side of a takeover is akin to the risk of owning stock in a company whose sole line of business is outlawed. In other words, it is an unsystematic risk, which the investor could eliminate through diversification. Accordingly, portfolio theory posits, investors need not—and should not—be compensated for voluntarily assuming nondiversified unsystematic risk. Because mutual funds and similar investments offer readily available opportunities for diversification at low cost, the law should not create special protections for investors who refuse to protect themselves by diversifying. Put another way, just as the tort law doctrine of assumption of risk bars recovery, the law should treat nondiversified investors as having "assumed the risk." Where a rule would benefit nondiversified investors at the expense of those who have diversified, the case for protecting the former seems particularly weak.

Conceding that we ought to privilege diversification, however, does not resolve the debate. As before, the analysis may change if certain conditions are not satisfied. If acquirers are systematically more likely to be privately held than are targets, for example, rational diversified investors could prefer a rule maximizing premiums. More important, if rational diversified investors believe that acquirer company boards and managers will fritter away the gains of takeovers in ways that do not benefit their shareholders, such investors may prefer to maximize cash

---

33. See, e.g., Victor Brudney, Equal Treatment of Shareholders in Corporate Distributions and Reorganizations, 71 Cal. L. Rev. 1072, 1100 n.85 (1983) ("The morality of a proposal which requires investors to diversify in order to protect themselves against the appropriative behavior of controllers, but which does not seek to prevent the appropriative behavior itself, is not self-evident.").

in hand. Recall the evidence that acquiring company shareholders on average do not gain from takeovers, which suggests that such frittering occurs. If so, rational investors will prefer a rule that maximizes the product of the number of deals and the average premium over rules that maximize one at the expense of the other. This analysis suggests a slightly different balancing test than the one adopted in *Flynn*. The appropriate balancing test weighs the "potential aid such information will give a shareholder" against the extent of the acquirer's proprietary interest in the information.

D. Procedural Rules

In addition to the basic disclosure provisions, the Williams Act provides a number of procedural protections for target shareholders. For example, shareholders are permitted to withdraw shares tendered to the bidder at any time prior to the closing of the offer. In Section 14(d)(5), the statute actually provides that tendered shares may only be withdrawn during the 7 days after the offer commences and at any time 60 days after commencement of the bid (assuming that the offer has not been closed and the shares taken up during that 60–day period). SEC Rule 14d–7, however, permits withdrawal for up to 15 days after commencement of the offer. The rule triggers withdrawal rights if a competing bid is made during the tender offer period. Shareholders thus have substantial opportunity to change their minds, especially if a better offer comes along.

Rule 14e–1 obligates the bidder to keep the tender offer open for at least 20 business days. In addition, the bidder must further extend the tender offer period by at least 10 business days after material changes in the offer's terms. In particular, the bidder must extend the offer by 10 days if it raises the offering price.

In partial tender offers, if more than the specified number of shares are tendered Rule 14d–8 requires the offeror to take up the tendered shares on a pro rata basis. This ensures that all shareholders who tender get a chance to receive a premium for at least part of their shares. The rule eliminates a favorite pre-Williams Act tactic, in which bidders made a partial offer on a first come-first served basis. This tactic pressures shareholders to tender, so as to avoid being left as minority shareholders in a company under new control. To eliminate a similar tactic, Rule 14d–10 provides that if the bidder, during the pendency of the offer, increases the consideration to be paid, shareholders who have already tendered their shares are entitled to receive that additional consideration.

E. Registration of Securities Issued in an Exchange Offer

An exchange offer is a tender offer in which the some or all of the consideration is paid in the form of stock or other securities instead of cash. Typically, the target's shareholders exchange their shares of target stock for stock or debt securities issued by the acquiring company, although other securities or property can also be used.

Securities Act § 2(3) of the 1933 Act broadly defines the terms "sale" or "sell" to "include every contract of sale or disposition of a security or interest in a security, for value." Since its adoption in 1933, this definition has encompassed exchange offers. Some private stock for stock (or other security) transfers may qualify for one of the exemptions for registration. A stock for security exchange effected pursuant to a public tender offer is unlikely to qualify for any of the exemptions and the securities issued in the transaction therefore must be registered.

As originally adopted in 1968, the Williams Act did not apply to exchange offers. The Act was intended to close a loophole in which proxy contests and exchange offers were subject to federal regulation under the Securities Exchange Act proxy rules and Securities Act registration requirements, respectively, while cash tender offers were unregulated. In 1970, however, the Act was amended to apply to both cash and exchange offers. Accordingly, an acquirer now must comply with the disclosure and procedural rules under both statutory schemes.

F. Target Obligations

As long as they are acting in good faith, the target's directors have no legal duty to negotiate with a prospective acquirer. The target's board likewise has no duty to make a detailed response to hypothetical questions or hypothetical offers. Once a firm, bona fide offer is on the table, however, the target's board has a state corporate law-based fiduciary obligation to consider carefully the proposed acquisition.[34] To be sure, the business judgment rule "leaves relatively wide discretion in management to act in what it considers to be the best interests of the corporation."[35] Recall, however, that an informed decision is an essential prerequisite for the rule's application.[36]

---

34. See, e.g., Norlin Corp. v. Rooney, Pace Inc., 744 F.2d 255, 267 (2d Cir.1984) ("we have required corporate managers to examine carefully the merits of a proposed change in control ... [and] have also urged consultation with investment specialists in undertaking such analysis.... [t]he purpose of this exercise ... is to insure a reasoned examination of the situation before action is taken, not afterwards"); Smith v. Van Gorkom, 488 A.2d 858, 872 (Del.1985) ("Representation of the financial interests of others imposes on a director an affirmative duty to protect those interests and to proceed with a critical eye in assessing information of the type and under the circumstances present....").

35. Berman v. Gerber Products Co., 454 F.Supp. 1310, 1319 (W.D.Mich.1978).

36. Smith v. Van Gorkom, 488 A.2d 858, 872 (Del.1985) (directors must inform themselves of "all material information reasonably available to them"). Depending on the circumstances, the views of non-management directors with regard to any proposal may be given particular weight. See Panter v. Marshall Field & Co., 646 F.2d 271, 294 (7th Cir.1981) ("The presumption of good faith the business judgment rule affords is heightened when the majority of the board consists of independent outside directors.").

In evaluating a bona fide proposal, the following factors are legitimate and relevant considerations:

1. The adequacy of the offering price in terms of variables such as (i) current and past market prices of the target's stock,[37] (ii) book value and replacement cost of assets, (iii) earnings projections, (iv) "hidden" or off balance sheet assets, (v) future prospects for improvements in earnings or market value, (vi) market conditions, (vii) liquidation value of assets, (viii) if all shares are sought, the potential sales price of the business (a full financial picture of the target should be prepared), (ix) recent sales prices of other similarly situated companies, (x) premiums over book value paid in recent "friendly" acquisitions and hostile takeovers of other similar companies, and (xi) the probability that a higher price could be obtained from another offeror.

2. The nature of the consideration offered, e.g., cash or securities (and, if securities, the prospects of the company to which they relate).

3. Whether the acquirer is seeking all or a portion of the target stock; if a partial offer, the effect upon remaining shareholders, i.e., what generally would be the prospects for the minority in the case of a successful partial offer, and in particular, whether there would be a subsequent merger and if so, on what terms.[38]

4. If applicable, the regulatory implications of the offer and the likelihood that the suitor could obtain regulatory approvals.

5. The offeror's background, business practices and intention towards the company.

The latter two considerations are especially pertinent with respect to the target board's potential duty to affirmatively oppose an offer. Where the directors know or have reason to know that a potential acquirer would loot or mismanage the target company, for example, they have a duty to

---

37. In evaluating the adequacy of an offer, the mere fact that a target's shares may trade below the offer price does not mean that the price was sufficient, since the ordinary trading market does not reflect the target's value in an acquisition. The proper comparison is not between the price of the stock in the market and the offer price, but rather between the offer price and the price that could otherwise be obtained upon a sale of the entire company. As the Delaware supreme court has noted, "[a] substantial premium may provide one reason to recommend a merger, but in the absence of other sound valuation information, the fact of a premium alone does not provide an adequate basis upon which to assess the fairness of an offering price.... [Because] the Board had made no evalua-

tion of the Company designed to value the entire enterprise, nor had the Board ever previously considered selling the Company or consenting to a buy-out merger ... the adequacy of a premium is indeterminate unless it is assessed in terms of other competent and sound valuation information that reflects the value of the particular business." Smith v. Van Gorkom, 488 A.2d 858, 875–76 (Del.1985).

38. For example, the directors should consider the likely market liquidity of the shares held by the remaining shareholders, and whether this is the first step in a "freeze-out" of the minority in light of Weinberger v. UOP, Inc., 457 A.2d 701 (Del.1983).

oppose the offer.[39] Likewise, where the target's directors believe that an offer is illegal for regulatory reasons, they also have a duty to oppose it.[40]

Where the initial offer by the suitor includes an invitation to negotiate, the directors of the target may enter into negotiations if they so choose, of course. Negotiation may disclose useful information, as well as providing the target company more time to evaluate and respond to the situation. The target company may condition its willingness to enter into negotiations on the suitor's agreement not to make an unfriendly offer. On the other hand, there are several potential disadvantages to entering into negotiations with an unwanted suitor. Negotiating could also give the suitor the impression that an offer might be accepted if the terms were different. This could encourage the suitor to disbelieve management objections and to pursue its proposal persistently when it might otherwise withdraw. Any counter-offer made by the target could undermine subsequent arguments to shareholders attacking the suitor. If discussions included a consideration of management's or the directors' future with the target company, claims could be raised that management or directors received improper benefits.

If a tender offer is made, the Williams Act mandates a target board disclosure statement on Schedule 14D–9.[41] Before filing the Schedule 14D–9, the target may only send communications to its shareholders if those communications are limited to three matters: (i) identifying the offeror; (ii) stating that the target is studying the tender offer and will, before a specified date, advise as to its position; and (iii) requesting shareholders to defer making a determination on whether to accept or reject the tender offer until they have been advised of the target's position. Under SEC Rule 14e–2, the target must disclose to shareholders within 10 business days of the commencement of a tender offer whether the target's board: (i) recommends acceptance or rejection of the tender offer; (ii) expresses no opinion and is remaining neutral with respect to the tender offer; or (iii) is unable to take a position with respect to the tender offer. The statement also must include the board's reason or reasons for its position. Pursuant to Rule 14d–9(f), this communication is deemed to be a recommendation or solicitation and therefore requires the filing of Schedule 14D–9 with the SEC. The Schedule 14D–9 must disclose: (i) the reasons supporting the board's recommendations, (ii) any arrangements or understandings between members of management or the board and the offeror, (iii) the identity

39. Harman v. Willbern, 374 F.Supp. 1149, 1158–59 (D.Kan.1974), aff'd, 520 F.2d 1333 (10th Cir.1975).

40. Panter v. Marshall Field & Co., 646 F.2d 271, 297 (7th Cir.1981); Berman v. Gerber Products Co., 454 F.Supp. 1310, 1323 (W.D.Mich.1978).

41. Before the offer has actually commenced, the issue is whether a proposal is material information the target is required to disclose. In general, no announcement need be made of invitations to negotiate or of casual inquiries. Panter v. Marshall Field & Co., 646 F.2d 271, 296 (7th Cir.1981) ("Directors are under no duty to reveal every approach made by a would-be acquiror or merger partner.").

and employment capacity of the persons making the recommendations, and (iv) information as to all transactions by officers or directors effected during the 60 days prior to the filing of the Schedule 14D–9 in the securities that are the subject of the offer.

§ 6.5 Tender Offer Litigation

Tender offers generate a lot of litigation: the target sues the bidder; the bidder sues the target; target shareholders sue the target board and/or the bidder; the SEC sues the target and/or the bidder. It is a litigator's dream and a transactional lawyer's nightmare. None of the relevant statutes explicitly grant a cause of action to private parties. As with § 13(d) litigation, the questions therefore are (1) whether an implied private right of action exists and (2) if so, does the party in question have standing?

Over time, the United States Supreme Court has set out at least four distinct approaches to creating implied private rights of action:

1. The old *Borak* rule, under which the court creates an implied right of action whenever private enforcement of the statute is necessary to supplement SEC efforts.[42] Although *Borak* has not been expressly overruled, it has been effectively limited to the proxy setting.[43]

2. A four factor standard announced in *Cort*,[44] which asks: "First, is the plaintiff one of the class for whose especial benefit the statute was enacted ... ? Second, is there any indication of legislative intent, explicit or implicit, either to create such a remedy or to deny one? ... Third, is it consistent with the underlying purposes of the legislative scheme to imply such a remedy for the plaintiff? ... And finally, is the cause of action one traditionally relegated to state law, in an area basically the concern of the States, so that it would be inappropriate to infer a cause of action based solely on federal law?"[45]

3. The strict constructionist approach announced in *Touche Ross*, which mandates a very narrow focus on legislative intent.[46]

4. The legal context approach of *Curran*, also known as the re-enactment approach, which asks whether Congress has amended the statute in question without overruling judicial decisions creating an implied right of action under a federal statute.[47] If

---

42. J.I. Case Co. v. Borak, 377 U.S. 426 (1964).

43. See, e.g., Reschini v. First Fed. Sav. & Loan Ass'n of Ind., 46 F.3d 246, 255 (3d Cir.1995) (holding that *Borak* "is still good law as a construction of the 1934 Act and Rule 14a–9," but noting that "it is not clear that *Borak*, if it arose for the first time today, would be decided the same way").

44. Cort v. Ash, 422 U.S. 66 (1975).

45. California v. Sierra Club, 451 U.S. 287, 293 (1981).

46. Touche Ross & Co. v. Redington, 442 U.S. 560 (1979).

47. Merrill Lynch, Pierce, Fenner & Smith, Inc. v. Curran, 456 U.S. 353 (1982).

so, it will be assumed that Congress expressly intended to preserve the implied remedy.

Unfortunately, the only Supreme Court guidance on implied private rights of action under the Williams Act pre-dates the latter two approaches. In *Piper v. Chris–Craft*,[48] the Court addressed the standing of a defeated tender offeror to sue a successful competing bidder and the target for damages under § 14(e)'s antifraud provision. In late 1968, Chris–Craft mounted a takeover bid for Piper. The Piper board of directors enlisted Bangor–Punta as a white knight—a competing bidder more acceptable to the target's incumbent directors and managers. Bangor–Punta agreed to make an exchange offer, in which Piper shareholders would receive a package of Bangor–Punta securities in exchange for the Piper stock. By the time Bangor–Punta's competing offer commenced, Chris–Craft had already acquired about 13% of Piper's outstanding shares. Nevertheless, Bangor–Punta ultimately prevailed, acquiring just over 50% of the stock. Chris–Craft was left owning just over 40% of the shares. Chris–Craft sued Piper, its underwriter, and Bangor–Punta. Chris–Craft's main allegation was that Bangor–Punta listed a railroad as a subsidiary in a filing sent to Piper's shareholders in connection with the exchange offer. Chris–Craft alleged that Bangor–Punta failed to disclose that the railroad was about to be sold at a loss, which allegedly violated § 14(e)'s prohibition of fraud in connection with a tender offer. This nondisclosure allegedly caused Piper's shareholders to accept Bangor–Punta's offer in reliance on the inflated value given Bangor–Punta's fixed assets.

It is critical to your understanding of this case for you to understand the nature of the alleged injury at issue. Bear in mind that Chris–Craft ended up as the minority shareholder of Piper, with Bangor–Punta as the controlling shareholder. Chris–Craft, of course, had paid a substantial premium over market in buying its Piper shares. But once the Bangor–Punta offer succeeded, the value of Chris–Craft's Piper holdings fell sharply. As we know, the value of any share of stock reflects the market's consensus as to the present value of the bundle of rights conferred by stockownership. Among the relevant valuation factors are: the value of the stream of future dividends, voting rights, and the probability of future takeover attempts at a premium. The decline in value of Chris–Craft's holdings reflected two basic facts of takeover life: First, Bangor–Punta now had a controlling stock position, such that the voting rights of the minority shareholders were now essentially worthless. Second, since Bangor–Punta had a controlling stock position, nobody could obtain control by buying the rest of Piper's outstanding stock. Thus, the possibility of future takeover premiums was also lost.

The lower court held that Chris–Craft had a cause of action for damages against Bangor–Punta and Piper under § 14(e). The court

48.   430 U.S. 1 (1977).

measured the amount of Chris–Craft's damages by the difference between what Chris–Craft paid to buy its block and the much lower price Chris–Craft could have obtained by selling that block in a public offering immediately after Bangor–Punta obtained control, which worked out to about $37 per share. The Supreme Court reversed on standing grounds—defeated tender offerors lack standing to sue for damages arising out of a violation of § 14(e).

Two years before *Piper*, the Supreme Court had decided *Cort v. Ash*, in which it created a four factor test to be used by courts in creating new implied private rights of action. Post–*Piper* cases have purported to overrule *Cort*. As Justice Scalia has explained, the Court "effectively overruled the *Cort v. Ash* analysis in *Touche Ross* . . . and *Transamerica* . . . converting one of [*Cort's*] four factors (congressional intent) into the *determinative factor*."[49] Having said that, however, the other three *Cort* factors remain relevant insofar as they assist in determining congressional intent.[50] Consequently, it is still useful to analyze *Piper* by working through the original four factor test.

The first *Cort* factor asks whether plaintiff was part of the class for whose especial benefit the statute was enacted. Chris–Craft was a Piper shareholder—it started out owning about 13% and ended up owning over 40% of Piper's stock. Chris–Craft, however, was not the kind of shareholder that Congress wanted to protect. Congress was worried about public shareholders caught between the offeror and management. Congress was trying to regulate offerors for the benefit of independent shareholders. Chris–Craft was thus part of the regulated class, not the benefited class.

The second *Cort* factor, now deemed determinative, is whether there is any indication of a legislative intent, explicit or implicit, either to create or deny a remedy. The strongest argument for Chris–Craft's position thus is based on the claim that Congress intended the Williams Act to be neutral as between bidders and target management. In a frequently used analogy, Congress supposedly intended to preserve a "level playing field" between the contending parties. Hence, the argument went, Congress must have wanted the courts to let managers and bidders sue each other for violations of the statute so as to ensure that the competition is fair. In *Piper,* the Supreme Court acknowledged that Congress adopted a policy of neutrality as between bidders and target management, but said the neutrality policy has nothing to do with the protection of tender offerors or their standing to sue for violations of the statute. Rather, the neutrality policy was designed to help achieve the principal purpose of the Williams Act; namely, the protection of independent shareholders through a regime of full and fair disclosure by offer-

49. Thompson v. Thompson, 484 U.S. 174, 189 (1988) (Scalia, J., concurring) (emphasis in original).

50. Touche Ross & Co. v. Redington, 442 U.S. 560, 575–76 (1979).

ors. In addition, statements in the legislative history about the neutrality policy were intended to rebut criticisms that the legislation favored target management. Because Congress' intent was to regulate the previously unregulated conduct of bidders, however, it is hard to see why Congress would have wanted to give bidders an additional weapon. The whole point was to protect shareholders from offerors—not to enhance the rights of offerors.

The third *Cort* factor is whether it is consistent with the underlying purposes of the legislative scheme to imply such a remedy for the plaintiff. Chris–Craft lost on this point too. The court emphasized that it was difficult to accept the contention Chris–Craft's recovery would benefit the other Piper shareholders. Although a recovery would benefit the old Piper shareholders who are now shareholders of Chris–Craft, it would harm the larger group of old Piper shareholders who are now shareholders of Bangor–Punta and who would therefore bear the burden of the damages payment. The Supreme Court's argument made sense in this case, because the Bangor–Punta tender offer was an exchange offer in which the consideration was paid in the form of Bangor–Punta shares. Would the court's argument still make sense if Bangor–Punta had paid cash, such that the old Piper shareholders would not now be Bangor–Punta stockholders? Yes, although you lose the make-weight argument that a recovery would harm the majority of old Piper shareholders. The point is that a recovery by Chris–Craft would benefit Chris–Craft and Chris–Craft alone—this was not a class action brought to champion the rights of all Piper shareholders.[51] This was a lawsuit arising out of the fact that Chris–Craft was stuck with a minority position and had lost the difference between the price it paid for Piper stock and the present value of Piper shares. Thus, even if Bangor–Punta's offer had been for cash, a Chris–Craft recovery would not have benefited the old Piper shareholders.

The fourth *Cort* factor is whether the cause of action is one traditionally relegated to state law. The Supreme Court held that granting Chris–Craft a cause of action on these facts would be tantamount to creation of a federal cause of action for tortious interference with a prospective commercial advantage. This cause of action has traditionally been a matter of state tort law. Hence, so offerors should be relegated to their state law remedies, if any, until Congress acts.

So on all the relevant factors, Chris–Craft lost. Hence, the Court held, there is no standing for tender offerors for damages. As one might

---

51. Chris–Craft could not have brought its suit as a class action on behalf of all Piper shareholders, because nobody but Chris–Craft was injured. The shareholders who sold to Chris–Craft got a premium from Chris–Craft, and in any event obviously didn't rely on the alleged misstatements. The shareholders who sold to Piper also weren't injured—selling the railroad at a loss caused the value of their new Bangor–Punta shares to rise, not fall. The shareholders who didn't sell to either side also weren't injured, as there is nothing to suggest that the misstatement caused them to hold on to their shares.

expect, lower courts have extended *Piper* to preclude standing by target companies to bring an implied private right of action for damages under all of the applicable statutes. In doing so, they have relied mainly on *Piper*'s emphasis on the notion that target managers and bidders were part of the regulated class, not the special class benefited by the statute. As for shareholders, the majority rule denies damages standing to target shareholders under virtually all provisions except § 14(e). As with § 13(d) litigation, all three relevant players—bidders, targets, and target shareholders—generally have been given standing to bring an implied private right of action for equitable relief under all of the Williams Act's various provisions.

The distinction between equitable and damage remedies makes sense. Since *Borak*, the basic justification for implied private rights of action has been the concept of private attorneys general. As Chris–Craft argued, defeated bidders have a special interest in uncovering violations. Consequently, granting Chris–Craft standing to bring a cause of action will benefit shareholders by furthering enforcement of the federal securities laws. Yet, while deterrence is desirable, it ought to be achieved in an efficient manner. Deterrence is a function of the nominal sanction imposed and the probability of detection and conviction. When detection is costly or difficult and hence unlikely, the nominal sanction must increase to compensate and effect deterrence. In the case of Williams Act violations, the probability of detection is relatively high. The offeror must file with the SEC and both target and bidder have plenty of incentive to look for illegal conduct. Consequently, the nominal sanction does not need to be very large in order for there to be adequate levels of deterrence. Indeed, if the sanction is large in these cases you may have over-deterrence—you may deter beneficial conduct that falls close to the line between legal and illegal actions. If we think takeovers, especially takeovers in which there is competitive bidding, are a good thing, we don't want too much deterrence. This principle explains why damage relief is uniformly denied—the courts, following the Supreme Court's lead in *Piper*, must believe that damage penalties would create too high a level of deterrence. Conversely, if one side is free to lie and cheat, subject only to the risk of SEC enforcement, the level playing field may tip in that party's favor. Injunctive relief—especially when limited to corrective disclosure—seems like a fairly nonintrusive means of helping to maintain the level playing field envisioned by the Act. The party with the most incentive to seek legal relief will be given an opportunity to prevent misstatements and other violations, while not creating excessive levels of deterrence.

In any event, having identified who has standing to seek what remedies for violations of the tender offer statutes, the obvious next task is identifying the elements of the cause of action. The elements of the injunctive action are essentially the same as those for injunctive relief under the proxy rules—assuming you can show the traditional grounds for equitable relief, all you have to show is that the defendant failed to file a required document or that the defendant's filing contains a material misstatement or omission.

§ 6.6 Insider Trading and Tender Offers

If you know of an impending takeover prior to its announcement, you can buy up stock at the low pre-announcement price and sell or tender at the higher post-announcement price. The earlier one knows of the bid, of course, the greater the spread between your purchase and sale prices and the greater the resulting profit. By using options, rather than actually buying target stock, you can further increase your profits, because options permit one to control larger blocks of stock for the same investment. If you succumb to the temptation to do so, however, you will run up against the federal prohibition of insider trading.

The modern federal insider trading prohibition began taking form in *SEC v. Texas Gulf Sulphur Co.*[52] *TGS*, as it is commonly known, rested on a policy of equality of access to information. Accordingly, under *TGS* and its progeny, virtually anyone who possessed material nonpublic information was required either to disclose it before trading or abstain from trading in the affected company's securities. If the would-be trader's fiduciary duties precluded him from disclosing the information prior to trading, abstention was the only option.

In *Chiarella v. United States*[53] and *Dirks v. SEC*,[54] however, the United States Supreme Court rejected the equal access policy. Instead, the Court made clear that liability could be imposed only if the defendant was subject to a duty to disclose prior to trading. Inside traders thus were no longer liable merely because they had more information than other investors in the market place. Instead, a duty to disclose only arose where the inside traders breached a pre-existing fiduciary duty owed to the person with whom they traded.[55]

---

52. 401 F.2d 833 (2d Cir.1968), cert. denied, 394 U.S. 976 (1969).

53. 445 U.S. 222 (1980).

54. 463 U.S. 646 (1983).

55. Creation of this fiduciary duty element substantially narrowed the scope of the disclose or abstain rule. But the rule remains quite expansive in a number of respects. In particular, it is not limited to true insiders, such as officers, directors, and controlling shareholders, but picks up corporate outsiders in two important ways. Even in these situations, however, liability for insider trading under the disclose or abstain rule can only be found where the trader—insider or outsider—violates a fiduciary duty owed to the issuer or the person on the other side of the transaction.

First, the rule can pick up a wide variety of nominal outsiders whose relationship with the issuer is sufficiently close to the issuer of the affected securities to justify treating them as "constructive insiders," but only in rather narrow circumstances. The outsider must obtain material nonpublic information from the issuer. The issuer must expect the outsider to keep the disclosed information confidential. Finally, the relationship must at least imply such a duty. If these conditions are met, the putative outsider will be deemed a "constructive insider" and subjected to the disclose or abstain rule in full measure. See *Dirks*, 463 U.S. at 655 n.14. If they are not met, however, the disclose or abstain rule simply does not apply. The critical issue thus re-

Chiarella and *Dirks* created significant gaps in the insider trading prohibition's coverage. Consider this standard law school hypothetical: A law firm is hired by Raider Corporation to represent it in connection with a planned takeover bid for Target Company. Ann Associate is one of the lawyers assigned to the project. Before Raider publicly discloses its intentions, Associate purchases a substantial block of Target stock. Under the disclose or abstain rule, she has not violated the insider trading prohibition. Whatever the scope of the duties she owed Raider, she owed no duty to the shareholders of Target. Accordingly, the requisite breach of fiduciary duty is not present in her transaction. Rule 14e–3 and the misappropriation theory were created to fill this gap.

A. Rule 14e–3

Rule 14e–3 was the SEC's immediate response to *Chiarella*.[56] The Rule was specifically intended to reach the wave of insider trading activity associated with the increase in merger and acquisition activity during the 1980s. The rule prohibits insiders of the bidder and target from divulging confidential information about a tender offer to persons that are likely to violate the rule by trading on the basis of that information. This provision (Rule 14e–3(d)(1)) does not prohibit the bidder from buying target shares or from telling its legal and financial advisers about its plans. What the rule prohibits is tipping of information to persons who are likely to buy target shares for their own account. In particular, the rule was intended to strike at the practice known as warehousing. Anecdotal evidence suggests that before Rule 14–3 was on the books bidders frequently tipped their intentions to friendly parties. Warehousing increased the odds a hostile takeover bid would succeed by increasing the number of shares likely to support the bidder's proposal.

Rule 14e–3 also, with certain narrow and well-defined exceptions, prohibits any person that possesses material information relating to a

---

mains the nature of the relationship between the parties.

Second, the rule also picks up outsiders who receive inside information from either true insiders or constructive insiders. There are a number of restrictions on tippee liability, however. Most important for present purposes, the Supreme Court explained in *Dirks* that a tippee's liability is derivative of the tipper's, "arising from his role as a participant after the fact in the insider's breach of a fiduciary duty." As a result, the mere fact of a tip is not sufficient to result in liability. What is proscribed is not merely a breach of confidentiality by the insider, but rather a breach of the duty of loyalty imposed on all fiduciaries to avoid personally profiting from information entrusted to

them. Thus, looking at objective criteria, the courts must determine whether the insider personally will benefit, directly or indirectly, from his disclosure. So once again, a breach of fiduciary duty is essential for liability to be imposed: a tippee can be held liable only when the tipper has breached a fiduciary duty by disclosing information to the tippee, and the tippee knows or has reason to know of the breach of duty.

56. 17 C.F.R. § 240.14e–3. In fact, Rule 14e–3 was pending at the time *Chiarella* was decided, see Chiarella v. United States, 445 U.S. 222, 234 n. 18 (1980), almost as though the Commission knew that its attempts to reach warehousing of takeover securities under Rule 10b–5 were of questionable validity.

tender offer by another person from trading in target company securities if the bidder has commenced or has taken substantial steps towards commencement of the bid. The requisite "substantial step" can be found even if formal announcement of a tender offer has not yet occurred and, perhaps, even if a tender offer never takes place. Substantial steps include such things as voting on a resolution by the offering person's board of directors relating to the tender offer; the formulation of a plan or proposal to make a tender offer by the offering person; activities which substantially facilitate the tender offer, such as arranging financing for a tender offer, or preparing or directing or authorizing the preparation of tender offer materials.[57] The trader must know or have reason to know that the information is nonpublic. The trader also must know or have reason to know the information was acquired from the bidder or the target company or agents of either.

Unlike both the disclose or abstain rule and the misappropriation theory under Rule 10b–5, Rule 14e–3 liability is not premised on breach of a fiduciary duty. There is no need for a showing that the trading party or tipper was subject to any duty of confidentiality, and no need to show that a tipper personally benefited from the tip. In light of the well-established fiduciary duty requirement under Rule 10b–5, however, the rule arguably ran afoul of *Schreiber v. Burlington Northern, Inc.*,[58] in which the Supreme Court held that § 14(e) was modeled on § 10(b) and, like that section, requires a showing of misrepresentation or nondisclosure. If the two sections are to be interpreted *in pari materia*, as *Shreiber* indicated, and § 10(b) requires a showing of a breach of a duty in order for liability to arise, the SEC appeared to have exceeded its statutory authority by adopting a rule that makes illegal a variety of trading practices that do not involve any breach of duty. In *United States v. O'Hagan*,[59] however, the Supreme Court upheld Rule 14e–3 as a valid exercise of the SEC's rulemaking authority despite the absence of a fiduciary duty element.

While Rule 14e–3 thus escapes the fiduciary-duty based restrictions of the *Chiarella/Dirks* regime, the Rule nevertheless is quite limited in scope. One prong of the rule (the prohibition on trading while in possession of material nonpublic information) does not apply until the offeror has taken substantial steps towards making the offer. More important, both prongs of the rule are limited to information relating to

---

57. SEC Release No. 34–17,120 (1980). See, e.g., SEC v. Maio, 51 F.3d 623 (7th Cir.1995) (signing a confidentiality agreement constituted a substantial step where one of the corporate parties had earlier solicited a tender offer); SEC v. Musella, 578 F.Supp. 425 (S.D.N.Y.1984) (retaining law firm to advise on an impending offer constituted a substantial step); Camelot Indus. Corp. v. Vista Resources, Inc., 535 F.Supp. 1174 (S.D.N.Y.1982) (meeting between target managers, prospective acquiror, and an investment banker deemed a substantial step); O'Connor & Assoc. v. Dean Witter Reynolds, Inc., 529 F.Supp. 1179 (S.D.N.Y.1981) (Rule 14e–3 can be violated even if offer never becomes effective).

58. 472 U.S. 1 (1985).

59. 521 U.S. 642, 666–76 (1997).

a tender offer. As a result, most types of inside information remain subject to the duty-based analysis of *Chiarella* and its progeny.

Although most lawsuits under 14e–3 have been brought by the SEC, it seems likely that a private right of action exists under the rule and is available to investors trading in the target's securities at the same time as the persons who violated the rule.[60]

B. Misappropriation

In response to the set-backs it suffered in *Chiarella* and *Dirks*, the SEC began advocating a new theory of insider trading liability: the misappropriation theory. Unlike Rule 14e–3, the SEC did not intend for the misappropriation theory to be limited to tender offer cases (although many misappropriation decisions have in fact involved takeovers). Accordingly, the Commission posited misappropriation as a new theory of liability under Rule 10b–5. Which meant, in turn, that the SEC had to find a way of finessing the fiduciary duty requirement imposed by *Chiarella* and *Dirks*.

1. Origins

The misappropriation theory is commonly (but incorrectly) traced to Chief Justice Burger's *Chiarella* dissent. Burger contended that the way in which the inside trader acquires the nonpublic information on which he trades could itself be a material circumstance that must be disclosed to the market before trading. Accordingly, Burger argued, "a person who has misappropriated nonpublic information has an absolute duty [to the persons with whom he trades] to disclose that information or to refrain from trading."[61] The majority did not address the merits of this theory; instead rejecting it solely on the ground that the theory had not been presented to the jury and thus could not sustain a criminal conviction.

Consequently, the way was left open for the SEC to urge, and the lower courts to adopt, the misappropriation theory as an alternative basis of insider trading liability.[62] The Second Circuit swiftly moved to

60. See, e.g., O'Connor & Assoc. v. Dean Witter Reynolds, Inc., 529 F.Supp. 1179 (S.D.N.Y.1981).

61. Chiarella v. United States, 445 U.S. 222, 240 (1980) (Burger, C.J., dissenting).

62. On the post-*Chiarella* definition of insider trading, see generally Douglas Branson, Discourse on the Supreme Court Approach to SEC Rule 10b–5 and Insider Trading, 30 Emory L.J. 263 (1981); James D. Cox, Choices: Paving the Road Toward a Definition of Insider Trading, 39 Ala. L. Rev. 381 (1988); Jill E. Fisch, Start Making Sense: An Analysis and Proposal for Insider Trading Regulation, 26 Ga. L. Rev. 179

(1991); Donald C. Langevoort, Insider Trading and the Fiduciary Principle: A Post–Chiarella Restatement, 70 California Law Review 1 (1982); Jonathan R. Macey, From Judicial Solutions to Political Solutions: The New, New Direction of the Rules Against Insider Trading, 39 Ala. L. Rev. 355 (1988); Lawrence E. Mitchell, The Jurisprudence of the Misappropriation Theory and the New Insider Trading Legislation: From Fairness to Efficiency and Back, 52 Albany L. Rev. 775 (1988); William K. S. Wang, Post–Chiarella Developments in Rule 10b–5, 15 Rev. Sec. Reg. 956 (1982); William K. S. Wang, Recent Developments in the Fed–

take advantage of that opportunity. In *United States v. Newman*,[63] employees of an investment bank misappropriated confidential information concerning proposed mergers involving clients of the firm. As was true of Vincent Chiarella, the Newman defendants' employer worked for prospective acquiring companies, while the trading took place in target company securities. As such, the Newman defendants owed no fiduciary duties to the investors with whom they traded. Moreover, neither the investment bank nor its clients traded in the target companies' shares contemporaneously with the defendants.

Unlike Chief Justice Burger's *Chiarella* dissent, the Second Circuit did not assert that the Newman defendants owed any duty of disclosure to the investors with whom they traded or had defrauded. Instead, the court held that by misappropriating confidential information for personal gain, the defendants had defrauded their employer and its clients, and this fraud sufficed to impose insider trading liability on the defendants with whom they traded.[64] As eventually refined, the (pre-*O'Hagan*) misappropriation theory thus imposed liability on anyone who: (1) misappropriated material nonpublic information; (2) thereby breaching a fiduciary duty or a duty arising out of a similar relationship of trust and confidence; and (3) used that information in a securities transaction, regardless of whether he owed any duties to the shareholders of the company in whose stock he traded.[65]

Like the traditional disclose or abstain rule, the misappropriation theory thus required a breach of fiduciary duty before trading on inside information became unlawful.[66] The fiduciary relationship in question, however, was a quite different one. Under the misappropriation theory, the defendant did not need to owe a fiduciary duty to the investor with whom he traded, nor did he need to owe a fiduciary duty to the issuer of the securities that were traded. Instead, the misappropriation theory applied when the inside trader violated a fiduciary duty owed to the source of the information.[67] Had the misappropriation theory been available against Chiarella, for example, his conviction could have been upheld even though he owed no duties to those with whom he had traded. Instead, the breach of the duty he owed to Pandick Press would have sufficed.

---

eral Law Regulating Stock Market Inside Trading, 6 Corp. L. Rev. 291 (1983).

63. 664 F.2d 12 (2d Cir.1981).

64. See United States v. Newman, 664 F.2d 12, 17 (2d Cir.1981); see also United States v. Carpenter, 791 F.2d 1024 (2d Cir. 1986), aff'd on other grounds, 484 U.S. 19 (1987); SEC v. Materia, 745 F.2d 197 (2d Cir.1984), cert. denied, 471 U.S. 1053 (1985).

65. See United States v. Bryan, 58 F.3d 933, 945 (4th Cir.1995).

66. See SEC v. Switzer, 590 F.Supp. 756, 766 (W.D.Okla.1984) (stating that it is not unlawful to trade on the basis of inadvertently overheard information).

67. See, e.g., United States v. Carpenter, 791 F.2d 1024, 1028–29 (2d Cir.1986) (applying misappropriation theory to a journalist who breaches his duty of confidentiality to his employer).

The misappropriation theory should be seen as the vehicle by which the SEC sought to recapture as much as possible the ground it had lost in *Chiarella* and *Dirks*. In the years following those decisions, the SEC (and the lower courts) seemed to view the fiduciary duty element as a mere inconvenience that should not stand in the way of expansive insider trading liability. They consistently sought to evade the spirit of the fiduciary duty requirement, while complying with its letter. Even a former SEC Commissioner admitted as much, acknowledging that the misappropriation theory was "merely a pretext for enforcing equal opportunity in information."[68] Put another way, the SEC used the misappropriation theory as a means of redirecting the prohibition back towards the direction in which *Texas Gulf Sulphur* had initially set it.[69]

2. *O'Hagan and Bryan: The Misappropriation Theory is Called into Question*

The Supreme Court first took up the misappropriation theory in *Carpenter v. United States*,[70] in which a Wall Street Journal reporter and his confederates misappropriated information belonging to the Journal. The Supreme Court upheld the resulting convictions under the mail and wire fraud statutes, holding that confidential business information is property protected by those statutes from being taken by trick, deceit, or chicanery.[71] As to the defendants' securities fraud convictions, however, the court split 4–4. Following the long-standing tradition governing evenly divided Supreme Court decisions, the lower court ruling was affirmed without opinion, but that ruling had no precedential or stare decisis value.

68. Charles C. Cox & Kevin S. Fogarty, Bases of Insider Trading Law, 49 Ohio St. L.J. 353, 366 (1988).

69. One of the more puzzling features of the federal insider trading prohibition is the willingness of courts to aid and abet the Commission's efforts. Although the SEC's incentive to erect a broad insider trading prohibition seems easily explainable as a matter of political economy, it is far less clear why courts would be willing to go along. Yet they have consistently done so. The *Cady, Roberts* power grab was validated by *Texas Gulf Sulphur Co.*. *Newman* followed the reversal suffered in *Chiarella*. The SEC's most recent reversals in *O'Hagan* and *Bryan* were swept aside by the Supreme Court. At every turn, judges have aided and abetted the SEC. For an attempt to explain this course of judicial conduct, see Stephen M. Bainbridge, Insider Trading Regulation: The Path Dependent Choice between Property Rights and Securities Fraud, 52 SMU L. Rev. 1589, 1635–40 (1999).

70. 484 U.S. 19 (1987).

71. The federal mail and wire fraud statutes, 18 U.S.C. §§ 1341 and 1343, respectively prohibit the use of the mails and "wire, radio, or television communication" for the purpose of executing any "scheme or artifice to defraud." The mail and wire fraud statutes protect only property rights, McNally v. United States, 483 U.S. 350 (1987), but confidential business information is deemed to be property for purposes of those statutes. Carpenter v. United States, 484 U.S. 19, 25 (1987). Hence, the Supreme Court held, the Wall Street Journal owned the information used by Winans and his co-conspirators and, moreover, that their use of the mails and wire communications to trade on the basis of that information constituted the requisite scheme to defraud. Arguably, after *Carpenter* and *O'Hagan*, if there is a Rule 10b–5 violation there will also be a mail and wire fraud violation and vice-versa.

The way was thus left open for lower courts to reject the misappropriation theory, which the Fourth and Eighth Circuits subsequently did in, respectively, *United States v. Bryan*[72] and *United States v. O'Hagan*.[73] These courts held that Rule 10b–5 imposed liability only where there has been deception upon the purchaser or seller of securities, or upon some other person intimately linked with or affected by a securities transaction. Because the misappropriation theory involves no such deception, but rather simply a breach of fiduciary duty owed to the source of the information, the theory could not stand. The Supreme Court took cert in *United States v. O'Hagan* to resolve the resulting split between these circuits and the prior Second Circuit holdings validating the misappropriation theory.

3. *O'Hagan*

James O'Hagan was a partner in the Minneapolis law firm of Dorsey & Whitney. In July 1988, Grand Metropolitan PLC (Grand Met), retained Dorsey & Whitney in connection with its planned takeover of Pillsbury Company. Although O'Hagan was not one of the lawyers on the Grand Met project, he learned of their intentions and began buying Pillsbury stock and call options on Pillsbury stock. When Grand Met announced its tender offer in October, the price of Pillsbury stock nearly doubled, allowing O'Hagan to reap a profit of more than $4.3 million.

O'Hagan was charged with violating 1934 Act § 10(b) and Rule 10b–5 by trading on misappropriated nonpublic information. As with Chiarella and the *Newman* defendants, O'Hagan could not be held liable under the disclose or abstain rule because he worked for the bidder but traded in target company stock. He was neither a classic insider nor a constructive insider of the issuer of the securities in which he traded.[74]

In *O'Hagan*, a majority of the Supreme Court upheld the misappropriation theory as a valid basis on which to impose insider trading liability. A fiduciary's undisclosed use of information belonging to his principal, without disclosure of such use to the principal, for personal gain constitutes fraud in connection with the purchase or sale of a

---

72. 58 F.3d 933 (4th Cir.1995).

73. 92 F.3d 612 (8th Cir.1996), rev'd, 521 U.S. 642 (1997).

74. O'Hagan was also indicted for violations of Rule 14e–3, which proscribes insider trading in connection with tender offers, and the federal mail fraud and money laundering statutes. The Eighth Circuit overturned O'Hagan's convictions under these provisions. As to Rule 14e–3, the court held that the SEC lacked authority to adopt a prohibition of insider trading that does not require a breach of fiduciary duty. United States v. O'Hagan, 92 F.3d 612, 622–27 (8th Cir.1996), rev'd, 521 U.S. 642 (1997). As to

O'Hagan's mail fraud and money laundering convictions, the Eighth Circuit also reversed them on grounds that the indictment was structured so as to premise the charges under those provisions on the primary securities fraud violations. Id. at 627–28. Accordingly, in view of the court's reversal of the securities fraud convictions, the latter counts could not stand either. The Supreme Court reversed on all points, reinstating O'Hagan's convictions under all of the statutory violations charged in the indictment. United States v. O'Hagan, 521 U.S. 642 (1997).

security, the majority (per Justice Ginsburg) opined, and thus violates Rule 10b–5.[75]

The court acknowledged that misappropriators such as O'Hagan have no disclosure obligation running to the persons with whom they trade. Instead, it grounded liability under the misappropriation theory on deception of the source of the information. As the majority interpreted the theory, it addresses the use of "confidential information for securities trading purposes, in breach of a duty owed to the source of the information." Under this theory, the majority explained, "a fiduciary's undisclosed, self serving use of a principal's information to purchase or sell securities, in breach of a duty of loyalty and confidentiality, defrauds the principal of the exclusive use of that information." So defined, the majority held, the misappropriation theory satisfies § 10(b)'s requirement that there be a "deceptive device or contrivance" used "in connection with" a securities transaction.[76]

C. Short Swing Profits

In addition to the complicated insider trading rules under § 10(b), Congress has also provided a much simpler prophylactic rule under Securities Exchange Act § 16(b). In brief, § 16(b) holds that any profits an insider earns on purchases and sales that occur within six months of each other must be forfeited to the corporation.[77] As with all prophylactic

---

75. United States v. O'Hagan, 521 U.S. 642 (1997). See generally Donna Nagy, Reframing the Misappropriation Theory of Insider Trading Liability: A Post–*O'Hagan* Suggestion, 59 Ohio St. L.J. 1223 (1998).

76. The Supreme Court thus rejected Chief Justice Burger's argument in *Chiarella* that the misappropriation theory created disclosure obligation running to those with whom the misappropriator trades. United States v. O'Hagan, 521 U.S. 642, 655 n. 6 (1997). Instead, it is the failure to disclose one's intentions to the source of the information that constitutes the requisite disclosure violation under the *O'Hagan* version of the misappropriation theory. Id. at 653–55.

77. Section 16(b) provides:

For the purpose of preventing the unfair use of information which may have been obtained by such beneficial owner, director, or officer by reason of his relationship to the issuer, any profit realized by him from any purchase and sale, or any sale and purchase, of any equity security of such issuer (other than an exempted security) within any period of less than six months, unless such security was acquired in good faith in connection with a debt previously contracted, shall inure to and be recoverable by the issuer, irrespective of any intention on the part of such beneficial owner, director, or officer in entering into such transaction of holding the security purchased or of not repurchasing the security sold for a period exceeding six months. Suit to recover such profit may be instituted at law or in equity in any court of competent jurisdiction by the issuer, or by the owner of any security of the issuer in the name and in behalf of the issuer if the issuer shall fail or refuse to bring such suit within sixty days after request or shall fail diligently to prosecute the same thereafter; but no such suit shall be brought more than two years after the date such profit was realized. This subsection shall not be construed to cover any transaction where such beneficial owner was not such both at the time of the purchase and sale, or the sale and purchase, of the security involved, or any transaction or transactions which the Commission by rules and regulations may exempt as not comprehended within the purpose of this sub-section.

rules, § 16(b) is both over- and under-inclusive. It captures all sorts of trades unaffected by the use of inside information, while missing many trades flagrantly based on nonpublic information.

Unlike Rule 10b–5, § 16(b) applies only to officers, directors, or shareholders who own more than 10% of the company's stock. It also applies only to insider transactions in their own company's stock. There is no tipping liability, no misappropriation liability, and no constructive insider doctrine.

There are two other important limitations on § 16(b)'s scope. First, it applies only to firms that must register under the Securities Exchange Act. Second, it applies only to stocks and convertible debt. In both respects, it is narrower than under Rule 10b–5.

Although there must be both a sale and a purchase within six months of each other in order to trigger § 16(b), it applies whether the sale follows the purchase or vice versa. Accordingly, shares are fungible for § 16(b) purposes. The trader thus need not earn his or her gains from buying and selling specific shares of stock. Instead, if the trader unloads 10 shares of stock and buys back 10 different shares of stock in the same company at a cheaper price, he or she is liable.

Form almost always triumphs over substance in § 16(b) cases. There are some exceptions, however, the most notable of which is the unconventional transaction doctrine. The Exchange Act defines "sale" very broadly: it includes every disposition of a security for value. For purposes of § 16(b), however, certain transactions are not deemed sales; namely, so-called unconventional transactions.

The leading case in this area is *Kern County Land Co. v. Occidental Petroleum Corp.*[78] In 1967, Occidental launched a tender offer for 500,-000 shares of Kern County Land Co. (Old Kern). The offer later was extended and the number of shares being sought was increased. When the offer closed in June, Occidental owned more than 10% of Old Kern's stock. To avoid being taken over by Occidental, Old Kern negotiated a defensive merger with Tenneco. Under the merger agreement, Old Kern stock would be exchanged for Tenneco stock. In order to avoid becoming a minority shareholder in Tenneco, Occidental sold to a Tenneco subsidiary an option to purchase the Tenneco shares Occidental would acquire in the merger, which could not be exercised until the § 16(b) six month period had elapsed. Tenneco and Old Kern merged during the six month period following Occidental's tender offer. Somewhat later, more than 6 months after the tender offer, Occidental sold Tenneco stock pursuant to the option.

The successor corporation to Old Kern (New Kern) sued under § 16(b). It offered two theories. First, the merger and resulting exchange of Old Kern for Tenneco stock constituted a sale, which had occurred

78.   411 U.S. 582 (1973).

less than six months after the purchase effected by the tender offer. Second, the tender offer constituted a purchase and that the grant of the option (rather than the exercise of the option) constituted a sale. Because the option was granted less than six months after the tender offer, New Kern argued that Occidental was liable for any profit earned on the shares covered by the option. The Supreme Court rejected both of New Kern's arguments, holding that Occidental had no § 16(b) liability. Both the merger and the grant of the option were unconventional transactions and, as such, were not deemed a sale for § 16(b) purposes.

Courts have identified three factors to be considered in deciding whether a transaction is conventional or unconventional: (1) whether the transaction is volitional; (2) whether the transaction is one over which the beneficial owner has any influence; and (3) whether the beneficial owner had access to confidential information about the transaction or the issuer. In the case at bar, Occidental as a hostile bidder had no access to confidential information about Old Kern or Tenneco. In addition, as to the merger, the exchange was involuntary—as the other shareholders had approved the merger, Occidental had no option but to exchange its shares.

Chapter 7

TARGET DEFENSES AGAINST HOSTILE TAKEOVER BIDS

§ 7.1 Takeover Defenses: The Arsenal

As we have seen, the target's board of directors functions as a sort of gatekeeper in statutory acquisitions. A key feature of the non-statutory acquisition forms, from the acquirer's perspective, thus is the ability to bypass the target board and make an offer directly to the target's shareholders. When the hostile tender offer emerged in the 1970s as an important acquirer tool, lawyers and investment bankers working for target boards began to develop defensive tactics designed to impede such offers. Takeover defenses reasserted the board's primacy, by extending their gatekeeping function to the non-statutory acquisition setting. The takeover arms race remains unrelenting. As fast as new acquisition techniques are developed, new defenses spring up.

A. Shark Repellents

A shark repellent is an amendment to the firm's articles of incorporation designed to persuade potential bidders to look elsewhere. Broadly speaking, shark repellents fall into two principal categories: provisions relating to the board of directors and supermajority voting requirements for certain transactions.

1. *Classified Boards*

Classified board provisions, which are also known as staggered boards, divide the board of directors into three classes of which only one is elected annually. The offeror thus must go through two annual meeting cycles before it has elected a majority of the board. This defense will be most effective as to an acquirer who needs quick access to target assets to pay off acquisition debt. If the acquirer can wait out the current board, the provisions will be of little benefit. Many factors will tend to lead the current board to play along with a successful acquirer—even if the board has the right to hold-out. Why should any director, except maybe an insider, risk being sued by the acquirer every time they do something he or she opposes?[1]

---

1. Ronald J. Gilson, The Case Against Shark Repellent Amendments: Structural Limitations on the Enabling Concept, 34 Stan. L. Rev. 775, 793 (1982). Although the classified board seemingly has limited utility standing alone, we shall see below that it

The classification scheme must be protected from the possibility that the acquirer will (1) remove the directors without cause or (2) pack the board with his or her own appointments. This can be done by reserving to the board the sole right to determine the number of directors and the sole right to fill any vacancies. If permitted by state law, a classified board shark repellent can be further strengthened by limiting or abolishing the right of shareholders to call a special shareholders meeting or to remove directors without cause (defining cause as narrowly as possible).

Delaware permits a classified board to be created either in the articles of incorporation or in the bylaws.[2] In contrast, the MBCA requires that a classified board be created through the articles.[3] In general, a classified board scheme established in the articles will be more difficult for to a hostile bidder to undo. Because shareholders may initiate changes to the bylaws, but initial board approval is required to amend the articles, a classified board scheme contained solely in the bylaws is more vulnerable to repeal than a classified board scheme contained in solely in the articles.[4]

can become a very effective device when coupled with a poison pill. See generally John C. Coates IV, Takeover Defenses in the Shadow of the Pill: A Critique of the Scientific Evidence, 79 Tex. L. Rev. 271, 325–28 (2000).

2. DGCL § 141(d).

3. MBCA § 8.06.

4. At early common law, only shareholders had the power to amend the bylaws. Many states thereafter adopted statutes allowing shareholders to delegate the power to amend the bylaws to the board of directors. DGCL § 109(a) typifies this approach: It provides that only shareholders have the power to amend bylaws, unless the articles of incorporation expressly confer that power on the board of directors. An article provision authorizing the board to amend the bylaws, moreover, does not divest the shareholders of their residual power to amend the bylaws.

In contrast, the MBCA reflects a modern trend of vesting the power to amend the bylaws in both the directors and the shareholders. MBCA § 10.20(b) allows the directors to amend the bylaws unless (1) the articles of incorporation give that power solely to the shareholders or (2) the shareholders amend the bylaw in question and provide that the directors cannot thereafter further amend the bylaw. By implication, MBCA § 10.20(a) authorizes the shareholders to amend the bylaws even though the directors also have that power. Notice that amendment of the bylaws is one of the few

corporate actions the shareholders are entitled to initiate. Unlike the articles of incorporation, where the board must first recommend an amendment, no prior board action is required on a bylaw amendment.

The concurrent power of both shareholders and boards to amend the bylaws raises the prospect of cycling amendments and counter amendments. Suppose the shareholders adopted a bylaw declassifying the board. Disliking that decision, the board then repeals the new bylaw provision using its concurrent power to amend the bylaws. The MBCA allows the shareholders to forestall such an event. As noted, MBCA § 10.20(b)(2) authorizes the board to adopt, amend, and repeal bylaws unless "the shareholders in amending, repealing, or adopting a bylaw expressly provide that the board of directors may not amend, repeal, or reinstate that bylaw." In the absence of such a restriction, however, the board apparently retains its power to amend or even repeal the bylaw. If the board does so, the shareholders' remedies presumably are limited to readopting the term limit amendment, this time incorporating the necessary restriction, and/or electing a more compliant board.

Delaware § 109 is more problematic, as it lacks any comparable grant of power to the shareholders. Worse yet, because the board only has power to adopt or amend bylaws if that power is granted to it in the articles of incorporation, a bylaw prohibiting board amendment would be inconsistent with the

2. *Supermajority Vote Requirements*

Supermajority provisions focus on preventing back-end freeze-out mergers. Rarely does a successful hostile tender offeror acquire 100% of the shares. The bidder therefore will usually follow a successful offer with a freeze-out merger to eliminate any remaining minority shareholders.

In some cases, a bidder may intentionally use a back-end merger to ensure success. In a so-called "two-tier offer," the bidder makes a partial tender offer and simultaneously announces its intention to subsequently acquire the remaining shares of the company in a subsequent merger. Often, the price paid in the second step merger will be lower than the tender offer price and/or be paid in a less desirable form of consideration. Such offers are said to be structurally coercive.[5] Such an offer works because collective action problems preclude shareholders from communicating with each other and from credibly binding themselves to reject offers not in their collective best interests. Suppose the bidder makes a tender offer for 51% of the target's stock at $50 per share in cash, while announcing an intent to follow up a successful offer with a freeze-out merger at $40 per share to be paid in the form of subordinated debt securities. An individual shareholder might believe that the offer is unacceptable, but worry that a majority of the other stockholders will accept the offer. A shareholder who does not tender thus risks having all of his shares acquired in the less desirable back-end transaction, which creates an incentive to tender into the front-end transaction. If the shareholder tenders, however, some pro rata portion of his shares will be taken up in the higher paying front-end.

A freeze-out merger generally only requires approval by a majority of the outstanding shares. As a result, the outcome of the shareholder vote often will be a foregone conclusion in light of the acquirer's holdings. Supermajority voting shark repellents erect barriers to second-

---

articles and, therefore, invalid. In American Int'l Rent a Car, Inc. v. Cross, 1984 WL 8204 (Del.Ch.1984), the Delaware Chancery Court suggested that, as part of a bylaw amendment, the shareholders "could remove from the Board the power to further amend the provision in question." Dicta in several other Delaware precedents, however, are to the contrary. In General Data-Comm Industries, Inc. v. State of Wisconsin Investment Board, 731 A.2d 818 (Del.Ch. 1999), for example, Vice Chancellor Strine noted the "significant legal uncertainty" as to "whether, in the absence of an explicitly controlling statute, a stockholder adopted bylaw can be made immune from repeal or modification by the board of directors." Id. at 821 n.1. In Centaur Partners, IV v. National Intergroup, Inc., 582 A.2d 923 (Del.

1990), the Delaware Supreme Court addressed a shareholder proposed bylaw limiting the number of directors. As proposed, the bylaw contained a provision prohibiting the board from amending or repealing it. Noting that the corporation's articles gave the board authority to fix the number of directors through adoption of bylaws, the Supreme Court opined that the proposed bylaw "would be a nullity if adopted." Id. at 929. Consequently, it seems doubtful that restrictions on the board's power over the bylaws will pass muster in Delaware or other states likewise lacking a MBCA style provision.

   5. See, e.g., Chesapeake Corp. v. Shore, 771 A.2d 293, 331 (Del.Ch.2000); City Capital Assoc. Ltd. Partnership v. Interco Inc., 551 A.2d 787, 797 (Del.Ch.1988).

step transactions by imposing a supermajority-voting requirement for mergers, asset sales, and like transactions. A typical formulation requires that 80% of all outstanding shares and a majority of the outstanding shares not owned by the bidder approve any merger. Such provisions are authorized by DGCL § 102(b)(4), which authorizes the articles of incorporation to include: "Provisions requiring for any corporate action, the vote of a larger portion of the stock or of any class or series thereof. . . ."[6]

Supermajority vote shark repellents usually provide that the supermajority provision can be deleted or amended only by a vote equal to the supermajority vote. Hence, for example, amending an 80% vote requirement would have to be approved by 80% of all outstanding shares. This requirement is obviously intended to prevent the offeror from avoiding the supermajority vote by the simple expedient of amending the charter. In order to permit friendly transactions, most of these provisions provide that transactions approved by a majority or supermajority of the continuing directors—those in office when the raider first acquired a substantial interest in the target (say 10%)—shall not be subject to the supermajority shareholder vote requirement.

3.   The Fair Price Variant

Fair price shark repellents are a variant on the supermajority vote provision. This version exempts transactions from the supermajority vote where the price to be paid exceeds a specified amount. The specified "fair price" usually is not less than the price paid in the first-step transaction. In addition, fair price provisions also typically require that the second-step payment be made in the same form of consideration. Hence, they prevent the offeror from paying cash in the first-step and junk bonds in the second. A related alternative is a compulsory redemption provision that allows minority shareholders to demand to be bought out at a price at least equal to the price paid in the first-step transaction.

4.   Supermajority and Fair Price Provisions in Action

The supermajority vote and fair price variants of shark repellents will be most effective when the aggregate holdings of insiders and persons with demonstrated loyalty to present management are sufficient to block the second-step transaction. If the necessary vote is 80% of the outstanding shares, for example, and insiders own more than 20%, it will be difficult for an acquirer to obtain the necessary approval. Supermajority vote shark repellents, however, are effective only against bidders who

---

6. See Seibert v. Milton Bradley Co., 405 N.E.2d 131 (Mass.1980) (upholding by-law requiring 75% approval of a merger unless the merger was approved by a two-thirds vote of the board of directors); Seibert v. Gulton Indus., Inc., 1979 WL 2710 (Del.Ch.1979) (upholding a supermajority vote shark repellent requiring an 80% vote to approve mergers with another person or entity owning 5% or more of the outstanding stock).

want to acquire 100% ownership. If the acquirer is willing to live with a frozen-in minority, the second-step barrier is essentially meaningless. Note that compulsory redemption provisions may deter even that class of raiders, because they require the bidder to buy out the minority at a fair price.

The effectiveness of these provisions largely depends on the minority having not only the power, but also the will, to exercise their rights. Exercising one's rights under these charter provisions often results in current managers being frozen into a substantially less liquid minority investment. In many cases, management may not want to be caught in that position. As with staggered board provisions, they may prefer to waive their rights and get out from under a determined bidder, albeit at a price.

B. Poison Pills

Poison pills take a wide variety of forms, but today most are based on the class of security known as a right. Hence, the pill's official name, the "shareholder rights plan." A traditional right, such as a warrant, grants the holder the option to purchase new shares of stock of the issuing corporation. The modern poison pill adds three additional elements not found in traditional rights: a "flip-in" element; a "flip-over" element; and a redemption provision.[7]

1. First Generation Pills

Lenox adopted the first poison pill in 1983.[8] Like most of the first generation pills, the Lenox plan was based on so-called blank check preferred stock. Many corporate charters authorize a class of preferred stock whose rights are not detailed in the articles. Instead, the board of directors defines the preferred stock's rights at the time the stock is issued. Typically, these provisions do not require any shareholder action—hence, the name "blank check." The Lenox pill was issued as a special dividend consisting of nonvoting convertible preferred stock, the dividend issuing at the ratio of one preferred share for every forty shares of common stock.

The anti-takeover effect of the preferred stock lay in the conversion rights conferred on its holders. If Lenox was merged into another corporation, the preferred stock became convertible into common stock of the acquiring corporation at a price well below market. Any such

---

7. Warrants are traded as separate securities, having value because they typically confer on the holder the right to buy issuer common stock at a discount from the prevailing market price. In contrast, the poison pill right usually is "stapled" to the common stock and does not trade separately until some triggering event occurs.

8. See generally Martin M. Cohen, "Poison Pills" as a Negotiating Tool: Seeking a Cease-Fire in the Corporate Takeover Wars, 1987 Colum. Bus. L. Rev. 459, 468–469.

conversion would result in undesirable balance sheet effects for the bidder and dilute the holdings of pre-existing bidder shareholders, which would make an acquisition of Lenox less attractive.

The Lenox plan was an early variant of what is now known as a flip-over pill. Modern flip-over plans start not with preferred stock as did the Lenox pill, but with the issuance of rights as a pro rata dividend on the common stock to the shareholders of the target corporation. Rights are corporate securities that give the holder of the right the option of purchasing shares. Because issuance of rights does not require shareholder approval, the board of directors without any shareholder action may adopt a rights-based pill.[9] When adopted, the rights initially attach to the corporation's outstanding common stock, cannot be traded separately from the common stock, and are priced so that exercise of the option would be economically irrational. The rights become exercisable, and separate from the common stock, upon a so-called distribution event, which is typically defined as the acquisition of, or announcement of intent to acquire, some specified percentage of the issuer's stock by a prospective acquirer. (Twenty percent is a commonly used trigger level.) Although the rights are now exercisable, and will remain so for the remainder of their specified life (typically ten years), they remain out of the money.

The pill's flip-over feature typically is triggered if, following the acquisition of a specified percentage of the target's common stock, the target is subsequently merged into the acquirer or one of its affiliates. In such an event, the holder of each right becomes entitled to purchase common stock of the acquiring company, typically at half-price, thereby impairing the acquirer's capital structure and drastically diluting the interest of the acquirer's other stockholders. In other words, once triggered, the flip-over pill gives target shareholders the option to purchase acquiring company shares at a steep discount to market. As with the older style preferred stock pills, this causes dilution for the bidder's pre-existing shareholders and may have undesirable balance sheet effects.

In *Moran v. Household International*,[10] as we'll see below in detail, the Delaware Supreme Court upheld a flip-over pill against challenges based on both the board's authority and the board's fiduciary duties. The plan at issue in that case nicely illustrates in more detail how such pills worked. There were two triggering events: (1) the making of a tender offer for 30 percent or more of Household's shares; and (2) the acquisition of 20% or more of Household's outstanding shares by any person or group. If issued, the rights were immediately exercisable and would entitle the holders to purchase 1/100th of a share of Household preferred

---

9. See Account v. Hilton Hotels Corp., 780 A.2d 245 (Del.2001) (noting the power of "directors of a Delaware corporation" to "adopt a rights plan unilaterally").

10. 500 A.2d 1346 (Del.1985).

stock at a price of $100. Because that price was way out of the money, there was no expectation that the rights would be exercised.

Why were the underlying rights initially stapled to the common stock? This common provision is intended to ensure that the rights trade with the common. If the rights traded separately, the potential target corporation would have to issue a separate security. More important, if the rights did not trade with the common, holders might sell common without selling the rights—or vice-versa if a separate secondary trading market developed for the rights.

Why did the rights detach from the stock in a way that initially made them unattractive to exercise? By detaching the rights once a bidder is on the scene, the target ensures that the bidder has to buy up the rights separately. Some stockholders will tender their common or sell their common shares on the market, but retain the rights. Consequently, the bidder has to deal with two distinct groups. As for the provision under which the rights are initially convertible into preferred (out of the money) and only convertible into common (in the money) in the event of a second-step transaction, it is intended to preclude an argument that the right was a sham security. DGCL § 157 allows the corporation to issue rights, but does not facially authorize the issuance of rights for takeover defenses purposes. Presumably, the transaction planner who devised the pill intended that this provision would make it appear as though the rights had economic value.

Note that the Household pill, if triggered by the making of a tender offer for 30% or more of the stock, was redeemable. The board could redeem the rights at a price of 50 cents per right at any time prior to their being exercised. If the pill was triggered by the acquisition of 20% or more of the stock, however, the rights were not redeemable. The transaction planner presumably intended this distinction to deter hostile beachhead acquisitions exceeding 20% of the shares, while still allowing a friendly deal to be accomplished by means of a tender offer.

2.   Second Generation Pills

The first generation flip-over pills proved ineffective in deterring takeovers. Bidders continually found flaws in the plans. The classic example of a bidder turning such a pill to its own advantage was Sir James Goldsmith's takeover of Crown Zellerbach. Like most first generation pills, the Crown Zellerbach pill only kicked in if the bidder sought to effect a freeze-out merger. Goldsmith acquired a controlling interest in Crown Zellerbach, but decided not to squeeze out the remaining Crown Zellerbach shareholders. This had a rather nifty effect. Since Goldsmith wasn't going to do a merger, he didn't suffer any poisonous effects. On the other hand, since the rights were now exercisable in the event of a merger, what had happened? The pill had become a double-edged sword, which Goldsmith had redirected at the target's throat. By triggering the pill, Goldsmith precluded anyone from merging with Crown Zellerbach—any merger partner would suffer the poisonous effects. As a result, he had effectively precluded the board from attracting a white knight.

There were other ways around the first generation plans. For example, the Goldsmith strategy only worked because the Zellerbach pill was not redeemable. Suppose the target included a redemption provision, which would allow the board to repurchase the preferred shares at a nominal cost. That would defeat the Goldsmith strategy, but created its own set of problems. The bidder could simply condition its tender offer on the redemption of the plan by the target's board of directors. If the board refused to redeem the pill in the face of a fair any and all cash offer, the board took a substantial risk with its constituency.[11]

As the defects in the first generation of pills became increasingly obvious, takeover lawyers developed new features to close the various loopholes that had been identified. Among the most important of these was the so-called flip-in element, which prevents a bidder from implementing the Goldsmith strategy. In a flip-in plan, rights again are issued and become exercisable upon the same sort of triggering events. The difference between the two plans is that the flip-in plan enables shareholders of the target to purchase target stock at a discount. Today, they are usually adopted in tandem with flip-over plans.

The second-generation pill's flip-in element is typically triggered by the actual acquisition of some specified percentage of the issuer's common stock. (Again, 20 percent is a commonly used trigger.) If triggered, the flip-in pill entitles the holder of each right—except, and this is key, the acquirer and its affiliates or associates—to buy shares of the target issuer's common stock or other securities at half price. In other words, the value of the stock received when the right is exercised is equal to two times the exercise price of the right. The flip-in plan's deterrent effect thus comes from the dilution caused in the target shares held by the acquirer. For example, in Grand Metropolitan's bid for Pillsbury, Pillsbury's flip-in plan would have reduced Grand Met's interest in Pillsbury from 85% to 56 percent. The value of Grand Met's holdings would have declined by more than $700 million dollars.

3. Redemption Provisions

Proponents of poison pills argue that such plans give the target bargaining leverage that it can use to extract a higher price in return for redeeming the pill. Because the rights trade separately from the issuer's common stock, an acquirer remains subject to the pill's poisonous effects

---

11. One could also get around a flip-over pill by placing anti-dilution provisions into the bidder's corporate charter. This would involve the issuance of shares to preexisting acquirer shareholders in proportion to the shares issued to target shareholders exercising their flip-over rights. Another possible defense to the flip-over pill involved the acquirer's giving itself a call on any shares issued in a merger at below-market prices.

even if an overwhelming majority of the target's shareholders accept the bidder's tender offer. In the face of a pill, a prospective acquirer thus has a strong incentive to negotiate with the target's board.

Flexible redemption provisions are imperative for this purpose; the transaction planner must give the board the option of redeeming the rights at a nominal cost in order to allow desirable acquisitions to go forward. Typical redemption provisions include: the window redemption provision, in which the board retains the ability to redeem the rights for a specified time period following the issuance of the rights, and the white knight redemption provision, in which the target may redeem the rights in connection with a transaction approved by a majority of the continuing directors.

Note that combining a poison pill with a classified board shark repellent gives the board an especially powerful negotiating device.[12] The pill will deter the bidder from buying a control block of stock prior to the pill being redeemed. Instead, in the face of board resistance, the acquirer must go through two successive proxy contests in order to obtain a majority of the board. Prevailing in two such successive contests, without owning a controlling block of stock, would be a significant obstacle.

4.   *Variants on the Second Generation Pill*

Back-end plans involve issuing rights to the shareholders upon some triggering event—normally the acquisition of a specified percentage of the target's shares. The target's shareholders may then exchange their rights for a package of target company securities valued at the present minimum fair value of the target. The back-end plan thus establishes a minimum takeover price for the target, since such pills typically are redeemable if the bidder's offer meets or exceeds the price set by the board.

Back-end plans are designed to deter partial tender offers, structurally coercive two-tier tender offers, and open-market purchases by establishing a minimum fair price at which the holders of the rights may be

---

12. Lucian Arye Bebchuk et al., The Powerful Antitakeover Force of Staggered Boards: Theory, Evidence, and Policy, 54 Stan. L. Rev. 887 (2002) (presenting empirical data showing that the combination of a pill and classified board is an effective takeover defense); Ronald J. Gilson, Unocal Fifteen Years Later (And What We Can Do About It), 26 Del. J. Corp. L. 491, 504 (2001) (noting that "institutional investors [have] decided that, because of the interaction of staggered boards with poison pills, they would not vote for them"); Neil C. Rifkind, Note, Should Uninformed Shareholders be a Threat Justifying Defensive Action by Target Directors in Delaware?:
"Just Say No" After Moore v. Wallace, 78 B.U.L. Rev. 105, 111 (1998) (observing that "[w]hen poison pills and classified boards are used in tandem, the bidder either must mount two consecutive proxy contests to elect a majority of directors, or convince a court that the target directors' opposition to the offer constitutes a breach of the directors' fiduciary duties."); Robert B. Thompson, Shareholders as Grown–Ups: Voting, Selling, and Limits on the Board's Power to "Just Say No," 67 U. Cin. L. Rev. 999, 1017–18 (1999) (using legal treatment of poison pill and classified board provisions as a measure of jurisdictional commitment to shareholder primacy).

cashed out. Moreover, the debt securities to be issued under the plan typically include provisions precluding the bidder from selling target assets or taking on additional debt. This prevents the bidder from using the target's own resources as collateral for financing the acquisition.

Poison debt relies solely on debt securities. The target issues bonds or notes whose terms are designed to deter a hostile takeover. The indentures for such debt forbid the acquirer from burdening the target with further debt. They also usually forbid the bidder from selling target assets. Poison debt also usually makes a change of control an event of default. As a result, the bondholders may accelerate the loan and force the bidder to immediately redeem the bonds, which has a significant adverse effect on the company's cash flow.

Poison debt is an effective defense against leveraged takeovers. In a leveraged acquisition, the bidder borrows funds to finance the acquisition. These loans are typically given with the assumption that the bidder will be able to sell off target assets and make use of the target's cash flow in order to repay the debt. The theory is that the bidder will not be able to get financing if lenders know about the restrictive provisions of the poison debt.

Voting plans were briefly in vogue during the late 1980s. In some respects, they were a return to the first generation pills. Most voting plans go back to the idea of using preferred stock. One version gives the preferred shares the right to vote, but denies that right to bidders who acquire more than a specified percentage of the common or preferred stock. An alternative version permits the preferred shareholders, other than the bidder, to vote as a separate class in electing directors and gives them the right to elect a specified number of directors to represent their interests.

5.   The Third Generation: Dead Hand and No Hand Pills

Standard poison pills have a major weakness. Most pills are subject to redemption at nominal cost by the target's board of directors. Such redemption provisions purportedly allow the target's board to use the pill as a negotiating device: The poison pill makes an acquisition of the target prohibitively expensive. If the prospective acquirer makes a sufficiently attractive offer, however, the board may redeem the pill and allow the offer to go forward unimpaired by the pill's dilutive effects. Although such redemption provisions gave the target's board considerable negotiating leverage, and were one of the justifications used to defend the whole idea of the poison pill, they also made the target vulnerable to a combined tender offer and proxy contest. The prospective acquirer could trigger the pill, conduct a proxy contest to elect a new board, which, if elected, would then redeem the pill to permit the tender offer to go forward.

The dead hand pill was developed to close this loophole by depriving any such newly elected directors of the power to redeem the pill. In addition to fairly standard flip in and flip over features, the dead hand pill provides that it may be redeemed only by those directors who had been in office when the shareholder rights constituting the pill had become exercisable (or their approved successors). Unlike a dead hand pill, the so-called no hand pill contains no provision for redemption by continuing directors. Instead, the pill contains provisions making it nonredeemable for six months after a change in control of the board. Again, the purpose of this pill is to close the proxy contest loophole in standard pills. Because a prospective acquirer can take control of the board of directors, however, the no hand pill is far less of a showstopper than is a dead hand pill. Acquirers who need rapid access to the target's assets, so as to help finance the takeover, however, may still be deterred. The validity of these pills has been cast into doubt by recent Delaware cases, although they have been upheld in other jurisdictions.[13]

C. Dual Class Stock

Shares of common stock represent a bundle of ownership interests: a set of economic rights, such as the right to receive dividends declared by the board of directors; and a right to vote on certain corporate decisions. As it has long done, state law today generally provides corporations with considerable flexibility with respect to how this bundle will be packaged. Virtually all state corporate codes adopt one vote per common share as the default rule, but allow corporations to depart from the norm by adopting appropriate provisions in their organic documents.[14]

Although departures from the one share-one vote standard were well-known historically, dual class stock had largely fallen into disuse after the 1930s.[15] One comprehensive survey, for example, found only 30 issuers with nonvoting or dual class common stock that had been traded on any U.S. secondary market between 1940 and 1978.[16] As hostile takeovers of large corporations became more common, however, dual class capital structures became much more popular with corporate managers. One survey found that 37 of 44 publicly-traded firms adopting disparate voting rights plans between 1962 and 1984 did so after

---

13. See § 7.3.B.

14. For cases upholding departures from the one vote per share norm, see Groves v. Rosemound Improvement Ass'n, Inc., 413 So.2d 925, 927 (La.App.1982); Providence & Worcester Co. v. Baker, 378 A.2d 121, 122–24 (Del.1977); Hampton v. Tri–State Fin. Corp., 495 P.2d 566, 569 (Colo.App.1972); Shapiro v. Tropicana Lanes, Inc., 371 S.W.2d 237, 241–42 (Mo. 1963): Deskins v. Lawrence County Fair & Dev. Corp., 321 S.W.2d 408, 409 (Ky.1959).

15. For a history of dual class stock, see Stephen M. Bainbridge, Revisiting the One–Share/One–Vote Controversy: The Exchanges' Uniform Voting Rights Policy, 22 Sec. Reg. L.J. 175 (1994).

16. Ronald C. Lease et al., The Market Value of Control in Publicly–Traded Corporations, 11 J. Fin. Econ. 439, 450–52 (1983). Even more strikingly, in no year during that period were there more than 11 such issuers. Id. at 456 (table 2).

January 1980.[17] According to yet another survey, 34 more corporations created dual class capital structures between March 1986 and May 1987 alone.[18] Most commentators believed this revival was motivated by managerial fears of hostile takeovers.[19]

The basic dual class recapitalization provides a useful example of how dual class stock plans were used in the 1980s to defend against hostile takeovers. Shareholders were asked to approve a charter amendment creating two classes (typically referred to as Class A and Class B) of common stock. The Class A shares were essentially the preexisting common stock under a new name, retaining all of its former attributes, including the usual one vote per share. The Class B shares had all of the attributes of common stock, with three exceptions: (1) ownership of Class B stock was effectively nontransferable; (2) Class B shares could be converted into shares of Class A, however, which were freely transferable; and (3) the Class B stock had a larger number of votes, usually 10, per share. The Class B shares were then distributed to the shareholders as a stock dividend on their existing common shares.

As the Class B shares were not transferable, if a shareholder wished to sell his shares of Class B stock, he had to convert them into shares of Class A. Over time, as the normal process of shareholder turn-over proceeded, the number of outstanding Class B shares accordingly fell. In contrast, because incumbent managers were more likely to retain their Class B shares, the superior voting shares gradually concentrated in their hands. A dual class recapitalization thus eventually gave management voting control without requiring it to invest any additional equity in the firm.

A closely related alternative involved issuing the Class B shares, previously created by appropriate charter amendments, in an exchange offer. Shareholders were invited to exchange their existing Class A stock for the higher voting rights Class B shares. In these cases, however, the Class B shares were typically given lesser dividend rights and a concomi-

---

17. Megan Partch, The Creation of a Class of Limited Voting Common Stock and Shareholder Wealth, 18 J. Fin. Econ. 313, 314 (1987).

18. SEC Office of the Chief Economist, Update—The Effects of Dual–Class Recapitalizations on Shareholder Wealth: Including Evidence from 1986 and 1987 2 (July 16, 1987). An earlier study by the same authors found 65 dual class capital structures created between 1976 and 1986, three-quarters of which were adopted between 1983 and 1986. SEC Office of the Chief Economist, The Effects of Dual–Class Recapitalizations on the Wealth of Shareholders 11–12 (June 1, 1987).

19. See, e.g., Stephen M. Bainbridge, The Short Life and Resurrection of SEC Rule 19c–4, 69 Wash. U.L.Q. 565, 570–71 (1991); Richard M. Buxbaum, The Internal Division of Powers in Corporate Governance, 73 Cal. L. Rev. 1671, 1713–15 (1985); George W. Dent, Jr., Dual Class Capitalization: A Reply to Professor Seligman, 54 Geo. Wash. L. Rev. 725, 726 (1986); Jeffrey N. Gordon, Ties that Bond: Dual Class Common Stock and the Problem of Shareholder Choice, 76 Cal. L. Rev. 1, 4 (1988); Joel Seligman, The Transformation of Wall Street 10 (1982); Richard S. Ruback, Coercive Dual–Class Exchange Offers, 20 J. Fin. Econ. 153 (1988). But see Daniel R. Fischel, Organized Exchanges and the Regulation of Dual–Class Common Stock, 54 U. Chi. L. Rev. 119, 149–51 (1987).

tant lower dividend rate. Accordingly, it was expected that most public investors would not exchange their shares. If, in fact, only management and its allies acquired the higher voting right shares, an exchange offer dual class recapitalization could give management immediate voting control.

The effectiveness of such plans as anti-takeover devices is obvious. For managers of potential takeover targets, the surest takeover defense is possession of voting control. A hostile bidder by definition cannot oust incumbents who can outvote it. Even less than majority control may help managers fend off hostile takeovers, as by making it easier to obtain shareholder approval of other types of takeover defenses. Moreover, the plans' anti-takeover effects were immediate, even if management did not hold a majority of the superior voting rights shares, because the restrictions on transferability precluded an offeror from acquiring any of the Class B stock.

In the late 1980s, dual class stock provided the setting for the principal test to date of federal regulatory power over shareholder voting rights. The story illustrates not only the limits of the SEC's regulatory purview, but also the SEC's ability to evade those limits.

The NYSE long refused to list issuers having either a class of nonvoting common outstanding or multiple classes of common stock with disparate voting rights. The AMEX likewise refused to list nonvoting common stock, but its policy with respect to disparate voting rights plans was more flexible. Issuers adopting such plans would be listed as long as the plan satisfied certain guidelines designed to create a minimum level of participation to which the lesser voting rights class was entitled. In contrast, the NASD imposed no voting rights listing standards in either the over-the-counter market or the NASDAQ system.

With the renewal of corporate interest in dual class stock during the 1980s, however, issuers began pressuring the NYSE to adopt a more flexible listing standard. In 1988, the SEC responded by adopting Rule 19c–4, which effectively amended the rules of all the exchanges (and the NASD) to prohibit them from listing an issuer's equity securities if the company issued securities or took other corporate action nullifying, restricting, or disparately reducing the voting rights of existing shareholders.[20] As such, Rule 19c–4 was the SEC's first direct attempt to regulate substantively a matter of corporate governance applicable to all public corporations. The Business Roundtable challenged the Rule, arguing that corporate governance regulation is primarily a matter for state law and that the SEC therefore had no authority to adopt rules affecting substantive aspects of corporate voting rights. The D.C. Circuit agreed,

---

20. For a detailed treatment of Rule 19c–4 and the surrounding legal issues, see Stephen M. Bainbridge, The Short Life and Resurrection of SEC Rule 19c–4, 69 Wash. U. L.Q. 565 (1991).

striking down the rule as beyond the Commission's regulatory authority.[21]

Slippery slope arguments are often the last refuge of those with no better case, but Rule 19c–4 was indeed the proverbial camel's nose. There simply was no firebreak between substantive federal regulation of dual class stock and a host of other corporate voting issues raising similar concerns. Nor did laws affecting shareholder voting rights differ in principle or theory from any other corporate governance rules. Having once entered the field of corporate governance regulation, the SEC would have been hard-pressed to justify stopping with dual class stock. Creeping federalization of corporate law was a plausible outcome. The D.C. Circuit quite properly foreclosed this possibility.

The SEC could have sought U.S. Supreme Court review of the *Business Roundtable* decision, but did not. The SEC could have sought appropriate countervailing legislation from Congress, but did not. Instead, the Commission made use of what has been aptly called its "raised eyebrow" powers.[22] By virtue of the unique relationship between the SEC and the exchanges, the Commission naturally has considerable informal influence over exchange rulemaking. When the D.C. Circuit invalidated Rule 19c–4, SEC Chairman Arthur Levitt encouraged the three principal domestic securities exchanges—NYSE, AMEX, and NAS-DAQ—to adopt a uniform voting rights policy essentially tracking Rule 19c–4.[23]

D. Other Defenses

The most common response to a hostile takeover bid is litigation, usually raising some violation or another of the tender offer rules we studied earlier. In this section, we consider some other commonly used defenses.

1. *Pre-offer Planning*

In olden days, say circa 1980, corporations would develop so-called "black books" that provided a pre-determined set of responses to unsolicited offers. Today, however, most takeover lawyers recommend against pre-planned defensive packages. In reviewing target board actions, courts have emphasized the board's duty to evaluate a particular offer.[24]

21. Business Roundtable v. SEC, 905 F.2d 406 (D.C.Cir.1990).

22. Donald E. Schwartz, Federalism and Corporate Governance, 45 Ohio St. L.J. 545, 571 (1984).

23. For a more detailed treatment of the post-*Business Roundtable* developments, see Stephen M. Bainbridge, Revisiting the One–Share/One–Vote Controversy:

The Exchanges' Uniform Voting Rights Policy, 22 Sec. Reg. L.J. 175 (1994). See generally Roberta S. Karmel, The Future of Corporate Governance Listing Requirements, 54 SMU L. Rev. 325 (2001).

24. See, e.g., Moran v. Household Int'l, Inc., 500 A.2d 1346, 1354 (Del.1985) ("When the Household Board of Directors is faced with a tender offer and a request to

Canned responses will fail the "smell test" many courts seem to use when reviewing the consistency of a defense with the fiduciary duties of management.[25]

2. Early Warning Systems

In order to successfully resist an unsolicited takeover, the target must know at the earliest possible moment that a bid is being planned. Waiting for a Schedule 13D to be filed could mean the difference between a successful defense and a successful takeover. Counsel commonly advise potential targets to conduct daily reviews of trading in the company's stock to detect unusual price or volume movements. Regular contact with the firm's market maker or floor specialists was encouraged so as to alert the target of any large block transactions. The target was advised to regularly review the stockholder lists, looking for concentrated accumulations under individual or nominee names.

3. Defensive Acquisitions

In the old days, a potential target would try to create barriers for potential purchasers by acquiring companies that cause antitrust problems for the most likely bidders. In the 1970s, for example, the Marshall Field & Co. department store chain acquired numerous other retail chains for the purpose of creating such antitrust barriers. Although the acquisitions were uniformly unprofitable, the acquired chains operated in the same geographic areas as the most probable potential bidders for Marshall Field.[26] An obvious problem with this tactic is that unprofitable defensive acquisitions will cause the target's stock price to fall, which may make the target more vulnerable to potential buyers who will not face antitrust concerns.[27]

4. Stock Repurchases

Stock repurchase programs involve setting up a regular program to buy target shares on the open market from time to time. Such programs should have the desirable effect of supporting the company's stock price by (1) lessening the number of outstanding shares and (2) acting as a signal that management is supportive of shareholder interests. As a high stock price is an excellent takeover defense, such repurchase programs have become a common feature of corporate governance.

redeem the Rights, they will not be able to arbitrarily reject the offer.").

25. See E. Norman Veasey, The New Incarnation of the Business Judgment Rule in Takeover Defenses, 11 Del. J. Corp. L. 503, 512 (1986) (noting that a defense may fail the "smell test" if "it looks like an effort to entrench the incumbents and ... there is a reasonable likelihood that stock-

holders are not getting the best price obtainable").

26. Panter v. Marshall Field & Co., 646 F.2d 271 (7th Cir.1981) (holding that the defensive acquisition strategy did not violate the target board's fiduciary duties).

27. See Mark L. Mitchell & Kenneth Lehn, Do Bad Bidders Become Good Targets?, 98 J. Pol. Econ. 372 (1990).

As a takeover defense, stock repurchases will be most effective when the corporation has a large amount of free cash (cash for which there are no positive net present value investments available), but no substantial free cash flows. If the corporation has on-going free cash flows, a one-time stock repurchase is unlikely to have a permanent stock price effect. In order to make such a target a less attractive takeover candidate, an on-going program of regular stock repurchases will be necessary.

There are some potential problems associated with stock repurchase programs. Securities fraud liability is a major risk. Issuers can be held liable for securities fraud under Rule 10bn5 when they purchase shares while in possession of material nonpublic information, just as officers and directors can be held liable for inside trading. In any repurchase plan, the corporation therefore must be careful to analyze whether there would be any basis for an insider trading claim. In large companies with diverse information flows, this can obviously be very difficult. The best times to engage in repurchases are therefore immediately after annual and quarterly disclosure reports are filed with the SEC, as there is somewhat less likelihood of undisclosed material information at those times.

A stock repurchase plan reduces the number of shares the bidder has to buy in order to achieve control. If the price effect of the repurchase plan is not substantial, the plan may backfire. This risk can be alleviated by having a friendly or controlled entity purchase the stock. Some firms therefore effect repurchases through a pension plan or employee stock ownership plan. In that way, the shares remain outstanding, with full voting rights, instead of becoming nonvoting treasury shares.

5. Lock-ups

Both negotiated acquisitions and unsolicited tender offers may trigger competitive bidding for control of the target. Like exclusivity provisions in a merger agreement, the lock-up developed as a response to these risks. A lock-up is any arrangement or transaction by which the target corporation gives the favored bidder a competitive advantage over other bidders.[28] So defined the term includes such tactics as an unusually large cancellation fee or an agreement by the target to use takeover defenses to protect the favored bid from competition. Lock-up options refer more narrowly to agreements (usually separate from the merger agreement) granting the acquirer an option to buy shares or assets of the target. The option commonly becomes exercisable upon the acquisition by some third party of a specified percentage of the target's outstanding shares.[29]

---

28. See generally Stephen M. Bainbridge, Exclusive Merger Agreements and Lock–Ups in Negotiated Corporate Acquisitions, 75 Minn. L. Rev. 239 (1990).

29. E.g., Hanson Trust PLC v. ML SCM Acquisition Inc., 781 F.2d 264, 267 (2d Cir.

Stock lock-up options give the favored bidder an option to purchase treasury or authorized but unissued target shares. If the option is exercised prior to the shareholder vote on the merger agreement, the favored bidder can vote the additional shares in favor of the merger, helping to assure that the requisite approval will be obtained. If a competing bidder prevails, the favored bidder can exercise the option and sell the additional shares on the open market or tender them to the successful bidder, thereby recouping some or all of its sunk costs. Finally, the risk that the option will be exercised, thereby driving up the number of shares that must be acquired in order to obtain control and thus increasing the overall acquisition cost, may deter competing bids in the first instance.

Asset lock-up options grant the favored bidder an option to purchase a significant target asset. While asset lock-ups often are used to entice a prospective bidder, they are principally intended to end or prevent competitive bidding for the target. Accordingly, the subject of the option is usually either the asset most desired by a competing bidder or those essential to the target's operations.[30] Asset lock-ups are sometimes referred to as "crown jewel options," the name coming from the notion that the asset subject to the option is the target's crown jewel, i.e., its most valuable or desirable asset.

§ 7.2　Takeover Defenses and the Target Board's Fiduciary Duties Through *QVC*

The concern raised by the defenses just reviewed should be readily apparent:

> When managers are busy erecting obstacles to the taking over of the corporation by an investor who is likely to fire them if the takeover attempt succeeds, they have a clear conflict of interest, and it is not cured by vesting the power of decision in a board of directors in which insiders are a minority.... No one likes to be fired, whether he is just a director or also an officer. The so-called outsiders moreover are often friends of the insiders. And since they spend only part of their time on the affairs of the corporation, their knowledge of those affairs is much less than that of the insiders, to whom they are likely therefore to defer.[31]

The question is how courts ought to respond. The Delaware Supreme Court early recognized that the traditional doctrinal options were inadequate to the task at hand. Characterizing the action of a corporation's

---

1986); Mobil Corp. v. Marathon Oil Co., 669 F.2d 366 (6th Cir.1981), cert. denied, 455 U.S. 982 (1982); DMG, Inc. v. Aegis Corp., 1984 WL 8228 (1984).

30. See, e.g., Hanson Trust PLC v. ML SCM Acquisition Inc., 781 F.2d 264, 267 (2d

Cir.1986); Mobil Corp. v. Marathon Oil Co., 669 F.2d 366 (6th Cir.1981), cert. denied, 455 U.S. 982 (1982).

31. Dynamics Corp. of Am. v. CTS Corp., 794 F.2d 250, 256 (7th Cir.1986), rev'd on other grounds, 481 U.S. 69 (1987).

board of directors as a question of care or of loyalty has potentially outcome determinative consequences.[32] This is so because, if the court treated takeover defenses as a loyalty question, with its accompanying intrinsic fairness standard, takeover defenses would rarely pass muster. The defendant directors would be required, subject to close and exacting judicial scrutiny, to establish that the transaction was objectively fair to the corporation.[33] Because this burden is an exceedingly difficult one to bear, and thus would likely result in routine judicial invalidation of takeover defenses, a duty of loyalty analysis makes sense only if we think all takeovers are socially desirable and that all takeover defenses are therefore bad social policy.

On the other hand, if the court treated takeover defenses as a care question, virtually all takeover defenses would survive judicial review. Before the target's directors could be called to account for their actions, plaintiff would have to rebut the business judgment rule's presumptions by showing that the decision was tainted by fraud, illegality, self-dealing, or some other exception to the rule. Absent the proverbial smoking gun, plaintiff is unlikely to prevail under this standard. A duty of care analysis thus makes sense only if we think management resistance to takeovers is always appropriate.

The Delaware Supreme Court has therefore tried to steer a middle path. In this section, we trace the evolution of this complex body of law.

A. *Cheff v. Mathes*: Delaware's First Try

Cheff v. Mathes[34] long was Delaware's leading case on the validity of takeover defenses. In it the Delaware Supreme Court laid down a set of rules that purported to restrict a target board's ability to resist hostile takeovers, but in fact did very little to do so. The target was a company called Holland Furnace, which marketed its products using a set of remarkably fraudulent tactics. Holland salesmen went door-to-door posing as government or utility inspectors. Once they had received access to the homeowner's furnace, the salesmen would dismantle the furnace and refuse to reassemble it. The salesmen would inform the homeowner that the furnace was unsafe and that parts necessary to make it safe were unavailable. The homeowner would then be sold a replacement Holland furnace.[35] Because of government investigations into these unsavory practices, the firm was under-performing.

---

32. Both the Delaware supreme and chancery courts have recognized that choice of standard can be outcome determinative in this context. Mills Acquisition Co. v. Macmillan, Inc., 559 A.2d 1261, 1279 (Del. 1989); AC Acquisitions Corp. v. Anderson, Clayton & Co., 519 A.2d 103, 111 (Del.Ch. 1986).

33. See Robert M. Bass Group, Inc. v. Evans, 552 A.2d 1227, 1239 (Del.Ch.1988); cf. Sinclair Oil Corp. v. Levien, 280 A.2d 717 (Del.1971) (application of intrinsic fairness standard to fiduciary duties of majority shareholders).

34. 199 A.2d 548 (Del.1964).

35. Holland Furnace Co. v. FTC, 295 F.2d 302 (7th Cir.1961).

Arnold Maremont proposed a merger between Holland and Maremont's Motor Products Corporation. Holland's president, one Cheff, rejected Maremont's overtures. Maremont then began buying Holland stock. When he announced his purchase publicly and demanded a place on the board, Cheff again refused. Holland claimed Maremont often bought corporations to liquidate them for a profit. Because of this reputation, Cheff claimed, Holland employees who were aware of Maremont's interest were beginning to show signs of discontent.

Having met resistance, Maremont offered to sell his stock to the firm at a premium over his purchase price and over the current market price.[36] Holland's board agreed, causing the corporation to repurchase Maremont's shares using corporate funds. Other shareholders then challenged that repurchase transaction in a derivative suit.

In *Cheff*, the Delaware Supreme Court announced the so-called "primary purpose test" for review of takeover defenses. Under that standard, the court did not give the directors the immediate benefit of the business judgment rule's presumption of good faith. Rather, the directors had the initial burden of showing that they had reasonable grounds to believe that a danger to corporate policy and effectiveness existed and did not act for the primary purpose of preserving their own incumbency. Only if the board could make such a showing would they be entitled to the business judgment rule's protection. However, the directors merely had to show good faith and reasonable investigation; they could not be held liable for an honest mistake of judgment.[37]

---

36. During the 1980s, the purchase by a corporation of a potential acquirer's stock, at a premium over the market price, came to be called "greenmail." Buying off one person, however, provides no protection against later pursuers, except possibly to the extent that the premium paid to the first pursuer depletes the corporate resources and makes it a less attractive target. Managers could of course achieve such reduction in corporate resources simply by paying a dividend to all shareholders or by buying the corporation's shares from all shareholders wanting to sell. Section 5881 of the Internal Revenue Code, enacted in 1987, imposes a penalty tax of 50 percent on the gain from greenmail, which is defined as gain from the sale of stock that was held for less than two years and sold to the corporation pursuant to an offer that "was not made on the same terms to all shareholders." Despite its many critics, greenmail actually may be beneficial in that it may allow the board to seek higher bids or to enhance value (above the greenmail bidder's price) by making changes in

management or strategy. The question whether greenmail deserves its bad reputation therefore is essentially an empirical one. The evidence supports the proposition that greenmail actually benefits nonparticipating shareholders overall, and does not appear to be a device for entrenching incumbent management. Consequently, a greenmailer may be a catalyst for change from within or for a bidding war and may therefore deserve to make a profit. Jonathan R. Macey & Fred S. McChesney, A Theoretical Analysis of Corporate Greenmail, 95 Yale L.J. 13 (1985); Fred S. McChesney, Transaction Costs and Corporate Greenmail: Theory, Empirics, and a Mickey Mouse Case Study, 14 Managerial & Decision Econ. 131 (1993).

37. See Cheff v. Mathes, 199 A.2d 548 (Del.1964); see also Royal Indus., Inc. v. Monogram Indus., Inc., [1976–1977 Transfer Binder] Fed.Sec.L.Rep. (CCH) ¶ 95,863 at 91,136–38, 1976 WL 860 (C.D.Cal.1976) (applying Delaware law); Bennett v. Propp, 187 A.2d 405, 408 (Del.1962); Kors v. Carey, 158 A.2d 136, 140–42 (Del.Ch.1960).

The *Cheff* court was well aware of the conflict of interest inherent in target resistance to unsolicited bids. Hence, the court imposed the primary purpose test as a purportedly more stringent standard than the business judgment rule. To be sure, the court downplayed the conflict slightly by comparing the conflict posed by takeovers to that "present, for example, when a director sells property to the corporation." As we shall see below, however, this comparison is a perfectly plausible one, although it also is one that has essentially escaped most academic commentators.

In practice, however, the burden placed on target directors by the primary purpose test proved illusory. Liability could be imposed only if entrenching the incumbent officers and directors in office was the primary motive for the defensive actions.[38] Management therefore simply directed its counsel to carefully scrutinize the bidder's tender offer documents to find some issue of policy as to which they differed. And, of course, it was always possible to find some policy disagreement between incumbent management and the outside bidder. Why else would the bidder be trying to oust the incumbents? Once found, such a policy difference was all that was necessary to justify the use of defensive tactics, because the board could not be held liable for its actions, even if hindsight showed them to be unwise, so long as they were motivated by a sincere belief that they were necessary to maintain proper business policy and practices.[39] The primary purpose analysis thus added little to the highly deferential treatment of board decisions mandated by the traditional business judgment rule and therefore proved an ineffective response to the conflict of interest present when target boards and management respond to a takeover bid.

B.　*Unocal*

In *Unocal v. Mesa Petroleum*,[40] the Delaware Supreme Court addressed the flaws inherent in the *Cheff* standard by promulgating what has been called an "intermediate" or "enhanced business judgment" standard of judicial review, but is perhaps best described as a "conditional business judgment rule."[41] Famed corporate raider T. Boone Pickens,

---

38. Royal Industries, Inc. v. Monogram Industries, Inc., [1976–1977 Transfer Binder] Fed.Sec.L.Rep. (CCH) ¶ 95,863 at 91,- 136–38, 1976 WL 860 (C.D.Cal.1976) (applying Delaware law); Condec Corp. v. Lunkenheimer Co., 230 A.2d 769 (Del.Ch. 1967).

39. See Ronald J. Gilson, A Structural Approach to Corporations: The Case Against Defensive Tactics in Tender Offers, 33 Stan. L. Rev. 819, 829 (1981).

40. Unocal Corp. v. Mesa Petroleum Co., 493 A.2d 946 (Del.1985).

41. Michael P. Dooley, Fundamentals of Corporation Law 547 (1995). Like the traditional business judgment rule, the conditional *Unocal* rule can be applied only to actions that are within the power or authority of the board. As a preliminary inquiry one must ask whether the board had the authority under the governing statutes and the corporation's organic documents to take this specific action. Moran v. Household Int'l, Inc., 500 A.2d 1346, 1350 (Del.1985).

whom the court referred to as having "a national reputation as a 'greenmailer,' " controlled Mesa, which in turn owned 13% of Unocal's voting stock. Mesa launched a hostile two-tiered tender offer, pursuant to which it initially offered to buy slightly over 37% of the remaining shares for $54 per share. According to Mesa, if the initial bid succeeded, Mesa would then eliminate the remaining shares by means of a freeze-out merger, in which the consideration would be junk bonds ostensibly worth $54 per Unocal share.

Two-tier offers like Mesa's are generally regarded as being structurally coercive. Suppose Target's pre-bid stock price was $50. Bidder 1 makes a two-tier offer with differing prices: $80 cash in the first step tender offer and $60 cash in the second step freeze-out merger. Assuming the first step tender offer seeks 50% of the shares plus one, the blended offer price is $70 with a blended premium of $20 per share (calculated by taking the weighted average of the two steps). Bidder 2 offers $75 in cash for any and all shares tendered, a premium of $25 per share. As a group shareholders are better off with Bidder 2. Yet, Bidder 1's offer creates a prisoners' dilemma. Those shareholders who "cheat," by taking Bidder 1's front-end offer, end up with $80 rather than $75. With a large non-cohesive group in which defectors bear no cost—such as shame or reprisals—rational investors should defect. Because everyone's individual incentive is to defect, the shareholders end up with the offer that is worst for the group. Mesa's offer differed from this example by offering the same price in both steps, but the far less attractive form of consideration to be paid in the second step would have similarly coercive effects.

In hopes of fending off Mesa's bid, Unocal's board of directors authorized a discriminatory self-tender offer for Unocal's own stock. Under Unocal's counter offer, if Mesa's front-end tender offer succeeded in giving Mesa a majority of Unocal's stock, Unocal would then offer to repurchase the remaining minority shares with debt securities purportedly worth $72 per share. Unocal's self-tender offer was intentionally discriminatory in that any shares tendered by Pickens would not be accepted. If effected, the self-tender offer would drain Unocal of most of its significant assets and leave it burdened by substantial debt. Even more cleverly, however, Unocal might never need actually complete the self-tender offer. Its offer only applied if Mesa acquired more than 50% of Unocal's voting stock. Because Unocal offered a higher price than did Mesa, however, Unocal's shareholders were likely to tender to it rather than to Mesa. If no shareholders tendered to Mesa, Mesa would not acquire 50%, and Unocal would be able close its offer without taking down any of the tendered shares. When Unocal's shareholders complained about this aspect of the defense, Unocal agreed to buy 50 million of the shares tendered to it the stock tendered to it even if Mesa did not acquire 50%.

Mesa sued to enjoin the self-tender offer, alleging that Unocal's board of directors had violated its fiduciary duties to both Mesa and Unocal's other shareholders. In particular, Mesa objected to the discriminatory nature of the proposed self-tender offer. The Delaware Supreme Court rejected Mesa's arguments.[42] Given the coercive nature of Mesa's bid, the bid's probable price inadequacy, and Pickens' reputation as a greenmailer, Unocal was entitled to take strong measures to defeat the Mesa offer. Because excluding Mesa from the self-tender offer was essential to making the defense work, the directors could discriminate against Mesa without violating their fiduciary duties.[43]

In *Unocal*, the Delaware Supreme Court reaffirmed the target's board general decision-making primacy, which includes an obligation to determine whether the offer is in the best interests of the shareholders. In light of the board's potential conflict of interest vis-à-vis the shareholders, however, judicial review was to be somewhat more intrusive than under the traditional business judgment rule: "Because of the omnipresent specter that a board may be acting primarily in its own interests, rather than those of the corporation and its shareholders, there is an enhanced duty which calls for judicial examination at the threshold before the protections of the business judgment rule may be conferred."

The initial burden of proof is on the directors, who must first show that they had reasonable grounds for believing that a danger to corporate policy or effectiveness existed. The directors satisfy this burden by showing good faith and reasonable investigation. The good faith element requires a showing that the directors acted in response to a perceived threat to the corporation and not for the purpose of entrenching themselves in office. The reasonable investigation element requires a demonstration that the board was adequately informed, with the relevant standard being one of gross negligence.[44] Assuming the directors carry their initial burden, they next must prove that the defense was reasonable in relationship to the threat posed by the hostile bid. Note that both

42. After the *Unocal* decision, the SEC demonstrated its disapproval of discriminatory tender offers by amending its Williams Act rules to prohibit tender offers other than those made to all shareholders. See Exchange Act Rule 13e–4(f)(8) (issuer self-tender offers); Exchange Act Rule 14d–10(a)(1) (third party offers).

43. Unocal and Mesa eventually negotiated an agreement that allowed Mesa to participate in Unocal's self-tender. A Unocal shareholder then sued Mesa under the short swing profit provisions of Securities Exchange Act § 16(b). Mesa argued that the self-tender qualified as an unorthodox

transaction exempt from § 16(b). In Colan v. Mesa Petroleum Co., 951 F.2d 1512 (9th Cir.1991), however, the court rejected that argument, holding that the so-called *Kern County* exception applies solely to involuntary transactions. Mesa's decision to tender to Unocal was voluntary and, therefore, subject to § 16(b) liability.

44. Moran v. Household Int'l, Inc., 500 A.2d 1346, 1356 (Del.1985); Harvey L. Pitt, On the Precipice: A Reexamination of Directors' Fiduciary Duties in the Context of Hostile Acquisitions, 15 Del. J. Corp. L. 811, 878 n. 264 (1990).

the decision to adopt and any subsequent decision to implement a set of takeover defenses are subject to challenge and judicial review.[45]

Not surprisingly, the board's "initial" burden of proof quickly became the whole ball game. If the directors carried their two-step burden, the business judgment rule applied, but if the directors failed to carry their initial burden, the duty of loyalty's intrinsic fairness test applied.[46] It is for this reason that the *Unocal* test is more properly seen as a conditional version of the business judgment rule, rather than an intermediate standard. The *Unocal* rule solved the problem of outcome determination not so much by creating a different standard of review, as by creating a mechanism for determining on an individual basis which of the traditional doctrinal standards was appropriate for the particular case at bar.

C. *Revlon*

In *Revlon v. MacAndrews & Forbes Holdings*, the Delaware Supreme Court developed a modified version of the *Unocal* standard to deal with a particular problem; namely, the use of takeover defenses to ensure that a white knight would prevail in a control auction with the hostile bidder.[47] In response to an unsolicited tender offer by Pantry Pride, Revlon's board undertook a variety of defensive measures, culminating in the board's authorization of negotiations with other prospective bidders. Thereafter the board entered into a merger agreement with a white knight, which included a lock-up arrangement, as well as other measures designed to prevent Pantry Pride's bid from prevailing. Revlon's initial defensive tactics were reviewed (and upheld) under standard *Unocal* analysis. In turning to the lock-up arrangement, however, the court struck out in a new direction:

> The Revlon board's authorization permitting management to negotiate a merger or buyout with a third party was a recognition that the company was for sale. The duty of the board had thus changed from the preservation of Revlon as a corporate entity to the maximization of the company's value at a sale for the stockholders' benefit. This

---

45. In Moran v. Household Int'l, Inc., 500 A.2d 1346 (Del.1985), plaintiffs sued when the poison pill was first adopted, before any takeover bid had been made. The court upheld the pill as valid, but explained that: "When the Household Board of Directors is faced with a tender offer and a request to redeem the [pill], they will not be able to arbitrarily reject the offer. They will be held to the same fiduciary standards any other board of directors would be held to in deciding to adopt a defensive mechanism, the same standard as they were held to in originally approving the [pill]." Id. at 1355. See also Hills Stores Co. v. Bozic, 769 A.2d

88, 106–07 (Del.Ch.2000) (opining that: "Delaware case law has assured stockholders that the fact that the court has approved a board's decision to put defenses in place on a clear day does not mean that the board will escape its burden to justify its use of those defenses in the heat of battle under the *Unocal* standard.").

46. Shamrock Holdings, Inc. v. Polaroid Corp., 559 A.2d 257, 271 (Del.Ch.1989).

47. Revlon, Inc. v. MacAndrews & Forbes Holdings, Inc., 506 A.2d 173 (Del. 1986).

significantly altered the board's responsibilities under the *Unocal* standards. It no longer faced threats to corporate policy and effectiveness, or to the stockholders' interests, from a grossly inadequate bid. The whole question of defensive measures became moot. The directors' role changed from defenders of the corporate bastion to auctioneers charged with getting the best price for the stockholders at a sale of the company.

Because the lock-up ended the auction in return for minimal improvement in the final offer, it was invalidated.

Thus was born the jurisprudential territory that came to be known as *Revlon*-land. Finding one's way around it proved surprisingly troublesome. For example, did *Revlon* establish special duties to govern control auctions or were the so-called "*Revlon* duties" really just the general *Unocal* rules applied to a special fact situation? The courts have waffled on this issue, although the latter interpretation seems to have ultimately prevailed. In 1987, for example, the Delaware Supreme Court drew a rather sharp distinction between the *Unocal* standard and what it then called "the *Revlon* obligation to conduct a sale of the corporation."[48] Two years later, however, the court indicated that *Revlon* is "merely one of an unbroken line of cases that seek to prevent the conflicts of interest that arise in the field of mergers and acquisitions by demanding that directors act with scrupulous concern for fairness to shareholders."[49] The doctrinal differences between *Unocal* and *Revlon* nevertheless still loom quite large at times or, at least, in some eyes.

Whether the *Revlon* duties were distinct or just a sub-set of *Unocal*, what exactly were directors supposed to do once their role changes from "defenders of the corporate bastion to auctioneers"? Prior to the pivotal *Paramount* decisions discussed below, we thought a few things could be said with confidence. We knew, for example, that target directors need not be passive observers of market competition.[50] The board's objective, however, "must remain the enhancement of the bidding process for the benefit of the stockholders."[51] Favored treatment of one bidder at any stage of the process was therefore subjected to close scrutiny. Ultimately, the board's basic task was to get the best possible deal, which usually but not always meant the best possible price, for their shareholders. Directors did not need to blindly focus on price to the exclusion of other relevant factors. The board could evaluate offers on such grounds as the proposed form of consideration, tax consequences, firmness of financing, antitrust or other regulatory obstacles, and timing.[52] Easy standards to state perhaps, but often quite difficult ones to apply.

48. Ivanhoe Partners v. Newmont Mining Corp., 535 A.2d 1334, 1338 (Del.1987).

49. Barkan v. Amsted Indus., Inc., 567 A.2d 1279, 1286 (Del.1989).

50. CRTF Corp. v. Federated Dep't Stores, Inc., 683 F.Supp. 422, 441 (S.D.N.Y. 1988) (applying Delaware law).

51. Mills Acquisition Co. v. Macmillan, Inc., 559 A.2d 1261, 1287 (Del.1989).

52. Cottle v. Storer Communication, Inc., 849 F.2d 570, 577 (11th Cir.1988).

Finally, and even more fundamentally, when did directors stop being "defenders of the corporate bastion" and become "auctioneers"? Again, prior to the *Paramount* decisions, it seemed well-settled that the auction-eering duty is triggered when (but apparently only when) a proposed transaction would result in a change of control of the target corporation. For example, if a defensive recapitalization, which most of these cases involved, transferred effective voting control to target management, or some other identifiable control block, the courts treated the transaction as a "change in control" of the corporation requiring adherence to *Revlon*'s auction rule.[53] If no identifiable control block formed (or changed hands), however, defensive measures were subject solely to standard *Unocal* review.[54]

D. Evolution: The Pivotal *Paramount* Cases

As the *Unocal* rules evolved, two recurring questions arose. First, what threats to the corporation and its shareholders were legally cogni-zable under the first prong? Second, what defenses were proportional to a given threat?

At least for a time, the Delaware Chancery Court defined the category of cognizable threats quite narrowly. Only threats to sharehold-er interests had any real analytical significance.[55] Nor were all threats to shareholder interests cognizable. Rather, at least in the context of an offer for all of the target's outstanding shares, the trend was towards limiting cognizable threats to inadequate value and structural coercion.[56] Inadequate value refers, obviously enough, to a claim that the price offered by the bidder is too low. Structural coercion refers to bidder tactics creating a "risk that disparate treatment of non-tendering share-holders might distort shareholders' tender decisions."[57]

---

53. Mills Acquisition Co. v. Macmillan, Inc., 559 A.2d 1261, 1285 (Del.1989) (hold-ing that the requisite "sale" could take "the form of an active auction, a manage-ment buyout or a 'restructuring' "); see also Robert M. Bass Group, Inc. v. Evans, 552 A.2d 1227, 1243 (Del.Ch.1988); cf. Ivanhoe Partners v. Newmont Mining Corp., 535 A.2d 1334, 1345 (Del.1987) (*Revlon* not trig-gered where management ally had less than 50% voting control after defensive recapital-ization); accord Black & Decker Corp. v. American Standard, Inc., 682 F.Supp. 772, 781 (D.Del.1988) (reading Delaware law to require directors of a company to maximize the amount received by shareholders once it is clear to them that the "corporation is to be subject to a change of control").

54. Paramount Communications, Inc. v. Time Inc., [1989 Transfer Binder] Fed.Sec.

L.Rep. (CCH) ¶ 94,514 at 93,279–80, 1989 WL 79880 (Del.Ch.), aff'd on other grounds, 571 A.2d 1140 (Del.1989).

55. See § 6.3.A.

56. See, e.g., City Capital Assoc. Ltd. Partnership v. Interco Inc., 551 A.2d 787, 797 (Del.Ch.1988).

57. Ronald J. Gilson & Reinier Kraak-man, Delaware's Intermediate Standard for Defensive Tactics: Is there Substance to Proportionality Review, 44 Bus. Law. 247, 267 (1989). Two-tier tender offers are per-haps the most commonly recognized form of structural coercion. If shareholders believe that the offeror is likely to obtain a control-ling interest in the front-end transaction, they face the risk that they will be squeezed out in the back-end for less desirable con-sideration. Thus they are coerced into ten-dering into the front-end to avoid that risk,

The Delaware courts gave target directors a more-or-less free hand to deal with structurally coercive bidder tactics. Defenses designed to preclude such offers, to minimize their coercive effect, or to provide a more viable alternative to the shareholders all were deemed proportional. Indeed, when structural coercion was the identified threat, proportionality review usually was perfunctory at best.[58]

When inadequate value was the sole threat, however, proportionality review became more exacting. As most observers interpreted the so-called poison pill cases,[59] *Unocal* permitted target management to use takeover defenses as negotiating leverage to obtain a better deal for the shareholders or, more realistically, to delay the hostile offer while an alternative transaction was arranged. In either case, however, target management supposedly had to let the shareholders make the ultimate decision.[60] According to the conventional wisdom, once it became clear the best possible alternatives were on the table, the board was required to redeem the pill and permit the shareholders to choose between the available alternatives. The target board could neither "just say no," nor could it structure the transaction in such a way as to force shareholders to accept a management-sponsored alternative. On close examination of the cases, however, this conventional wisdom missed a subtle, but important nuance.

---

even if they believe the front-end transaction itself is undesirable.

58. In *Unocal*, for example, the court's proportionality analysis can be described most charitably as concise. See Unocal Corp. v. Mesa Petroleum Co., 493 A.2d, 946, 956 (Del.1985). Note that Delaware law on coercive bidder tactics is easily squared with our authority-accountability framework. On the one hand, corporate law grants sweeping powers to the board in part so that the board can protect shareholder financial interests. If a coercive bid threatens those interests, authority values thus justify board resistance. On the other hand, giving the board power to resist coercive offers does not implicate significant accountability concerns. To be sure, the board's decision to resist a structurally coercive bid may be motivated by personal considerations unrelated to shareholder welfare. But so what? In the first place, the category of structurally coercive tactics is a well-defined one, making it possible to objectively determine whether the board was responding to a true threat to shareholder interests. In the second, why should it matter that incumbents get some protection if resistance also protects shareholder interests? The bidder, after all, controls its own

fate in this regard. If the bidder drops the structurally coercive aspects of its offer, this justification for defensive tactics is no longer availing.

59. The name refers to a group of cases in which targets used poison pills to protect a restructuring plan from interference by a hostile bidder. See, e.g., Grand Metropolitan PLC v. Pillsbury Co., 558 A.2d 1049 (Del.Ch.1988); City Capital Assoc. Ltd. Partnership v. Interco Inc., 551 A.2d 787 (Del.Ch.1988); see also BNS Inc. v. Koppers Co., Inc., 683 F.Supp. 458 (D.Del.1988) (applying Delaware law); CRTF Corp. v. Federated Dep't Stores, Inc., 683 F.Supp. 422 (S.D.N.Y.1988) (same).

60. Cases purporting to stand for the proposition that the board must ultimately permit the shareholders to choose include: Shamrock Holdings, Inc. v. Polaroid Corp., 559 A.2d 257 (Del.Ch.1989); Grand Metropolitan PLC v. Pillsbury Co., 558 A.2d 1049, 1058 (Del.Ch.1988); City Capital Assoc. Ltd. Partnership v. Interco Inc., 551 A.2d 787, 799–800 (Del.Ch.1988); AC Acquisitions Corp. v. Anderson, Clayton & Co., 519 A.2d 103, 113–14 (Del.Ch.1986). But see Moran v. Household Int'l, Inc., 490 A.2d 1059, 1070 (Del.Ch.), aff'd, 500 A.2d 1346 (Del. 1985).

What the conventional wisdom ignored was the extent to which the Delaware cases suggested that the board of directors' motive actually was the key issue. As former Delaware Chancellor Allen explained in the closely related context of management buyout transactions: "The court's own implicit evaluation of the integrity of the ... process marks that process as deserving respect or condemns it to be ignored." Assuming that a special committee of independent directors would be appointed to consider the proposed transaction, Allen went on to explain: "When a special committee's process is perceived as reflecting a good faith, informed attempt to approximate aggressive, arms-length bargaining, it will be accorded substantial importance by the court. When, on the other hand, it appears as artifice, ruse or charade, or when the board unduly limits the committee or when the committee fails to correctly perceive its mission—then one can expect that its decision will be accorded no respect."[61] The same is true with respect to board resistance to unsolicited tender offers. If the conflict of interest inherent in such resistance has matured into actual self-dealing, the court will invalidate the defensive tactics. If the board acted from proper motives, even if mistakenly, however, the court will leave the defenses in place.

Former Delaware Supreme Court Justice Moore argued, for example, that his court's "decisions represent a case-by-case analysis of some difficult and compelling problems."[62] He later elaborated:

> We did not approach [takeover] cases with the question of whether to allow the corporation to continue in its present form or to permit someone else to acquire the company.... [T]he question before the court was whether the directors acted properly in accepting or rejecting the competing offers.... As long as the directors adhered to their fiduciary duties, it would have been most inappropriate for any court to intrude upon a board's business decision. No court has a role in disciplining directors for the proper exercise of business judgment, even if it turns out to be wrong.[63]

Former Delaware Chancellor Allen made much the same point in *RJR Nabisco*, where he indicated that the basic question is whether the board acted with due care and in good faith:

> Surely the board may not use its power to exercise judgment in [an auction of control] as a sham or pretext to prefer one bidder for inappropriate reasons.... But the board of directors continues, in the auction setting as in others, to bear the burden imposed and

---

61. William T. Allen, Independent Directors in MBO Transactions: Are They Fact or Fantasy?, 45 Bus. Law. 2055, 2060 (1990); see generally Michael P. Dooley, Two Models of Corporate Governance, 47 Bus. Law. 461, 517–24 (1992) (discussing the significance of board motives in Delaware's takeover jurisprudence).

62. Andrew G.T. Moore, II, State Competition: Panel Response, 8 Cardozo L. Rev. 779, 782 (1987).

63. Andrew G.T. Moore, II, The 1980s— Did We Save the Stockholders While the Corporation Burned?, 70 Wash. U.L.Q. 277, 287–89 (1992).

exercise the power conferred by Section 141(a). Assuming it does exercise a business judgment, in good faith and advisedly, concerning the management of the auction process, it has, in my opinion, satisfied its duty.[64]

A federal court similarly described the *Unocal* standard as asking "whether a fully informed, wholly disinterested, reasonably courageous director would dissent from the board's act in any material part."[65] Motive is a consistent theme throughout these summations of Delaware law.[66]

Motive also turns out to be a major theme of *Interco*, the case most often cited as standing for the conventional wisdom. In *Interco,* the target's board of directors refused to redeem its poison pill. By doing so, the board prevented a hostile bid from going forward until a management-sponsored restructuring could be completed, which would make Interco an unattractive takeover target. Chancellor Allen enjoined the board's obstructive tactics, using dicta that broadly endorsed the shareholder choice position.[67] Tellingly, however, he concluded "that reasonable minds not affected by an inherent, entrenched interest in the matter, could not reasonably differ with respect to the conclusion that the [bidder's] $74 cash offer did not represent a threat to shareholder interests sufficient in the circumstances to justify, in effect, foreclosing shareholders from electing to accept that offer." If the right to decide belongs to the shareholders, however, what relevance does the board's motives have? A motive analysis is only necessary—or appropriate, for that matter—if the board in fact has decisive authority in takeover battles.[68]

The emphasis on motive is further confirmed by a case outside the line of poison pill decisions: the Delaware Supreme Court's *Macmillan*

64. In re RJR Nabisco, Inc. Shareholders Litigation, [1988–89 Transfer Binder] Fed.Sec.L.Rep. (CCH) ¶ 94,194 at 91,715, 1989 WL 7036 (Del.Ch.1989).

65. Southdown, Inc. v. Moore McCormack Resources, Inc., 686 F.Supp. 595, 602 (S.D.Tex.1988).

66. This is not to suggest that motive is always dispositive. In Omnicare, Inc. v. NCS Healthcare, Inc., 818 A.2d 914 (Del. 2003). The Delaware Supreme Court invoked Unocal and its progeny to invalidate a lockup arrangement in a negotiated acquisition. In dissent, Justice Steele observed (correctly, in my view) that the target's "board of directors acted selflessly pursuant to a careful, fair process and determined in good faith that the benefits to the stockholders and corporation flowing from a merger agreement containing reasonable deal protection provisions outweigh any speculative benefits that might result from

entertaining a putative higher offer." If motive were controlling, the court therefore should have upheld the merger agreement.

67. City Capital Assoc. Ltd. Partnership v. Interco, Inc., 551 A.2d 787 (Del.Ch.1988). See generally Michael P. Dooley, Two Models of Corporate Governance, 47 Bus. Law. 461, 519–21 (1992).

68. This reading of Allen's *Interco* opinion is supported by his subsequent *TW Services* decision, in which he distinguished *Interco* and the other poison pill cases from the case at bar on the ground that the former did not "involve circumstances in which a board had in good faith (which appears to exist here) elected to continue managing the enterprise in a long term mode and not to actively consider an extraordinary transaction of any type." TW Servs. v. SWT Acquisition Corp., 1989 WL 20290 (1989).

decision.[69] In May 1987, Macmillan's senior management recognized that it was a likely takeover target. Management therefore began studying a restructuring plan that would effectively transfer voting control to senior managers. Before the restructuring could be completed, the Robert M. Bass Group emerged as a potential bidder. The board then lowered the threshold at which its poison pill would become operative and took various other defensive steps designed to stave off the Bass Group until the restructuring could be completed. Unfortunately for Macmillan's management, Vice Chancellor Jacobs found that the restructuring was not only economically inferior to the Bass Group bid, but also was designed to preclude the shareholders from accepting that bid.[70] Concluding that *Unocal* obliged Macmillan's directors to give their shareholders "a choice," the Vice Chancellor enjoined the restructuring. So far all is perfectly consistent with the conventional wisdom.

Undaunted by their initial failure, the Macmillan board immediately began exploring a management-sponsored leveraged buyout. Shortly thereafter, a company controlled by Robert Maxwell entered the fray. Macmillan's incumbent CEO conducted the initial negotiations with Maxwell. The CEO misled Maxwell, while information about Maxwell's bid was tipped to management's leveraged buyout partner. Nor did the Macmillan board of directors act to restrain management; instead, the board essentially abdicated its oversight function, allowing management to skew the auction process in favor of their partner. Finally, the board granted a lock-up option to management's partner, effectively precluding Maxwell from presenting a competing tender offer to the target's shareholders. The ultimate decision thus was made not by the disinterested board members or the shareholders, but by the same managers who were trying to buy the company.

Now we reach the point at which the conventional wisdom begins to unravel. In the course of invalidating the lock-up, the Supreme Court distinguished between lock-ups that draw an otherwise unwilling bidder into the contest and those that end an active auction by effectively foreclosing further bidding. While neither type is per se unlawful, the latter is subject to exacting judicial scrutiny. Where the target obtains only a minimal increase in the final bid in return for an auction-ending lock-up, the agreement is unlikely to pass muster. On the other hand, where the favored bidder offers a significant price increase in return for an end to competitive bidding, judicial review will be more favorable.

If this distinction is to be taken seriously, *Macmillan* effectively permits the board to foreclose shareholder choice.[71] Lock-ups can pose a

---

69. Mills Acquisition Co. v. Macmillan, Inc., 559 A.2d 1261, 1265 (Del.1989).

70. Robert M. Bass Group, Inc. v. Evans, 552 A.2d 1227, 1241–44 (Del.Ch.1988).

71. In theory, of course, shareholders retain some degree of choice even in this context. They can reject the favored bidder's proposal, by voting down a merger agreement or refusing to sell into a tender

severe threat both to free shareholder choice and to continued competitive bidding. While *Macmillan* holds bid-preclusive lock-ups to a high standard, it also leaves open the possibility that the board can justify their use in appropriate cases. What then happened to the principle of free shareholder choice? The answer is that *Macmillan* rested not on shareholder choice but on motive. *Macmillan* implies that the board retains full decision-making authority—including the authority to foreclose shareholder choice—unless it acted from improper motives.

This interpretation of *Macmillan* is forcefully confirmed by the contrast between that decision and Chancellor Allen's opinion in the RJR Nabisco takeover fight. Drawn with a broad brush, these cases appear to be quite similar. In both, the sequence of events opened with a proposal to give incumbent management control of the company. In both, a competing bid then emerged. In both, an auction of corporate control developed. In both, the board ultimately had to select between two bids that were quite close in price. Yet the results were quite different. In *Macmillan*, the board selected the nominally higher bid, but was found guilty of breaching its fiduciary duties. In *RJR Nabisco*, the board rejected the nominally higher bid, but its decision was protected by the business judgment rule. Why this disparity of result? As always, the answer is in the details.

In *RJR Nabisco*, a special committee of outside directors was formed as soon as the board was told that a group led by Russ Johnson, the President and Chief Executive Officer, wanted to take the company private in a management-sponsored leveraged buyout.[72] The board carefully did not permit Johnson to have any role in the selection of the special committee; nor did the committee permit Johnson any role in selecting its financial or legal advisers. No member of the special committee had any direct or indirect financial interest in the transaction. The committee's independence paid off handsomely in its insistence on fair competition. The management group's role in the auction was limited to that of a bidder, with no special advantages. Indeed, plaintiffs asserted that the committee and the board were biased against management, a claim Chancellor Allen found "baseless." As a result, there was no basis for believing that the board's decisions were motivated by self-interest.

In *Macmillan*, by contrast, there was a lengthy delay before a special board committee was formed. The special committee was "hand picked" by the incumbent chief executive officer, who along with Macmillan's other senior managers was to receive up to a 20 percent equity stake in the firm if their leveraged buyout proposal succeeded. The supposedly

offer, in the hopes that competing bids will then be made. In practice, however, the factors outlined in the text often render even this vestige of shareholder choice illusory.

72. RJR Nabisco, [1988–89 Transfer Binder] Fed.Sec.L.Rep. (CCH) ¶ 94,194 at 91,703.

independent committee, moreover, included a former college classmate of the CEO's father. The CEO selected the committee's financial and legal advisers. Not surprisingly, the committee failed to adequately oversee the competitive process, allowing management to skew the process in its favor.

Circumstantial evidence of the board's motives thus proved critical to the outcomes of both cases. In *RJR Nabisco*, for example, Chancellor Allen ultimately treated plaintiff's complaint as "an attack upon a decision made by an apparently disinterested board in the exercise of its statutory power to manage the business and affairs of the corporation." Finding no evidence that undermined the appearance of disinterest, Chancellor Allen upheld the RJR Nabisco board's conduct even though the two bids were substantially equivalent. He did so even though the nominally higher bid was rejected. He did so even though the board expressly refused to reopen the bidding. This last is particularly striking. The stated reason for the board's refusal to reopen the bidding, despite the closeness of the two bids, was a concern that the non-management bidder would drop out if the auction was extended. Although Allen believed that was unlikely, in light of the absence of any evidence that the board had acted from conflicted interests he deferred to the board's decision to endorse one of the bids, just as our analysis suggests he should have done. In contrast, the strong evidence of self-interested behavior by Macmillan's officers and directors rendered the board's decisions unworthy of deference.[73] Shareholder choice thus is not important in its own right, but rather has significance only because attempts to foreclose it may suggest that the board of directors' inherent conflict of interest has shifted from being a potential problem to an actual one.

The ability of Delaware's takeover doctrine to address cases in which improper motives tainted the board's decision-making process was at first undermined but ultimately restored in a pair of well-known cases involving Paramount Communications. In the first of these cases, *Paramount Communications v. Time Inc.*,[74] the Delaware courts addressed a

---

73. Other examples of the outcome-determinative nature of motive include Gilbert v. El Paso Co., 575 A.2d 1131, 1146 (Del.1990) (upholding settlement of a hostile takeover contest because "there is not a scintilla of evidence to intimate that this arrangement was the result of improper motives" on the board's part); Ivanhoe Partners v. Newmont Mining Corp., 535 A.2d 1334, 1344 (Del.1987) (upholding defensive tactics because the "board acted to maintain the company's independence and not merely to preserve its own control"); Henley Group, Inc. v. Santa Fe Southern Pacific Corp., 13 Del J. Corp. L. 1152, 1178 (Del.Ch.1988) (upholding corporate restructuring where the board's "diligent efforts"

to sell the company before embarking on the restructuring "deprive[d] the plaintiffs' argument—that the defendants were motivated to entrench themselves—of its force."); Freedman v. Restaurant Assoc. Indus., [1987–1988 Transfer Binder] Fed.Sec. L.Rep. (CCH) ¶ 93,502, 1987 WL 14323 (Del.Ch.1987) (board committee's handling of management-led leveraged buyout proposal to be reviewed under the business judgment rule because plaintiffs had "failed utterly to offer any legal justification for the court's second-guessing of the special committee.").

74. Paramount Communications, Inc. v. Time Inc., [1989 Transfer Binder] Fed.Sec.

takeover struggle between Time, Warner Communications, and Paramount. After first developing a long-term strategic plan and searching for acquisitions that would advance that plan, Time's board of directors agreed to a merger with Warner Communications in which former Warner shareholders would receive newly issued Time shares representing approximately 62 percent of the shares of the combined entity. As is typical in negotiated acquisitions, the parties also sought "to discourage any effort to upset the transaction" by agreeing to a lock-up option giving each party the option to trigger an exchange of shares. In addition, the merger agreement included a no shop clause, which they supplemented by obtaining commitments from various banks that they would not finance a takeover bid for Time.

Shortly before Time' shareholders were to vote on the merger agreement,[75] Paramount made a cash tender offer for Time. Time's board rejected the offer as inadequate, without entering into negotiations with Paramount. To forestall Paramount, the Time and Warner boards then agreed to a new structure for the transaction, under which Time would make a cash tender offer for a majority block of Warner shares to be followed by a merger in which remaining Warner shares would be acquired, thus obviating the need for shareholder approval. The new plan required Time to incur between 7 and 10 billion dollars in additional debt. Finally, and perhaps most damningly from the perspective of a Time shareholder, it foreclosed the possibility of a sale to Paramount. If the new plan succeeded, Time's shareholders therefore would end up as minority shareholders in a company saddled with substantial debt and whose stock price almost certainly would be lower in the short run than the Paramount offer.

The substantial differences in shareholder wealth likely to result from a decision to merge with Warner rather than to sell to Paramount forcefully presented the question of who should make that decision. As Chancellor Allen put it, the "overarching question is where legally (an easy question) and equitably (more subtle problem) the locus of decision-making power does or should reside in circumstances of this kind." Paramount naturally insisted that Time's board had an obligation to give the "shareholders the power and opportunity to decide whether the company should now be sold." Chancellor Allen, however, squarely rejected that proposition. Allen acknowledged that reasonable people could believe that the Paramount offer was the better deal for the shareholders, that many of Time's shareholders undoubtedly so believed, and that the Time directors' preference for the Warner deal might turn

L.Rep. (CCH) ¶ 94,514, 1989 WL 79880 (Del.Ch.), aff'd, 571 A.2d 1140 (Del.1989).

75. The plan of merger called for Warner to be merged into a Time subsidiary in exchange for Time common stock. Although Time was not formally a party to the merger and approval by its shareholders therefore was not required under Delaware law, New York Stock Exchange rules required a vote of Time shareholders because of the number of shares to be issued.

out to be a terrible mistake. Having said all that, however, the board nonetheless had the authority to go forward with the Warner acquisition:

> [T]he financial vitality of the corporation and the value of the company's shares is in the hands of the directors and management of the firm. The corporation law does not operate on the theory that directors, in exercising their powers to manage the firm, are obligated to follow the wishes of a majority of shares. In fact, directors, not shareholders, are charged with the duty to manage the firm.[76]

Time's emphasis on board prerogative at the expense of shareholder choice reminds us that shareholder choice has little, if any, independent normative significance. Instead, the real question is whether the Time board's foreclosing of shareholder choice was based on proper or improper motives. In other words, did the board exercise its prerogative in ways suggesting that the transaction was driven by management self-interest?

Granted, Time's decisions were made by a board comprised principally of outsiders with no readily apparent conflicts of interest. Once the Paramount bid emerged, however, the directors undertook a drastic course of action whose sole purpose was preventing their shareholders from accepting Paramount's offer. As in *Macmillan* and *Interco*, the attempt to foreclose shareholder choice without first conducting a fair competition for control implicates accountability concerns because it provides circumstantial evidence from which one might reasonably infer the presence of self-interested decision making.

Both decisions in *Time* responded at least implicitly to this concern. Both courts concluded that the Time board's initial decision to merge with Warner was protected by the business judgment rule. Both courts also concluded that the lock-up, the decision to recast the transaction as a tender offer for Warner, and the various other measures undertaken to stave off Paramount's competing bid involved a conflict of interest sufficiently severe to require application of a more exacting standard of review. The preliminary question then was whether the *Unocal* or *Revlon* standard governed.

For somewhat different reasons both Chancellor Allen and the Supreme Court concluded that *Revlon* had not triggered. Chancellor Allen followed the poison pill cases by holding that *Revlon* applies to any transaction constituting a change in control, but he determined that the merger agreement would not result in a transfer of control because

---

76. Paramount Communications, Inc. v. Time Inc., [1989 Transfer Binder] Fed.Sec. L.Rep. (CCH) ¶ 94,514 at 93,284, 1989 WL 79880 (Del.Ch.1989). The supreme court agreed: "Delaware law confers the management of the corporate enterprise to the stockholders' duly elected board representatives.... That duty may not be delegated to the stockholders." Paramount Communications, Inc. v. Time Inc., 571 A.2d 1140, 1154 (Del.1989). The supreme court further observed, however, that courts should not substitute their "judgment as to what is a 'better' deal for that of a corporation's board of directors." Id. at 1153.

control of the combined entity remained "in a large, fluid, changeable and changing market."

Although the Delaware Supreme Court indicated Allen's analysis was correct "as a matter of law," it rejected plaintiff's *Revlon* claims on "different grounds":

> Under Delaware law there are, generally speaking and without excluding other possibilities, two circumstances that may implicate *Revlon* duties. The first, and clearer one, is when a corporation initiates an active bidding process seeking to sell itself or to effect a business reorganization involving a clear break-up of the company. However, *Revlon* duties may also be triggered where, in response to a bidder's offer, a target abandons its long-term strategy and seeks an alternative transaction also involving the breakup of the company.[77]

This passage is not exactly crystal clear. What are the other possibilities the court did not exclude? What is the difference between the first and second identified possibilities? If they were deciding the case on broader grounds than Allen, can change of control transactions not involving a break-up of the company still trigger *Revlon*?[78] In particular, does *Revlon* apply when the target "initiates an active auction process seeking to sell itself," but the auction participants do not contemplate breaking-up the company?[79] What does the court mean by a break-up of the company?[80] One could spin out such questions indefinitely, but the key point

77. Paramount Communications, Inc. v. Time Inc., 571 A.2d 1140, 1150 (Del.1989).

78. Suppose the target company, which is following some long-term business strategy, receives a hostile takeover bid. In response, the target's board decides to effect a recapitalization, which will transfer control to an identifiable control block comprised of target management and its allies, but will not require the sale of any target assets. Does *Revlon* apply? Arguably not. Even if this is a business reorganization, it does not involve a break-up of the company, so neither the first nor the second prong appear to be triggered.

79. Suppose that a target company sought out a white knight bid. Assume the white knight intends to keep the target intact and to continue the target's long-term strategy. Does *Revlon* apply? The second prong of the court's test is inapplicable, because there has been no abandonment of the strategy and there is to be no break up of the company. The answer therefore depends on how you read the first prong. The target has "initiate[d] an active bidding process seeking to sell itself." But query

whether this prong triggers Revlon in the absence of an intention to break up the company. Does the language "involving a clear break-up of the company" in that sentence modify both clauses or only the latter? In this regard, note that the court premised its rejection of plaintiff's Revlon argument on "the absence of any substantial evidence to conclude that Time's board, in negotiating with Warner, made the dissolution or breakup of the corporate entity inevitable, as was the case in Revlon." Paramount Communications, Inc. v. Time Inc., 571 A.2d 1140, 1150 (Del.1989).

80. Presumably they have in mind the species of transactions commonly referred to as "bust-up" takeovers, in which a bidder finances the transaction through highly leveraged debt securities and then sells substantial portions of the target's assets in order to help finance the acquisition. If so, however, it also remains unclear what percentage of the firm must be sold off in order for the transaction to be regarded as a break-up. See Marc I. Steinberg, Nightmare on Main Street: The Paramount Picture Horror Show, 16 Del. J. Corp. L. 1, 16–17 (1991).

remains that the court appears to have used *Time* as a vehicle for sharply limiting *Revlon's* scope, albeit in an unusually murky manner.

The court's rejection of *Revlon* is curious because *Revlon,* as it had been interpreted before *Time,* seemed well-designed to address the problem at hand. There was a growing recognition that the *Revlon* "duties" were in fact simply the general *Unocal* rules applied to a special fact situation. Hence, *Revlon* did not create a special duty of the board, and corresponding right of the shareholders, to maximize the short-term value of the target company's shares through a control auction.[81] Instead, consistent with our analysis of *Unocal* and its progeny, *Revlon* is principally concerned with capturing cases of conflicted interests.[82] *Revlon* thus provided a useful vehicle by which the court might have determined whether the board had acted from improper motives. But the *Time* court not only ignored this option, its limitation of *Revlon's* doctrinal scope restricted the ability of Delaware courts to do so in future cases. This weakening of *Revlon* thus threatened to permit cases in which the board acted from improper motives to escape judicial review.

To be sure, the *Time* courts did not leave the lock-up and other bid-preclusive measures immune from challenge. Instead, both courts concluded that the lock-up and Time's subsequent recasting of the acquisition as a tender offer were defensive measures to be analyzed under *Unocal.* Relying on *Interco* and its progeny, Paramount argued that bid-preclusive defensive tactics were excessive in light of the minimal threat of inadequate value posed by a non-coercive tender offer at a substantial premium. Chancellor Allen distinguished those cases on the grounds that the original decision to merge with Warner was motivated by Time's long-term business plan. Unlike the poison pill cases, in which the management-sponsored transaction was principally intended to defeat an unsolicited tender offer, Chancellor Allen saw the revised structure of the Time–Warner transaction as being principally intended to facilitate accomplishment of the board's long-term strategy. Given that the tender offer thus arose out of preexisting legitimate, non-defensive business considerations, Time had a "legally cognizable interest" in going forward with the acquisition of Warner, which satisfied the first prong of *Unocal.*

---

81. See, e.g., Barkan v. Amsted Indus., Inc., 567 A.2d 1279, 1286 (Del.1989); In re J.P. Stevens & Co., Inc. Shareholders Litig., 542 A.2d 770, 778 (Del.Ch.1988).

82. From this perspective, *Revlon* itself can be seen as a case in which the board's actions strongly suggest self-interest. Why else would an honest auctioneer approve a transaction other than the highest bid if not for improper motives, at least assuming the competing proposals are identical in all respects other than price? While the court did not find that the board acted out of self-interest, the inherently conflicted position of a target board coupled with the suggestive conduct of the board at hand sufficed to taint their course of action. In fact, it appears that Revlon's directors were mainly concerned with protecting themselves from litigation by the company's debtholders. See Revlon, Inc. v. MacAndrews & Forbes Holdings, Inc., 506 A.2d 173 (Del.1986).

Allen believed the second prong of the *Unocal* analysis required him to evaluate, among other things, the importance of the corporate policy at stake and the impact of the board's actions. With respect to the first point, Chancellor Allen reiterated his view that pursuing the board's long-term strategy was a legitimate and important corporate goal. As to the latter, he observed that the offer for Warner "was effective, but not overly broad." Time's board thus "did only what was necessary to carry forward a preexisting transaction in an altered form."

As with Allen's *Revlon* analysis, the Supreme Court affirmed his *Unocal* analysis, but once again did so with important differences. The Supreme Court expressly rejected Paramount's argument that structural coercion and inadequate value were the only threats cognizable under *Unocal*. Instead, *Unocal* was to be applied on a case-by-case basis and in a flexible, open-ended manner. Among the flexible, open-ended threats the court identified in this case were the possibility that shareholders might incorrectly value the benefits of sticking with management's long-term business plan, the difficulty of comparing Paramount's bid to the benefits of the Warner acquisition, and the possibility that Paramount's bid might "upset, if not confuse," the shareholder vote. Applying the second, proportionality prong of the *Unocal* analysis, the court found that Time's recasting of the transaction was a reasonable response to the identified threats.

Just as had been the case with its analysis of *Revlon*, the Supreme Court's approach marked a major turning point in the evolution of *Unocal*. It expanded the list of cognizable threats and arguably weakened the proportionality standard. In doing so, it appeared to undermine the ability of the *Unocal* framework to capture cases in which conflicted interests drove the board's decision-making process.

Consider, for example, that many commentators concluded that *Time* validated the so-called "just say no" defense, pursuant to which the target's board simply refuses to allow the firm to be acquired, backing up that refusal by a poison pill or other takeover defenses.[83] We find this reading unpersuasive. At the Chancery court level, Allen's analysis hinged on his observation that Time's acquisition of Warner did not legally preclude "the successful prosecution of a hostile tender offer" for the resulting entity. More important, he also indicated that defensive tactics used against a hostile offer by Paramount or some other bidder for the combined entity after Time's acquisition of Warner would present a different issue.

---

83. See Wall St. J., Feb. 28, 1990, at A3. Prior cases had at least implicitly rejected the just say no defense. In *Interco*, for example, Chancellor Allen indicated that "in most instances" the use of takeover defenses was only legitimate in connection with attempts by the board to negotiate with the unsolicited bidder or to assemble an alternative transaction. City Capital Assoc. Ltd. Partnership v. Interco Inc., 551 A.2d 787, 798 (Del.Ch.1988). In other words, the board can not simply just say no.

The Supreme Court's opinion is similarly limited. While it is true that the court rejected any inference that directors are obliged to abandon a pre-existing business plan in order to permit short-term shareholder gains, Time's plan was deemed reasonable and proportionate to the Paramount threat precisely because it was "not aimed at 'cramming down' on its shareholders a management-sponsored alternative," but was only intended to carry forward "a preexisting transaction in an altered form." The Supreme Court also expressly affirmed Chancellor Allen's finding that Time's actions "did not preclude Paramount from making an offer for the combined Time–Warner company."

These limitations on the court's holding are important, because they eliminate the just say no defense, as well as some of the other more apocalyptic interpretations of *Time*. The just say no defense does cram down a particular result—independence—on the shareholders, and also attempts to preclude anyone from making an offer for the combined company, both of which the court said management could not do. *Time* thus does not necessarily compel one to conclude that the just say no defense will be deemed to be proportional to an adequate, non-coercive offer.

The trouble is that this limitation on *Time*'s scope is not sufficient, because it in fact creates it own problems. The courts' concern with the legal effect of Time's actions appeared to signal a retreat from the use of *Unocal* to constrain target defensive measures. Consider, for example, the poison pill cases. Suppose management responds to an unsolicited tender offer by proposing a restructuring that effectively transfers voting control to the incumbent management team. The target's board endorses this proposal and, to insure its success, refuses to redeem the target's outstanding poison pill. Because of the substantial financial injury a pill would work on the bidding company and its shareholders, a bidder rarely seeks to complete its tender offer while an effective pill remains in place. Unless there has been a fair competition between the competing proposals, this course of conduct necessarily permits an inference of management self-interest. Yet, just as Time's actions did not legally preclude Paramount from pursuing a bid for the combined Time–Warner entity, a poison pill does not legally preclude a bidder from going forward. Accordingly, one could have plausibly argued that it was proper under *Time*'s interpretation of *Unocal*.

Although *Time*'s doctrinal implications are troubling, the actual result in that case is far less troubling. In most of the poison pill cases, for example, the pill was deployed in order to delay a hostile bid while the target undertook a defensive restructuring intended to give management effective voting control or to otherwise make the target unpalatable to potential bidders.[84] Such a restructuring's deterrent effect is not

---

84. In a typical defensive restructuring, the target company pays a dividend consist- ing of cash (often borrowed) and debt securities, reducing the post-dividend value of

dependent upon the target's size; it works even for very small companies. In contrast, the success of Time's defensive actions depended almost wholly on the combined entity's great size. While the extent of the combined entity perhaps made it unlikely that a subsequent buyer would emerge to unwind the transaction, the possibility existed. The market for corporate control thus could exert some constraining influence on Time's board, which reduced the likelihood that the board was acting for improper motives, especially in comparison to the defensive restructurings just described.

In addition, it's critical to the outcome here that Time's business strategy was motivated by a desire to advance legitimate corporate interests; it had not been cobbled together simply to justify takeover defenses. As a result, Paramount was essentially asking the court to enjoin Time's board from continuing to operate the corporation's business and affairs during the pendency of the takeover bid. The Delaware courts were properly reluctant to do so, as a hostile bidder has no right to expect the incumbent board of directors to stop an ongoing business strategy in mid-stream.

In sum, *Time* presented a highly unusual set of facts, which rebutted the inference that the board acted from improper motives and rendered the result—if not the reasoning—in that particular case relatively unobjectionable. Many fruitful avenues for limiting *Time*'s reasoning thus presented themselves. The question was whether the Delaware Supreme Court would avail themselves of those options or would continue down the road of retreat *Time*'s reasoning appeared to mark out.

Ironically, the vehicle by which the Delaware Supreme Court revisited its *Time* decision was provided by Paramount, which now found itself playing Time's role and advocating the very same arguments that had been its downfall in the prior case.[85] Paramount, run by Martin Davis, entered into merger negotiations with Viacom, run and largely owned by Sumner Redstone. The parties sought to preclude competing bids with an array of defensive measures, including: (1) A no shop clause in their merger agreement, pursuant to which Paramount's board could not

the target's stock to the extent of the distribution. While the process is usually rather complex, target managers and/or the target's employee stock ownership plan effectively receive the dividend in the form of stock, rather than cash or debt, at an exchange rate based on the stock's post-dividend value. E.g., Black & Decker Corp. v. American Standard, Inc., 682 F.Supp. 772 (D.Del.1988); Ivanhoe Partners v. Newmont Mining Corp., 535 A.2d 1334, 1345 (Del. 1987); Robert M. Bass Group, Inc. v. Evans, 552 A.2d 1227, 1243 (Del.Ch.1988). Alternatively, the target may conduct a tender offer in which public shareholders exchange their

stock for cash and debt. E.g., AC Acquisitions Corp. v. Anderson, Clayton & Co., 519 A.2d 103 (Del.Ch.1986). In either case, management's equity interest increases substantially relative to public shareholders. In *AC Acquisitions*, for example, the restructuring would have transferred 25% of the firm's voting stock to a newly formed employee stock ownership plan. Coupled with management's stock holdings, this would have created a formidable barrier for any post-transaction bidder.

85. Paramount Communications Inc. v. QVC Network Inc., 637 A.2d 34 (Del.1994).

discuss any business combination with a third party unless (i) the third party could show that its proposal was not subject to financial contingencies, and (ii) the Paramount board decided that its fiduciary duties required it to talk to the third party. (2) A termination fee, under which Paramount was obliged to pay Viacom $100 million if the Paramount–Viacom deal fell through. The termination fee was payable regardless of whether the deal cratered because Paramount terminated the Viacom deal to accept a competing offer or the Paramount stockholders voted down the Viacom deal. (3) A stock lock-up option, under which, if the Viacom deal fell through for any reason that triggered the termination fee, Viacom would have the option of buying 24 million shares of outstanding Paramount stock at $69 per share (roughly 20% of the outstanding shares). Viacom could buy these shares with a senior subordinated note or could demand instead that Paramount pay it the difference between $69 and the market price of the stock for 24 million shares.

Despite this seemingly formidable array of defenses, QVC made a competing offer. Hollywood egos seem to have played some role, as Davis had once fired QVC's CEO and major shareholder, Barry Diller, and the two apparently hated each other. Following several rounds of bidding, Paramount's board announced that it would recommend acceptance of the Viacom proposal and would continue to resist QVC's offer.

In the inevitable litigation, Paramount relied on *Time* to argue that the *Revlon* duties had not triggered. Given *Time*'s description of the requisite triggering events, this was not an implausible argument. Paramount had neither initiated an active bidding process nor approved a breakup of the company.

QVC thus sharply illustrated the potential mischief done by *Time*. Assuming that *Revlon* had not triggered, the issue would be whether Paramount's defensive actions could be sustained under a *Unocal*-style analysis, which would have raised the distinction between legally and factually precluding competing bids. A successful Paramount–Viacom merger would not have legally precluded QVC from attempting to purchase the combined Viacom–Paramount entity. Accordingly, there was a strong argument that Paramount's actions should pass muster under *Time*'s reading of *Unocal*.

Even assuming QVC could have financed a bid for the combined entity, however, its efforts to acquire Paramount would have faced an insurmountable practical barrier; namely, the presence of Sumner Redstone. As controlling shareholder of Viacom, Redstone would have controlled the combined Paramount–Viacom entity. The presence of a controlling shareholder substantially changes the conflict of interest mix.

In theory, so long as acquisitions of publicly held corporations are conducted by other publicly held corporations, diversified shareholders will be indifferent as to the allocations of gains between the parties.

Assume that the typical acquisition generates gains equal to 50 percent of the target's pre-bid market price. A fully diversified investor is just as likely to own acquiring company shares as target shares. Indeed, he may own both. Allocation of the available gain between targets and acquirers is thus irrelevant to the diversified shareholder. Increasing the target's share of the gains by increasing the premium the acquirer pays to obtain control necessarily reduces the acquirer's share, which from the shareholder's perspective is simply robbing Peter to pay Paul. Worse yet, to the extent that gain allocation rules increase transaction costs, they leave a fully diversified shareholder worse off. In practice, of course, this argument is undermined by the implicit assumption that gains to the acquirer flow through to its shareholders.

Whatever one makes of the theory, however, situations like *QVC* unquestionably raise serious gain allocation concerns for target shareholders. If the acquiring entity is privately held, even a fully diversified shareholder by definition cannot be on both sides of the transaction. If the acquiring entity is publicly held, but is controlled by a single very large shareholder, a fully diversified shareholder may not be able to fully share in the gains to be reaped by the acquiring company because the large shareholder's control enables it to reap a non-pro rata share of any such gains. In the *QVC* situation, shareholders therefore would not be indifferent to gain allocation. Instead, they would prefer to see gains allocated to the target.

For this reason, *QVC* raised accountability concerns in a way that *Time* simply did not. There is special reason to fear that the controlling shareholder's positional and informational advantages will affect the allocation of gains. In particular, the controlling shareholder's ability to reap a disproportionate share of post-transaction gains gives it an unusually high incentive to cause the acquiring entity to offer side-payments to target directors in order to obtain their cooperation. In turn, the controlling shareholder's ability to reject acquisition proposals insulates the combined entity from the constraining influence of the market for corporate control.[86] As a result, the normal conflict of interest to be found in any acquisition is substantially magnified in the *QVC* situation.

In *QVC*, the Delaware Supreme Court demonstrated its sensitivity to this concern. Consider the otherwise rather obscure way in which the court described the nature of the shareholder interest that was imperiled by the Paramount board's conduct. The court several times "noted that voting control is generally achieved only at the price of paying a 'premium' to the minority shareholders for the loss of their voting

---

86. While a controlling shareholder owes fiduciary duties to the minority, it would not be obliged to sell its shares to another bidder. Indeed, the Delaware Supreme Court has held that *Revlon* duties do not apply when a controlling shareholder effects a cash-out merger with the subsidiary target corporation. *Bershad v. Curtiss–Wright Corp.*, 535 A.2d 840, 844–45 (Del. 1987).

influence (fluid and dispersed though it is), and that public shareholders lose the expectation of receiving any such premium once control has been transferred to and consolidated in a majority shareholder."[87] In addition, the court offered an equally curious explanation of why board action in a sale of control context is subject to enhanced judicial scrutiny: "Such scrutiny is mandated by: (a) the threatened diminution of the current stockholders' voting power; (b) the fact that an *asset belonging to public shareholders (a control premium)* is being sold and may never be available again; and (c) the traditional concern of Delaware courts for actions which impair or impede stockholder voting rights."[88] If generalized to all takeovers, these references are rather puzzling, as they have little to do with the conflicted-interest focus of *Unocal* and *Revlon* and, in fact, might presage some new analytic mode in which the principal emphasis will be on protecting shareholder property rights in control premia. As applied to the specific facts of *QVC*, however, references to the shareholders' interest in the control premium make perfect sense. They reflect the possibility that conflicted interests on the part of Paramount's directors would lead them to take actions that transferred gains from their shareholders to Viacom and Redstone.

Of course, it is not enough to recognize a conflict of interest, one must go on to do something about it. The *QVC* court not only recognized the enhanced conflict of interest present in this situation, but also seemingly recognized the doctrinal limitations *Time* imposed on efforts to deal with this conflict. Granted, the court did not overrule *Time*, but it did limit *Time* to its unique facts. It did so by rejecting Paramount's reading of *Time*. Recall the relevant passage from *Time*: "Under Delaware law there are, generally speaking and *without excluding other possibilities*, two circumstances which may implicate *Revlon* duties," which are initiation of an active bidding process and approval of a break-up of the company.[89] In *QVC*, the court emphasized the phrase "without excluding other possibilities." In this case, the court opined, one of the other possibilities was present; namely, a change of control. Accordingly, *Revlon* was triggered.[90]

The court's analysis of *Time*, of course, was disingenuous at best. In *Time*, the court had passed over the change of control test in favor of the break-up and self-initiated auction triggers. The "other possibilities" language was little more than judicial boilerplate. Yet, from a precedential perspective, that boilerplate became the mechanism by which the court was able to avoid the need to overrule its own *Time* decision while still repairing the damage that decision had done to *Unocal* and *Revlon*.

---

87. Michael P. Dooley, Fundamentals of Corporation Law 577 (1995).

88. Paramount Communications Inc. v. QVC Network Inc., 637 A.2d 34, 45 (Del. 1994) (emphasis supplied).

89. Paramount Communications, Inc. v. Time Inc., 571 A.2d 1140, 1150 (Del.1989) (emphasis supplied).

90. Paramount Communications Inc. v. QVC Network Inc., 637 A.2d 34, 46–48 (Del. 1994).

The end, however, perhaps justifies the means. By rehabilitating Chancellor Allen's *Time* opinion, which the *QVC* court went out of its way to describe as "well-reasoned," and by resurrecting the change of control test, *QVC* specifically addressed the potential for conflicted interests on the part of directors in transactions like the one at hand. Indeed, the court laid great stress on the fact that a transaction in which control changes hands to an identifiable owner leaves the target's shareholders vulnerable to both ex ante and ex post misconduct by the incumbent directors and the new owner.

In addition to consigning *Time*'s interpretation of *Revlon* to the dustbin of history, the court made a subtle but very important doctrinal shift. Where *Time* had treated *Unocal* and *Revlon* as involving separate modes of inquiry directed at distinct issues, *QVC* restored the pre-*Time* view that they are part of a single line of cases in which the significant conflict of interest found in certain control transactions justified enhanced judicial scrutiny. The court, for example, opined that "the general principles announced in *Revlon*, in *Unocal v. Mesa Petroleum Co.*, and in *Moran v. Household International, Inc.* govern this and every case in which a fundamental change of corporate control occurs or is contemplated."

Likewise, while *Time* had emphasized the formal tests announced in *Unocal* and *Revlon*, the *QVC* court struck out in a less rigid direction. As described by *QVC*, the enhanced scrutiny test is basically a reasonableness inquiry to be applied on a case-by-case basis: "The key features of an enhanced scrutiny test are: (a) a judicial determination regarding the adequacy of the decision-making process employed by the directors, including the information on which the directors based their decision; and (b) a judicial examination of the reasonableness of the directors' action in light of the circumstances then existing." The burden of proof is on the directors with respect to both issues. They need not prove that they made the right decision, but merely that their decision fell within the range of reasonableness.

QVC, moreover, strongly indicated that a court should not second-guess a board decision that falls within the range of reasonableness, "even though it might have decided otherwise or subsequent events may have cast doubt on the board's determination." In *Interco*, Chancellor Allen had warned that "Delaware courts have employed the Unocal precedent cautiously.... The danger that it poses is, of course, that courts—in exercising some element of substantive judgment—will too readily seek to assert the primacy of their own view on a question upon which reasonable, completely disinterested minds might differ."[91] *QVC* made clear that, so long as the board's conduct falls within the bounds of

---

91. City Capital Assoc. Ltd. Partnership v. Interco, Inc., 551 A.2d 787, 796 (Del.Ch. 1988).

reasonableness, Delaware courts will not second-guess the board's decisions.

The new reasonableness standard is a logical culmination of the argument that motive is what counts. The implicit assumption is that a reasonable decision is unlikely to be motivated by conflicted interest or, at least, that improper motives are irrelevant so long as the resulting decision falls within a range of reasonable outcomes. The operating norm seems to be "no harm, no foul," which seems sensible enough.

§ 7.3 *Unocal* **Post–QVC**

The Delaware judiciary's reluctance to second-guess decisions that fall within the range of reasonableness was driven home in unmistakable terms by the Delaware Supreme Court's subsequent decision in *Unitrin v. American General Corp.*, in which the court approved an everything but the kitchen sink array of defensive tactics.[92] Unitrin's board adopted a poison pill, amended the bylaws to add some shark repellent features, and initiated a defensive stock repurchase. The Chancery Court found the latter "unnecessary" in light of the poison pill. The Supreme Court reversed. The court deemed "draconian" defenses—i.e., those that are "coercive or preclusive"—to be invalid. (Note the parallel to our discussion of the post-*Time* status of the just say no defense.) Defenses that are not preclusive or coercive are to be reviewed under *QVC*'s "range of reasonableness" standard. On the facts before it, the court concluded that the shareholders were not foreclosed from receiving a control premium in the future and that a change of control was still possible. Accordingly, the defensive tactics were neither coercive nor preclusive. More important, the Supreme Court held that the Chancery Court had "erred by substituting its judgment" for that of the board. The Supreme Court explained:

> The *ratio decidendi* for the "range of reasonableness" standard is a need of the board of directors for latitude in discharging its fiduciary duties to the corporation and its shareholders when defending against perceived threats. The concomitant requirement is for judicial restraint. Consequently, if the board of directors' defensive response is not draconian (preclusive or coercive) and is within a "range of reasonableness," a court must not substitute its judgment for the board's.

Thereafter the courts elaborated on these themes in a number of different contexts, adapting the analysis as necessary to the circumstances in which the standard was to be applied.

---

92. Unitrin, Inc. v. American General Corp., 651 A.2d 1361 (Del.1995).

A. *Unocal* and Poison Pills

In *Moran v. Household International*,[93] two Household shareholders sued to have the pill described above invalidated. Among other charges, plaintiffs argued that the relevant provision of the Delaware General Corporation Law, § 157, did not authorize the issuance of the rights as structured by Household. DGCL § 157 provides, in pertinent part: "every corporation may create and issue, whether or not in connection with the issue and sale of any shares of stock or other securities of the corporation, rights or options entitling the holders thereof to purchase from the corporation any shares of its capital stock of any class or classes." This statutory language presented two significant issues.[94] First, were the rights and/or the preferred stock into which they were initially convertible sham securities? Although the rights are initially convertible into preferred (at a conversion rate far out of the money) and only convertible into common (in the money) in the event of a second-step transaction, they did separate from the common stock in the event of a triggering event. At that point, they presumably would develop a secondary market in which they could be bought and sold. If a second-step merger occurred, moreover, sensible shareholders would exercise the rights. Presumably, the transaction planner who devised the pill intended that these provisions would make it appear as though the rights had economic value. If so, the planner succeeded, because the court rejected the argument that Household's poison pill consisted of sham securities.

A second issue, however, was presented by § 157's authorization of rights "entitling the holders thereof to purchase from the corporation any shares of *its* capital stock." Plaintiff argued that § 157 thus only authorized Household to issue rights convertible into Household stock. Household therefore could not issue rights purporting to give Household shareholders the right to buy shares of another corporation. The court rejected this argument, analogizing the Household pill to anti-destruction provisions commonly found in convertible securities. Anti-destruction clauses give holders of target company convertible securities the right to convert their securities into whatever securities the acquiring company is offering in exchange for target company common stock. Because anti-destruction provisions are valid, the court upheld the pill.

---

93.   500 A.2d 1346 (Del.1985).

94.   In addition, plaintiff made two other minor arguments. First, that § 157 "has never served the purpose of authorizing a takeover defense." Moran v. Household Int'l, Inc., 500 A.2d 1346, 1351 (Del.1985). The court found no basis in the statute or its legislative history, however, to suggest that the legislature intended to limit § 157 to rights issued "for the purposes of corporate financing." Id. Second, plaintiff argued that Delaware had adopted a very limited anti-takeover statute. Hence, plaintiff argued, the legislature must have intended to allow tender offers to go forward essentially unimpeded. Id. at 1352–53. The court rejected this argument on grounds that legislative intent to "have little state regulation of tender offers cannot be said to also indicate a desire to also have little private regulation." Id. at 1353.

Plaintiffs' final set of authority arguments asserted that the board had no power to block shareholders from receiving proxy contests or tender offers. As to the former, Delaware law provides that a board may not erect takeover defenses that disenfranchise its shareholders without a "compelling justification."[95] But while the board thus cannot preclude proxy contests, the *Moran* court concluded that Household's pill did not do so. Soliciting proxies did not trigger the pill, even if the challenger held proxies for more than 20% of the shares. Moreover, although the court acknowledged that the pill would effectively prohibit one from buying more than 20% of the shares before conducting a proxy contest, the court opined that that restriction was unlikely to have a significant impact on the success rate of such contests.

Finally, while *Moran* implied that the board must leave some mechanism by which the bidder can present an offer to the shareholders, it strongly emphasized that the board of directors has authority to erect defenses with teeth. As to the Household pill, the court identified several methods by which a hostile bidder could structure its offer so as to avoid the pill's poisonous effects, including conditioning the offer on redemption of the pill by board, soliciting written consents to remove the board at same time that the offer is made, and conducting a proxy contest to oust the incumbent board.[96]

Having determined that the board of directors has authority to adopt poison pills and re-emphasized the more general principle that a board of directors has authority to resist unsolicited offers, the Delaware Supreme Court then turned to whether the Household board had violated its fiduciary duties by adopting the pill. In this portion of the opinion, the court relied heavily on its then-still novel *Unocal* decision.[97] The Delaware Supreme Court concluded that Household's pill was a reasonable response to the generalized threat of coercive takeover tactics then being employed by bidders. In doing so, however, the court was careful to emphasize that Household was not then faced with an actual takeover bid. The court stressed that: "When the Household Board of Directors is faced with a tender offer and a request to redeem the [pill], they will not

---

95. See, e.g., Unitrin, Inc. v. American Gen. Corp., 651 A.2d 1361, 1379 (Del.1995); Stroud v. Grace, 606 A.2d 75, 92 n. 3 (Del. 1992); Blasius Indus., Inc. v. Atlas Corp., 564 A.2d 651 (Del.Ch.1988).

96. Plaintiff argued that Household's pill precluded shareholders from exercising their right to conduct a proxy contest. Delaware law provides that a board may not erect takeover defenses that disenfranchise its shareholders without a "compelling justification." See, e.g., Unitrin, Inc. v. American Gen. Corp., 651 A.2d 1361, 1379 (Del. 1995); Stroud v. Grace, 606 A.2d 75, 92 n. 3 (Del.1992); Blasius Indus., Inc. v. Atlas Corp., 564 A.2d 651 (Del.Ch.1988). While

the board thus cannot preclude proxy contests, the *Moran* court concluded that Household's pill did not do so. Soliciting proxies did not trigger the pill, then even if the challenger held proxies for more than 20% of the shares. Moreover, the court concluded that even though the pill would effectively prohibit one from buying more than 20% of the shares before conducting a proxy contest that restriction was unlikely to have a significant impact on the success rate of such contests. Moran v. Household Int'l, Inc., 500 A.2d 1346, 1355 (Del.1985).

97. See § 6.2.C.

be able to arbitrarily reject the offer. They will be held to the same fiduciary standards any other board of directors would be held to in deciding to adopt a defensive mechanism, the same standard as they were held to in originally approving the [pill]."[98] Having said that, however, the key point is that the court deemed the pill to be a "reasonable defensive mechanism."

The Delaware Supreme Court recently invoked the principle of *stare decisis* to reject a post-*Moran* challenge to poison pills: "It is indisputable that *Moran* established a board's authority to adopt a rights plan" without shareholder approval or consent.[99] "To recognize viability of the [plaintiff's] claim would emasculate the basic holding of *Moran*, both as to this case and *in futuro*, that directors of a Delaware corporation may adopt a rights plan unilaterally. The Chancellor determined that the doctrine of *stare decisis* precluded that result and we agree."

Curiously, however, when it came time to litigate the validity of dead hand and no hand pills, the Delaware Supreme Court struck out in a different direction. The no hand pill at issue in *Quickturn Design Sys., Inc. v. Mentor Graphics Corp.,*[100] was nonredeemable for six months after a change in control of the board. Instead of invoking the standard *Unocal* analysis, the Delaware Supreme Court held that Delaware law "requires that any limitation on the board's authority be set out in the" articles of incorporation. The no hand pill limited a newly elected board's authority by precluding redemption of the pill—and thereby precluding an acquisition of the corporation—for six months. Consequently, the no hand pill tended "to limit in a substantial way the freedom of [newly elected] directors' decisions on matters of management policy." Accordingly, it violated "the duty of each [newly elected] director to exercise his own best judgment on matters coming before the board." Absent express authorization of such a limitation in the articles, the no hand pill therefore was invalid as beyond the board's authority.

An alternative line of attack on poison pills focused on the enhanced effect of a pill when combined with a classified board of directors. As we saw above, a bidder could attempt to end run the pill by conducting a proxy contest to elect a new board of directors that would redeem the pill so as to allow the offer to go forward. If the target also has a classified board, however, the bidder would have to win two consecutive proxy contests in order to effect this strategy, because it would take two successive wins to elect a majority of the board. Not surprisingly, the

98. 500 A.2d at 1355. See also Hills Stores Co. v. Bozic, 769 A.2d 88, 106–07 (Del.Ch.2000) (opining that: "Delaware case law has assured stockholders that the fact that the court has approved a board's decision to put defenses in place on a clear day does not mean that the board will escape its burden to justify its use of those defenses in the heat of battle under the *Unocal* standard . . .").

99. Account v. Hilton Hotels Corp., 780 A.2d 245, 249 (Del.2001).

100. 721 A.2d 1281 (Del.1998).

combination of a pill and classified board has been a highly effective takeover technique.

In *Versata Enterprises, Inc. v. Selectica, Inc.*,[101] Selectica was a financially struggling company with substantial net operating losses (NOLs):

> NOLs are tax losses, realized and accumulated by a corporation, that can be used to shelter future (or immediate past) income from taxation. If taxable profit has been realized, the NOLs operate either to provide a refund of prior taxes paid or to reduce the amount of future income tax owed. Thus, NOLs can be a valuable asset, as a means of lowering tax payments and producing positive cash flow. NOLs are considered a contingent asset, their value being contingent upon the firm's reporting a future profit or having an immediate past profit.

> Should the firm fail to realize a profit during the lifetime of the NOL (twenty years), the NOL expires. The precise value of a given NOL is usually impossible to determine since its ultimate use is subject to the timing and amount of recognized profit at the firm. If the firm never realizes taxable income, at dissolution its NOLs, regardless of their amount, would have zero value.

> In order to prevent corporate taxpayers from benefiting from NOLs generated by other entities, Internal Revenue Code Section 382 establishes limitations on the use of NOLs in periods following an "ownership change." If Section 382 is triggered, the law restricts the amount of prior NOLs that can be used in subsequent years to reduce the firm's tax obligations. Once NOLs are so impaired, a substantial portion of their value is lost.

> The precise definition of an "ownership change" under Section 382 is rather complex. At its most basic, an ownership change occurs when more than 50% of a firm's stock ownership changes over a three-year period. Specific provisions in Section 382 define the precise manner by which this determination is made. Most importantly for purposes of this case, the only shareholders considered when calculating an ownership change under Section 382 are those who hold, or have obtained during the testing period, a 5% or greater block of the corporation's shares outstanding.[102]

Versata and its affiliates had offered to acquire Selectica and, after those offers had been rejected, had bought a beachhead stake of over 5% of Selectica's common stock. Thereafter, Selectica's board of directors reviewed a Section 382 analysis, which informed them that additional acquisitions of roughly 10% of the company's outstanding shares by existing or new 5% shareholders would result in permanent limitations

101. 5 A.3d 586 (Del. 2010). **102.** Id. at 589 (footnotes omitted).

on the company's ability to use the NOLs. "The Board then unanimous-ly passed a resolution amending Selectica's Shareholder Rights Plan, by decreasing the beneficial ownership trigger from 15% to 4.99%, while grandfathering in existing 5% shareholders and permitting them to acquire up to an additional 0.5% (subject to the original 15% cap) without triggering the NOL Poison Pill."[103]

After further jockeying, including a deliberate triggering of the pill by Versata and its affiliates, Selectica sued seeking a declaratory judg-ment that the pill was valid.

The court held that *Unocal* applied. The potential loss of the NOLs was a cognizable threat to corporate policy. "The court of Chancery found the record 'replete with evidence' that, based upon the expert advice it received, the Board was reasonable in concluding that Selecti-ca's NOLs were worth preserving and that [Versata's] actions presented a serious threat of their impairment."[104] The Chancery Court further found that the very low 4.99% trigger was justified because it arose out of the tax laws not from some arbitrary choice by the board of directors. The Supreme Court agreed.

In applying the second prong of the *Unocal* standard, the Supreme Court relied on the *Unitrin* formulation, holding that the pill would pass muster if it was preclusive or coercive, which would render it unreason-able per se, and, if neither, whether the pill was otherwise reasonable in relation to the threat posed. Versata and its allies argued that Selectica's pill was unreasonable because the combination of a 5% threshold and Selectica's classified board of directors constituted a preclusive defense, claiming that "Selectica's charter-based classified board effectively fore-closes a bid conditioned upon a redemption of the NOL Poison Pill, because it requires a proxy challenger to launch and complete two successful proxy contests in order to change control."

The Delaware Supreme Court rejected that argument, holding that:

Classified boards are authorized by statute and are adopted for a variety of business purposes. Any classified board also operates as an antitakeover defense by preventing an insurgent from obtaining control of the board in one election. More than a decade ago, in Carmody, the court of Chancery noted "because only one third of a classified board would stand for election each year, a classified board would delay—but not prevent—a hostile acquiror from obtaining control of the board, since a determined acquiror could wage a proxy contest and obtain control of two thirds of the target board over a two year period, as opposed to seizing control in a single election." The fact that a combination of defensive measures makes it more

103. Id. at 595.   **104.** Id. at 600.

difficult for an acquirer to obtain control of a board does not make such measures realistically unattainable, i.e., preclusive.[105]

Further, the combination was reasonable in relation to the threat to the NOLs, which the court described as a valuable corporate asset whose loss was threatened absent the pill.

The *Selectica* case offers a number of instructive points. First, contextual evidence of good faith and proper motives are critical to a favorable outcome for the target. The court emphasized that Selectica's board was trying to protect unique asset of uncertain value. Economist Mark Humphrey–Jenner's paper *Anti–Takeover Provisions as a Source of Innovation and Value Creation* argues for greater than usual judicial deference to a target board's decisions in such cases. He argues that:

> Managers are risk averse. Excessive risk-aversion can destroy share-holder wealth. A key source of risk is the threat of an opportunistic takeover designed to take advantage of depressed market prices. This is especially the case in innovative or hard-to-value ("HtV") companies whose price may be depressed due to valuation difficul-ties rather than managerial under-performance. For these HtV firms, the threat of an opportunistic takeover can destroy value by inducing agency conflicts of managerial risk aversion. Managers and regulators argue that [anti-takeover protections ("ATPs")] can ame-liorate this problem. This article presents a theoretical model and empirical results that show that for HtV firms, ATPs encourage managers to make value-creating takeovers and increase innovation and do not induce agency conflicts of managerial entrenchment. This implies that for innovative or hard-to-value firms, ATPs can ameliorate managerial risk aversion and encourage value-creation.

Assuming that's true, how would one incorporate his conclusions into Delaware's *Unocal* framework for judicial review of takeover defenses? *Selectica* did it by largely deferring to the board's analysis of the NOL issue. But the much older case of *Shamrock Holdings, Inc. v. Polaroid Corp.*[106] is even more instructive.

Shamrock made a hostile takeover bid for Polaroid. The target responded by issuing convertible preferred stock to friendly investors and initiating a substantial stock buyback program. Polaroid also had a poison pill "containing 'flip-in' and 'flip-over' provisions. In addition, although the company does not have a staggered board of directors, several provisions limit a dissident stockholder's ability to gain control of the company. Polaroid's charter prohibits stockholder action by written consent. Pursuant to the bylaws, stockholders may not call special meetings and must give written notice of their intention to nominate directors for election ninety days prior to the annual meeting." Sham-rock sued, claiming the defensive tactics violated the *Unocal* standard.

---

105. Id. at 604 (footnotes omitted).   **106.** 559 A.2d 278 (Del.Ch. 1989).

The court held that:

> Polaroid directors [satisfied the first *Unocal* prong because they] acted in good faith and reasonably investigated Shamrock's offer. The board met on at least six occasions over a four month period to review Shamrock's original and amended offer and to discuss appropriate responses with management as well as its financial and legal advisers. Only two of Polaroid's thirteen board members are present or former officers of the company and there is no evidence from which the court could make a preliminary finding that the outside directors were seeking to entrench themselves.

> The second prong of *Unocal* is the proportionality test under which Polaroid's response must be balanced against the Shamrock threat....

Here is where the case becomes relevant to Humphrey–Jenner's paper. In assessing whether the Shamrock bid posed a threat to Polaroid, the court took into consideration that fact that Polaroid was hard to value. Polaroid had recently won the liability phase of a major patent lawsuit against Kodak. Critically, however, the damages phase of the suit remained unresolved. Nobody knew exactly what the damages were likely to be, but it seemed fair to assume that the damage claim represented a very significant chunk of Polaroid's value. Hence, as the court explained, Polaroid argued that:

> Shamrock's offer is also considered a threat because, in the board's view, it does not offer full value for the Kodak judgment. That judgment is, by far, Polaroid's most valuable asset. The directors fear that Shamrock will either exploit or impair that asset: "(a) ... Shamrock may undervalue the award because of its uncertainty and Shamrock's lesser knowledge of the full merits of Polaroid's claim; (b) ... because of Shamrock's need to pay down its acquisition debt promptly, Shamrock may be willing to quickly settle the litigation for less than full value; and (c) ... the court in the Kodak action may be inclined to award less damages to a takeover acquiror than to the original victim."

The court agreed:

> In sum, Polaroid is anticipating a monetary recovery that may exceed $5 billion as the result of a complicated patent infringement claim that spans more than a decade. In the foreseeable future, the amount of the damage award will be quantified if not paid. Until that time, it seems appropriate to consider a non-coercive but inadequate tender offer to be a threat. Although the stock market has "valued" the Kodak judgment and analysts have made estimates, Polaroid's stockholders really have very little way of assessing the present worth of this extremely valuable asset. Under these circumstances, there is a real possibility that the Polaroid stockhold-

ers will undervalue the Kodak judgment and it does not appear that the mere dissemination of information will cure this problem. Thus, I am satisfied that the Polaroid directors were entitled to treat the Shamrock tender offer as a threat. There is evidence that the offered price is inadequate (and the board so found) and there is a valid basis for concern that the Polaroid stockholders will be unable to reach an accurate judgment as to intrinsic value of their stock in light of the current status of the Kodak litigation.

The issue then becomes whether the Management Transactions constitute a reasonable response to the threat presented by this arguably inadequate bid. The purported purpose of the self-tender and buyback is to offer some immediate value to those stockholders interested in cash while increasing the equity interest held by the remaining stockholders. The Preferred Stock issuance is said to be an advantageous form of financing for the repurchase program. . . .

In sum, although I am not entirely satisfied that the issuance of the Preferred Stock was simply a financing device, I am unable to conclude preliminarily that either the Corporate Partners transaction alone or the Management Transactions as a whole are unreasonable either because they are disproportionate to the Shamrock threat or because they were improperly motivated.

Humphrey–Jenner's paper suggests that the court in *Shamrock Holdings* got it exactly right. Where targets are hard to value, even more deference than usual may be appropriate in applying the *Unocal* standard.

A second point driven home by the *Selectica* decision is the importance of independent directors getting the benefit of independent advisors. A board committee comprised solely of independent directors made the relevant decisions. The committee was advised by multiple independent experts, especially including outside tax experts upon whose analysis of the Section 382 issues that board relied. This combination drove the Chancery court's decision that the reasonable investigation prong of *Unocal* was satisfied. The Supreme Court likewise laid great emphasis on the extensive advice the committee received from its outside advisors. In addition to confirming that the committee had made a fully informed decision based upon a reasonable investigation, the use of independent directors who rely on independent experts tends to show that the target was acting from proper motives rather than selfish desires to entrench the incumbents in office. If motive is as important in *Unocal* cases as we have argued herein, Selectica's board did everything right to show that its' motives were pure.

In contrast, the court seems to have viewed Versata and its affiliates as the bad actors. The court emphasized that the pill had been amended in response to an effort by "a longtime competitor . . . to intentionally impair corporate assets." One is reminded here of the way in which the supreme court chose to emphasize T. Boone Pickens' "national reputation" as a greenmailer in the original *Unocal* decision. If the target board's motives matter, perhaps so do those of the acquirer. Perhaps the court suspected that Versata's efforts were directed not so much at acquiring Selectica but at destroying the value of Selectica's NOLs and thus making it even more difficult for Selectica to work its way out of its financial difficulties.

A year after *Selectica* was decided, the Delaware Chancery court had occasion to pass on the combination of a poison pill and classified board in *Air Products & Chemicals, Inc. v. Airgas, Inc.*[107] Airgas had adopted a classified board more than a decade before it adopted a poison pill in 2007. Only the latter decision was prompted by the prospect of a hostile takeover offer, moreover. Chancellor Chandler nevertheless concluded that they were inextricably related and therefore had to be considered as a unitary defensive tactic.

In a long opinion (81 pages with 514 footnotes), which extensively reviewed both the relevant facts and the applicable Delaware law, Chancellor Chandler repeatedly demonstrated the dilemma faced by a trial court judge bound by appellate precedent with which he disagrees. To cite but one example, Chandler wrote that:

> Although I have a hard time believing that inadequate price alone (according to the target's board) in the context of a non-discriminatory, all-cash, all-shares, fully financed offer poses any "threat"—particularly given the wealth of information available to Airgas's stockholders at this point in time—under existing Delaware law, it apparently does. ... [The cognizable threat is that] Airgas's stockholders will disbelieve the board's views on value (or in the case of merger arbitrageurs who may have short-term profit goals in mind, they may simply ignore the board's recommendations), and so they may mistakenly tender into an inadequately priced offer.

> Trial judges are not free to ignore or rewrite appellate court decisions. Thus, ... I am constrained by Delaware Supreme Court precedent to conclude that defendants have met their burden under *Unocal* to articulate a sufficient threat that justifies the continued maintenance of Airgas's poison pill. That is, assuming defendants have met their burden to articulate a legally cognizable threat (prong 1), Airgas's defenses have been recognized by Delaware law as reasonable responses to the threat posed by an inadequate offer— even an all-shares, all-cash offer (prong 2).

> In my personal view, Airgas's poison pill has served its legitimate purpose. Although the "best and final" $70 offer has been on the table for just over two months (since December 9, 2010), Air Products' advances have been ongoing for over sixteen months, and

---

107. 16 A.3d 48 (Del. Ch. 2011).

Airgas's use of its poison pill—particularly in combination with its staggered board—has given the Airgas board over a full year to inform its stockholders about its view of Airgas's intrinsic value and Airgas's value in a sale transaction. ... It has given Airgas more time than any litigated poison pill in Delaware history—enough time to show stockholders four quarters of improving financial results, demonstrating that Airgas is on track to meet its projected goals. And it has helped the Airgas board push Air Products to raise its bid by $10 per share from when it was first publicly announced to what Air Products has now represented is its highest offer. ... In short, there seems to be no threat here—the stockholders know what they need to know (about both the offer and the Airgas board's opinion of the offer) to make an informed decision.

That being said, however, as I understand binding Delaware precedent, I may not substitute my business judgment for that of the Airgas board. The Delaware Supreme Court has recognized inadequate price as a valid threat to corporate policy and effectiveness. The Delaware Supreme Court has also made clear that the "selection of a time frame for achievement of corporate goals ... may not be delegated to the stockholders." Furthermore, in powerful dictum, the Supreme Court has stated that "[d]irectors are not obliged to abandon a deliberately conceived corporate plan for a short-term shareholder profit unless there is clearly no basis to sustain the corporate strategy." Although I do not read that dictum as eliminating the applicability of heightened *Unocal* scrutiny to a board's decision to block a non-coercive bid as underpriced, I do read it, along with the actual holding in *Unitrin*, as indicating that a board that has a good faith, reasonable basis to believe a bid is inadequate may block that bid using a poison pill, irrespective of stockholders' desire to accept it.[108]

Did Chancellor Chandler thus validate the argument of those who contend that a target's board can "just say no"? The opinion claims that:

A board cannot "just say no" to a tender offer. Under Delaware law, it must first pass through two prongs of exacting judicial scrutiny by a judge who will evaluate the actions taken by, and the motives of, the board. Only a board of directors found to be acting in good faith, after reasonable investigation and reliance on the advice of outside advisors, which articulates and convinces the court that a hostile tender offer poses a legitimate threat to the corporate enterprise, may address that perceived threat by blocking the tender offer and forcing the bidder to elect a board majority that supports its bid.

In other words, a board cannot "just say no." Instead, the board must conduct a reasonable investigation. It must hire independent outside

---

108. Id. at 56–58 (footnotes omitted).

experts. It must then determine that at least the threat of inadequate value is present. Only then can the target board "say no."

The difference between the "just say no" defense and Chandler's approach of saying no after jumping through certain hoops, however, seems trivial. So long as the incumbent board is willing to rely on independent directors advised by independent advisors paid out of the corporate treasury, they will always be able to say no. As we have seen, takeover valuation is at best an art rather than a science. A target will always be able to find credible experts who put a higher value on the company than the hostile bidder's offer.

The bidder thus is left with the onerous task of fighting and winning two consecutive proxy contests in order to elect a board that will redeem the pill so that the offer may go forward. Even though the pill and classified board were to be reviewed as a unitary defense, and even though Chandler acknowledged that "no bidder to my knowledge has ever successfully stuck around for two years and waged two successful proxy contests to gain control of a classified board in order to remove a pill," the combination was not fatal to the target. Citing *Selectica*, Chandler described himself as "bound by this clear precedent to proceed on the assumption that Airgas's defensive measures are not preclusive if they delay Air Products from obtaining control of the Airgas board (even if that delay is significant) so long as obtaining control at some point in the future is realistically attainable."

In evaluating *Airgas*, it's worth starting with our discussion above of the just say no defense in connection with the *Time* case, which argued that that precedent involved a highly unusual set of facts, which rebutted the inference that the board acted from improper motives. In contrast, we have repeatedly seen cases in which Delaware courts found ways to strike down takeover defenses erected by boards acting from the improper motive of entrenching the incumbents in office. In *Airgas*, there was a particularly striking set of facts that tip the motive analysis in favor of the target's board of directors. Air Products (the bidder) had already managed to get three of its nominees elected to Airgas's board of directors. In a somewhat atypical development, the three Air Product nominees "wholeheartedly" supported the decision to keep the poison pill in place:

> [W]hat is more, [the three Air Product nominees] believe it is their fiduciary duty to keep Airgas's defenses in place. And Air Products' own directors have testified that (1) they have no reason to believe that the Airgas directors have breached their fiduciary duties, (2) even though plenty of information has been made available to the stockholders, they "agree that Airgas management is in the best position to understand the intrinsic value of the company," and (3) if the shoe were on the other foot, they would act in the same way as Airgas's directors have.

If our claim that motive is dispositive, these facts tip the motive analysis strongly in the target's direction.

Having said that, however, the striking thing about *Airgas* is that, despite its great length and detail, the court actually applied the relevant tests in a way that strikes this observer as mechanical and formalistic. When that observation is coupled with Chandler's repeated laments that, as a Chancellor, he was bound by Supreme Court precedent, one cannot help but wonder whether Chandler used this opinion to prod the Supreme Court to eliminate inadequate value as a cognizable threat and to otherwise toughen the *Unocal* standard of review. If so, to date it has not succeeded.

B. *Unocal* and Deal Protection Devices

As we saw in Chapter 3, parties to a negotiated acquisition often enter into a merger agreement containing exclusivity provisions or lockups designed to deter competitive bidding. In this chapter, we saw similar devices used in cases like *Revlon* and *Time* to ensure that one of two or more competing bidders prevailed in corporate control contests arising out of a hostile takeover bid. Recall that *Time* held that *Unocal* is the appropriate standard for reviewing such deal protection devices.

1. Omnicare

In *Omnicare, Inc. v. NCS Healthcare, Inc.*,[109] the Delaware Supreme Court confirmed that *Unocal* is the appropriate standard even in connection with deal protection devices included in a negotiated acquisition. The standards for reviewing exclusivity agreements discussed in Chapter 3 thus have been supplemented—indeed, effectively supplanted—by *Unocal*, at least in Delaware. NCS was an insolvent health care company considering a "pre-packaged" bankruptcy reorganization. Omnicare, a competitor health care firm, offered to acquire NCS' assets for $225 million (later raised to $270 million and then to over $313 million) in a bankruptcy sale pursuant to § 363 of the Bankruptcy Code. Omnicare's proposal was substantially less than NCS' outstanding debt, which meant that NCS' shareholders would get nothing and many creditors would be paid only in part. Negotiations broke down and were discontinued.

A few months later NCS was approached by Genesis, another health care firm. Genesis proposed a merger that would have paid off most of NCS' creditors in full, provided substantial recovery for holders of NCS' notes, and given NCS' shareholders a small return on their investments. NCS formed a special committee of independent directors to conduct the negotiations. Because Genesis had lost a prior bidding war to Omnicare, Genesis insisted on an exclusivity arrangement pursuant to which NCS

---

109. 818 A.2d 914 (Del.2003).

would not conduct merger negotiations with any other potential bidder while the negotiations between NCS and Genesis were underway. When Omnicare tried to reopen negotiations, the independent committee decided to honor the exclusivity agreement with Genesis because they believed there was a substantial risk that Genesis would walk away from the deal, allowing Omnicare to press its bankruptcy sale plans. In light of Omnicare's bid, NCS' independent directors did extract significantly better terms from Genesis. In return, however, Genesis' insisted on substantial deal protections. First, it required a termination fee of $6 million. Second, NCS' board agreed to submit the Genesis deal to a shareholder vote even if the board withdrew its recommendation that the shareholders approve the deal.[110] Third, the agreement contained a no shop clause. Finally, Genesis insisted on a shareholder lockup. NCS had two classes of common stock. Class A was standard common with one vote per share. Class B was super-voting rights stock with 10 votes per share. NCS' board chairman and its CEO owned the vast majority of the Class B stock. The chairman and CEO thereby had effective voting control of NCS. At Genesis' insistence, the chairman and CEO agreed to vote in favor of the merger. NCS was a party to that agreement, apparently to validate it under Delaware's antitakeover statute. Despite these deterrents, Omnicare nevertheless made a higher offer to acquire NCS. Omnicare and some NCS shareholders thereafter sued to invalidate the deal protection devices NCS had granted Genesis.

By a 3–2 vote, the Delaware Supreme Court struck down the NCS–Genesis merger agreement.[111] The majority acknowledged that "[a]ny board has authority to give [a bidder] reasonable structural and economic defenses, incentives, and fair compensation if the transaction is not completed." In addition, the majority acknowledged that the controlling

---

110. In Smith v. Van Gorkom, 488 A.2d 858 (Del.1985), the Delaware Supreme Court had held that directors could not submit a merger to shareholders without making a recommendation that it be approved. The Delaware legislature later overturned that result by adopting DGCL § 251(c), which provides: "The terms of the agreement may require that the agreement be submitted to the stockholders whether or not the board of directors determines at any time subsequent to declaring its advisability that the agreement is no longer advisable and recommends that the stockholders reject it." The NCS–Genesis merger agreement contained such a provision. In *Omnicare*, however, the Delaware Supreme Court held that § 251 did not trump the fiduciary duties of directors: "Taking action that is otherwise legally possible, however, does not *ipso facto* comport with the fiduciary responsibilities of directors in all circumstances.... Section 251 provisions ...

are 'presumptively valid in the abstract.' Such provisions in a merger agreement may not, however, 'validly define or limit the directors' fiduciary duties under Delaware law or prevent the [NCS] directors from carrying out their fiduciary duties under Delaware law.'" 818 A.2d at 937–38. If so, however, what is the point of § 251? The court seems to have eviscerated § 251 of any utility.

111. In his dissent, Chief Justice Veasey noted that "[s]plit decisions by this court, especially in the field of corporation law, are few and far between." 818 A.2d at 940 n.90. There is a strong unanimity norm in that court. David A. Skeel, Jr., The Unanimity Norm in Delaware Corporate Law, 83 Va. L. Rev. 127 (1997). The willingness of Justices Veasey and Steele to dissent indicates the high profile nature of the *Omnicare* decision.

shareholders "had an absolute right to sell or exchange their shares with a third party at any price." Yet, the majority nevertheless concluded that NCS' board "was required to contract for an effective fiduciary out to exercise its continuing fiduciary responsibilities to the minority stockholders."

Citing *QVC*, the majority observed that the defendants had to prove that the directors were "adequately informed and acted reasonably." Citing *Unitrin*, the majority noted that deal protection devices that are preclusive or coercive are "draconian and impermissible." Applying those standards to the facts at bar, the majority explained that, taken together, the various deal protection devices presented the minority shareholders of NCS with a *fait accompli*. There was no way they could reject the deal as long as the two controlling shareholders voted for it, as they were obliged to do. In order to prevent that result, an effective fiduciary out should have been included in the merger agreement.

The majority explained neither what it meant by "an effective fiduciary out," what the NCS board should have done if Genesis refused to agree to a fiduciary out, nor what it expected the NCS board to do if the controlling shareholders wanted to go forward with the Genesis deal. In sum, *Omnicare* is a most unsatisfying opinion that poses as many questions—if not more—than it answers.

Would the NCS board be obliged, for example, to issue stock to other investors so as to dilute the controlling shareholders' voting power? Presumably not, as such a requirement would be contrary to Delaware precedent.[112] Instead, the majority most likely contemplated a fiduciary out pursuant to which the NCS board could refuse to hold a shareholder vote on the Genesis deal if a better deal came along. But why? Suppose the NCS board had insisted on such a fiduciary out. The board then declines to put the Genesis deal to a shareholder vote after Omnicare makes a higher bid. Instead, the board puts the Omnicare deal to a shareholder vote. What happens if the controlling shareholders then vote down the Omnicare deal? NCS would be left up the proverbial creek without the proverbial paddle.

2. Policy

The Delaware courts' hostility to lockups and exclusive merger agreements is very puzzling. Such provisions are nothing more than corporate versions of precommitment strategies.

---

112. See Mendel v. Carroll, 651 A.2d 297 (Del.Ch.1994) ("The board's fiduciary obligation to the corporation and its shareholders, in this setting, requires it to be a protective guardian of the rightful interest of the public shareholders. But while that obligation may authorize the board to take extraordinary steps to protect the minority from plain overreaching, it does not authorize the board to deploy corporate power against the majority stockholders, in the absence of a threatened serious breach of fiduciary duty by the controlling stock.").

In *The Odyssey*, Homer tells a story illustrating the use of a precommitment strategy to achieve a desired goal. Circe warned Odysseus that his course would lead him past the Sirens, whose song famously enchanted all who passed near them. Once they trapped passing sailors, the Sirens warbled the sailors to death. Following Circe's advice, Odysseus adopted a plan by which he would be able to hear the Sirens' song but still escape their trap. Odysseus charged his men to lash him to the mast of their boat and not to release him until they were far beyond the Sirens. Odysseus then stopped up his sailor's ears with beeswax, so they could hear nothing.[113] As his ship passed the Sirens, their song overwhelmed Odysseus' will power and he tried desperately to get his men to approach the Sirens. Unable to hear the song, and thus being free of its enchantment, however, his men merely tied him even more tightly to the mast and sailed on. Only once they were safely past the Sirens did they release Odysseus.

Precommitment strategies of this sort abound in everyday life. The dieter who cleans all the junk food out of his pantry before starting a new diet precommits to the diet by disabling himself from enjoying a late night snack. The Congress that passed First Amendment to the U.S. Constitution precommitted to a policy of free speech, by disabling itself from regulating speech and assembly.[114] Indeed, that Congress went even further by disabling future Congresses from doing so as well, a point that becomes quite significant for our analysis. And so on. But what, you may be asking, does any of this have to do with corporate law?

Precommitment strategies also abound in business life. When a corporation's board of directors authorizes the inclusion of a negative pledge clause in a bond indenture, the board disables the corporation from issuing certain types of secured debt.[115] When the board and/or shareholders adopt a mandatory indemnification amendment to the bylaws, they precommit the corporation to a policy of indemnifying officers and directors under circumstances in which the statute does not

---

113. As Homer's tale illustrates, self-disablement is a critical aspect of any pre-commitment strategy. Odysseus knew he would not be able to trust himself once he heard the Siren's song. Hence, he had to create a situation in which he would be unable to effect a change in the course to which he was committed. As Homer's tale also illustrates, however, precommitment strategies sometimes require one to disable others. Odysseus also knew, after all, that he would not be able to trust his crew if they could hear the Siren's song.

114. See, e.g., Cass R. Sunstein, Constitutionalism and Secession, 58 U. Chi. L. Rev. 633, 641 (1991) (suggesting that "constitutional precommitment strategies might serve to overcome myopia or weakness of will on the part of the collectivity, or to ensure that representatives follow the considered judgments of the people. Protection of freedom of speech ... might represent an effort by the people themselves to provide safeguards against the impulsive behavior of majorities."). But see Jon Elster, Ulysses Unbound 92 (2000) (calling into question the extent to which constitutions can be considered as precommitment devices).

115. Cf. William A. Klein and John C. Coffee, Jr., Business Organization and Finance 244 (8th ed. 2002) (describing negative pledge clauses).

mandate such indemnification.[116] And so on.

Judicial hostility to precommitment strategies thus does not follow a fortiori from the mere fact that directors are fiduciaries. Why should informed directors acting in good faith not be allowed to lash themselves to the mast of a particular deal? Case law in other jurisdictions allows them to do precisely that.[117] No Delaware court has yet offered a persuasive reason for their hostility to no shop clauses and the like. Instead, the invalidity of such strategies has been asserted by mere fiat.

C. *Unocal* and Shareholder Disenfranchisement

Recall that one of the arguments plaintiffs made in *Moran* was that poison pills were invalid because they adversely impacted a shareholders' ability to wage a proxy contest. The Delaware Supreme Court rejected that argument on the empirical basis that the pill would not deter someone from conducting a proxy contest. Suppose, however, that the board of directors undertook some course of action that did impact shareholder voting rights. What standard of review would the court apply in that case?

In *Schnell v. Chris–Craft Industries, Inc.*,[118] the defendant's board of directors amended company's the bylaws to change the date of the corporation's annual meeting, which was a legally permissible amendment, for the equitably impermissible purpose of defeating a proxy contest in which insurgent shareholders sought to oust the incumbent board. The court struck down the amendment, holding that that "inequitable action does not become permissible merely because it is legally possible."

In *Blasius Industries, Inc. v. Atlas Corp.*,[119] the Delaware Supreme Court went even further, holding that where the board of directors takes actions for the "primary purpose" of interfering with the free exercise of the shareholder franchise, the board must demonstrate that it had a "compelling justification" for doing so. *Blasius* involved a pure proxy contest, however. Where a board action affecting the shareholder franchise takes place in other contexts, such as a simultaneous tender offer

---

116. Section 145(f) of the Delaware General Corporation Law provides that statutory indemnification rights "shall not be deemed exclusive of any other rights" to indemnification created by "bylaw, agreement, vote of the stockholders or disinterested directors or otherwise." Del. Code Ann. tit. 8, § 145(f) (2002). Most public corporations have availed themselves of this provision to extend "indemnification guarantees via bylaw to cases where indemnification is typically only permissive" by statute. VonFeldt v. Stifel Fin. Corp., 714 A.2d 79, 81 n. 5 (Del.1998).

117. See, e.g., Jewel Cos., Inc. v. Pay Less Drug Stores Northwest, Inc., 741 F.2d 1555 (9th Cir.1984), which specifically validated no shop clauses by permitting the target's board to "lawfully bind itself in a merger agreement to forbear from negotiating or accepting competing offers until the shareholders have had an opportunity to consider the initial proposal." Id. at 1564.

118. 285 A.2d 437 (Del.1971).

119. 564 A.2d 651 (Del.Ch.1988).

and proxy contest, *Unocal* provides the basic standard of review for the board's actions. In applying *Unocal*'s proportionality prong, however, the courts will treat board action that purposefully disenfranchises the shareholders as "strongly suspect."[120]

Three distinguished Delaware Chancery court jurists complained that the *Unocal* and *Blasius* standards "are not easily separable."[121] One of them (Chancellor Leo Strine) later elaborated on the point, explaining that:

> The great strength of *Blasius*—its reminder of the importance of the director election process and the barrier the decision draws to the acceptance of the bizarre doctrine of "substantive coercion" as to the question of who should constitute the board—came along with some overbroad language that rendered the standard of review articulated in the case too crude a tool for regular employment. As has been noted elsewhere, the trigger for the test's application-director action that has the primary purpose of disenfranchise-ment—is so pejorative that it is more a label for a result than a useful guide to determining what standard of review should be used by a judge to reach an appropriate result.[122]

courts therefore have had considerable difficulty determining which standard to apply to specific cases. Indeed, as Strine wryly noted, post-*Blasius* cases commonly "threshold exertions in reasoning as to why director action influencing the ability of stockholders to act did not amount to disenfranchisement, thus obviating the need to apply *Blasius* at all." Accordingly, he proposed scrapping the *Blasius* standard in favor of a reasonableness test based on the post-*QVC Unocal* formulation. Although this strikes many observers as a useful reform proposal, to date the Delaware Supreme Court has not adopted it.

§ 7.4   *Revlon* Post–*QVC*

As we've seen, any effort to map *Revlon*-land requires resolution of two critical questions: First, when do directors stop being "defenders of the corporate bastion" and become "auctioneers"? Second, do the *Revlon* duties really differ from those imposed by *Unocal*?

A.   *Revlon*-Land's Borders

The legal standard for determining whether *Revlon* had come into play repeatedly expanded and contracted during the first decade after the decision was rendered. Ultimately, however, the Delaware Supreme Court settled on a standard with three triggers:

120. Stroud v. Grace, 606 A.2d 75 (Del. 1992).

121. William T. Allen et al., Function Over Form: A Reassessment of Standards of Review in Delaware Corporation Law, 56 Bus. Law. 1287, 1314 (2001).

122. Mercier v. Inter–Tel (Delaware), Inc., 929 A.2d 786, 805–06 (Del. Ch. 2007).

The directors of a corporation have the obligation of acting reasonably to seek the transaction offering the best value reasonably available to the stockholders, in at least the following three scenarios: (1) when a corporation initiates an active bidding process seeking to sell itself or to effect a business reorganization involving a clear break-up of the company; (2) where, in response to a bidder's offer, a target abandons its long-term strategy and seeks an alternative transaction involving the break-up of the company; or (3) when approval of a transaction results in a sale or change of control. In the latter situation, there is no sale or change in control when "[c]ontrol of both [companies] remain[s] in a large, fluid, changeable and changing market."[123]

Outside those three situations, which do not even encompass all corporate control bidding contests, let alone all acquisitions, *Unocal* remained the defining standard. Indeed, in *Unitrin,* the Delaware Supreme Court emphasized the target board of directors' continuous gatekeeping function by flipping the famous *Revlon* metaphor around:

When a corporation is not for sale, the board of directors is the defender of the metaphorical medieval corporate bastion and the protector of the corporation's shareholders. The fact that a defensive action must not be coercive or preclusive does not prevent a board from responding defensively before a bidder is at the corporate bastion's gate.[124]

B. Directors' Duties in *Revlon*-land

As for the limited classes of cases for which *Revlon* was the controlling precedent, the Delaware Supreme Court eventually brought the relevant standard of review into line with *Unocal.* Granted, even after *QVC* was decided, some cases and commentators still occasionally used phrases like "*Revlon* duties" or even "*Revlon*-land." In general, however, the court has continued to indicate that *Revlon* is properly understood as a mere variant of *Unocal* rather than as a separate doctrine.

Having said that, however, the analysis of cases falling within the borders of *Revlon*-land does differ somewhat in degree if not in kind from those governed solely by *Unocal.* As the Delaware Chancery Court observed in *In re Lukens Inc. Shareholders Litig.,*[125] the term "*Revlon* duties" refers "to a director's performance of his or her duties of care, good faith, and loyalty in the unique factual circumstance of a sale of control over the corporate enterprise." In other words, one of the factors to be considered in applying the heightened scrutiny test is the context

---

123. Arnold v. Society for Sav. Bancorp, Inc., 650 A.2d 1270, 1289–90 (Del. 1994) (citations, footnotes, and internal quotation marks omitted).

124. Unitrin, Inc. v. American Gen. Corp., 651 A.2d 1361, 1388 (Del. 1995).

125. 757 A.2d 720 (Del. Ch. 1999)

of the transaction. As a result, what is reasonable under *Unocal* may not be reasonable in *Revlon*-land.[126]

1. *Discrimination and Favoritism*

Many takeover defenses that pass muster under the *Unocal* standard involve discrimination between the bidder and other shareholders. The stock repurchase at issue in *Unocal* itself started out by excluding Mesa from participation. The flip-in element of a poison pill inherently discriminates against the bidder, who is not allowed to exercise that right.

When only *Unocal* is in play, the target's board of directors thus is allowed to use defensive measures to achieve its favored outcome; namely, keeping the company independent. This is subject to the *Unitrin* proviso, of course, that in doing so the board does not use preclusive or coercive tactics.

In contrast, once *Revlon* triggers, the target's board of directors loses most of its power to affect the outcome of the contest. The target's board must "endeavor to secure the highest value reasonably attainable for the stockholders."[127] The board must take an "active and direct role in the sale process."[128]

To be sure, "there is no single blueprint that a board must follow to fulfill its [*Revlon*] duties."[129] Accordingly, "[n]o court can tell directors exactly how to accomplish that goal, because they will be facing a unique combination of circumstances, many of which will be outside their control."[130]

Moreover, in a holding that supports the argument that motive is key, the court held that a board is not liable where it "unintentionally fails, as a result of gross negligence ..., to follow up on a materially higher bid and an exculpatory charter provision is in place ...."[131] Instead, liability arises only where the board acted from "bad faith or self-interest."

Favoritism towards one bidder over the other has been the paradigm case in which courts have inferred that the target board is acting from improper motives:

126. The clearest example of how Revlon duties differ from those imposed by Unocal is the proper role, if any, of director concerns for corporate stakeholders other than shareholders. See § 7.5 below, where the differences between the two cases are discussed in detail.

127. McMillan v. Intercargo Corp., 768 A.2d 492, 502 (Del.Ch. 2000).

128. Citron v. Fairchild Camera & Instrument Corp., 569 A.2d 53, 66 (Del.1989).

129. Barkan v. Amsted Industries, Inc., 567 A.2d 1279, 1287 (Del.1989).

130. Lyondell Chemical Co. v. Ryan, 970 A.2d 235, 242 (Del. 2009).

131. McMillan, 768 A.2d at 502(the court here refers to an exculpatory provision added to the corporation's articles of incorporation per DGCL § 102(b)(7), which eliminates monetary liability for breaches of the duty of care.)

When *Revlon* duties devolve upon directors, this court will continue to exact an enhanced judicial scrutiny at the threshold, as in *Unocal*, before the normal presumptions of the business judgment rule will apply. However, as we recognized in *Revlon*, the two part threshold test, of necessity, is slightly different . . . .

At the outset, the plaintiff must show, and the trial court must find, that the directors of the target company treated one or more of the respective bidders on unequal terms. It is only then that the two-part threshold requirement of *Unocal* is truly invoked, for in *Revlon* we held that '[f]avoritism for a white knight to the total exclusion of a hostile bidder might be justifiable when the latter's offer adversely affects shareholder interests, but . . . the directors cannot fulfill their enhanced *Unocal* duties by playing favorites with the contending factions.'

In the face of disparate treatment, the trial court must first examine whether the directors properly perceived that shareholder interests were enhanced. In any event the board's action must be reasonable in relation to the advantage sought to be achieved, or conversely, to the threat which a particular bid allegedly poses to stockholder interests.[132]

In general, a target board thus may not bring an auction of control to an end by granting a lockup to the favored bidder or using other bid preclusive devices to the same end. While such devices are not per se illegal, as *Macmillan* taught, such devices can only be used to benefit shareholders. As noted above, the *Macmillan* court tried to steer a path through that doctrinal maze by distinguishing between lockups that draw an otherwise unwilling bidder into the contest and those that end an active auction by effectively foreclosing further bidding. But this distinction makes no sense at all. Suppose a prospective white knight tells the target's board that it will not bid unless the board grants the bidder a lockup amounting to 10% of the target's outstanding shares. In response, the initial bidder says that it will walk if the lockup is granted. If both parties are credible, the lockup will simultaneously induce an unwilling bid and end the auction process. Accordingly, while the draws in/ends dichotomy "has the virtue of appearing to encourage a desirable end-competitive bidding in acquisition transactions-it is not particularly helpful in determining the validity of any particular option because all lock-up options, by their nature, encourage the bid of the person receiving the lock-up and discourage the bids of all other persons."[133] Accordingly, "classifying a lockup as a permissible type that promotes bidding,

---

132. Mills Acquisition Co. v. Macmillan, Inc., 559 A.2d 1261, 1288 (Del. 1989) (citations omitted).

133. Kenneth J. Nachbar, Revlon, Inc. v. MacAndrews & Forbes Holdings, Inc.—

The Requirement of a Level Playing Field in Contested Mergers, and its Effect on Lock-ups and Other Bidding Deterrents, 12 Del. J. Corp. L. 473, 488 (1987) (footnote omitted).

or a harmful strain that discourages bidding, appears to be no more than conclusory judicial labels that are affixed by hindsight after the lockup has been scrutinized by the courts."[134]

The Eleventh Circuit cut through the confusion in *Cottle v. Storer Communication, Inc.,* holding that:

> All auctions must end sometime, and lock-ups by definition must discourage other bidders. The question therefore is not whether the asset lock-up granted to KKR effectively ended the bidding process. The question is whether [the target] conducted a fair auction, and whether KKR made the best offer.[135]

This observer believes that Delaware courts would agree. After all, what matters is motive. A board that conducts a fair auction is a board whose motives will withstand scrutiny.

2.   Best Practices in Revlon-land

The cases thus give no clear-cut guidance as to how to satisfy the *Revlon* duties. Directors have no "single blueprint." Nor have courts been willing to tell "directors exactly how to" find their way through *Revlon*-land. But the cases do allow us to infer best practices that clearly would satisfy the most demanding application of *Revlon*.

To be sure, "Delaware law does not ... hold fiduciaries liable for failure to comply with the aspirational ideal of best practices."[136] A board that seeks to do the bare minimum rather than aspiring to best practice, however, is asking for trouble.

Consider a hypothetical based on a stylized version of the *RJR Nabisco* case, as described above. There was an extended period of competitive bidding between a hostile offeror and a white knight. The target board formed a committee comprised solely of independent directors to conduct the auction. That committee hired independent legal and financial advisors. With the assistance of those advisors, the committee members fully informed themselves of the material facts relevant to valuing the target. At the direction of the committee, the financial advisors aggressively—but unsuccessfully—attempted to interest other potential buyers to enter the bidding. The committee allowed both bidders a reasonable opportunity to conduct due diligence.

After several rounds of bidding, the committee consults an independent economist with expertise in designing auctions. The expert suggests that when one is dealing with a unique asset trading in a thin market a sealed-bid auction is a useful way of inducing the bidders to make offers at their reservation price. Accordingly, the committee advises both

---

134.   Leo Herzel, Misunderstanding Lockups, 14 Sec. Reg. L.J. 150, 177 (1986).

135.   849 F.2d 570, 576 (11th Cir. 1988).

136.   In re Walt Disney Co. Derivative Litigation, 907 A.2d 693, 697 (Del.Ch. 2005), aff'd, 906 A.2d 27 (Del. 2006).

bidders to submit their best offer in a sealed envelope to be opened by the committee at a time and date certain. The bidders agree.

The white knight offers $100 per share in cash. The hostile bidder offers $105, but $45 consists of illiquid debt securities whose value is contested. Although the bidder's financial advisors have offered an opinion that the securities are in fact worth $45, the committee's independent financial advisor has opined that their value is speculative and could be as low as $35 per share. The target board opts for the white knights offer, ending the auction by granting a lockup to the favored bidder.

Can there be any doubt that the hypothetical committee has satisfied its *Revlon* duties? While the board has a duty to get the best deal for the shareholders, that did not always mean that the board had to favor the highest priced offer. Instead, as had been the case pre-*QVC*, the board is not obliged to focus on price to the exclusion of other relevant factors. As noted above, the board may evaluate offers on such grounds as the proposed form of consideration, tax consequences, firmness of financing, antitrust or other regulatory obstacles, and timing.

On our hypothetical's facts there is no evidence that the target board committee improperly favored one bidder over the other. Instead, the committee treated both even handedly. The committee made informed decisions. The process was constructed in a way that seems reasonably designed to elicit the best possible offer.

The Delaware Supreme Court has made clear that where a board is found to be independent, disinterested, and adequately informed, which is the case in our hypothetical, the decision to enter into a change in control transaction should be upheld unless the directors "utterly failed to attempt to obtain the best sale price."[137] That result, of course, is perfectly consistent with the argument that motive is what counts. Indeed, where the target's board can offer credible contemporaneous evidence that it new what it was doing and that it was doing its best to advance shareholder interests, a motive-based analysis fully justifies the favorable outcome such a board can expect from Delaware courts.

3. Frankle's Best Practices

Prominent corporate counsel Diane Holt Frankle offers these best practices for board in *Revlon*-land:

> First, the board should be informed about the value of the company, if not before the offer, then after it is made.

> Second, the board should be actively involved in the process, not necessarily negotiating the deal, but certainly reviewing and guiding overall strategy.

---

137. Lyondell Chem. Co. v. Ryan, 970 A.2d 235, 243 (Del. 2009).

Third, the board should consider all alternatives available to the company, including independence and other possible bidders.

Fourth, if the board does not have a "body of reliable evidence" about the company's value, the board must consider what it reasonably believes is the appropriate process to obtain that information, which may be through a pre-signing market check, or in some cases a post-signing market check or the go shop process, or some other reasonable process, and pursue that process as appropriate in the exercise of its business judgment.

. . . A prospective buyer will sometimes propose an exclusivity agreement to a target, arguing that the buyer does not want to be a stalking horse and is unwilling to undertake significant expense in diligence efforts and negotiation of an acquisition agreement without such an exclusivity agreement. These types of arrangements are subject to significant scrutiny by the courts, particularly in a cash transaction, given the board's duty to maximize stockholder value, and should be evaluated with caution. These arrangements should not be entered into without board approval and only after considering all the factors relevant to the arrangement, including the likelihood of other bidders, the duration and extent of any market check undertaken, the amount of time requested for exclusivity, the status of negotiations relating to price and terms and the relative attractiveness of the offer compared to other alternatives reasonably available to the company, the risk of losing the transaction at hand in the event exclusivity is not granted and any other relevant factors.[138]

All of which strikes this observer as excellent advice.

C. The Chancery Court Gets Lost in Revlon–Land

By 2000 or thereabouts, it seemed that *Revlon*-land was well mapped. We thought we knew when one entered its borders and what one was obliged to do therein. In subsequent years, however, the Chancery Court blurred that map. Our analysis of these developments begins with a case, *Ryan v. Lyondell Chemical Co.*,[139] which threatened to fundamentally remake *Revlon* duties. Because it did so by misapplying the emerging concept of good faith in the *Revlon* context, we must start with a short digression into the emerging law of good faith.

1. Background: The "Duty" of Good Faith

The notion that directors ought to act in good faith pervades Delaware's corporate governance jurisprudence. Only directors who,

---

138. Diane Holt Frankle, Fiduciary Duties of Directors Considering a Proposal For an Acquisition of a Privately Held Company, 1885 PLI/Corp 845, 864–65 (2011).

139. 2008 WL 2923427 (Del. Ch. 2008), rev'd, 970 A.2d 235 (Del. Supr. 2009).

inter alia, act in good faith are entitled to indemnification of legal expenses.[140] Only directors who, *inter alia*, rely in good faith on corporate books and records or reports from corporate officers or certain advisors are "fully protected" against shareholder claims.[141] Related party transactions are partially insulated from judicial review, *inter alia*, only if the disinterested directors or shareholders in good faith approve them.[142] The business judgment rule presumes that directors acted, *inter alia*, in good faith.[143] And so on.

Despite these longstanding references to good faith, however, it is fair to say that the concept remained essentially undefined until quite recently. Instead, a director's obligation to act in good faith traditionally was subsumed into the duties of care and loyalty. If there was no breach of either of those duties, courts did not perform a separate inquiry on the issue of good faith.

The process of giving content to good faith began with the Delaware Supreme Court's decision in *Cede & Co. v. Technicolor, Inc.*:

> [A] shareholder plaintiff challenging a board decision has the burden at the outset to rebut the rule's presumption. To rebut the rule, a shareholder plaintiff assumes the burden of providing evidence that directors, in reaching their challenged decision, breached any one of *the triads of their fiduciary duty-good faith, loyalty or due care*. If a shareholder plaintiff fails to meet this evidentiary burden, the business judgment rule attaches to protect corporate officers and directors and the decisions they make, and our courts will not second-guess these business judgments. If the rule is rebutted, the burden shifts to the defendant directors, the proponents of the challenged transaction, to prove to the trier of fact the "entire fairness" of the transaction to the shareholder plaintiff.[144]

The court's use of the term "triad" signaled the then-novel proposition that good faith was a freestanding fiduciary obligation having equal dignity with the traditional concepts of care and loyalty. The novel triad formulation quickly took on potentially major significance when coupled with the growing use by corporations of exculpatory charter provisions under DGCL § 102(b)(7).

DGCL § 102(b)(7) provides that a corporation's articles of incorporation may (but need not) contain:

> A provision eliminating or limiting the personal liability of a director to the corporation or its stockholders for monetary damages

---

140. DGCL § 145.

141. DGCL § 141(e).

142. DGCL § 144(a)(1)–(2).

143. See, e.g., Aronson v. Lewis, 473 A.2d 805, 812 (Del. 1984) (defining the business judgment rule as "a presumption that in making a business decision the directors

of a corporation acted on an informed basis, in good faith and in the honest belief that the action taken was in the best interests of the company").

144. 634 A.2d 345, 361 (Del. 1993) (emphasis supplied).

for breach of fiduciary duty as a director, provided that such provision shall not eliminate or limit the liability of a director: (i) For any breach of the director's duty of loyalty to the corporation or its stockholders; (ii) for acts or omissions not in good faith or which involve intentional misconduct or a knowing violation of law; (iii) under § 174 of this title [relating to liability for unlawful dividends]; or (iv) for any transaction from which the director derived an improper personal benefit.[145]

Notice that the statute distinguishes violations of the duty of loyalty ("improper personal benefit") and good faith, for both of which monetary liability remains available, from a breach of the duty of care, for which it is not.[146]

The widespread adoption of § 102(b)(7) exculpatory provisions by Delaware corporations thus prompted plaintiff lawyers to begin exploring whether duty of care claims could be recast as sounding in the new "duty" of good faith. They did so because the statute makes clear that "acts or omissions not in good faith" are not exculpable. Presumably, they reasoned, there must be a class of cases in which there was no breach of the duty of loyalty—since such breaches were excluded by other subclauses of § 102(b)(7)—but did entail a breach of the duty of

---

145. Several aspects of the Delaware statute are noteworthy. First, it applies only to directors. Although officers also are subject to a duty of care, they are denied exculpation by charter provision. In Arnold v. Society for Savings Bancorp, Inc., 650 A.2d 1270 (Del. 1994), the supreme court held that, as to a defendant who is both a director and an officer, an exculpatory § 102(b)(7) provision applies only to actions taken solely in his capacity as a director.

Second, the statute limits only the monetary liability of directors. Equitable remedies are still available. Because the real party in interest in many shareholder suits is the plaintiff's attorney rather than the shareholders, and because attorneys' fees can be recovered in connection with equitable remedies, § 102(b)(7) does not eliminate the incentive to bring shareholder litigation.

Third, the Delaware Supreme Court held in Emerald Partners that a § 102(b)(7) provision is an affirmative defense. Emerald Partners v. Berlin, 726 A.2d 1215, 1223–24 (Del. 1999). See also McMullin v. Beran, 765 A.2d 910, 926 (Del. 2000). Defendant directors thus have the burden of proving that they are entitled to exculpation under the statute. If aggressively applied, *Emerald Partners* could mean that a § 102(b)(7) provision rarely will entitle directors to a dismissal on grounds that plaintiff's complaint

fails to state a cause of action. Consequently, plaintiffs will be entitled to discovery, which some might call a fishing expedition, and the settlement value of such claims will go up.

146. Interestingly, Chancellor Allen suggested that *Van Gorkom* itself can be interpreted as a loyalty case. Gagliardi v. TriFoods Int'l, Inc., 683 A.2d 1049, 1052 n.4 (Del. Ch. 1996) ("I see it as reflecting a concern with the Trans Union board's independence and loyalty to the company's shareholders"). Similarly, the Delaware Supreme Court has opined that *Van Gorkom* included a disclosure violation and implied that such violations have a loyalty component. Cinerama, Inc. v. Technicolor, Inc., 663 A.2d 1156, 1166 n.18 (Del. 1995) ("In *Van Gorkom*, it was unnecessary for this court to state whether the disclosure violation constituted a breach of the duty of care or loyalty or was a combined breach of both since 8 Del. C. § 102(b)(7) had not yet been enacted."). In addition, according to the Sixth Circuit, a § 102(b)(7) liability limitation provision may not insulate directors from duty of care claims based on intentional or reckless misconduct. McCall v. Scott, 250 F.3d 997, 1000–01 (6th Cir. 2001). Ironically, a § 102(b)(7) provision thus might not have insulated the directors from liability in the very transaction that motivated the statute's adoption.

good faith. After all, presumably the legislature did not intend for "acts or omissions not in good faith" to be an empty set. As Delaware Chief Justice Myron Steele observed, "we can't overlook the fact that good faith is mentioned by our legislature in our statutes."[147]

2. Good Faith Refined and Confined

In *Walt Disney Co. Deriv. Litig.*,[148] the Delaware Supreme Court began to clarify the meaning of the triad formulation by defining good faith as encompassing "all actions required by a true faithfulness and devotion to the interests of the corporation and its shareholders. A failure to act in good faith may be shown, for instance, where the fiduciary intentionally acts with a purpose other than that of advancing the best interests of the corporation, where the fiduciary acts with the intent to violate applicable positive law, or where the fiduciary intentionally fails to act in the face of a known duty to act, demonstrating conscious disregard for his duties." The court held that a plaintiff could rebut the business judgment rule by showing that the board of directors acted in bad faith. The court declined to decide whether good faith was an independent fiduciary duty whose breach would give rise to liability absent a breach of the duty of care or loyalty, however.

In *Stone v. Ritter*,[149] the court resolved the issue left open in *Disney*. In doing so, the court oddly recast the triad formulation as a mere "colloquialism," explaining that "the obligation to act in good faith does not establish an independent fiduciary duty that stands on the same footing as the duties of care and loyalty." Instead, the obligation to act in good faith is now subsumed within the duty of loyalty:

> [T]he fiduciary duty of loyalty is not limited to cases involving a financial or other cognizable fiduciary conflict of interest. It also encompasses cases where the fiduciary fails to act in good faith. As the Court of Chancery aptly put it ..., "[a] director cannot act loyally towards the corporation unless she acts in the good faith belief that her actions are in the corporation's best interest."

This formulation appears to be a compromise between those who wanted to elevate good faith to being part of a triad of duties and those who did

---

147. Myron T. Steele, Is Good Faith a Viable Standard of Conduct for Corporate Governance, or Vehicle for Second–Guessing By Hindsight? 6 (October 5, 2006). The trouble with this argument is that it requires the court to overlook the serious flaws in § 102(b)(7), which has been aptly described as "an internally contradictory botch job." Christopher Bruner, Good Faith, State of Mind, and the Outer Boundaries of Director Liability in Corporate Law, 41 Wake Forest L. Rev. 1131, 1155 (2006).

Much trouble could have been avoided if the Delaware Supreme Court had simply followed Vice Chancellor Leo Strine's argument that § 102(b)(7)'s "subparts all illustrate conduct that is disloyal." Guttman v. Huang, 823 A.2d 492, 506 n.34 (Del. Ch. 2003). If it had done so, there would have been no statutory necessity to carve out a separate doctrine of good faith.

148. 906 A.2d 27 (Del. 2006).

149. 911 A.2d 362 (Del. 2006).

not, with the former losing as a matter of form, and the latter losing as a matter of substance.

On close examination, however, the *Stone* formulation makes little sense. First, the court took some pains to emphasize that a failure to act in good faith was "a 'necessary precondition to liability.' " Are there other conditions that must be satisfied in order for a bad faith act to constitute a breach of the duty of loyalty?

Second, and more important, the doctrinal consequences of subsuming good faith into loyalty are quite odd. The duty of loyalty traditionally focused on cases in which the defendant fiduciary received an improper financial benefit. Accordingly, the traditional remedy was to strip that benefit away from the defendant. In related party transactions whose terms are unfair to the corporation, for example, the transaction may be voided. Where a defendant usurps a corporate opportunity, the corporation gets a constructive trust on the opportunity.

By subsuming good faith into the duty of loyalty, however, *Stone* extends the domain of the duty of loyalty to cases in which the defendant received no financial benefit. In such cases, the traditional remedy is inapt. There is neither a transaction to be voided nor a *res* to be seized.

Liability for acts in bad faith thus will look a lot more like that imposed in cases involving a breach of the duty of care than the duty of loyalty. If someone "intentionally acts with a purpose other than that of advancing the best interests of the corporation," for example, it makes no sense to ask whether the action was fair to the corporation. Instead, the relevant question is whether the corporation was harmed and, if so, by what amount.

Good faith thus raises the issue of causation in a way that traditional loyalty concerns do not. After all, if one sets out to recover the amount by which the defendant harmed the corporation, presumably one needs to show that the defendant's conduct in fact harmed the corporation. Indeed, it would be unfair to impose liability without a showing of causation. To be sure, in *Technicolor*, the Delaware Supreme Court held that causation was not an element of the duty of care claim, a ruling that the court presumably will extend to the good faith context, but that decision made no sense.[150] In sum, by subsuming good faith into the duty of loyalty, *Stone* makes it doctrinally even more difficult to require causation, while simultaneously creating a conceptually difficult task of crafting appropriate remedies.

3. *Lyondell*

The board of directors of Lyondell Chemical Co. was approached in April 2006 by Basell AF, which expressed an interest in acquiring

150. See Stephen M. Bainbridge, Corporate Law 126–28 (2d ed. 2009).

Lyondell. The board thought the offered price was inadequate and said it was not interested in selling.

In May 2007, Access Industries, Basell's parent corporation, filed a Schedule 13D announcing that it had the right to acquire an 8.3% stake in Lyondell. Lyondell's board recognized that the Schedule 13D put it into play, but decided to take a wait and see approach.

On July 9, 2007, Access owner Leonard Blavatnik met with Lyondell CEO Dan Smith to propose a $40 per share acquisition of Lyondell. Smith rejected that offer as too low and Blavatnik countered with an offer of $44–45. Smith agreed to take that offer to the board, but said he suspected the board would reject it as too low. Later that day, Blavatnik raised his offer to $48 per share, conditioned on a demand for a $400 million break up fee and a merger agreement to be signed not later than July 16th.

A one-hour special meeting of the Lyondell board took place on July 10th. It thereafter authorized Smith to continue negotiations.

There was a certain amount of time pressure from Balavatnik's perspective. At the same time he was negotiating with Lyondell, he was also negotiating with an alternative target (Huntsman). Blavatnik had a deadline of July 11 to raise his offer for Huntsman if he wanted to go forward with that acquisition, so he asked Smith for Lyondell to provide a firm indication of interest by the end of the day on the 11th. Lyondell's board decided to provide the requested indication. Blavatnik announced he would not be raising his offer for Huntsman and Huntsman terminated its negotiations with Blavatnik. Lyondell tried to get better terms from Blavatnik, who rejected most of the requests because he had already made his best offer.

On July 16th, following a presentation by Lyondell's financial advisors that indicated $48 was a home run price, and that nobody else was likely to pay more, Lyondell's board approved the deal.

The Chancery court conceded that Lyondell's board "was active, sophisticated and generally aware of the value of the Company and the conditions of the markets in which the Company operated."[151] The board long had been kept up to date on the company's financial outlook and plans. The board had been kept fully abreast of the negotiations with Access and another potential bidder. The board had been briefed on Access' proposal by Lyondell's financial advisor.

Despite all this, however, the Chancery Court found the board's conduct deficient in a number of respects: (1) "The entire deal was negotiated, considered, and agreed to in less than seven days." This gave the court "pause as to how hard the Board really thought about this transaction and how carefully it sifted through the available market

---

151. Lyondell, 2008 WL 2923427 at *13.

evidence." This concern is consistent with an earlier Supreme Court caution that: "History has demonstrated boards 'that have failed to exercise due care are frequently boards that have been rushed.' "[152] Having said that, however, boards often must act quickly. If courts insist that boards beat the bushes in search of the proverbial two birds, they force boards to risk losing the equally proverbial bird in the hand.

(2) The Lyondell board did not conduct a "formal market test" by proactively seeking out competing bidders. But the Delaware Supreme Court had made clear that no such formal test was mandatory even in *Revlon*-land.[153]

(3) The Lyondell board did not actively insert itself into the negotiation and sale processes. But this complaint on the Chancery Court's part flew in the face of the clear teaching that there is no single roadmap directors must follow through *Revlon*-land. As long as the board was fully informed and was not acting from improper motives, the court should have rejected the *Revlon* claim.

Instead, the Chancery Court denied the defendant's motion for summary judgment, holding that there was significant doubt that the board had satisfied its *Revlon* duties:

> The record, as it presently stands, does not, as a matter of undisputed material fact, demonstrate the Lyondell directors' good faith discharge of their *Revlon* duties—a known set of 'duties' requiring certain conduct or impeccable knowledge of the market in the face of Basell's offer to acquire the Company. Perhaps with a more fully developed record or after trial, the court will be satisfied that the Board's efforts were done with sufficient good faith to absolve the directors of liability for money damages for any potential procedural shortcomings. With a record that does not clearly show the Board's good faith discharge of its *Revlon* duties, however, whether the members of the Board are entitled to seek shelter under the Company's exculpatory charter provision for procedural shortcomings amounting to a violation of their known fiduciary obligations in a sale scenario presents a question of fact that cannot now be resolved on summary judgment.[154]

Note how the Chancery Court thus not only exposed the board to the possibility that its decisions would be enjoined, the usual remedy in the *Unocal/Revlon* context, but also the very serious risk of non-exculpable monetary liability.

Based on the Chancery court decision, some observers worried that the emerging post-*Stone v. Ritter* jurisprudence on questions of good

152. McMullin v. Beran, 765 A.2d 910, 922 (Del. 2000).

153. Barkan v. Amsted Indus., Inc., 567 A.2d 1279 (Del. 1989).

154. Lyondell, 2008 WL 2923427 at *19.

versus bad faith tends to undermine the barrier to judicial review created by the business judgment rule. Although Vice Chancellor Noble's *Lyondell* opinion claimed that its good faith analysis did not gut the business judgment rule, the case in fact posed a serious risk of doing so. The business judgment rule is designed to prevent courts from asking "did the directors act with reasonable care?" In contrast, cases like *Lyondell* suggested that the emerging good faith rules allowed courts to ask "did the directors consciously disregard their duty to act with reasonable care." There is a difference between the two inquiries, to be sure, but perhaps only in semantics.

The Delaware Supreme Court's decision in *Lyondell* went a long way towards assuaging those concerns. In reversing the Chancery Court, the Supreme Court emphasized that an "extreme set of facts" is required to sustain a bad faith claim.[155]

> Only if [the target's board of directors] knowingly and completely failed to undertake their responsibilities would they breach their duty of loyalty. The trial court approached the record from the wrong perspective. Instead of questioning whether disinterested, independent directors did everything that they (arguably) should have done to obtain the best sale price, the inquiry should have been whether those directors utterly failed to attempt to obtain the best sale price.[156]

Importantly, the Supreme Court emphasized that the emergent doctrine of good faith did not change the longstanding principle that there is no single roadmap boards must follow in *Revlon*-land. The Chancery Court had held that *Revlon* duties required that "directors must 'engage actively in the sale process,' and they must confirm that they have obtained the best available price either by conducting an auction, by conducting a market check, or by demonstrating 'an impeccable knowledge of the market,' " but the Supreme Court reversed, holding that:

> [B]ad faith will be found if a fiduciary intentionally fails to act in the face of a known duty to act, demonstrating a conscious disregard for his duties. The trial court decided that the *Revlon* sale process must follow one of three courses, and that the Lyondell directors did not discharge that known set of [*Revlon*] duties. But, as noted, there are no legally prescribed steps that directors must follow to satisfy their *Revlon* duties. Thus, the directors' failure to take any specific steps during the sale process could not have demonstrated a conscious disregard of their duties. More importantly, there is a vast difference between an inadequate or flawed effort to carry out fiduciary duties and a conscious disregard for those duties.[157]

155. Lyondell, 970 A.2d at 243.
156. Id. at 243–44.

157. Id. at 243 (footnotes and internal quotation marks omitted).

Why would a board consciously disregard known duties if not for some improper motive? Accordingly, the Supreme Court's *Lyondell* decision is fully consistent with our argument that motive is what matters.

In sum, law professor William Bratton was quite correct when he observed that:

> Litigants and commentators have been mooting an expansive reading of Delaware's fiduciary duty of good faith. The Delaware Supreme Court recently made its most emphatic negative response to this proposition to date in Lyondell Chemical Company v. Ryan, a merger case. *Lyondell* simultaneously diminishes the intensity of scrutiny of target boards under the *Revlon* rubric. For one, the other, or both reasons, *Lyondell* will have more than its share of critics. But this comment enters a note of approbation. The current controversy regarding the good faith duty poses the question whether the fiduciary standard of conduct should be brought into congruence with prevailing standards of best practice, merging the soft law of corporate governance into the hard law of fiduciary duty. The Delaware courts have declined to effect the combination for two compelling reasons. First, they are not institutionally positioned to impose a liability standard directly grounded in best practices. Such a heavy-duty liability regime, quite simply, lies outside of their job description. Second, even if they were institutionally positioned to impose such a standard, the policy case for doing so is unpersuasive. Big stick fiduciary liability presumably would serve the deterrent purpose of forcing corporate boards to follow best practices. Yet best practices have become deeply rooted in the fabric of corporate decision-making, including boardroom processes respecting mergers, without the additional prod of a liability stick. It is accordingly difficult to project that a liability regime based on best practices has a productivity-enhancing role to play. In any event, *Lyondell* was decided correctly on its facts. Even as the board of directors in question arguably failed to follow the book of best practices, it did so in pursuit of a good deal, a deal that looks all the better in retrospect.[158]

D.   Chancery Redraws the Borders of *Revlon*-land

Recall that post-*QVC* one entered *Revlon* via three checkpoints: "(1) when a corporation initiates an active bidding process seeking to sell itself or to effect a business reorganization involving a clear break-up of the company; (2) where, in response to a bidder's offer, a target abandons its long-term strategy and seeks an alternative transaction involv-

---

158. William W. Bratton, Lyondell: A   http://ssrn.com/abstract=1692831.
Note of Approbation (March 31, 2011),

ing the break-up of the company; or (3) when approval of a transaction results in a sale or change of control. In the latter situation, there is no sale or change in control when [c]ontrol of both [companies] remain[s] in a large, fluid, changeable and changing market."[159] Since 2000 or thereabouts, however, a number of Chancery court decisions have redrawn *Revlon*-land's boundaries in ways that are inconsistent with Delaware Supreme Court precedent.

1. Hypotheticals

A stock for stock merger of equals: Acme and Ajax are both NYSE-listed public corporations. Acme offers to acquire Ajax in a merger of equals in which Acme shareholders would receive Ajax stock for their Acme shares.

This is an easy case. Recall that in *Time*, Chancellor Allen had said that *Revlon* was not triggered because there was no change of control. In turn, there was no change of control because control remained "in a large, fluid, changeable and changing market." The same is true here.[160]

A triangular merger: Same facts as in the preceding hypothetical, except that Acme proposes a triangular merger in which Ajax would be merged into a wholly-owned Acme subsidiary. The net effect of this transaction is precisely the same, however. The combined entity ends up being owned by dispersed shareholders "in a large, fluid, changeable and changing market." Only by elevating form over substance could *Revlon* apply here.

Bring cash into the picture: This time let's change the facts by changing the form of consideration. Version A entails a merger between Acme and Ajax in which Ajax shareholders get cash for their stock. Version B entails a triangular merger between Ajax and a wholly owned Acme subsidiary in which the Ajax shareholders get cash. Version C is a tender offer for any and all Ajax shares for cash to be followed by a freeze-out merger in which and remaining Ajax shareholders will be squeezed out in return for cash.

Checkpoint #1 is not triggered on these bare facts. Ajax did not initiate an active bidding process seeking to sell itself. (By the way, is that prong modified by "a clear break-up of the company"? The courts have never clearly resolved that question.) Likewise, the transaction will not result in a business reorganization involving a clear break up of the company.

159. Arnold v. Society for Sav. Bancorp, Inc., 650 A.2d 1270, 1290 (Del. 1994) (citations, footnotes, and internal quotation marks omitted).

160. See Krim v. ProNet, Inc., 744 A.2d 523, 527 (Del. Ch.1999) (noting that *Revlon*

"does not apply to stock-for-stock strategic mergers of publicly traded companies, a majority of the stock of which is dispersed in the market.").

Checkpoint #2 is not triggered, *inter alia*, because none of Ajax's actions were responsive to an unwanted offer.

As for checkpoint #3, the key issue is whether a cash sale constitutes "a sale or change of control." To answer that question, one must know whether control modifies both "sale" and "change" or only modifies "change." If the former, cash sales do not trigger *Revlon* duties if the acquirer is publicly held.

2.   *Chancery Precedents on Cash Sales*

A number of Chancery court decisions have found *Revlon* duties to be triggered by transactions in which all or part of the acquisition consideration consisted of cash.

NYMEX: NYMEX "was the largest commodity futures exchange in the world." In 2007, NYMEX's board set up a special committee to consider possible sales or acquisitions. The NYSE took a pass at NYMEX, but the deal did not develop. Instead, the CME made an offer to acquire NYMEX. CME offered a mix of cash and CME stock in exchange for the NYMEX stockholders' shares, which represented a mix of "56% CME stock and 44% cash."[161]

The Chancery Court teed up, but ultimately did not resolve the question of whether *Revlon* applied on those facts. In doing so, however, the court made clear that an all cash deal would trigger *Revlon*, holding that "in a transaction where cash is the exclusive consideration paid to the acquired corporation's shareholders, a fundamental change of corporate control occurs-thereby triggering *Revlon* because control of the corporation does not continue in a large, fluid market." The court clearly also contemplated that there "is a mix of cash and stock" that would trigger *Revlon*, even if the acquirer's "shares are held in a large, fluid market."

Lukens Inc.: In 1998, Lukens, Inc. and Bethlehem Steel Corporation agreed to an acquisition in which the latter would pay $30 per share in exchange for all of the Lukens common stock. The merger agreement provided that each Lukens shareholder would have the right to elect to receive cash, "subject to a maximum total cash payout equal to 62% of the total consideration."[162]

If all Lukens shareholders opted for cash, the split thus would be 62–38 cash and stock. In dicta, the Chancery Court observed that:

> [A]lthough there is no case directly on point, I cannot understand how the Director Defendants were not obliged, in the circumstances, to seek out the best price reasonably available. The defendants argue that because over 30% of the merger consideration was shares of Bethlehem common stock, a widely held company without any

---

161. In re NYMEX Shareholder Litig., 2009 WL 3206051 at *6 (Del. Ch. 2009).

162. In re Lukens Inc. Shareholders Litig., 757 A.2d 720, 725 (Del. Ch. 1999).

controlling shareholder, *Revlon* and *QVC* do not apply. I disagree. Whether 62% or 100% of the consideration was to be in cash, the directors were obliged to take reasonable steps to ensure that the shareholders received the best price available because, in any event, for a substantial majority of the then-current shareholders, there is no long run."

Smurfit–Stone Container Corp.: *In re Smurfit–Stone Container Corp. Shareholder Litig.*,[163] is the latest Chancery Court case to conclude that all or partial cash transactions trigger *Revlon*. The pertinent facts are simple. The case involved a triangular merger in which publicly held target Smurfit was to merge into a wholly owned subsidiary of a publicly held corporation named Rock–Tenn Co. In the merger, the shareholders of Smurfit would get $35 per share, with 50% of the consideration paid in cash and 50% paid in Rock–Tenn stock. Accordingly, as the Chancery Court observed:

> [T]his case provides cause for the court to address a question that has not yet been squarely addressed in Delaware law; namely, whether and in what circumstances *Revlon* applies when merger consideration is split roughly evenly between cash and stock.

Unfortunately, the court came up with the wrong answer.

There was no dispute that checkpoints 1 and 2 were not implicated. There was no claim that the target's board had initiated an active bidding process to sell itself or had sought to effect a reorganization involving a break up of Smurfit. There was no claim that the board had abandoned its long-term strategy in response to a bidder's offer or sought an alternative transaction involving a break up of the target.

As such, only checkpoint #3's reference to "a sale of change of control" was at issue. Because Smurfit's shareholders would get cash for a portion of their shares, the court concluded that the transaction came into *Revlon*-land via that checkpoint. This was so, the court argued, even though "control of Rock–Tenn after closing will remain in a large, fluid, changing, and changeable market" and the "Smurfit–Stone stockholders will retain the right to obtain a control premium in the future."

3. Conflict with Supreme Court Precedent

The most directly relevant Delaware Supreme Court precedent is *In re Santa Fe Pac. Corp. Shareholder Litig.*[164] Santa Fe and Burlington were both publicly held Delaware corporations. After negotiations, they agreed to a complicated deal in which the two companies would make a joint tender offer for up to 33% of Santa Fe's shares at $20 per share in cash. If successful, the offer would give Burlington 16% of Santa Fe's remaining outstanding shares. If the offer succeeded, a freeze-out merger

---

163. 2011 WL 2028076 (Del. Ch. 2011).   **164.** 669 A.2d 59 (Del.1995).

in which remaining Santa Fe shareholders would get Burlington shares in exchange for their Santa Fe stock would follow it.

The Supreme Court rejected the plaintiffs' argument that the deal triggered *Revlon* duties for Santa Fe's directors. It did so because the plaintiffs "failed to allege that control of Burlington and Santa Fe after the merger would not remain 'in a large, fluid, changeable and changing market.'" The clear implication is that the form of consideration was not the relevant issue. Instead, the issue was whether the Burlington shareholders would remain dispersed "in a large, fluid, changeable and changing market."

Yet, in *NYMEX*, the Chancery court recharacterized *Santa Fe* as simply setting a floor—33% cash—below which one did not enter *Revlon*-land. As for higher ratios, the Chancery court relied on *Lukens* for the proposition that the Delaware Supreme Court "has not set out a black line rule explaining what percentage of the consideration can be cash without triggering Revlon."

This recharacterization of *Santa Fe* is hard enough to square with the Supreme Court's analysis in the case, which makes no reference to floors or ceilings, but rather to the post-deal "the stock ownership structure of Burlington." It is even more difficult to square with *Arnold v. Soc'y for Sav. Bancorp, Inc.*'s three checkpoints.[165]

The *Smurfit* court finessed *Arnold* in the first instance by selective quotation. Recall the key passage setting out the three checkpoints. The *Smurfit* court quoted it as follows:

> The Delaware Supreme Court has determined that a board might find itself faced with such a duty in at least three scenarios: "(1) when a corporation initiates an active bidding process seeking to sell itself or to effect a business reorganization involving a clear break-up of the company[ ]; (2) where, in response to a bidder's offer, a target abandons its long-term strategy and seeks an alternative transaction involving the break-up of the company; or (3) when approval of a transaction results in a sale or change of control [.]"[166]

The observant reader will note that the Chancery court thereby omitted the critical qualifier *Arnold* added to checkpoint #3. Let's quote the pertinent part of *Arnold* again in full: "(3) when approval of a transaction results in a sale or change of control. *In the latter situation, there is no sale or change in control when [c]ontrol of both [companies] remain[s] in a large, fluid, changeable and changing market.*"[167]

Arnold's clear implication is that an acquisition by a publicly held corporation with no controlling shareholder that results in the combined

---

165. 650 A.2d 1270 (Del. 1994).

166. *In re Smurfit–Stone Container Corp.*, 2011 WL 2028076 at *12.

167. Arnold v. Society for Sav. Bancorp, Inc., 650 A.2d 1270, 1290 (Del. 1994) (citations, footnotes, and internal quotation marks omitted) (emphasis supplied).

corporate entity being owned by dispersed shareholders in the now proverbial "large, fluid, changeable and changing market" does not trigger *Revlon* whether the deal is structured as all stock, all cash, or somewhere in the middle. The form of consideration is simply irrelevant.

The Delaware Supreme Court's opinion in *Lyondell* confirms that reading of the earlier Supreme Court precedents. In addition to the substantive errors made by the Chancery Court in *Lyondell*, the court also took too expansive an approach to when *Revlon*-duties are triggered. The Chancery Court held that *Revlon* was triggered if the target's "board of directors undertakes a sale of the company for cash."[168]

In fact, however, checkpoint #1 was inapplicable on these facts, because the target board had not initiated "an active bidding process," let alone one that would involve a break up of the company. Checkpoint #2 was inapplicable because the transaction did not involve a hostile offer or an abandonment of its long-term strategy or a break up of the company.

In reversing, the Supreme Court acknowledged that once the target board decided to sell the company to Access, *Revlon* triggered because Access was a privately held corporation. The transaction therefore would have involved a change of control from disperse public shareholders in "a large, fluid, changeable and changing market" to a single controlling shareholder. At the same time, however, the court clarified checkpoint #3 by holding that:

> The problem with the trial court's analysis is that *Revlon* duties do not arise simply because a company is 'in play.' The duty to seek the best available price applies only when a company embarks on a transaction—on its own initiative or in response to an unsolicited offer—that will result in a change of control.

This passage confirms that, in the phrase "sale or change of control," as used in checkpoint #3, control must be understood to modify both the words sale and change. Accordingly, *Lyondell* confirms that our reading herein of *Arnold* and *Santa Fe* are the correct ones rather than those offered by the Chancery Court.

4. Policy

The Chancery Court decisions attempting to redraw the boundaries of *Revlon*-land are based on a concern that shareholders who get cash have no opportunity to participate in the potential post-acquisition gains that may accrue to shareholders of the combined company. In *Smurfit*, for example, the court argued that:

---

168. Ryan v. Lyondell Chemical Co., 2008 WL 2923427 (Del. Ch. 2008), rev'd, 970 A.2d 235 (Del. Supr. 2009).

Defendants emphasize that no Smurfit–Stone stockholder involuntarily or voluntarily can be cashed out completely and, after consummation of the Proposed Transaction, the stockholders will own slightly less than half of Rock–Tenn. While the facts of this case and Lukens differ slightly in that regard, Defendants lose sight of the fact that while no Smurfit–Stone stockholder will be cashed out 100%, 100% of its stockholders who elect to participate in the merger will see approximately 50% of their Smurfit–Stone investment cashed out. As such, like Vice Chancellor Lamb's concern that potentially there was no "tomorrow" for a substantial majority of Lukens stockholders, the concern here is that there is no "tomorrow" for approximately 50% of each stockholder's investment in Smurfit–Stone. That each stockholder may retain a portion of her investment after the merger is insufficient to distinguish the reasoning of Lukens, which concerns the need for the court to scrutinize under Revlon a transaction that constitutes an end-game for all or a substantial part of a stockholder's investment in a Delaware corporation.

But this argument makes no sense. As long as the acquirer is publicly held, shareholders who get cash could simply turn around and buy stock in the post-acquisition company. They could then participate in any post-transaction gains, including any future takeover premium. Only if there has been a change of control is that option foreclosed.

In any event, as the discussion above should make clear, the relevant policy concern is not whether there is a tomorrow. To be sure, *QVC* spoke of "that an asset belonging to public shareholders"; i.e., "a control premium." In doing so, however, the court was not showing concern for whether there will be a tomorrow for the shareholders. Instead, as discussed above, the court was concerned in *QVC* with the division of gains between target and acquirer shareholders because the post-transaction company would have a dominating controlling shareholder.

As the analysis of *QVC* explained, the relevant concern thus is the potential that conflicted interests will affect the target's board of directors' decisions. So long as acquisitions of publicly held corporations are conducted by other publicly held corporations, diversified shareholders will be indifferent as to the allocations of gains between the parties. In turn, those shareholders also will be indifferent as to the form of consideration.

In contrast, if the transaction results in a privately held entity, a diversified shareholder cannot be on both sides of the transaction. If the post-transaction entity remains publicly held, but will be dominated by a controlling shareholder, there is a substantial risk that the control shareholder will be able to extract non-pro rata benefits in the future and get a sweetheart deal from target directors in the initial acquisition.

In either situation, the division of gain matters a lot. As such, investors would prefer to see gains in such transactions allocated to the target. It is in these situations that *Revlon* therefore should come into play.

5. Summation

Revlon should be understood as a special case of the *Unocal* heightened scrutiny standard of review. The target board of directors' sole *Revlon* duty is to obtain the best deal for their shareholders. In so doing, any favoritism of one bidder over another must be motivated by a concern for immediate shareholder value and not by any improper motives.

One enters *Revlon*-land through any one of three checkpoints. (1) The target's board initiates an active bidding process to sell the corporation or to effect a business reorganization involving a clear break up of the company. (2) In response to an initial offer, the target's board causes the corporation to abandons the corporation's long-term strategy and seeks an alternative transaction involving the break up of the company. (3) The transaction results in a sale or change of control of the corporation.

Contrary to recent Chancery Court opinions, checkpoint #3 is not dependent on the form of the consideration paid by the acquirer. If dispersed shareholders own the post-transaction combined entity in "a large, fluid, changeable and changing market," *Revlon* does not apply. If the post-transaction entity has a controlling shareholder, however, regardless of whether the corporation goes private or remains listed on a stock market, *Revlon* does apply. In other words, there must be a change of control, whether by sale or otherwise.

§ 7.5 Consideration of Nonshareholder Constituency Interests

The takeover wars of the 1980s produced a host of target corporation defensive tactics. Early on, so-called nonmonetary factor provisions were a fairly common variant on the shark repellent theme. They permit, and in some cases require, directors to consider a variety of nonprice factors in evaluating a proposed acquisition. In particular, most allow directors to consider "the social, legal and economic effects of an offer upon employees, suppliers, customers and others having similar relationships with the corporation, and the communities in which the corporation conducts its business."[169]

From management's perspective, nonmonetary factor provisions have two principal drawbacks. First, except in the case of a newly

---

169. Proxy Statement and Text of Amendment for Nortek, Inc. (May 26, 1982), reprinted in I Robert L. Winter et al., Shark Repellents and Golden Parachutes: A Handbook for the Practitioner 197 (1983 and supp.) The full laundry list also usually included the legality of the offer, the bidder's financial condition, prospects, and reputation, the offer's structure, and the bidder's intentions for the target. See id. at 194.

incorporated firm, they must be adopted as amendments to the corporation's charter, which requires shareholder approval. Shareholder resistance to shark repellents steadily grew throughout the 1980s, especially among institutional investors. By 1989, for example, over half of the institutional investors responding to an industry survey reported that they had opposed some nonmonetary factors provisions, while another one-quarter reported that they did so routinely.[170] This growing opposition made nonmonetary factors provisions far less attractive and helped contribute to their apparent decline in popularity.

Second, and more seriously, state law arguably does not permit corporate organic documents to redefine the directors' fiduciary duties. In general, a charter amendment may not derogate from common law rules if doing so conflicts with some settled public policy.[171] In light of the well-settled shareholder wealth maximization policy, nonmonetary factors charter amendments therefore appeared vulnerable. As the 1980s wound down, this problem seemed especially significant for Delaware firms, as Delaware law became increasingly hostile to directorial consideration of nonshareholder interests in the takeover decision-making process.

A. Delaware Case Law

The business judgment rule typically precludes courts from reviewing board of director decisions that take into account the interests of nonshareholder constituencies.[172] Once Delaware adopted *Unocal*'s conditional business judgment rule as the standard of review for management resistance to takeovers, however, such decisions were no longer automatically protected. To be sure, under its first prong, *Unocal* apparently allowed directors to consider interests other than short-term shareholder wealth maximization. Under *Unocal*, target directors may balance the takeover premium a bidder offers shareholders against the bid's potential effects on the corporate entity. Among other factors, the board was explicitly permitted to consider "the impact of the bid on 'constituencies' other than shareholders (i.e., creditors, customers, employees, and perhaps even the community)."[173]

170. Lauren Krasnow, Voting by Institutional Investors on Corporate Governance Issues in the 1989 Proxy Season 37 (1989).

171. Sterling v. Mayflower Hotel Corp., 93 A.2d 107, 118 (Del.1952); Ernest L. Folk, III, The Delaware General Corporation Law: A Commentary and Analysis 10 (1972).

172. See, e.g., g., Shlensky v. Wrigley, 237 N.E.2d 776 (Ill.App.1968); see generally Stephen M. Bainbridge, Director Primacy: The Means and Ends of Corporate Governance, 97 Nw. U. L. Rev. 547, 601–05 (2003).

173. Unocal Corp. v. Mesa Petroleum Co., 493 A.2d 946, 955 (Del.1985). Several judicial opinions outside Delaware suggest that nonshareholder interests may be considered in making structural decisions. See, e.g., Norlin Corp. v. Rooney, Pace, Inc., 744 F.2d 255 (2d Cir.1984); Herald Co. v. Seawell, 472 F.2d 1081 (10th Cir.1972); GAF Corp. v. Union Carbide Corp., 624 F.Supp. 1016 (S.D.N.Y.1985); Enterra Corp. v. SGS Assoc., 600 F.Supp. 678 (E.D.Pa.1985);

Unfortunately, *Unocal* was not entirely clear as to what the language just quoted meant. *Unocal*'s board was faced with a structurally coercive bid by "a corporate raider with a national reputation as a 'greenmailer.' "[174] Accordingly, the directors reasonably believed that the bid was not in the best interests of any corporate constituency and, on the facts before the court, there arguably was no conflict between shareholder and stakeholder interests. Other situations are less clear-cut. Suppose, for example, the bidder makes a fairly priced, noncoercive offer, but also announces plans to close plants and lay off numerous workers. The target's board of directors reasonably concludes that the negative impact on its employees exceeds the gains shareholders will garner. Did *Unocal* permit the board to turn down such an offer?

In *Revlon, Inc. v. MacAndrews and Forbes Holdings, Inc.*, the Delaware Supreme Court concluded that *Unocal* did not.[175] *Revlon* added two crucial provisos to *Unocal*'s treatment of nonshareholder constituencies. The first is of general applicability, dealing with all structural decisions except those in which the so-called *Revlon* duties have triggered. If *Unocal* arguably allowed target boards to trade off a decrease in shareholder wealth for an increase in stakeholder wealth, *Revlon* forecloses that interpretation. *Revlon* expressly forbids management from protecting stakeholder interests at the expense of shareholder interests. Rather, any management action benefiting stakeholders must produce ancillary shareholder benefits.[176] In other words, directors may only consider stakeholder interests if doing so would benefit shareholders.[177]

Abramson v. Nytronics, Inc., 312 F.Supp. 519 (S.D.N.Y.1970). It is difficult to form a coherent picture from these cases, as most courts outside of Delaware face corporate law issues on a sporadic basis, which precludes sustained doctrinal development. Cf. Treadway Cos., Inc. v. Care Corp., 638 F.2d 357, 382 (2d Cir.1980) (stating that "[t]he law in this area is something less than a seamless web").

174. Unocal Corp. v. Mesa Petroleum Co., 493 A.2d 946, 956 (Del.1985).

175. Revlon, Inc. v. MacAndrews & Forbes Holdings, Inc., 506 A.2d 173 (Del. 1986). In Newell Co. v. Vermont American Corp., 725 F.Supp. 351 (N.D.Ill.1989), the court, applying the *Unocal* test, determined that the offer would maximize short-term shareholder profits, but nevertheless upheld the target's defensive measures. Although the principal threat appeared to be to nonshareholder interests, the court avoided the question posed in the text by finding that long-term shareholder interests were threatened. See id. at 372–76.

176. "A board may have regard for various constituencies in discharging its responsibilities, provided there are rationally related benefits accruing to the stockholders." Revlon, Inc. v. MacAndrews & Forbes Holdings, Inc., 506 A.2d 173, 182 (Del.1986). A somewhat weaker formulation was used in Mills Acquisition Co. v. Macmillan, Inc., 559 A.2d 1261 (Del.1989), which allows consideration of nonshareholder interests provided they bear "some reasonable relationship to general shareholder interests." Id. at 1282 n. 29.

177. Compare Buckhorn, Inc. v. Ropak Corp., 656 F.Supp. 209, 231–32 (S.D.Ohio), aff'd, 815 F.2d 76 (6th Cir.1987) (employee stock ownership plan invalidated because there was "no evidence in the record as to how the ESOP would benefit the stockholders nor as to how Ropak's tender offer posed a threat to Buckhorn's employees") with Shamrock Holdings, Inc. v. Polaroid Corp., 559 A.2d 257, 276 (Del.Ch.1989) (employee stock ownership plan upheld because it was "likely to add value to the company and all of its stockholders").

Second, where the *Revlon* duties have triggered, stakeholders become entirely irrelevant. Once a *Revlon* auction begins, it no longer matters whether benefiting nonshareholder interests may also benefit shareholders. Instead, shareholder wealth maximization is the board's only appropriate concern.[178] Indeed, in *Revlon*-land,[179] considering any factors other than shareholder wealth violates the board's fiduciary duties.[180]

In sum, *Revlon* sharply limits directors' ability to consider nonshareholder interests in structural decisions.[181] Moreover, by withholding the business judgment rule's protections from directors, *Revlon* puts considerable teeth into the shareholder wealth maximization norm. Unlike the operational context, directors who make structural decisions based on stakeholder interests rather than shareholder interests face the very real threat of personal liability.

B. A Note on the ALI Principles' Approach

The ALI PRINCIPLES adopted a rule bearing substantial similarity to *Unocal* minus the *Revlon* limitations thereon. Section 6.02 provides that the board, when making takeover decisions, may "have regard for interests or groups (other than shareholders) with respect to which the corporation has a legitimate concern if to do so would not significantly disfavor the long-term interests of shareholders."[182] Unlike *Unocal*, the burden is on plaintiff to prove that the defendant directors acted unreasonably. This rule applies to all takeover situations, including those in which a *Revlon*-like control auction has begun.

Section 6.02 is a very odd formulation. For one thing, the shareholders have long-term interests in the takeover context only if the target remains independent. The standard thus seems to put the cart before the horse. Additionally, how much injury to the shareholders can the target board work before the shareholders are "significantly disfavor[ed]"? The ALI failed to coherently answer that question. The unsatisfactory treatment of this issue by the ALI becomes more explicable when one realizes that Section 6.02 was one of the most hotly debated

178. Revlon, Inc. v. MacAndrews & Forbes Holdings, Inc., 506 A.2d 173, 182 (Del.1986).

179. "*Revlon* land" is the emerging term of art for corporate control contests in which the so-called *Revlon* duties have triggered.

180. Black & Decker Corp. v. American Standard, Inc., 682 F.Supp. 772, 786–87 (D.Del.1988); C–T of Virginia, Inc. v. Barrett, 124 Bankr. 689 (W.D.Va.1990); Revlon, Inc. v. MacAndrews & Forbes Holdings, Inc., 506 A.2d 173, 185 (Del.1986).

181. To be sure, some commentators contend that *Time* implicitly allows target managers greater freedom to consider nonshareholder interests. See, e.g., Alan E. Garfield, *Paramount*: The Mixed Merits of Mush, 17 Del. J. Corp. L. 33, 57–58 (1992); Lyman Johnson & David Millon, The Case Beyond *Time*, 45 Bus. Law. 2105 (1990); David Millon, Redefining Corporate Law, 24 Ind. L. Rev. 223, 237–38 (1991). But see Jeffrey N. Gordon, Corporations, Markets, and courts, 91 Colum. L. Rev. 1931, 1951–71 (1991).

182. ALI PRINCIPLES § 6.02(b)(2).

sections of the entire project. The final version is a compromise that seems to have satisfied no one.[183]

C. Nonshareholder Constituency Statutes

Over 30 states have adopted nonshareholder constituency statutes that authorize directors to consider nonshareholder interests when making corporate decisions, typically by amending the existing statutory statement of the director's duty of due care. These statutes typically provide that, in discharging their duty of care, directors may consider the effects of a decision on not only shareholders, but also on a laundry list of other constituency groups, commonly including employees, suppliers, customers, creditors, and the local communities in which the firm does business. In the operational setting, these statutes rarely will change the outcome of shareholder litigation. Because the business judgment rule precludes courts from deciding whether directors violated their duty of care, the court will not even reach the statutory issue in most cases.[184]

In the structural setting, however, the statutes could have outcome determinative effects. Despite some judicial holdings to the contrary,[185] it seems clear that nonshareholder constituency statutes were intended to reject *Revlon*'s constraints on director decision making. Like most state takeover laws, nonshareholder constituency statutes are typically adopted at the request of target corporation management actively engaged in resisting a hostile takeover bid. Unquestionably, the legislative intent was to make takeovers harder.[186] What better way do so than by

---

183. See Steven M. H. Wallman, Section 6.02: Is ALI Provision on Director Duties Consistent with Evolution in Thinking about Takeovers?, Corp. Couns. Wkly. (BNA) at 8 (Aug. 7, 1991).

184. On these statutes, see generally Stephen Bainbridge, Interpreting Nonshareholder Constituency Statutes, 19 Pepperdine L. Rev. 971 (1992).

185. See, e.g., Hilton Hotels Corp. v. ITT Corp., 978 F.Supp. 1342 (D.Nev.1997); Amanda Acquisition Corp. v. Universal Foods Corp., 708 F.Supp. 984, 1009 (E.D.Wis.), aff'd on other grounds, 877 F.2d 496 (7th Cir.1989).

186. In a legislative debate on Pennsylvania's package of takeover laws, which included a new nonshareholder constituency statute, one of the bill's sponsors observed, "To Sam Belzberg, to Carl Icahn, to Boone Pickens, to the Bass Brothers, to Don Trump and all you other corporate raiders, you do not have a friend in Pennsylvania." Pa.Legis.J., Sen., Dec. 13, 1989, at 1539 (Sen. Armstrong). See also id. at 1507 ("legislation in defense from corporate raiders is no vice") (Sen. Williams); Pa.Legis.J.House, Apr. 24, 1990, at 778 ("By passing this antitakeover measure, we will send a loud and clear message to those who would make our Pennsylvania corporations simple, quick-profit chop shops, and that is, Pennsylvania is no longer your playground."). Professors Johnson and Millon have argued that state takeover laws are generally intended "to protect nonshareholders from the disruptive impact of ... hostile takeovers." Lyman Johnson & David Millon, Missing the Point About State Takeover Statutes, 87 Mich. L. Rev. 846, 848 (1989). Whether or not this claim is true of state takeover laws generally, it is difficult to reject as to nonshareholder constituency statutes. See Robert D. Rosenbaum & L. Stevenson Parker, The Pennsylvania Takeover Act of 1990: Summary and Analysis 28–30 (1990) ("The basic argument made in support of the new [Pennsylvania] stakeholder provision was that public corporations are and should be more than vehicles

tempering the shareholder wealth norm exemplified by *Revlon?* This interpretation is especially apt for those statutes that expressly permit directors to consider the corporation's long-term interests even in takeover contests. These statutes can only be read as implicitly rejecting *Revlon's* command that short-term shareholder wealth maximization be the director's sole concern once a corporate control auction begins.

The rejection of *Revlon* implicit in most statutes was made explicit by Indiana's nonshareholder constituency statute. The legislation was obviously drafted in response to a pair of Seventh Circuit decisions striking down a series of poison pills adopted by a target corporation.[187] Because Indiana had no applicable precedents, the Seventh Circuit looked to *Unocal* and *Revlon* for guidance. The Indiana nonshareholder constituency statute was specifically intended to reverse that approach, giving courts astonishingly blunt guidance:

> Certain judicial decisions in Delaware and other jurisdictions, which might otherwise be looked to for guidance in interpreting Indiana corporate law, including decisions relating to potential change of control transactions that impose a different or higher degree of scrutiny on actions taken by directors in response to a proposed acquisition of control of the corporation, are inconsistent with the proper application of the business judgment rule under this article.[188]

Revlon is the statute's clear target, for the statute goes on to expressly reject the primacy of shareholder interests: "directors are not required to consider the effects of a proposed corporate action on any particular corporate constituent group or interest as a dominant or controlling factor." Moreover, the board's determinations in this respect are conclu-

to generate maximum profits—particularly in the short term—for shareholders.").

187. Dynamics Corp. of Am. v. CTS Corp., 805 F.2d 705 (7th Cir.1986), prior op., 794 F.2d 250 (7th Cir.1986), rev'd on other grounds, 481 U.S. 69 (1987). This takeover battle went on to fame as CTS Corp. v. Dynamics Corp. of Am., 481 U.S. 69 (1987), in which the supreme court upheld the constitutionality of a different Indiana takeover statute. No decision to date has squarely addressed the constitutionality of nonshareholder constituency statutes. In the course of upholding a different type of state takeover statute, however, Judge Easterbrook offered the following noteworthy dictum: "States could choose to protect 'constituencies' other than stockholders." Amanda Acquisition Corp. v. Universal Foods Corp., 877 F.2d 496, 500 n. 5 (7th Cir.), cert. denied, 493 U.S. 955 (1989).

188. Ind. Code Ann. § 23–1–35–1(f) (West 1990). Pennsylvania's nonshareholder constituency statute largely tracks the Indiana statute. Like Indiana, Pennsylvania makes the board's determinations conclusive unless a challenger proves that the board did not act "in good faith after reasonable investigation." 15 Pa. Cons. Stat. § 1721 (Supp.1991). Similarly, Pennsylvania also precludes courts from imposing any burden greater than the business judgment rule on directors seeking to justify takeover defenses. Id. Finally, the Pennsylvania statute does not require directors to treat any corporate constituency interest as having paramount importance. See id. Although Pennsylvania omitted any direct reference to Delaware law, the prohibition on imposition of a higher standard of review is clearly intended to follow Indiana in precluding courts from adopting *Unocal* or *Revlon*.

sive unless a challenger proves that the board did not act "in good faith after reasonable investigation."

So interpreted, these statutes are very unsound as a matter of public policy. To be sure, there is a lot of anecdotal evidence suggesting that corporate takeovers generate negative externalities with respect to nonshareholder constituencies. Yet, there is little systematic evidence that takeover bidders do any more damage to the interests of such constituencies than do entrenched "incumbents—who may (and frequently do) close or move plants to follow the prospect of profit."[189]

By contrast, there is a well-documented managerial conflict of interest in the takeover setting. There is a very real possibility that unscrupulous directors will use nonshareholder interests to cloak their own self-interested behavior. Selfish decisions easily could be justified by an appropriate paper trail of tears over the employees' fate. This then is the real vice of nonshareholder constituency statutes. While they allow honest directors to act in the best interests of all the corporation's constituents, they also may protect dishonest directors who are acting solely in their own interest. All of this tends to suggest that legislatures ought to think twice about adopting nonshareholder constituency statutes without first addressing management's conflict of interest.

What then should we do about the statutes that are on the books? Whatever the theoretical merits of a rule requiring management passivity in the face of a hostile takeover bid, the nonshareholder constituency statutes plainly reject any such requirement. Rather, their very premise is that shareholder and stakeholder interests conflict in corporate takeovers and that the target's directors are in the best position to reconcile those competing interests.

While the nonshareholder constituency statutes clarify that it is appropriate for directors to consider the interests of those constituencies in making structural decisions, corporate law need not ignore the very real risk that the directors' proffered justification is a ruse. Enabling directors to transfer part of the pie from shareholders to stakeholders is the stated purpose of nonshareholder constituency statutes. courts must be true to that purpose, but they need not interpret nonshareholder constituency statutes as allowing directors and managers to reallocate a bigger piece of the pie to themselves. In structural decisions, corporate law therefore should separate instances of honest director concern for nonshareholder interests from selfish director concern for their own positions. Happily, a mechanism for doing so is close at hand: *Unocal's* shifting burdens of proof will do quite nicely by analogy.

To be sure, nonshareholder constituency statutes reject the *Revlon* gloss on *Unocal*. Absent the unique provisions found in the Indiana and

---

189. Amanda Acquisition Corp. v. Universal Foods Corp., 877 F.2d 496, 500 n. 5   (7th Cir.), cert. denied, 493 U.S. 955 (1989).

Pennsylvania statutes, however, the nonshareholder constituency statutes need not be interpreted as barring a *Unocal*-type test. An apt precedent for this thesis is provided by the prevailing judicial interpretation of interested director transaction statutes. Not every interested director transaction involves self dealing, but the high probability of misconduct in this context led courts to permit review even of transactions that are properly ratified and to impose a very exacting standard on transactions that are not ratified. The significant risk of self-interested director behavior in corporate acquisitions similarly justifies exacting judicial scrutiny of claims that the directors were acting to protect nonshareholder interests. Accordingly, unless the legislature has clearly prohibited courts from imposing a heightened standard of review, courts should read a *Unocal*-type standard into the nonshareholder constituency statutes.

By analogy to the first *Unocal* prong, a court should first require the directors to show that the takeover bid poses a threat to one of the enumerated nonshareholder interests. Presumably, the requisite threats could take a variety of forms: lay-offs, plant closings, downgrading of bonds, and the like. A court should also require directors to show that they acted in good faith and after a reasonable investigation. The good faith element requires a showing that the directors acted in response to a perceived threat to the corporation and not for the purpose of entrenching themselves in office. As such, this element necessarily involves a subjective inquiry into the directors' motives. Absent the proverbial smoking gun it may be difficult to distinguish cases involving self-interested director behavior from cases involving legitimate director concern for stakeholders. Nonetheless, retaining a subjective component to the analysis can be justified on several grounds. First, judicial review is better than no review. Many takeover decisions are subject to review by the market. For example, when a board agrees to merge with one of several potential bidders, motive analysis is unnecessary. As long as the board fairly conducted an auction amongst the competing bidders, the market will have demonstrated the merger's fairness. However, when a board rejects a hostile takeover bid on nonmonetary grounds, by definition a market test is unavailable. In effect, the directors are asking to be exempted from a market test because of the takeover's alleged impact on nonshareholder constituents. As such, a motive based inquiry becomes more justifiable. At the very least, it captures gross cases in which there is good evidence—either direct or circumstantial—that the board acted for its own interest. Second, the test proposed here is not limited to a subjective motive analysis. Instead, the good faith element is primarily intended to force the directors to articulate a nonself-interested rationale for their action. The directors' stated rationale can then be tested against the model's objective standards, which have the primary responsibility for capturing cases of director misconduct. Finally, as further described below, the obligation to construct a disinterested rationale for the decision may deter many boards from self-interested behavior in the first place.

The second *Unocal* prong is the critical one if self-interested management behavior is to be controlled. Unless the requirement of proportionality between threat and response has real teeth, management can still use a threat to nonshareholder interests as a cloak for protecting their own jobs. Absent an effective proportionality standard, any threat to nonshareholder interests, no matter how mild or insignificant, would give management a free hand to develop takeover defenses to kill the hostile takeover bid. Because one cannot reasonably interpret the nonshareholder constituency statutes as codifying *Revlon*, the statute must be interpreted as allowing directors to make trade-offs between shareholder and stakeholder interests. At the same time, however, an effective proportionality standard requires that directors minimize the effect of their decision on shareholders. In other words, their decision must impose no greater burden on the shareholders than necessary to protect the nonshareholder constituencies. If measures less harmful to the shareholders' interest would have adequately protected the nonshareholder interests at stake, the target's chosen defensive measures should be invalidated.

Similar tests are used in other corporate conflict of interest transactions. Under Massachusetts law, for example, when a minority close corporation shareholder alleges a breach of fiduciary duty by the firm's controlling shareholder, the controlling shareholder must first demonstrate a legitimate business purpose for its actions. If the controlling shareholder does so, the minority shareholder can still prevail by showing that the same objective could have been accomplished through an alternative course less harmful to the minority's interest.[190]

The precise application of this standard will obviously vary from case to case. In general, however, judicial review should focus on questions of process. In making proportionality assessments, the court should thus scrutinize closely management's arguments and require a convincing demonstration that no less restrictive defense is available. In doing so, the court should look to such evidence as the specificity of management's plans, the record of the board's deliberations, and expert testimony from both sides. A showing that the directors were aware of and considered the threat to nonshareholder interests at the time they decided to resist the takeover bid is particularly important, because it lowers the likelihood that the threat is an ex post facto justification for selfish behavior.

Courts also should examine closely the negotiations, if any, between the bidder and target management. If there is any evidence that target management would set aside its concern for stakeholders in exchange for a higher acquisition price or side payments for itself, management's

---

190. Wilkes   v.   Springside   Nursing
Home, Inc., 353 N.E.2d 657 (Mass.1976).

purported fears for nonshareholder interests should be seen as mere pretense.

The most important evidence probably will be the history of the firm's treatment of nonshareholder constituencies. A long history of board concern for the firm's workers tells a more plausible story than a sudden interest in their welfare. This is particularly relevant for firms that have previously used threats to nonshareholder constituencies to justify takeover defenses. Not infrequently, an unsuccessful hostile bid will be followed months or years later by another hostile bid from a new bidder. If management has largely ignored stakeholder concerns in the interim, it will be hard for them to use those concerns to justify resisting the new bid.

By carrying its burden of proof under both prongs of this test, the board of directors demonstrates that it is not disabled by a conflict of interest. Absent a disabling conflict, courts generally defer to board decisions. Accordingly, if the board carries its burden, the court should not inquire into the reasonableness of the board's decision unless the plaintiff is otherwise able to rebut the business judgment rule's presumptions. But if the board fails to carry its burden, the court should enjoin the proposed corporate action and/or grant other appropriate relief.

An effective proportionality requirement may reduce management's ex ante incentives to cheat. Dishonest management may find it difficult to construct a plausible story of nonshareholder injury. Dishonest management may not be able to locate experts who can or will support credibly a false nonshareholder injury story; indeed, stakeholders themselves may decline to support dishonest management's story. Independent directors may be unwilling to risk the reputational injury of supporting a false story. Finally, the hostile bidder will be actively seeking to rebut management's story and, perhaps, will be recruiting stakeholder support. All of these factors should deter management misconduct and, moreover, give management incentives to evaluate fairly whether shareholder and stakeholder interests in fact diverge.

Chapter 8

STATE ANTI–TAKEOVER LEGISLATION

Although its intensity varies from year to year, the takeover arms race remains unrelenting. As fast as new acquisition techniques are developed, new defenses spring up. In the quest for more effective defenses, legislative avenues were by no means ignored. Although Congress remains on the sidelines, the states are active players. The states normally can be found on management's end of the playing field; state takeover laws are almost uniformly anti-takeover laws. Although the state law front has been relatively quiet since the mid–1990s, the old statutes remain on the books. Under current law, moreover, there are few obstacles to renewed state activism.

§ 8.1 The First Generation and *MITE*

Simultaneously with Congress' adoption of the Williams Act, the states began adopting what are now known as first generation state takeover laws.[1] Like the Williams Act, the first generation state laws were mainly disclosure statutes. Unlike the Williams Act, the first generation statutes also imposed certain procedural and substantive requirements creating substantial obstacles for takeover bidders.

The Illinois Business Takeover Act (IBTA), which the Supreme Court invalidated in *Edgar v. MITE Corp.*,[2] was typical of the first generation statutes. It differed from the Williams Act in three critical ways. First, the IBTA required bidders to notify the target and the Illinois Secretary of State twenty days before the offer's effective date. Second, the IBTA permitted the Secretary of State to delay a tender offer by holding a hearing on the offer's fairness. Moreover, the Secretary was required to hold such a hearing if one was requested by shareholders owning ten percent of the class of securities subject to the offer. Finally, the Secretary of State could enjoin a tender offer on a variety of bases, including substantive unfairness.

A. Preemption Standards

Three basic preemption tests are currently in use. First, the federal regulatory scheme may so thoroughly pervade the field as to suggest

---

1. Indeed, Virginia's first generation statute was adopted several months prior to the William Act's passage. Stephen M. Bainbridge, State Takeover and Tender Offer Regulations Post–MITE: The Maryland, Ohio and Pennsylvania Attempts, 90 Dickinson L. Rev. 731, 736 (1986).

2. Edgar v. MITE Corp., 457 U.S. 624 (1982).

Congress left no room for concurrent state regulation.[3] Nobody seriously contends that state takeover regulation is preempted by the Williams Act under this standard. Congress has never attempted broadly to supplant state regulation of corporate governance.[4] A cursory comparison of the federal tender offer rules and any state's corporation code demonstrates that the former occupies only a relatively small portion of the field. Among the many issues left to state law are the fiduciary duties of managers, the validity of post-offer freeze-out mergers, and so on. Federal regulation is thus by no means sufficiently pervasive as to justify preemption under this prong.

Second, where it is physically impossible for an actor to comply with both federal and state regulations, the supremacy of federal law requires that the actor comply with the federal rule.[5] This is a fairly constrained standard, however. The question here is not whether the state statute deters rational actors from going forward. Rather, the question is whether an actor could comply with both the federal and state laws if it chose to make the attempt.

Finally, federal law preempts state statutes if they are inconsistent with the purposes of the relevant federal law. Here the relevant standard is whether the state law "stands as an obstacle to the accomplishment and execution of the full purposes and objectives of Congress."[6] This preemption standard requires a court to resolve two questions: (1) What are the intended Congressional purposes of federal tender offer regulation? (2) Does the state statute under review interfere with the accomplishment of those purposes?

B.   Did the Williams Act Preempt the IBTA?

Lower courts were divided on the constitutionality of state takeover legislation pre-*MITE*, but the trend was decidedly hostile towards state regulation.[7] Courts found such statutes problematic under both the physical incompatibility and frustration of Congressional intent standards. The potential for delay inherent in the advance filing and the

3. Rice v. Santa Fe Elevator Corp., 331 U.S. 218, 230 (1947) (whether federal regulation is "so pervasive as to make reasonable the inference that Congress left no room for the States to supplement" federal law).

4. CTS Corp. v. Dynamics Corp. of Am., 481 U.S. 69, 85–86 (1987); Business Roundtable v. SEC, 905 F.2d 406, 411–13 (D.C.Cir.1990).

5. Florida Lime & Avocado Growers, Inc. v. Paul, 373 U.S. 132, 142–43 (1963).

6. Hines v. Davidowitz, 312 U.S. 52, 67 (1941).

7. Pre-*MITE* decisions invalidating state takeover statutes included: Kennecott Corp. v. Smith, 637 F.2d 181 (3d Cir.1980); Natomas Co. v. Bryan, 512 F.Supp. 191 (D.Nev.1981); Canadian Pac. Enter. (U.S.) Inc. v. Krouse, 506 F.Supp. 1192 (S.D.Ohio 1981); Kelly v. Beta–X Corp., 302 N.W.2d 596 (Mich.Ct.App.1981). But see AMCA Int'l Corp. v. Krouse, 482 F.Supp. 929 (S.D.Ohio 1979); City Investing Co. v. Simcox, 476 F.Supp. 112 (S.D.Ind.1979), aff'd, 633 F.2d 56 (7th Cir.1980).

administrative review requirements of many state statutes were found to excessively tilt the balance sought by the Williams Act to the side of target management.[8] The administrative review process, which could result in the state barring the tender offer on "fairness" or other grounds, was also found to conflict with a purported Congressional intent that shareholders make the decision as to whether to tender or not.

On January 19, 1979, MITE Corporation filed a Schedule 14D–1 with the SEC, indicating its intent to make a $28 per share cash tender offer for Chicago Rivet & Machine Company. On February 1, 1980, Illinois officials notified MITE that the proposed offer violated the IBTA and issued a cease and desist order and a notice of an administrative hearing. Chicago Rivet then notified MITE that it would file suit under the IBTA to restrain the tender offer. MITE thereupon sued in federal court, seeking to have the IBTA declared unconstitutional on both preemption and commerce clause grounds. The district court struck down the statute on both grounds and the Seventh Circuit affirmed.

Although the circuit court recognized that the federal scheme of regulating tender offers is not so pervasive that an implicit congressional intent to preempt parallel state legislation could be inferred from the Williams Act, it found that the IBTA empowered the Illinois Secretary of State to pass upon the substantive fairness of a tender offer and to prohibit it from going forward if the Secretary judged the offer inequitable. Thus, the circuit court stated, "Illinois' substitution of the judgment of its Secretary of State for an investor's own assessment of the equitability of a tender offer is patently inconsistent with the Williams Act, . . . which contemplates unfettered choice by well-informed investors." Consequently, the Williams Act preempted the IBTA. The circuit court also found that the IBTA unconstitutionally burdened interstate commerce. The circuit court relied on the balancing standard set forth by the Supreme Court in *Pike v. Bruce Church*: "Where the statute regulates evenhandedly to effectuate a legitimate local public interest, and its effects on interstate commerce are only incidental, it will be upheld unless the burden imposed on such commerce is clearly excessive in relation to the putative local benefits."[9] Illinois asserted two interests:

---

8. In 1979, the SEC had promulgated Rule 14d–2(b), which requires that a bidder meet the SEC's dissemination and Schedule 14D–1 disclosure requirements within five days of the announcement of the offer. The rule created a direct conflict between the federal tender offer rules and the first generation of state takeover laws. Because most first generation statutes required a substantial delay between the announcement and dissemination of the offer, it was no longer possible to time an offer to comply with both federal and state law. After

Rule 14d–2(b) was promulgated, the clear trend was towards finding state takeover statutes unconstitutional. See Mark A. Sargent, On the Validity of State Takeover Regulation: State Responses to *MITE* and *Kidwell*, 42 Ohio St. L.J. 689, 696–97 (1981).

9. Pike v. Bruce Church, Inc., 397 U.S. 137, 142 (1970) (citation omitted). The commerce clause of the U.S. constitution is both a grant of power to Congress and a limitation on state power. Under the su-

protection of resident shareholders and regulation of the internal affairs of Illinois corporations. The circuit court rejected both arguments. It found that the IBTA provided shareholders "marginal" benefits and that Illinois' "tenuous interest" was counterbalanced by the statute's "global impact" and its "significant potential to cause commercial disruption" by blocking an offer "even if it received the enthusiastic endorsement of all other States." Consequently, because the IBTA substantially obstructed interstate commerce, without significant countervailing local benefits, it violated the dormant commerce clause.

The Supreme Court affirmed in a badly divided opinion.[10] Rejecting an argument that the preliminary injunction rendered the case moot, the plurality reached the constitutional issues. Among the substantive portions of Justice White's opinion, only the *Pike* commerce clause analysis commanded a majority. On that issue, the Court found that Illinois had "no legitimate interest in protecting non-resident shareholders," and offered only "speculative" protection for resident shareholders. The Court agreed with the circuit court "that the possible benefits of the potential delays as required by the Act may be outweighed by the increased risk that the tender offer will fail due to defensive tactics employed by incumbent management." The Court also rejected Illinois' "internal affairs" argument, noting that: "[t]ender offers contemplate transfers of stock by stockholders to a third party and do not themselves implicate the internal affairs of the target company. Furthermore, . . . Illinois has no interest in regulating the internal affairs of foreign corporations." The Court therefore concluded that the IBTA was unconstitutional under the dormant commerce clause because it imposed a substantial burden on interstate commerce that outweighed the putative local benefits.

Writing for a plurality of the court, Justice White also argued that the Williams Act preempted IBTA. According to White, the Williams Act adopted a policy of neutrality as between bidders and targets. In an oft-used metaphor, Congress supposedly intended to create a level playing field for takeover contests. The IBTA's prenotification and hearing requirements imposed significant delays before a bid could commence, during which management could erect defenses and take other measures designed to prevent the offer from going forward, and thus frustrated Congressional purpose by tipping the playing field in target manage-

---

premacy clause a valid congressional exercise of the commerce power will preempt conflicting state regulation. However, even in the absence of congressional legislation, the "dormant" commerce clause bars direct state regulation of commerce. Edgar v. MITE Corp., 457 U.S. 624, 640 (1982) (White, J.).

10. Edgar v. MITE Corp., 457 U.S. 624 (1982). In his lead opinion, Justice White

determined that the Williams Act preempted the IBTA and also invalid under the commerce clause because (1) the IBTA directly regulated interstate commerce and (2) the IBTA's legitimate local benefits did not outweigh its indirect burden on interstate commerce. Only the latter holding, however, commanded a majority of the Court.

ment's favor. Drawing on the Williams Act's legislative history, White noted that Congress had rejected an advance-filing requirement precisely because "Congress itself 'recognized that delay can seriously impede a tender offer' and sought to avoid it." In addition, White concluded that the administrative veto granted the Secretary of State conflicted with a Congressional intent that shareholders be allowed make the final decision as to whether to accept a tender offer.

The *MITE* decision's immediate impact was unclear. Only those statutes with similarly "global" ability to block tender offers were directly rendered unconstitutional by the opinion of the Court. Because Justice White's preemption analysis commanded the votes of only two other Justices, it seemed possible that state statutes with a more narrow jurisdictional basis but still having a pro-target bias could pass constitutional muster. Indeed, in refusing to join the preemption analysis, Justice Stevens expressly stated that he was "not persuaded ... that Congress' decision to follow a policy of neutrality in its own legislation is tantamount to a federal prohibition against state legislation designed to provide special protection for incumbent management." Similarly, Justice Powell declined to join the preemption analysis, observing that the Court's "Commerce Clause reasoning leaves some room for state regulation" and that "the Williams Act's neutrality policy does not necessarily imply a congressional intent to prohibit state legislation [protecting] interests that include but are often broader than those of incumbent management." Surprisingly, however, subsequent lower court decisions almost uniformly adopted the plurality's preemption analysis.

§ 8.2   The Second Generation and *CTS*

Justice White's *MITE* opinion left open a narrow window of opportunity for states to regulate takeovers: the internal affairs doctrine, pursuant to which the state of incorporation's law governs questions of corporate governance. The second generation of state takeover statutes was carefully crafted to fit within that loophole.

A.   The Second Generation Statutes

The so-called "second generation" statutes were, for the most part, cautiously tailored to avoid direct regulation of tender offers. Instead, they addressed issues purporting to fall within the sphere of corporate governance concerns traditionally subject to state law. In the years between 1983 and 1987, many of these statutes were challenged and almost uniformly were struck down by the lower courts as unconstitutional. That trend reversed following the Supreme Court's decision in *CTS Corp. v. Dynamics Corp.*,[11] however.

There are four principal variants of "second generation" statutes: Control share acquisition statutes rely on the states' traditional power to

11. CTS Corp. v. Dynamics Corp. of
Am., 481 U.S. 69 (1987).

define corporate voting rights as a justification for regulating the bidder's right to vote shares acquired in a control transaction. A "control share acquisition" is typically defined as the acquisition of a sufficient number of target company shares to give the acquirer control over more than a specified percentage of the voting power of the target. The triggering level of share ownership is usually defined as an acquisition which would bring the bidder within one of three ranges of voting power: 20 to 33 1/3%, 33 1/3 to 50% and more than 50%. Most control share acquisition laws provide that shares acquired in a control share acquisition shall not have voting rights unless the shareholders approve a resolution granting voting rights to the acquirer's shares.[12] The shares owned by the acquirer, officers of the target and directors who are also employees of the target may not be counted in the vote on the resolution.

The stated purpose of control share statutes is providing shareholders with an opportunity to vote on a proposed acquisition of large share blocks that may result in or lead to a change in control of the target. These statutes are premised on the assumption that individual shareholders are often at a disadvantage when faced with a proposed change in control. If the target's shareholders believe that a successful tender offer will be followed by a purchase by the offeror of non-tendered shares at a price lower than that offered in the initial bid, for example, individual shareholders may tender their shares to protect themselves from such an eventuality, even if they do not believe the offer to be in their best interests.

By requiring certain disclosures from the prospective purchaser and by allowing the target's shareholders to vote on the acquisition as a group, control share acquisition statutes supposedly provide the shareholders a collective opportunity to reject an inadequate or otherwise undesirable offer. For example, since control share acquisition statutes generally require the offeror to disclose plans for transactions involving the target that would be initiated after the control shares are acquired, shareholders presumably would be unlikely to approve a creeping tender offer or street sweep which would be followed by a squeeze out back-end merger at a price less than or in a consideration different than that paid by the acquirer in purchasing the initial share block.

Fair price statutes are modeled on the approach taken in company charters that include fair price provisions. These statutes provide that certain specified transactions, sometimes called "Business Combinations," involving an "interested shareholder" must be approved by a specified supermajority shareholder vote unless certain minimum price and other conditions are met. The term "interested shareholder" is

---

12. E.g., Ind. Code Ann. § 23–1–42. A few states took a slightly different approach, under which the shareholders determine whether or not the proposed acquisition may be made. E.g., Ohio Rev. Code Ann. § 1701.831. This is a slightly more aggressive position than the more usual approach, which simply requires shareholder approval for voting rights to be accorded to the acquirer's shares.

typically defined by statute as a shareholder owning more than some specified percentage, often 10%, of the outstanding shares of the target.

Business combination statutes are an extension of the fair price statute concept, providing substantially greater teeth. The typical statute prohibits a target from engaging in any business combination with an interested shareholder of the target corporation for a set period of time, often five years, following the date on which the interested shareholder achieved such status. Following the initial freeze period, a business combination with an interested shareholder is still prohibited unless the business combination is approved by a specified vote of the outstanding shares not beneficially owned by the interested shareholder or the business combination meets specified fair price and other criteria.[13] The definition of interested shareholder typically is comparable to that used in fair price statutes. As with fair price statutes, the term "business combination" typically is defined to include a broader variety of transactions than just a statutory merger.

Cash-out statutes require an acquirer of more than a threshold percentage of a target's stock to offer to purchase the remaining shares of all of the other shareholders at a price which reflects the highest premium paid by the acquirer in accumulating target stock. Cash-out statutes typically apply to so-called "control transactions," which are defined as acquisitions by a person or group who, after the acquisition, will have the status of a "controlling person or group." A "controlling person or group" is a person who has, or a group of persons acting in concert that has, voting power over voting shares that would entitle the holders thereof to cast at least a specified percentage of votes that all shareholders would be entitled to cast in the election of directors.

B. Powell's *CTS* Opinion

In *CTS Corp. v. Dynamics Corp.*,[14] the Supreme Court upheld an Indiana control share acquisition statute. Justice Powell's majority opinion began by noting that the *MITE* plurality's preemption analysis was not binding on the Court, but he declined to explicitly overrule it. Instead, Powell claimed that the Indiana Act passed muster even under White's interpretation of the Williams Act's purposes. It is perhaps instructive, however, that Justice White was the lone dissenter from Powell's preemption holding.

In fact, *CTS*' preemption analysis differed from *MITE*'s in at least two key respects. Where Justice White emphasized Congress' neutrality

---

13. See, e.g., N.Y. Bus. Corp. Law § 912(c). Delaware § 203 is similar to the original business combination statutes in a number of respects, but there is no requirement of shareholder approval after the freeze period expires. Shareholder voting may still occur, however, because the freeze period will be waived if at any time during it a proposed transaction is approved by the board of directors and by the two-thirds of the outstanding shares not owned by the bidder. DGCL § 203.

14. CTS Corp. v. Dynamics Corp. of Am., 481 U.S. 69 (1987).

policy, Justice Powell emphasized Congress' desire to protect shareholders.[15] Where Justice White would preempt any state statute favoring management, Justice Powell upheld the Indiana Act even though he recognized that it would deter some takeover bids. Justice Powell did so because he believed that, despite the Indiana statute's deterrent effect,[16] Justice Powell believed that it protected shareholders by permitting them collectively to evaluate an offer's fairness. He laid particular emphasis on a bidder's ability to coerce shareholders into tendering, such as by making a two-tier tender offer. By allowing shareholders collectively to reject such offers, the Indiana statute defuses their coercive effect. That the statute also deters takeovers and thereby protects incumbent managers is merely incidental to its primary function of protecting shareholders. The Indiana act therefore did not conflict with the Williams Act; to the contrary, Justice Powell concluded that it furthered Congress' goal of protecting shareholders.

Although Justice Powell acknowledged the Indiana act imposed a substantial delay on bidders, he reinterpreted *MITE* to only bar states from injecting unreasonable delay into the tender offer process. He then concluded that a potential 50–day waiting period was not unreasonable. Justice Powell noted that a variety of state corporate laws, such as classified board and cumulative voting statutes, limit or delay the transfer of control following a successful tender offer: "[T]he Williams Act would pre-empt a variety of state corporate laws of hitherto unquestioned validity if it were construed to pre-empt any state statute that may limit or delay the free exercise of power after a successful tender offer. . . . The longstanding prevalence of state regulation in this area suggests that, if Congress had intended to pre-empt all state laws that delay the acquisition of voting control following a tender offer, it would have said so explicitly."

15. In dissent, Justice White argued that the Williams Act was primarily intended to protect individual investors. CTS Corp. v. Dynamics Corp. of Am., 481 U.S. 69, 98–99 (1987) (White, J., dissenting). In contrast, Justice Powell believed that the Williams Act was intended to protect shareholders. Id. at 82. The difference between investors and shareholders is more than just semantic. Under Justice White's view, a statute will be preempted if it interferes with an individual investor's ability to freely make his own decision. In contrast, Justice Powell would uphold state takeover statutes that make shareholders as a group better off, even if the wishes of some individual investors are thereby frustrated.

16. Arguably, the control shareholder acquisition statutes are an ineffective takeover deterrent. The bidder's ability to request a special shareholder meeting to consider its proposed acquisition provides corporate raiders with an opportunity to cheaply advertise a target's takeover vulnerability. Likewise, a bidder can reduce the impact of a control share acquisition statute by simply delaying consummation of a purchase until a shareholder vote has been held and requiring a favorable vote as a condition to its tender offer. Most control share statutes prohibit both bidders and target insiders from voting on the resolution, but do not impose any minimum holding period on the "disinterested" shareholders in order for them to be eligible to vote. As a result, the outcome of the vote likely will depend in large part on the views of takeover arbitragers and other speculators who can be expected to favor the bidder over target management.

Justice White's analysis implied that the Williams Act's neutrality policy meant that any state laws that derogated from the level playing field established by the Williams Act were to be preempted. However, there was another, perhaps equally plausible, interpretation of the Act; namely, that Congress wanted to assure that the Act itself not affect the balance of power between bidders and targets but did not intend to prohibit all state laws that affected that balance. Powell's opinion implicitly embraced the latter view.

Turning to the commerce clause issues, Powell held that the Indiana statute also passed muster under the dormant commerce clause. The statute did not discriminate against out of state entities. It did not bar tender offers, leaving a meaningful opportunity for the offeror to succeed. Because the statute was limited to Indiana corporations, the statute did not have significant extraterritorial effects. As to the local benefits aspect of the balancing test, Justice Powell held that the state had a legitimate interest in defining the attributes of its corporations and protecting shareholders of its corporations. He opined, for example, that "[n]o principle of corporation law and practice is more firmly established than a State's authority to regulate domestic corporations, including the authority to define the voting rights of shareholders."[17] Accordingly, it "is an accepted part of the business landscape in this country for States to create corporations, to prescribe their powers, and to define the rights that are acquired by purchasing their shares."[18]

C. Interpreting *CTS*

Clearly *CTS* contemplated a greater degree of state regulation than did *MITE*, but how much greater remained uncertain. Because Justice Powell so narrowly focused on the specific provisions of the Indiana Act, he failed to provide a generally applicable analysis. Indeed, both proponents and opponents of state takeover legislation can mine *CTS* for support for their arguments. Faced with this uncertainty, two distinct lower court readings of *CTS*'s preemption analysis developed.

1. A Meaningful Opportunity for Success

The more restrictive interpretation of *CTS* requires states to preserve a meaningful opportunity for successful hostile bids. This standard

---

17. CTS Corp. v. Dynamics Corp. of Am., 481 U.S. 69, 89 (1987).

18. Some ten years after the Supreme Court's decision, CTS Corporation (the target) agreed to acquire Dynamics Corporation of America (the bidder) for $210 million in cash and stock. Dynamics still owned a 44 percent stake in CTS, which dated back to the contested control share acquisition. Ironically, the CTS acquisition was intended to thwart WHX Corporation's hostile takeover bid for Dynamics. CTS' chair-

man described the acquisition as a major benefit to "our shareholders." He also observed that the two companies' product families were complementary. The deal was structured as a cash tender for part of the Dynamics shares, to be followed by a stock swap for the rest of the shares, which gave Dynamics shareholders an opportunity to reject the cash end and take CTS shares, thereby avoiding tax on unrealized gain. Wall St. J., May 12, 1997, at B9.

is most fully developed in a trilogy of cases involving the Delaware takeover statute's constitutionality.[19] DGCL § 203 is a variant on the older business combination statutes. Section 203 prohibits a Delaware corporation from entering into a business combination for a period of three years after an offeror becomes an interested stockholder. Business combination is defined to include freeze-out mergers and other common post-acquisition transactions.[20] Interested shareholder is defined, subject to various exceptions, as the owner of 15% or more of the target's outstanding shares.

Unlike the older business combination statutes, the Delaware statute does not impose either a supermajority approval or a fair price requirement in connection with business combinations after the freeze period expires. Thus, once the three-year period expires, the interested stockholder may complete a second-step business combination on whatever terms and conditions would be lawful under applicable corporate and securities law provisions. In addition, the three-year freeze period is waived if any of four conditions are satisfied: (1) prior to the date on which the bidder crosses the 15% threshold, the business combination or the triggering acquisition is approved by the target's board of directors; (2) the bidder, in a single transaction, goes from a stock ownership level of less than 15% to more than 85% of the target's voting stock (not counting shares owned by inside directors or by employee stock plans in which the employees do not have the right to determine confidentially whether shares held by the plan will be tendered); (3) during the three year freeze period, the transaction is approved by the board of directors and by two-thirds of the outstanding shares not owned by the bidder; or (4) the target's board of directors approves a white knight transaction. Section 203(b) also sets forth various other conditions under which the statute will not apply, most prominently an opt-out provision pursuant to which a corporation may exempt itself from the statute through appropriate charter or bylaw provisions.

In the leading case of the trilogy, *BNS Inc. v. Koppers Co.*,[21] Chief District Judge Schwartz began by interpreting *CTS* as meaning that neutrality between bidders and targets was no longer regarded as a purpose of the Williams Act in itself, but rather merely as a means towards the true congressional end of shareholder protection. State statutes having a substantial deterrent effect are now permissible, as are statutes favoring management, so long as these effects are merely

19. City Capital Assoc. Ltd. v. Interco, Inc., 696 F.Supp. 1551 (D.Del.1988), aff'd on other grounds, 860 F.2d 60 (3d Cir. 1988); RP Acquisition Corp. v. Staley Cont'l, Inc., 686 F.Supp. 476 (D.Del.1988); BNS Inc. v. Koppers Co., Inc., 683 F.Supp. 458 (D.Del.1988).

20. Section 203 puts fewer restrictions on the raider's use of target assets to fi-

nance an acquisition than do the older business combination statutes. For example, it permits the raider to sell off target assets to third parties (subject to the usual fiduciary duty and voting rules).

21. BNS Inc. v. Koppers Co., Inc., 683 F.Supp. 458 (D.Del.1988).

incidental to protecting shareholders.[22] This proviso, however, is critical. As Chief Judge Schwartz saw it, *CTS* does not permit states to eliminate hostile takeovers. Rather, states must preserve a "meaningful opportunity" for hostile offers that are beneficial to target shareholders to succeed. Chief Judge Schwartz offered a four part test to decide whether a state law did so: (1) does the state law protect independent shareholders from coercion; (2) does it give either side an advantage in consummating or defeating an offer; (3) does it impose an unreasonable delay; and (4) does it permit a state official to substitute his views for those of the shareholders. Concluding that Section 203 probably satisfied these standards, Chief Judge Schwartz declined to enjoin its enforcement.

2. Amanda Acquisition

The 1980s takeover wars took many a surprising turn. Perhaps none was more surprising, however, than Judge Frank Easterbrook's decision in *Amanda Acquisition Corp. v. Universal Foods Corp.*[23] Judge Easterbrook is an unabashed proponent of hostile takeovers.[24] Indeed, *Amanda Acquisition* itself sings their praises. Yet in upholding the Wisconsin business combination statute, Judge Easterbrook authored the most permissive preemption analysis of state takeover legislation to date.[25]

Like most post-*MITE* state takeover statutes, the Wisconsin law deters tender offers by regulating freeze-out mergers and other post-acquisition transactions. Like most business combination statutes, it imposes a statutory freeze period, here three years, following the acquisition during which business combinations are prohibited. The sole viable exception to the freeze period is prior approval by the incumbent directors: "In Wisconsin it is management's approval in advance, or wait three years."

---

22. Accord Hyde Park Partners, L.P. v. Connolly, 839 F.2d 837, 850 (1st Cir.1988) ("protection of management that is incidental to protection of investors does not per se conflict with the purpose or purposes of the Williams Act.").

23. Amanda Acquisition Corp. v. Universal Foods Corp., 877 F.2d 496 (7th Cir. 1989).

24. See, e.g., Frank H. Easterbrook & Daniel R. Fischel, Auctions and Sunk Costs in Tender Offers, 35 Stan. L. Rev. 1 (1982); Frank H. Easterbrook & Daniel R. Fischel, The Proper Role of a Target's Management in Responding to a Tender Offer, 94 Harv. L. Rev. 1161 (1981).

25. Some observers posit that Judge Easterbrook did not mean what he said, but said it only to goad the Supreme Court or Congress into preempting state takeover legislation. Perhaps so, but then why did he

not simply say so, instead of creating an elaborate justification for state takeover regulations? It is not uncommon for lower court judges to follow Supreme Court precedents they disagree with, while expressly urging the Supreme Court to reconsider its prior holdings. No one doubts the appropriateness of such behavior. At the very least, however, there would be something unseemly about a judge deliberately misrepresenting his position in an attempt to force the Supreme Court to reverse him. Accordingly, it seems better to take Judge Easterbrook at his word, as several subsequent cases have done. E.g., Hoylake Investments Ltd. v. Washburn, 723 F.Supp. 42, 48 (N.D.Ill.1989); Glass, Molders, Pottery, Plastics and Allied Workers Int'l Union v. Wickes Co., Inc., 578 A.2d 402, 406 (N.J.Super.L.1990).

Judge Easterbrook began with the Williams Act's neutrality policy. Congress unquestionably expected the federal tender offers rules to be neutral as between bidders and targets. In *MITE*, Justice White read that expectation as forbidding state statutes from tipping the balance between them. Both Justices Powell and Stevens rejected that reading in their concurrences. And, of course, *CTS* implicitly backpedals from the spirit of Justice White's analysis. Judge Easterbrook recognized that all of this might open the door for non-neutral state laws, but he claimed to "stop short of th[at] precipice." At a minimum, however, *Amanda Acquisition* implicitly treats neutrality as a means rather than an end in itself. Easterbrook's decision to uphold the Wisconsin statute in the face of its admitted deterrent effects only makes sense if he has rejected Justice White's analysis in *MITE* of the neutrality policy's preemptive power.

In any case, Judge Easterbrook thereafter essentially ignored the Williams Act's neutrality policy. Instead, he asserted that Congress intended the Williams Act to regulate the process by which tender offers take place and the disclosures to which shareholders are entitled. He then used this reading of congressional purpose to distinguish *MITE* from *CTS*. The IBTA threatened to preclude a bidder from purchasing target shares even if the bidder complied with federal law. In contrast, the Indiana control share acquisition statute did not interfere with the federally mandated tender offer process; indeed, it did not even come into play until that process was completed and the shares acquired.

The Wisconsin business combination statute, like the Indiana Act, left the tender offer process alone. According to Judge Easterbrook, the Wisconsin statute therefore could be preempted only if the Williams Act gives investors a federal right to receive tender offers. He determined, however, that no such federal right exists: "Investors have no right to receive tender offers. More to the point—since Amanda sues as bidder rather than as investor seeking to sell—the Williams Act does not create a right to profit from the business of making tender offers. It is not attractive to put bids on the table for Wisconsin corporations, but because Wisconsin leaves the process alone once a bidder appears, its law may coexist with the Williams Act." The state statute need not even leave the bidder an opportunity—meaningful or otherwise—for success. Accordingly, the issue is not whether the statute deters tender offers. The issue is whether the state law directly interferes with an undeterred bidder's ability to go forward on schedule and in compliance with federal law.

3. Commerce Clause Issues

As illustrated by both *CTS* and *MITE*, challenges to state takeover laws typically entail not only preemption but also dormant commerce clause claims. Recall that there are three core commerce clause questions: (1) does the state statute discriminate against interstate commerce; (2) does the state statute subject interstate commerce to inconsistent regulation; and (3) do the local benefits of the statute outweigh the burdens it places on interstate commerce (the legitimacy of this third test is a matter of considerable debate among constitutional scholars, but let's leave it in their capable hands).[26] Post–*CTS*, commerce clause challenges have not had much traction. As long as the state statute treats in-state bidders and out-of-state bidders the same, the statute will pass muster under the first test. Provided the state law applies only to firms incorporated within the regulating state, there is no possibility of inconsistent regulation and it will pass muster under the second test. Some state takeover law decisions have declined to apply the third test, concluding that even statutes whose costs exceed their benefits are constitutional.[27] Even those that retain the third test, however, generally uphold state takeover laws in light of the substantial state interest in regulating corporate governance.[28]

D. The Third Generation

Following *CTS*, many states began adopting increasingly draconian takeover statutes. Perhaps none was more blatantly anti-takeover, however, that the statute adopted by Pennsylvania in 1990.[29] The statute contained no fewer than five distinct anti-takeover provisions. First, pursuant to a fairly standard nonshareholder constituency statute, directors are allowed to take account of the interests not only of shareholders but also of "employees, suppliers, customers and creditors of the corporation, and ... communities in which offices or other establishments of the corporation are located." Perhaps even more significantly, however, target company directors are expressly relieved of any obligation to treat the interests of shareholders as "dominant or controlling." These rules expressly apply to takeover defenses, such as a board refusal to redeem a poison pill. To be sure, the statute requires that directors act in "good faith," but their lack of good faith must be proved by "clear and convincing evidence."

Second, Pennsylvania adopted a control share acquisition statute largely modeled on the Indiana statute upheld in *CTS*. A control share

---

26. See CTS Corp. v. Dynamics Corp. of Am., 481 U.S. 69, 87–93 (1987).

27. E.g., Amanda Acquisition Corp. v. Universal Foods Corp., 877 F.2d 496, 505–09 (7th Cir.1989).

28. See, e.g., City Capital Assoc. L.P. v. Interco, Inc., 696 F.Supp. 1551, 1555 (D.Del.1988), aff'd on other grounds, 860 F.2d 60 (3d Cir.1988); RP Acquisition Corp. v. Staley Cont'l, Inc., 686 F.Supp. 476, 487–88 (D.Del.1988).

29. On Pennsylvania's various takeover statutes, see Stephen M. Bainbridge, Redi-recting State Takeover Laws at Proxy Contests, 1992 Wis. L. Rev. 1071 (discussing 1990 legislation, especially with respect to its effect on proxy contests); Stephen M. Bainbridge, State Takeover and Tender Offer Regulations Post–*MITE*: The Maryland, Ohio and Pennsylvania Attempts, 90 Dickinson L. Rev. 731 (1986) (discussing earlier cash out statute); John Pound, On the Motives for Choosing a Corporate Governance Structure: A Study of Corporate Reaction to the Pennsylvania Takeover Law, 8 J. L. Econ. & Org. 656 (1992).

acquisition must be approved by a majority of the "disinterested" shares and a majority of all shares (other than those of the bidder). If approval is not forthcoming, the bidder's shares are stripped of their voting rights. Disinterested shares are defined by statute as those that have been held by their owner for (i) twelve months before the record date for voting or (ii) five days prior to the first disclosure of the takeover bid. This provision apparently is intended to address a perceived loophole in second-generation control share acquisition statutes; namely, the fact that takeover speculators often buy up large blocks of stock after a bid is announced.

Third, the statute contains a so-called "tin parachute" provision, under which an employee who is fired after a takeover is entitled to a week's pay for each year of prior employment to a maximum of 26 weeks' pay. In a related provision, the statute provides that after a takeover all labor contracts are to remain in force.

Finally, and perhaps most innovatively, a target corporation (or one of its shareholders suing derivatively) may sue a controlling person or group for disgorgement of any profits realized upon disposition of the latter's shares in the target if the disposition occurs within 18 months after the person or group achieved control status. The controlling person or group also must have acquired the shares within 24 months before or 18 months after they acquired control status. A person or group achieves control status by disclosing an intent to seek control of the firm or by acquiring, offering to acquire or disclosing an intent to acquire "voting power over voting shares of a registered corporation that would entitle the holder thereof to cast at least 20% of the votes that all shareholders would be entitled to cast in an election of directors of the corporation." A registered corporation is one registered with the SEC under the Securities Exchange Act of 1934. Control is defined as the "power, whether or not exercised, to direct or cause the direction of the management and policies of a person, whether through the ownership of voting shares, by contract or otherwise."

Note that the statutory definition of control status picks up not only successful bidders but also the holder of proxies representing more than 20 percent of the outstanding shares. It does so because such a proxy holder has the power to cast "at least twenty per cent of the votes that all shareholders would be entitled to cast in the election of directors of the corporation."[30] As originally introduced, the statute thus imposed the disgorgement penalty not only on tender offerors, but also on anyone soliciting proxies for any purpose from more than 20 percent of the

---

30. "Voting power" is not a defined term in the disgorgement statute. Pennsylvania's older cash-out statute defines it as the power to direct the voting of the shares "through any option, contract, arrangement, understanding, conversion or rela-

tionship." One or more of these should cover the proxy relationship, which is usually regarded as being a sub-species of agency relationships. Parshalle v. Roy, 567 A.2d 19, 27 (Del.Ch.1989).

target's shareholders. As adopted, however, the statute expressly exempted all management proxy solicitations. It also provided a safe harbor for insurgent solicitations satisfying two conditions: (1) the solicitation is made in accordance with applicable federal proxy rules; and (2) the proxies given do not empower the holder to vote the covered shares on any matter except those described in the proxy statement and in accordance with the instructions of the giver of the proxy. The first condition is problematic because it opens the door for application of the disgorgement remedy not only to fraudulent proxy solicitations, but also to those that fail to comply with some technical aspect of the federal proxy rules. The second is equally problematic. Proxies normally grant the holder discretionary authority to vote on procedural and other unanticipated matters that arise during a shareholders' meeting. The second condition precludes insurgents (but not management) from seeking that normal discretionary authority.[31]

Some insurgents no doubt can live with these conditions. Perhaps anticipating just such insurgents, the safe harbor was carefully crafted to exclude insurgents waging a proxy contest for control of the target. Recall that there are two ways one becomes a controlling person: (1) by acquiring voting power over 20% or more of the stock and (2) by announcing intent to seek control. The safe harbor is only applicable to

---

31. Although Pennsylvania's cash-out statute provides no comparable safe harbor for proxy solicitations, it does exempt persons who hold shares as an agent or nominee of a beneficial owner. The holder of a revocable proxy thus should fall within the literal definition of a controlling person, but be exempted by the exception for agents. In fact, it makes little sense to extend the cash-out statute to proxy contests. A proxy solicited under the Exchange Act is only a temporary transfer of voting power and an easily revocable one at that. Moreover, subject to the limited exception for discretionary voting authority, an Exchange Act proxy only authorizes the holder to vote the shares as directed by their beneficial owner. Control of the company will not change hands unless the insurgent succeeds and, even then, voting power returns to the shares' beneficial owner after the shareholder meeting. In a remarkably opaque opinion, however, U.S. District Court Judge Gawthrop apparently interpreted the statute as being triggered by a proxy solicitation. Centaur Partners wanted to call a special shareholders meeting to remove Pennwalt Corporation's incumbent directors and replace them with Centaur nominees. In order to demand a special meeting, it needed consents from 20 percent of the outstanding shares. Apparently

Centaur did not own sufficient shares to demand a meeting by itself, as it solicited consents from other Pennwalt shareholders. The solicitation provided that the consents would be nullified if a court determined that execution of the consent made the shareholder a member of a controlling group for purposes of the cash-out statute. Pennwalt, of course, contended that Centaur and the signing shareholders were acting in concert and therefore constituted a control group. Judge Gawthrop agreed. In so doing, he implied that the statute applies to proxy contests. He also appeared to hold that the agency exception did not apply to Centaur. *Pennwalt Corp. v. Centaur Partners,* 710 F.Supp. 111, 115 (E.D.Pa.1989). If *Pennwalt* stands for the proposition that the cash-out statute applies to proxy solicitations, an almost insurmountable deterrent to proxy contests arises. Because voting power over 20 percent of the shares triggers the statute, an insurgent could lose the proxy contest and still be obliged to offer to buyout all the remaining shareholders. In effect, the statute gives the other shareholders a put, which rational shareholders will exercise if the statutorily defined fair price exceeds the current market price. Presumably no rational insurgent would conduct a proxy contest under those circumstances.

persons achieving control status by virtue of the first method. As such, the disgorgement remedy still applies to any insurgent that announces intent to seek control of the company.[32]

Would the Pennsylvania statute pass constitutional muster? Several of the provisions clearly would do so on an individual basis. Because it was closely patterned after the Indiana statute, the control share acquisition provision's constitutionality should follow as a matter of course from *CTS*. Likewise, nobody seriously doubts the constitutionality of nonshareholder constituency statutes. In contrast, the tin parachute provision seems particularly vulnerable. A similar provision in Massachusetts law was held preempted by the federal Employee Retirement Income Security Act (ERISA), which explicitly preempts "any and all State laws" that "relate to any employee benefit plan."[33]

The disgorgement provision presents the most serious constitutional questions. Under *Amanda Acquisition*, of course, the provision doubtless passes muster. Provided a state statute does not interfere with the tender offer process (or, by way of analogy, the proxy solicitation process) if a bid appears, the statute's effectiveness in deterring bidders is irrelevant. As the Pennsylvania statute affects neither the federal tender offer nor the proxy solicitation process, a court following *Amanda Acquisition* must uphold it.

The meaningful opportunity for success standard poses significantly greater problems for the disgorgement provision. Applying *BNS'* four-pronged test, note that the provision does not delay a tender offer (or proxy contest) nor provides any role for state officials. The third and fourth *BNS* prongs are thus not applicable to this provision. Under the first prong, the question is whether the Pennsylvania statute's primary effect is to protect shareholders. Yet the word shareholder does not even appear in the act's statement of purpose. According to that statement, the statute protects the corporation and its constituents—which presumably includes, but is not limited to shareholders—from greenmail and the hazards of having the company put in play. Those hazards supposedly include instability and loss of confidence, the risk that speculators will appropriate corporate values at the expense of the corporation and its constituents, and reaping short-term profits. Because this statement of

---

32. A bidder who seeks to evade the disgorgement remedy by failing to disclose a control intent likely will run afoul of the federal securities laws. Any person who acquires more than 5% of a class of a corporation's equity securities must file a Schedule 13D with the SEC within 10 days after crossing the 5% threshold. Item 4 of Schedule 13D effectively requires the filer to state whether it intends to seek control. Even if the filer does not intend to seek control at the time the statement is first filed, a change in that intent would require filing of an amendment to the schedule to disclose the new intent. As Schedule 13Ds are publicly available documents, disclosure of a control intent therein will trigger this method of acquiring control status. So too would disclosure of an intent to seek control pursuant to Pennsylvania's control share acquisition statute, which requires such disclosures by persons seeking to acquire 20 percent or more of the firm's voting shares.

33. Simas v. Quaker Fabric Corp. of Fall River, 6 F.3d 849 (1st Cir.1993).

purpose emphasizes potential harms to nonshareholder interests, it may prove problematic under the meaningful opportunity for success standard.

Under the second *BNS* prong, the question is whether the statute gives either side an advantage. The question here is whether the disgorgement provision provides sufficient loopholes that an "appreciable number" of bidders will be able to proceed.[34] It seems unlikely. Other than some minor exceptions unlikely to be of significant utility to bidders, there are four principal exemptions. First, the safe harbor for proxy contests not involving control. By definition, this loophole is useless to bidders seeking control. Second, disgorgement is waived if the bidder's acquisition of shares receives prior approval of both the board of directors and the shareholders owning a majority of the outstanding shares. It is difficult to imagine the board of directors that would agree ex ante to exempt acquisitions by a potential bidder, so this exemption's utility is also minimal. Third, disgorgement is waived if the bidder's disposition of shares receives prior approval by both the board of directors and shareholders owning a majority of the outstanding shares, provided that the bidder controlled the corporation at the time the disposition was approved. This exemption is potentially useful to hostile bidders, but in order to make use of it they must prevail. Moreover, because they must be able to prove they controlled the corporation at the time they sought to dispose of their shares, successful bidders who own less than 50 percent of the outstanding shares prior to the disposition face some uncertainty when the question of whether they have control is inevitably litigated. Finally, a corporation may opt out of the statute by adopting an appropriate charter provision in its original articles of incorporation. A bidder could therefore urge that the firm be reincorporated, so as to exempt any subsequent dispositions of shares.[35] Because reincorporation requires board of director approval, the bidder effectively must prevail in order to have a meaningful opportunity to exercise this loophole. Because reincorporation also requires shareholder approval, however, the loophole's availability is not guaranteed even if the bidder prevails. In sum, all of the meaningful exemptions are available only to bidders insurgents who prevail—the class least likely to trigger the statute by disposing of their shares.[36] In contrast, all management proxy solicitations are specifically exempted from the disgorgement penalty. Even before considering the other statutory obstacles Pennsylvania has erected, the disgorgement statute thus may fail the *BNS* test.

34. BNS, Inc. v. Koppers Co., Inc., 683 F.Supp. 458, 470 (D.Del.1988).

35. Alan R. Palmiter, The *CTS* Gambit: Stanching the Federalization of Corporate Law, 69 Wash. U.L.Q. 445, 541 (1991).

36. A nonprevailing insurgent that made a sufficient nuisance of itself might be able to obtain the incumbent board's cooperation by agreeing to go away in return. Such agreements, would have to be disclosed, however, lowering the likelihood of shareholder approval where that is necessary and opening the insurgent to the legal consequences of greenmail.

The Delaware trilogy holds out one ray of hope for proponents of the Pennsylvania statute. Since *CTS*, courts faced with state takeover statutes have been disinclined "to second-guess the empirical judgments of lawmakers concerning the utility of [takeover] legislation."[37] In *BNS*, for example, Chief Judge Schwartz opined that the Delaware statute's plausible exemptions are stacked in the target's favor.[38] After reviewing the conflicting evidence on a bidder's prospects under the statute, however, Chief Judge Schwartz concluded that he could not conclusively predict whether a meaningful opportunity for success remained. He therefore deferred to the state legislature's implicit judgment that the statute's benefits outweighed its costs. Schwartz left open an opportunity for reconsideration of the statute's constitutionality if conclusive evidence subsequently developed. In each of the next two installments of the trilogy, hostile bidders offered substantial new evidence on the exemptions' pro-management effects. In each, the court again rejected the bidder's preemption arguments.[39] The disgorgement statute's exemptions raise a similar empirical issue: will bidders prevail frequently enough to say they have a viable opportunity to make use of these exemptions.

When the Pennsylvania statute is taken as a whole, moreover, its viability under the meaningful opportunity for success standard becomes even more problematic. Consider a bidder who owns less than 20 percent of the target's shares prior to initiating a contest for control. Such a bidder faces both the disgorgement and the cash-out statutes. A bidder who purchases more than twenty percent of the target's shares before beginning a control contest faces the disgorgement statute, the cash-out statute, and the control share acquisition statute. Then too, the non-shareholder constituency statute will help validate target defensive tactics. The proverbial kitchen sink necessarily comes to mind.

---

37. CTS Corp. v. Dynamics Corp. of Am., 481 U.S. 69, 92 (1987). Although this quotation is taken from the commerce clause portion of the majority opinion, other takeover cases have applied it to the preemption analysis as well. E.g., Amanda Acquisition Corp. v. Universal Foods Corp., 708 F.Supp. 984, 1000 (E.D.Wis.), aff'd, 877 F.2d 496 (7th Cir.1989), cert. denied, 493 U.S. 955 (1989).

38. BNS, Inc. v. Koppers Co., Inc., 683 F.Supp. 458, 470 (D.Del.1988).

39. City Capital Assoc. Ltd. v. Interco, Inc., 696 F.Supp. 1551, 1554–55 (D.Del. 1988), aff'd on other grounds, 860 F.2d 60 (3d Cir.1988); RP Acquisition Corp. v. Staley Cont'l, Inc., 686 F.Supp. 476, 482–86 (D.Del.1988). See also West Point–Pepperell, Inc. v. Farley Inc., 711 F.Supp. 1096, 1100–06 (N.D.Ga.1989) (in light of inconclusive evidence as to bidder's chances for success, presumption of constitutional validity used to uphold Georgia takeover statute).

TABLE OF CASES

References are to Pages.

INDEX

References are to Pages

BREACH OF CONTRACT
Remedies, 83

**BUSINESS CONTEXT OF M & A TRANS-
ACTIONS**
Generally, 30-50
Agency costs, 30
Downward sloping demand curve hypothesis, 49, 50
Economics of Securities Markets, this index
Investor vs. nonshareholder constituencies, wealth effects, 47-49
Principal-agent problem, 30-32
Shirking
Agents, 30, 31
Directors or management, 41
Strategic acquisitions
Generally, 43-45
Diversification, 44
Empire building, 44, 45
Market power, 44
Operating synergy, 43
Redressing potential hold up concerns, 43
Takeover motives
Generally, 40-45
Creating value by displacing inefficient managers, 40-43
Strategic acquisitions, below
Target vs. acquirer shareholders, wealth effects, 45, 46
Wealth effects
Generally, 45-50
Downward sloping demand curve hypothesis, 49, 50
Investor vs. nonshareholder constituencies, 47-49
Target vs. acquirer shareholders, 45, 46

BUSINESS JUDGMENT RULE
Generally, 60-63
Disinterested and in dependent decision makers, 60, 61
Exercise of judgment, 60
Fraud or illegality, absence of, 61
Informed decision, 62, 63
Parent-subsidiary transactions, 121, 122
Rationality, 61, 62

CONFLICTS OF INTEREST
Negotiated acquisitions, 58, 59
Target managers and target shareholders, 58

CONSIDERATION
Acquisition agreement, price and form of consideration terms, 73-79

CONSOLIDATION
Acquisition mechanics, 18

CONTRACTS (M & A)
Generally, 71-86

CONTRACTS (M & A)—Cont'd
Acquisition agreement
Generally, 72-83
Covenants, 81, 82
Earnout clauses, using to adjust price ex post, 73 et seq.
Non-cash transactions, calculating price, 77, 78
Price and form of consideration terms, 73-79
Shareholders, getting money to, 78, 79
Warranties and representations, 79-81
Best efforts clause, 87, 90, 91
Conditions precedent to closing, 82, 83
Covenants, 81, 82
Due diligence, 83-85
Earnout clauses, using to adjust price ex post, 73 et seq.
Exclusivity, this index
Letter of intent, 71, 72
No shop clauses, 88
Non-cash transactions, calculating price, 77, 78
Price and form of consideration terms, 73-79
Remedies for breach, 83
Shareholders, getting money to, 78, 79
Specific performance, 83
Termination fees, 83, 88
Warranties and representations, 79-81

**CONTROLLING SHAREHOLDER TRANS-
ACTIONS**
Generally, 118-149
Conducting sale of corporation in presence of controlling shareholder, 147-149
Corporate office, sale of, 125, 126
Corporate opportunity, usurping, 126-128
Fiduciary duties, 118
Freeze-out mergers and variants
Generally, 132-147
Appraisal rights of minority shareholders, 133, 139-141
Business purpose test, 135, 136
Fairness, 136-139
Fiduciary duties, 139-141
Reverse stock split, freeze-outs via, 145-147
Shareholder approval, effect of, 141
Short-form merger, freeze-outs via, 142-145
Supermajority vote requirements, 237 et seq.
Why freeze out minority, 133-135
Identifying, 118-120
Looter, sale to, 124, 125
Office, sale of, 125, 126
Parent-subsidiary transactions, 120-123
Presumption of control, 119
Refusals to sell, 130-132
Reverse stock split, freeze-outs via, 145-147

†